D1713873

Contradictions of
Accumulation in
AFRICA

Volume 10
SAGE SERIES ON AFRICAN MODERNIZATION AND DEVELOPMENT

Henry Bernstein
Bonnie K. Campbell
Editors

Contradictions of Accumulation in AFRICA

Studies in Economy and State

SAGE PUBLICATIONS Beverly Hills London New Delhi

Copyright © 1985 by Sage Publications, Inc.

For information address:

SAGE Publications, Inc.
275 South Beverly Drive
Beverly Hills, California 90212

SAGE Publications India Pvt. Ltd.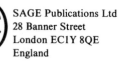
M-32 Market
Greater Kailash I
New Delhi 110 048 India

SAGE Publications Ltd
28 Banner Street
London EC1Y 8QE
England

Printed in the United States of America

Library of Congress Cataloging in Publication Data

Main entry under title:

Contradictions of accumulation in Africa.

(Sage series on African modernization and development ; v. 10)
English and French.
1. Africa—Economic conditions—Addresses, essays, lectures. 2. Africa—Dependency on foreign countries—Addresses, essays, lectures. 3. Capitalism—Africa—Addresses, essays, lectures. 4. Socialism—Africa—Addresses, essays, lectures. I. Bernstein, Henry. II. Campbell, Bonnie. III. Series.
HC800.C67 1984   330.96′0328   84-11640
ISBN 0-8039-2366-X

FIRST PRINTING

Contents

*This volume is dedicated to
the memory of Ruth First
1925-1982*

INTRODUCTION

HENRY BERNSTEIN AND
BONNIE K. CAMPBELL

**The current
crisis** of sub-Saharan Africa is frequently and amply diagnosed, its
manifestations listed and deplored, in an ever-growing number of
publications and commentaries by academic and non-academic writers. The chapter by Björn Beckman in this volume begins with one
such catalogue of "crisis" in the case of Nigeria, showing how its manifestations are assimilated to the vocabulary of the "development of
underdevelopment," "dependency," and the like. Notions such as
these, initially associated with the work of Andre Gunder Frank and
others on Latin America, have acquired the status of a general (and
generic) perspective on the contemporary Third World, a new conventional wisdom about the impossibility of economic and social
development in the conditions of contemporary capitalism, and hence
the necessity of "socialism" to any prospect of progress. The application
of this perspective to Africa, elaborated in the writings of Walter
Rodney, Samir Amin, and Dan Nabudere, among others, provides
the central thrust of much of anti-imperialist ideology in Africa today.[1]

In recent years a number of criticisms have been advanced of some
of the characteristic features of underdevelopment and dependency
theory. In theoretical terms, these encompass the confrontation of
different understandings of capitalism as a mode of production, and
of the historical investigation of its pervasively uneven development.
In terms of method, they encompass a reaction against the mechanical determinism of much "world system" type analysis, and, in political terms, the need for more rigorous and refined analyses of the
prospects *and* limitations of particular conjunctures of struggle—the
concrete analysis of concrete situations. This, in particular, requires
engagement with the difficult dialectic of class and nation: the search

for a means of constituting the national question from the standpoint of class struggle, rather than assimilating (and losing sight of) the latter in the former.[2]

This schematic outline indicates the kinds of issues addressed, explicitly and implicitly, by the chapters in this collection. While they reflect no unitary position or "line," their authors share a common commitment to producing knowledge of Africa that is adequate to its profoundly contradictory realities. Such knowledge—which can only result from confronting problematic issues of theory and method, of history and politics (first recognizing them as problematic)—is itself a condition of and contribution to more informed and effective political practices in the struggle for a better future. As suggested, this project expresses a dissatisfaction with much of recent and current debates about Africa and the terms in which they are conducted. Consequently, these chapters with all their variety should be seen as contributions to a *critique* in the full and ramified sense of that term: the critical investigation of both ideas *and* the social realities they claim to represent and explain (Colletti, 1972). The activity of critique aims to expose the systematic limitations of existing knowledge, and to transcend those limitations as a necessary aspect of transforming social reality itself.

One task of critique is necessarily concerned with clarifying what is at stake in the uses of an apparently convergent and shared vocabulary—in this context, the language of capitalism, imperialism, social class, class struggle and the state, ideology and consciousness. The widespread use of such terms is no guarantee of a common theoretical content and analytical effectiveness. The opposite is more likely to be the case: that the use of a relatively limited number of "key words" obscures the variety of their meanings, applications, and effects, as employed in different discourses. As always, what *is* at stake is not the words themselves but what lies behind them: the precise content of the concepts to which the words (more or less plausibly) refer, and how these concepts are *put to work* in the investigation of social reality.

These propositions are illustrated by the chapters in this volume. Three substantial papers contained here are constructed explicitly in the form of a critique, a particular type of intervention in current debates (or aimed at changing the terms of debate). Despite their differences of object and style, the chapters by Beckman, Kitching, and Gibbon and Neocosmos, articulate the basis of their disagreement with existing bodies of radical writing on Africa, as a means of establishing the groundwork of alternative approaches and interpretations.

Björn Beckman considers capitalist development in Nigeria, particularly as it has been affected by the oil boom of the 1970s. In tracing the economic and social contours of this development his principal concern is to formulate the nature of the state formation that has been an integral part of the process. His relationship to the analysis of Nigeria provided by dependency theory is a complex one. He seems to accept much of a dependency account at the level of *descriptive* validity, while registering his disagreement with its theoretical framework (or certain aspects of it). Beckman points to the dangers of a simple model of neo-colonial dependence (determination by "external" forces) which denies indigenous social forces their own dynamics—the expression of class and other social contradictions within the country. This effect of dependency theory is connected with its tendency (at least as applied to Africa, if not in the Latin American context) to deny the possibility of any significant indigenous capital accumulation. In turn this produces an instrumental version of the neo-colonial state as a mechanism of domination by international capital, in alliance with a strictly subordinated bureaucratic-military apparatus and/or comprador bourgeoisie.

Beckman's approach aims to transcend the preoccupation of dependency theory with the asymmetrical relationship between an apparently omnipotent international capitalism and an indigenous bourgeoisie that is "distorted," "deformed," or otherwise constrained by its subordination (hence failing to qualify as an authentically national bourgeoisie). At a general level he rejects the dichotomous logic of the "development of underdevelopment" (that a social formation is either "independent" and "developing" *or* "dependent" and "underdeveloping"), proposing instead that "in Nigeria continued deepening neocolonial dependence goes *hand in hand with* a dynamic process of capitalist transformation and class formation" (emphasis added). Interestingly, while Beckman specifies the enormous impact of oil revenues for accumulation and accelerated capitalist development, he concludes that oil revenues are not a necessary condition of the expanded reproduction of capital in future.

More specifically, his analysis of the Nigerian state is distinctive for several reasons. First, the nature (and changing nature) of the state can only be grasped properly through studying the process of its *formation*. Second, the state is a *site of struggle* between various social forces, including fractions and groupings of particular capitalist interests, (of which the differentiation between international and indigenous capitals is not necessarily, nor always, the most salient). Third, there is Beckman's major substantive argument that the state formed in the conjuncture of Nigeria's oil "boom"—with its various "repressive, regulative, productive, reproductive and ideological activities"—is an organ of *capital in general*: "The primary role of the Nigerian state is to establish, maintain, protect and expand the conditions of capitalist accumulation in general, without which neither foreign nor Nigerian capital can prosper."

This position is illustrated and tested through a review of recent "indigenization" policies and their interpretation. Beckman argues that these policies are best understood within the theoretical framework of the state as an organ of capital in general, although he concedes that the accounts of "indigenization" measures given by the alternative perspectives of the state as an organ of international capital, and as an organ of indigenous capital, have a certain plausibility. This recognition raises two issues. One is that *empirical* judgments cannot be evaluated in an *empiricist* fashion, that is, they are necessarily indeterminate until their theoretical and political content is uncovered and considered (a central argument of Kitching's contribution to this volume). The other issue concerns what may be a residual ambiguity in Beckman's relationship to the dependency framework even as he attempts to transcend it, for example, in his view of the ostensible ideological indeterminacy of a dependency position: that it can be appropriated both by nationalism and by socialism. Whether such "openness" constitutes political virtue (the basis of a broad anti-imperialist alliance) or political vice (losing class struggle in nationalism) is not entirely clear, despite Beckman's statement that the "question of national emancipation . . . cannot be divorced from the concrete class content of the strategies by which it is pursued."

No such trace of ambiguity is revealed by Gavin Kitching, whose rejection of dependency theory is complete. His chapter sets out the reasons for this—together with an assessment of other positions in the "Kenyan debate"—with forensic precision.[3] His critical exposition both illuminates some central issues in twentieth-century Kenyan history and represents a sophisticated and challenging essay on method in the widest (and deepest) sense: the relation between theoretical and political positions, the relation of both to empirical debate ("the relative significance and importance of different facts"), the requirements of a mode of investigation able to provide a coherent account of the contradictions of social reality (rather than registering those contradictions in theoretical confusion, evasion, or elision).

Just as Beckman notes the empirical plausibility of quite different interpretations of aspects of the Nigerian state, Kitching shows how the same empirical data have been used in the Kenyan debate to substantiate opposite conclusions (or premises?). A major purpose of his chapter is to show why this kind of thing happens, as well as how it can be avoided. In pursuing this theme, Kitching demonstrates not only how different theoretical positions produce different meanings of the same facts, but also how political positions (usually submerged) also contribute to this effect.

Like Beckman, Kitching criticizes the mechanical determinism of much dependency theory for its one-sided obsession with determination by "external" forces, which denies Africans any role as effective agents of social change. In contrast to the linear historiography that is particularly evident in cruder versions of underdevelopment and dependency theory—whereby "developing" or "underdeveloping" is the definitive attribute a social formation acquires from the initial moment and manner of its entry into the world market (and seems to retain thereafter)—Kitching emphasizes, first, that "capitalist development is *of necessity* both episodic ('conjunctural') and unstable, a thing of spurts and pauses, booms and slumps," and, second, that "the potentialities and limits of capitalist development in Kenya . . . are not simply ineluctable 'givens' but products and objects of struggle and human praxis, whether by indigenous Kenyan capitalists, 'middle peasants,' or representatives of different forms of multinational capital."

These two fundamental perceptions (or, more precisely, theoretical protocols) inform his own major historical study of Kenya (Kitching, 1980) and the equally central work of Michael Cowen, which Kitching summarizes and assesses with exemplary clarity. Both have investigated the development of commodity production in Kenya during the colonial period as well as in the two decades of independence and Cowen has also made a pioneering contribution concerning the salience of pre-colonial (Kikuyu) social forces for economic and social change in the twentieth century. Kitching explains the theoretical and methodological importance of the study of long historical periods; it is only within a framework of long periods that the significance of the conjunctural can be established satisfactorily, whether this refers to the uneven rhythms of capitalist development, the demarcation of its phases, the major shifts in modes of accumulation, in patterns of state formation, and so on.

The principle of contradiction, and its manifestation in social and political struggle, is also applied in Kitching's discussion of the nature of the Kenyan state. Like Beckman he views the state as a site of continual struggle between different social forces and interests, one effect of which is "the *fracturing* of the state, and indeed of particular state institutions, which themselves enter into conjunctural alliances and oppositions." The complexity that results "is not reducible to a 'last instance' hegemony of national or transnational capital because in the current historical moment . . . *the question of that hegemony is precisely one of the central issues which are at stake."* Here it is worth pointing out that the *forms of appearance* often assumed by that complexity—the incoherence or "messiness" of the state, the pursuit of inconsistent policies, the prevalent corruption and "inefficiency," to which a number of the authors in this volume refer—have been increasingly described and deplored in recent years by both conservative and radical critics of the post-colonial state in Africa.

Whether, like Beckman, Kitching would locate the state as a site of struggle within a process of formation of the state as an organ of capital in general is an intriguing question, the answer to which is not easily inferred from Kitching's chapter. Having shown that there are no "ineluctable 'givens,'" and having argued that the terrain of social investigation is constituted by contradictions and occupied by struggles between social forces generated by those contradictions, what are the further steps? What is the method of distinguishing *principal contradictions* from secondary contradictions? How is the *balance of forces* in particular conjunctural conditions of struggle to be assessed?

The need to establish the principal (or in their term, "determinative") contradiction is a central purpose of the chapter by Peter Gibbon and Michael Neocosmos, which represents an original and provocative intervention concerning the social identification of the peasantry in contemporary Africa, and the character of the state (especially in so-called "African socialist" regimes). Kitching criticizes those who equate capitalism with "the universalisation of the capital/wage-labor relationship" conceived in empiricist terms as the proportional growth of wage labor in an economy. He also refers to "the development of commodity production under capitalism." The prevalence of petty commodity production under capitalism (not least in Africa, and above all in agriculture) is the enduring and seemingly intractable object of debate with which Gibbon and Neocosmos are concerned.

Like Kitching they reject the reduction of capitalist development to "linear proletarianisation," and they also reject any theorization of "peasants" (as petty commodity producers in contemporary conditions) that places them *outside* capitalist relations of production (including formulations of peasantry as a pre-/ or non-capitalist mode/form of production articulated with capitalism).[4] Their alternative approach comprises (1) what may be called a generic theory of petty commodity production under capitalism, and (2) a dynamic theory of how capitalism constantly reproduces "places" for petty commodity production through the logic of its own functioning.

The inspiration for this two-fold theorization derives from a rigorous reading and interpretation of *Capital* and *Theories of Surplus*

Value, in the course of which contradictory tendencies in Marx's thought are identified and evaluated. The generic theory, as we have termed it, hinges on "the combination in petty commodity production of the functions of both capital and wage-labor . . . the combination in the concentrated form of the single individual/household of the contradictory class places common to all capitalist enterprises." The dynamic theory suggests how capitalism constantly reproduces "places" for petty commodity production as an *effect* of its own logic (the operation of the law of value). This represents a very different position from those "articulationist" theories that explain the so-called persistence of petty commodity production (especially by peasants) as meeting certain "needs" of capital (in other words, a functionalist explanation).

In formulating this theory of petty commodity production, Gibbon and Neocosmos make a vitally important—and generally neglected—point about the contradictory dynamics and effects of capitalism, which can be added to those made by Kitching quoted above. This concerns the distinction between the constant reproduction of "places" for petty commodity production under capitalism, and the inherent instability (hence high "turnover") of *individual* petty commodity enterprises. They attribute the latter to the peculiar way in which the capital/wage-labor relation is concentrated in such enterprises, but one can add to this that the "places" of petty commodity production are themselves constantly shifting (e.g., between particular branches and lines of production) as a result of the uneven development of capitalism.[5]

It is also worth noting that the analysis by Gibbon and Neocosmos entails a particular view of the *generalization of commodity production.* For them, it is a sufficient index of the generalization of commodity production that households or individuals are unable to reproduce themselves outside of commodity production and exchange. This contrasts with another important recent attempt to establish a generic theory of "simple" commodity production under capitalism by Harriet Friedmann (1980). For Friedmann "simple" commodity production as a generic form of production under capitalism exists only when *all* the conditions of production, realization, and distribution, are satisfied through exchange (including the complete commoditisation of land and labor-power). Accordingly, she regards the notion of "peasantry" as a residual, denoting all those agricultural producers whose conditions of production and reproduction are satisfied partly through non-market (hence "non-capitalist") relations.

To summarize: The distinctiveness of Gibbon and Neocosmos' theorization of the peasantry lies in their analysis of the peculiar form in which petty commodity production is constituted through the capital/wage-labor relation, by contrast with formulations based on a logic of simple reproduction (examined in their critique of the work of Henry Bernstein), or on conditions of existence ("external" to the enterprise) of generalized commodity production in the sense employed by Friedmann. In short, their theorization rests entirely on the specification of a *relation of production*. The conclusions of their analysis are these: petty commodity producing enterprises are *capitalist enterprises of a particular type*; middle peasants (as well as some poor, and some rich, peasants) belong to *the petty bourgeoisie*; since capitalist enterprises do not exploit each other, the *conflicts between peasant and state (capitalist) enterprises in Africa* (notably over the realization and distribution of the value of agricultural commodities), *are not the expression of a principal or "determinative" contradiction.*

These starkly summarized points are applied in the last part of Gibbon and Neocosmos' chapter, which elaborates and illustrates the elements of an analysis of "class and state in African socialism" with reference to Tanzania. In this account, no less than in Kitching's, the state is seen as a site of continual struggle but its incoherence and ineffectiveness, in this case, are the outcome of the characteristically petty bourgeois class practices of the state with its "tendency to vacillate between the principal class forces, local and international." Gibbon and Neocosmos would concur with the gist of Kitching's judgment that the Tanzanian ruling class is unwilling or unable "to abide by the most elementary rules of accumulation," although Kitching might not agree with their explanation of why this has proved to be the case.[6]

We have introduced these three chapters first because their presentation in the form of a critique gives them a programmatic quality. In all of them, substantive positions are criticized and alternatives established through the explicit consideration of theoretical, methodological, and political issues. One of their common merits is that they conclude with statements of their authors' own political positions. The other four chapters in this volume, while constructed somewhat differently, investigate themes that are related to the programmatic considerations of theory, method, empirical interpretation, and political effects provided by Beckman, Kitching, and Gibbon and Neocosmos.

The chapter by Judy Kimble adds another dimension to the consideration of the issues outlined so far. First, because its object and period of study lie outside the orbit of the other chapters (with the exception of parts of Kitching's and of Campbell's chapters), namely the formation of a colonial state from the 1890s to the 1930s. Second, her analysis is constructed within an "articulationist" framework of considerable theoretical sophistication, which avoids any recourse to functionalism, and which is disciplined by the detailed empirical investigation of the historian. In these two respects, her work is perhaps closest to that line of theorizing the articulation of modes of production associated with Pierre-Philippe Rey (1971). In addition, her research on Lesotho is located in the context of wide-ranging and vigorous debates about southern Africa, concerning the nature of its pre-capitalist social formations (both indigenous and settler), their modes of incorporation with and transformation by successive phases of capitalist development in South Africa, the processes of class and state formation that have characterized the course of that development, and the nature of the social and political struggles it has generated (including the precise nature of the national question in southern Africa).[7]

Rather like Rey, Kimble is as much concerned with *the articulation of political instances* constituted within different modes of production, as with the articulation of economic instances. In fact, her chapter reveals an unusual degree of synthesis of the issues of historical political economy with those concerning the complex and contradictory process of state formation in colonial Basutoland. She is able to show how the regional transition to capitalism in this period changed the conditions of reproduction of class rule by the Sotho chiefs, simultaneously constraining them and presenting them with new opportunities in their relations with their subjects on one hand, and with the colonial administration on the other. Kimble's analysis generates two hypotheses of considerable political relevance to the current conjuncture in southern Africa: first, that the political weight (and determination) of the Sotho chiefs in the colonial state apparatus during its formative period, prevented the absorption of Basutoland in the Union of South Africa; second, that the chieftainship acquired a particular symbolic significance in the discourse of Sotho anti-imperialism.

The chapters by Alain Cournanel and Jean-Loup Amselle provide interesting and different counterpoints to the analysis of "African socialism" by Gibbon and Neocosmos. Cournanel's research on Guinea over many years, and the analysis resulting from it, has paralleled and in some ways anticipated the theory of the "bureaucratic bourgeosie" in "African socialist" regimes best known in the anglophone world through the work of Issa Shivji (1975) on Tanzania. The basis of the *state bourgeoisie* (as Cournanel terms this class) is the creation and centralization of state property, as the means of collective (class) appropriation and accumulation, free from any popular control. (The latter is highlighted in Cournanel's discussion of the nature and role of the single party, an important topic which would have to be incorporated in any extension of Gibbon and Neocosmos' analysis of Tanzania). The distinctive feature of this type of ruling class and of the mode of its formation is that the economic instance is subordinated to the political and administrative instances.

In the case of Tanzania many critics of the state (and the state class) have been mesmerized by the "bureaucratic irrationalism" through which the subordination of the economic to the political instance presents itself. For Cournanel, the "anarchy" and "disorder" of the state economic sector, as well as its prevalent corruption and ineffectiveness, result from the *tension within the state bourgeoisie between maintaining its collective means of appropriation and the tendency to private appropriation and accumulation by individual members of the class*. This has been, to date, probably the most convincing explanation of the economic chaos of "African socialist" regimes, which Cournanel documents for Guinea, particularly from 1965 to 1977. It should now be considered in the light of the interpretation by Gibbon and Neocosmos, for whom the incoherence of state economic enterprises in Tanzania represents "not simply a lack of control and autonomy stemming from the petty-bourgeois character of the state but also a certain petty-bourgeois political position with respect to socialism." The content of this position is a "strategy of seeking to create 'non-capitalist' institutions which are simultaneously divorced from the masses."

In his conclusion, Cournanel provides a revision of his earlier work, which relied on the dependency-style argument that private capital is unable to generate a sufficiently dynamic process of accumulation in formations like Guinea, while at the same time its typically mercantile and speculative activities undermine the process of accumulation through the state, qualified by the extent to which the state bourgeoisie can use its political power to "tap" the channels of appropriation of private capital; on the other hand, the tendency of the state bourgeoisie is to partly transform itself into a bourgeoisie of private capital. Cournanel now argues that in view of the dismal record of state capitalism masquerading as "socialism"—including its inhibition of the formation of private capital—the most positive prospect for the foreseeable future is *an acceleration of capitalist development effected through an alliance of state and private capitals*, which provided Guinea's best period of economic growth in the past, between 1960 and 1965. Presumably, then, Cournanel would support the measures of economic "liberalization" introduced since 1977, although he notes that a successful expansion of both state and private capital (entailing negotiation and regulation of the links between them) requires political changes at the top levels of the regime. It should be noted that Cournanel's chapter went to press before the death of President Sékou Touré on March 26, 1984. Consequently, Cournanel did not have the opportunity to analyze the important changes that have occurred since that date.

The convergence of Cournanel's conclusion with that of Kitching's chapter is striking. The chapter by Amselle on Mali provides a somewhat different angle on the state bourgeoisie. To begin with, like Cournanel (and Shivji on Tanzania), Amselle sketches the formation of a state bourgeoisie from the petty bourgeois leadership of the independence movement. He calls this class in Mali a "nomenklatura," a term from the Soviet Union that refers to the privileged layers of the bureaucracy. The specificity of the "nomenklatura" is that access to state office, and the creation of state property, provide its avenues of appropriation. Through state sector industrialization, and through its relations with the peasantry (state marketing of cash crops and sporadic attempts to directly control peasant production), the state bourgeoisie extracts a "bureaucratic rent" that is both a collective form of appropriation and provides opportunities for individual appropriation. Amselle's account of the food aid that poured into Mali from 1968 with the Sahelian drought, shows that any form of income accruing to the state, whether in money or goods supplied through foreign aid, such as food and agricultural machinery, can be and is channelled into private appropriation by members of the "nomenklatura."

To this familiar account of the state bourgeoisie, Amselle contributes some additional and distinctive features. First, readers will note that having initially established itself during Mali's "socialist" period (1960–1968), the state bourgeoisie continued to reproduce itself after the military intervention of 1968. Second, and most critically, Amselle argues that the forms (and uses) of appropriation by the "nomenklatura" in Mali do not represent *accumulation* in the capitalist sense (expanded reproduction of capital and the development of the productive forces), but *predatory exaction of a pre-capitalist type* ("prédation"), whereby goods and money are centralized in the control of the ruling class and redistributed to establish and expand groups of followers. In this way, the nomenklatura inherits the practices of the ruling class of the pre-colonial mode of production, the landed and military aristocracy (whose suppression following independence was an aspect of the formation of the state bourgeoisie).

Accordingly, the expansion of the state economy is primarily determined by the politics of "clientilism," rather than by any economic imperative of profit or developing production and productivity. The use of the state for pillage and "clientilist" redistribution is the principal characteristic of the "nomenklatura," although individual appropriation of state revenues through rampant corruption and embezzlement is partly directed to private accumulation (in transport, real estate, and farming), as well as to luxury consumption.

By the late 1970s the capacity of state revenues to support this expanded reproduction of "clientilism" was exhausted, and provoked overt opposition from students no longer guaranteed state employment on graduation, and from the increasingly "squeezed" urban masses (especially in Bamako in 1980). The response to the crisis of the predator state has been to try to limit the extent to which the "nomenklatura" disposes of state income (through both salaries and corruption), and to rationalize the state sector through measures of austerity, liberalization, and privatization, connected with the growing role of finance provided by the IMF and the World Bank.

Several issues arise from this analysis. One concerns the unusual characterization of the state bourgeoisie as combining the attributes of a Soviet "nomenklatura" and of a predatory "pre-capitalist" ruling class. Whatever else may be said about the former, its historical trajectory is indissociable from the massive accumulation and industrialization of the Soviet Union. As for the latter, the appellation "pre-capitalist" is not based in a specification of *relations of production* (and their relation to particular state forms), such as are proposed for "African socialist" formations by Gibbon and Neocosmos in the case of Tanzania, and by Cournanel in the case of Guinea, and in a different context, by Kimble for colonial Basutoland.

Another issue concerns the present conjuncture. Having portrayed the formation and functioning of a predatory and authoritarian state in the 1960s and 1970s (based in "unproductive" forms of exploitation and oppression of the urban and rural masses), Amselle is equally critical of current measures of liberalization and privatization that, he suggests, benefit only merchant capital in Mali (and neither the urban and rural masses nor the "nonmenklatura"). The shadowy but evidently central role played by merchant capital throughout this period, above all in the organization of commodity circuits in the countryside, is an intriguing feature of the analysis that could be usefully extended. (Amselle, in fact, describes the conflict of bureaucrats and merchants as "l'éternelle donne de la politique malienne," contrasting with Cournanel's revised and more "optimistic" opinion about the prospects of an alliance between state and private capitals in Guinea.) In the light of Amselle's trenchant and vivid critique of the Malian state, one wonders what a more "positive" path out of the current situation (as a movement to a longer-term transformation) might be: the question that leads Kitching and Cournanel to "endorse" capitalist development in Kenya and Guinea, respectively.

The conjuncture from the late 1970s, marked by the cumulative effects of international recession and the growing "fiscal crisis of the state," also provides the context of Bonnie Campbell's chapter on the Ivory Coast. In contrast with Amselle's analysis of the revenue crisis in Mali as a product of the state's predatory and "pre-capitalist" mode of expansion, Campbell views the "fiscal crisis of the state" in the Ivory Coast as one manifestation of the *exhaustion of a particular pattern of accumulation* during the 1960s and 1970s—although, as she shows, some of its specific mechanisms were established in the late colonial period. The periodization employed exemplifies the observation made above that accumulation is a process subject to particular rhythms and phases, and that particular types of accumulation rest on specific conditions and mechanisms including those provided by the state and specific forms of class alliances. Both of these are sites of contestation, the effects of which can undermine, strengthen, or in other ways modify the conditions of accumulation. (Thus accumulation is neither unproblematically and indefinitely guaranteed, on one hand, nor necessarily forever denied, on the other.)

Campbell's chapter provides a framework for establishing "long" historial periods in the Ivory Coast, first outlining some of the specific conditions and mechanisms of accumulation in the colonial period, initially corresponding to a familiar "primitive accumulation" model of the development of commercial agriculture in peasant and capitalist enterprises, whose links to the world market are controlled by metropolitan merchant capital in alliance with the colonial state. Two of Campbell's findings resonate with themes of wider applicability, confirming the increasingly recognized crucial importance of the late colonial period, the second half of the 1940s and the 1950s. One concerns indigenous class formation resulting from the accelerated development of commodity production and the political strategies of the colonial state. In the Ivory Coast this was expressed in an emergent agrarian bourgeoisie (the "planter" class) which acquired African political leadership before independence and subsequently gained control of the state. The second concerns the ways in which the activities of the colonial state were expanded, and its apparatuses to some extent restructured, in the transitional conjuncture of "decolonization."

In the Ivory Coast, "decolonization" provided some of the elements of the pattern of accumulation that characterized the 1960s and

1970s, in which investment in manufacturing for the domestic market was supported by transfers from the export agricultural sector. These transfers were effected and regulated by the state and Campbell provides a detailed empirical account of some of the central mechanisms and institutional means through which this occurred. She also shows, in some detail, how this process affected the conditions of production in agriculture and industry and highlights the particular contradictions of this pattern of accumulation. It is important to emphasize the latter, that Campbell's concern is to uncover the *contradictory nature of a particular pattern of accumulation* rather than to deny the actuality of accumulation, by viewing some of its effects (the "squeezing" of certain branches of agriculture, the limited and protected character of the industrialization that took place) as merely indices of the further "development of underdevelopment."

Other important conditions and effects of this pattern of accumulation include the strategic alliance of the Ivorian state with certain international capitals, the fact that the ruling class was able to extend and diversify its social base from its "planter" origins (while inhibiting the formation of a local industrial bourgeoisie that might present itself as a competitor for class power), and that the regime was able to secure considerable political stability during this period. The exhaustion of the possibilities of this particular pattern of accumulation manifests itself in a number of ways, not least in the growing pressure on the state budget, providing all the indications of a "fiscal crisis of the state." In the last part of her chapter, Campbell discusses the issues confronting the ruling class in any effective attempt to establish the conditions for a new pattern of accumulation, involving "the extension and deepening of capitalist relations of production." She observes that this will require different kinds of alliances with international capital, or sections of it, as well as new patterns of class formation and connected shifts in internal class alliances. In the light of Kitching's analysis it is important to emphasize, however, that Campbell's conclusion sketches a *possible* scenario: she provides an interpretation of the changing conjunctural conditions of struggle within the state, as well as in society more generally, and not a prediction of an inevitable outcome.

In introducing the themes and issues of this collection, we have barely indicated the depth and diversity of the ways in which they are analyzed in its individual chapters. We have concentrated instead on emphasizing some central (and connected) areas of concern in the investigation of processes of accumulation and of state and class formation in contemporary Africa and the contradictions they express and generate. Our purpose in selecting certain issues is to illustrate some of the theoretical and methodological conditions necessary to any coherent and effective analysis of profoundly contradictory social realities, involving recognition of and confrontation with, what is problematic about those realities, as well as what is problematic about the means we use to grasp and explain them. In relation to the latter, we have pointed out a few of the possible ambiguities and lacunae of the arguments presented in this volume among the many that doubtless exist. However, as Gibbon and Neocosmos put it, "even the minutest advance in theory is only conceivable with these drawbacks or, to be exact, these marks of struggle." More important, we have tried to locate the positions advanced by our contributors not only in relation to other radical and socialist interpretations of Africa today but also in relation to each other. The necessary engagement with ideas through debate is thus reflected *between*, as well as within, the chapters that follow.

Of central importance to all our contributors are the political and ideological imperatives of effective analysis in a conjuncture of "crisis" in Africa, when frustration and despair on the part of radical critics (who are mostly detached from the concrete struggles taking place) is often expressed in views that perversely converge with those of bourgeois commentators. One such channel of convergence, already alluded to several times, is a growing consensus on what could be termed the "pathology" of the post-colonial state—its practices of corruption, "inefficiency," its instability and inability to promote "development," and so on). This has become a strong theme in a number of topical works reflecting a position of frustrated "modernization," and articulated through a market-versus-state dichotomy.

The concurrence of those on the left with such views of the "pathology" of the post-colonial state, which we suggested reflect only the *forms of appearance* of the contradictions through which the state is constituted, is not mitigated by attributing all its manifestations to the depredations of "dependency," nor by appealing to a vague (and usually "peasantist") populism, both of which Kitching's chapter anatomizes. He also points out that the precise identification of the enemy is not sufficient for an effective political strategy, which requires just as much the formulation of a viable *alternative* that can be pursued in current conditions of struggle. In this respect he is skeptical of any "model" presented by actually existing "African socialisms," a skepticism that is reinforced by the diagnoses of "African socialist" ideology and practice in the chapters by Gibbon and Neocosmos, Cournanel, and Amselle. Kitching emphasizes, too, how the mechanical ("external forces") determinism of much underdevelopment and dependency theory produces a syndrome of hopelessness, hence political paralysis—or, one could add, its dialectical counterpart: a voluntarism undisciplined by any real consideration of the conditions of struggle and the balance of forces in particular conjunctures. The experiences of the outcome of a voluntarist politics (i.e., defeat and disillusion) only serve to reinforce a deterministic pessimism.[8]

As Immanuel Wallerstein has recently written: "After the long period of defamation and the short period of too-easy triumphalism, we are now arrived at the moment of hard work and renewed reflection about the structures of the Third World, and hopefully the transformation of many of them."[9] The papers collected in this volume are presented as a contribution to this project of "hard work and renewed reflection." We hope that in engaging with the arguments that follow, readers will be as stimulated by them, and as provoked to debate with them, as we have been. Finally we would like to express our appreciation to Sage Publications for agreeing to include two of the chapters in French, and to Mitch Allen of Sage and Peter Gutkind for their patience, and for their support of this volume since it was first proposed some years ago.

NOTES

1. We do not have the space here, nor perhaps is there any need, to rehearse the arguments of this approach and to provide a list of references. It is enough to point out that analyses exemplifying the perspective of the "development of underdevelopment," "dependency," "neo-colonialism," and so on, are well represented (with a variety of emphases and degrees of sophistication) in the previous volumes of this series; see, in particular, Gutkind and Wallerstein (1976).

2. Systematic critiques of the underdevelopment and dependency "school" include those by Brenner (1977), Leys (1977), Bernstein (1979), and Warren (1980).

3. As the Kenyan debate took place without reference to his own outstanding historical monograph on Kenya (Kitching, 1980), and as he has subsequently diversified his research interests from East Africa to Brazil, we are particularly glad that Gavin Kitching agreed to contribute a review of the Kenyan debate to this volume.

4. The fact that Gibbon and Neocosmos begin their chapter with a detailed critique of the work on peasantry by one of the editors of this collection is coincidental.

5. This point is well demonstrated in two excellent recent studies of petty commodity production in Turkey by Dikerdem (1980) and Ayata (1982).

6. An interpretation of the Tanzanian experience by Kitching can be found in his book on populism (Kitching, 1982: chap. 5).

7. Something of the themes and flavor of these debates can be seen in Kimble's chapter; unfortunately, reasons of space did not allow us to include a systematic account by her of the various positions in the debates.

8. The utopian quality of the "socialism" advocated from a dependency position is specified by Leys (1977); the combination of determinism and voluntarism in the analy-

sis of "global crisis" by Andre Gunder Frank, and his consequent pessimism, is discussed in Bernstein and Nicholas (1983).

9. This appeared in a letter published in *Third World Book Review*, 1(1), 1984.

REFERENCES

AYATA, S. (1982). Differentiation and capital accumulation: case studies of the carpet and metal industries in Kayseri (Turkey). Ph.D. thesis, University of Kent.

BERNSTEIN, H. (1979). "Sociology of underdevelopment vs. sociology of development?," in D. Lehmann (ed.) Development Theory: Four Critical Studies. London: Frank Cass.

———and H. NICHOLAS (1983). "Pessimism of the intellect, pessimism of the will? A response to Gunder Frank," Development and Change 14(4).

BRENNER, R. (1977). "The origins of capitalist development: a critique of neo-Smithian Marxism." New Left Review 104.

COLLETTI, L. (1972). "Marxism: science or revolution?" in R. Blackburn (ed.) Ideology in social science: Readings in critical social theory. London: Fontana.

DIKERDEM, M.A. (1980). Factory and workshop. An investigation into forms of small-scale production in Turkey. D.Phil. thesis, University of Sussex.

FRIEDMANN, H. (1980). "Household production and the national economy: concepts for the analysis of agrarian formations." Journal of Peasant Studies 7 (2).

GUTKIND, P.C.W. and I. WALLERSTEIN [eds.] (1977). The Political Economy of Contemporary Africa. Beverly Hills, CA: Sage.

KITCHING, G. (1980). Class and Economic Change in Kenya: The making of an African Petite Bourgeoisie. New Haven: Yale University Press.

———(1982). Development and Underdevelopment in Historical Perspective: Populism, Nationalism and Industrialization. London: Methuen.

LEYS, C. (1977). "Underdevelopment and dependency: critical notes." Journal of Contemporary Asia 7(1).

REY, P.-P. (1971). Colonialisme, néo-colonialisme et transition au capitalisme: Exemple de la "Comilog" au Congo-Brazzaville. Paris: Maspéro.

SHIVJI, I. (1975). Class Struggles in Tanzania. Dar es Salaam and London: Tanzania Publishing House and Heinemann.

WARREN, B. (1980). Imperialism: Pioneer of Capitalism. London: Verso.

1

"CLINGING TO THE CHIEFS"
Some Contradictions of Colonial Rule
in Basutoland, c.1890–1930

JUDY KIMBLE

[O]ur reasons, in 1868, for passing over the Republican governments of the Orange River and the Transvaal and surrendering to England, was that we had been told that the Government of England was under hereditary chieftainship, which we preferred. . . . [W]e see Native Chiefs being deposed one after another. . . . We therefore pray the Government of the King to make a permanent letter for Basutoland which will disallow the Union Government making any boundaries which would amount to a deprivation of the land, which act would be tantamount to the destruction of the chieftainship [Chiefs of Basutoland to the High Commissioner, on the Act of Union of South Africa, 1910].

Remember this, Basutos. Your salvation rests in the maintenance of your ancestrial [sic] organization. If it ever gets broken, it will be the end of you as a nation, and all those who co-operate to that end . . . act as enemies of the nation. Every Mosuto who loves his country ought then to cling to his chiefs, to his language, to the traditions which bind the nation together. Everything loosening the links weakens the nation [*Naledi* editorial, 19 January 1912].

Author's Note: This is part of a broader historical study of Lesotho which engages with theoretical debates concerning imperialism and African social formations, and those of southern Africa in particular. In this essay the name Basutoland is used for the period of colonial domination (1868 to 1966), and the name Lesotho for independence before 1868 and after 1966. I would like to thank Henry Bernstein, Norman Levy, and Harold Wolpe for their comments on an earlier draft.

We must defend our hereditary chieftainship despite the fact that it is more and more becoming troublesome and an unbearable burden to the people and try to reform it in our own interests because it is a part ... of the conditions under which Basutoland came under the protection of England ... and if we may let the foundation get destroyed without being repaired by us we shall suffer an irreparable loss of the political status enjoyed by Basutoland as a protectorate under England [*Lekhotla la Bafo*, 1930].

[H]owever great the grumbling about the oppression and misconduct of the individual chiefs there is still an immense respect for the institution of chieftainship. An attack on the institution would find the Nation practically solid in its support [Pim Report, 1935].

Two distinctive features of colonial Basutoland were the maintenance of the hereditary institution of chieftainship and the retention of the kingdom as a national polity under direct British rule. Despite its manifest integration with the regional political economy of southern Africa, and the clear intention of the British to hand over the territory to the Union of South Africa, the experience of Basutoland (along with Swaziland and Bechuanaland, now Botswana) provides an important contrast with the fate of most other African kingdoms in the subcontinent. These two features are still of interest in contemporary Lesotho. The hereditary chieftainship, with the king at its apex, persists as an institution of political and economic importance (Weisfelder, 1977), although the reforms of 1938 to 1946, formal independence in 1966, and the 1979 Land Act have effected major changes (Hailey, 1953; Jones, 1951; Rugege, 1980).

The "separateness" of the state in Lesotho, which is sovereign yet hardly "independent," is of tremendous importance to the lives of its citizens in the current political confrontation in southern Africa, raising questions about the degree of autonomy of its dominant class in relation to South Africa and its differences from the state apparatuses of the "Bantustans." Most recent Marxist discussion of Lesotho (as of the "Bantustans") has tended to focus on economic underdevelopment with little attention to questions concerning the state (exceptions are Santho, 1981, and Rugege, 1980). This chapter, while relevant to both a fuller historical investigation and the analysis of current struggles, is more limited in scope. Its object is to locate colonial Basutoland, and particularly its state, in the context of the political economy of southern Africa in the period c. 1890 to 1930.

Recent studies of imperialist colonial domination have tended to concentrate on the economics of expropriation, exploitation, and underdevelopment. In recent southern African historiography the broad parameters of primitive accumulation, emergent capitalist production, and the transformation of the regional hinterland into a vast reservoir of cheap labor power have been well established. There is now a need for a more differentiated history exploring variant forms of capitalist penetration, and reconstructing transition as a process of struggle. Analysis of the colonial state—its structures, contradictions and development—is a strategic part of this project. Colonial Basutoland provides an instructive case since it came to occupy an uneasy position between Westminster and Pretoria and underwent extremely interesting political developments during colonialism.

Despite the continuing debate over its effectiveness, the concept of articulation of modes of production has proved very fruitful for investigating the process of transition in southern Africa at the turn of the twentieth century (Kimble, 1980, 1981; Wolpe, 1980a, 1983). By drawing attention to the internal structures and dynamics of African social formations and to the complexity of concrete social relations, it is possible to combat the tendency to "functionalist" explanations of capital accumulation.

Furthermore, analysis of the colonial state requires consideration of the articulation of political instances (Berman and Lonsdale, 1979; Lonsdale, 1981; Temu and Swai, 1981: 35–40), rather than viewing the state as simply an instrument or a unified agent (Mamdani, 1976; Omvedt, 1980). In Basutoland, a major element of the pre-colonial state apparatus, the chieftainship, was articulated with the institutions of colonial rule and administration. The term "colonial state" is used here to refer to this articulation, while "colonial administration" is restricted to those apparatuses run by colonial officials. In analyzing the chieftainship, it is necessary to distinguish between the chiefs as an economic class category, positioned within specific social relations of production, and the institutions and practices through which their class power was defined and reproduced—institutions with ideological and political as well as economic dimensions.

The *state*, then, is simultaneously an articulation of political institutions and a central element in the overall articulation of modes of production and social relations under colonialism. It is inevitably a complex object of analysis as the relationship between class and state in the capitalist mode of production is not equivalent to that in precapitalist modes. How the colonial state—colonial officials and chiefs in this case—intervened directly in the economy and in other ways affected the conditions of existence of different social classes and categories, is of critical importance in analysing the transition to capitalism. At the same time such an analysis must take into account the specificities of colonialism in the era of imperialism.

To establish the character and dynamics of the pre-capitalist mode of production and the pre-colonial state in Lesotho, it is necessary to explore briefly some economic and political developments in the mid-nineteenth century. The first section, therefore, deals with Moshoe-shoe's kingdom from c. 1830 to annexation by the Cape Colony in 1868, and the ensuing decade of Cape colonial rule. The major part of the chapter, the second section, concerns British colonial domination from c. 1890 to 1930, during which the key parameters of the political relations and struggles of the later colonial period were established. This account of the genesis of the colonial state demonstrates the initial ambivalence of British rule in Basutoland and suggests how this stamped the character of the political alliance between senior chiefs and colonial officials.

The institutional content of political articulation is then explored, with particular reference to the areas of utmost concern to all parties: the courts and taxation. The nature of production relations and class formation is indicated to show how the development of the colonial state was tied to the entrenchment of the system of migrant labor.

The chapter concludes with an attempt to demonstrate how the chieftainship had both changed through its articulation within the colonial state and yet become central to the discourse of almost all competing political forces within the country. As illustrated by the above quotations, the hereditary chieftainship with its laws, courts, and control of the land, came to symbolize Basutoland's special relationship with Britain. In my view, it was ultimately an obstacle to the incorporation of Basutoland in the Union of South Africa, although this requires further analysis outside the scope of the present essay.

PRE-COLONIAL LESOTHO AND CAPE ANNEXATION: 1830-1885

The history of Lesotho as a social formation in the geographical location it occupies today goes back approximately 160 years. While the history of the southern highveld prior to this awaits a Marxist exploration as challenging as the work of Slater (1976) on the southeast of the subcontinent, we can note that the emergence of the Sotho kingdom was a product of two major processes. The first was an internal transformation of African societies in this area, the second the penetration of European settlers into the interior of the highveld north of the great rivers Senqu and Vaal. These two developments were not unconnected, but whereas the racist historiography of apartheid attributed the former entirely to the latter, it is now widely recognized that the consolidated and centralized kingdoms of Moshoeshoe, Shaka, Khama, Sobhuza and others, were the result of a protracted historical transition, culminating in the crisis of the *lifaqane* wars of the early nineteenth century (Legassick, 1969; Slater, 1976).

Displacing a large number of fragmented and autonomous chiefdoms, the new kingdoms demonstrated a capacity to concentrate populations, mobilize labor and organize production on a large scale, and displayed a far more complex division of labor and political and military organization. While the interpretation of this process remains controversial, my view is that amongst the Sotho-Tswana peoples the transition from a lineage to an embryonic tributary mode of production had occurred long before, and that by the beginning of the nineteenth century the basis of the real, as opposed to formal, domination of producers by new ruling classes was being established. (These terms are taken from Rey, 1979.)

The penetration of white traders and settlers dramatically altered the context in which changes in African societies were to take place. In particular, it served to hasten the consolidation of class domination in African formations by posing a threat to the major means of production: land. Prior to the nineteenth century, contact between black and white had been focused around the initial annexation of the Cape by the Dutch. By the mid-eighteenth century a local commercial bourgeoisie had emerged in the Cape, based in the slave production of wine and grain and in growing trade links with the peoples of the interior.

With the establishment of British economic and political hegemony at the end of the eighteenth century, this local bourgeoisie began to expand its influence in the interior, while white cattle farmers moved north into the highveld region in search of land. The confrontation of these forces with African societies in the course of the nineteenth century took many forms, from land expropriation and exchange to war and colonial annexation. But at the core of colonial conquest lay the economic transformation of African formations: the commoditization of production, making the satisfaction of needs more dependent on the sale than on the immediate use of products (Marx, 1974: 325). The rhythm and extent of this process and the precise forms it took, varied with the particular African formations and settler groups involved and the nature of their interaction.

Moshoeshoe's Kingdom, c. 1830–1870[1]

Moshoeshoe's kingdom was primarily the outcome of internal social contradictions amongst the Sotho-Tswana formations of the southern highveld, but it was also affected by the penetration of merchant capital and struggles against settler expansion. Between 1825 and 1850 or so, Moshoeshoe's following expanded from about 3,000 to 80,000; by 1870 the population numbered about 125,000.

Basotho conquest of their natural environment was effected through the development of a complex and impressive system of agro-pastoralism. The uniqueness of the Caledon highlands lies in its high average rainfall; but given its markedly seasonal character and periodic drought (occurring with regularity every five years), the soils and vegetation structure require extremely skillful management to maintain the concentrated population and mixed farming patterns that have marked Sotho history. Moshoeshoe's kingdom exemplified three patterns of settlement and production, which had their roots in earlier Sotho practices. (1) To maintain the precarious ecology of the veld, pastoral production required extensive grazing patterns which were organized through the development of the *mafisa* system: the practice widespread in Africa of loaning stock with the "caretaker" enjoying rights of usufruct. (2) *Maboella*, a system for reserving local resources, especially of grazing, was developed to ensure access to wide reaches of pasture in years of drought and provide winter grazing within close range of lowland settlement. (3) Cultivation was based on two staple cereals, sorghum and maize. These provide a useful combination for lowlands farming, since sorghum is drought resistant while maize requires a relatively short growing system (thereby evading the danger of frost), and the stalks remaining in the fields are an important source of winter fodder.

In brief, the general pattern of Sotho development in the fifty years of Moshoeshoe's reign was of fairly dense but scattered settlement in the lowland region, with the well-watered plateaus and foothills used for grazing. The highlands were used only for hunting and as a retreat for herds in wartime. The intrinsic dangers of Sotho land use were, first, that of a secular decline in soil fertility since, in the absence of sources of wood, animal manure was required as a source of fuel; second, the vulnerability of the soil (common to many agro-pastoral systems but particularly acute in the geological and climatic conditions of Lesotho) which was to suffer irreparable damage in the twentieth century.

By the 1870s, the pattern of land use in Lesotho had begun to change (Sayce, 1924; Sheddick, 1954; Turner, 1978; Kimble, 1979).

First, some degree of concentration of settlement had begun to take place, particularly around the central residencies of the senior Koena chiefs—Moshoeshoe and his sons. Second, the expansion of settlement and arable cultivation in the lowlands, compounded by the limited introduction of a new cash crop, wheat, had led to a change in grazing patterns. Patterns of seasonal transhumance were beginning with the development of more regular cattle-posts in the upland and mountain regions, while some cultivation had begun to develop on the foothills. The early colonial period was to see further changes in production and land use, with the discovery that the mountain region was not only habitable and could support (admittedly poor) harvests of the two staple crops, but proved in succession to be some of the best wheatlands and sheep and goat grazing pasture in the entire subcontinent.

The key to the tremendous expansion of population and productive forces in the nineteenth century lay in the changing social relations and political organization of Sotho society under Moshoeshoe's kingdom. In seeking to understand the class nature of African formations in this period, one has to overcome the formidable obstacle presented by dominant perceptions of the chiefs, both then and now, and in academic as well as popular discourse. These perceptions, evident in Sotho sayings and proverbs and in historical writing (Thompson, 1975; Mofoka, 1980; Phoofolo, 1981) stress the role of chief as patriarch; identification of a chief by lineage; the chief as redistributor of wealth to his followers; and the relationship of chief and follower as one of personal dependence. The effect of these views is, first, to attribute the basis of a chief's power to his lineage identity which is characterized as the homestead, or family writ large, and, second, to divert attention from the mechanisms whereby chiefs accumulated wealth in the first place. In short, these conceptions obscure the fact that the relation between chiefs and followers was one of exploitation (extraction of surplus labor) *and* that this relation entailed mechanisms for the reproduction of chiefs as a social class (and not simply as individuals). In my view, the crucial transition from "lineage-based" to class society had taken place long before the social revolution unleased by the *lifaqane* wars of the early nineteenth century. The case for this position is, schematically, as follows.

According to the major writers on the lineage mode of production (Meillassoux, 1979, 1981; Terray, 1979; Dupré and Rey, 1980; Rey, 1979), it involves three principal elements: (1) the "major principles of social life and in particular the essential units of production are built up on the basis of real or fictive kinship" (Rey, 1979: 51); (2) power resides in control over the means of human reproduction (i.e., women) rather than the means of production (Meillassoux, 1981: 49; Dupré and Rey, 1980: 145); (3) relations of exploitation are predominantly between (male) elders and the dominated categories of (male) cadets, women and children (Terray, 1979; Rey, 1979; Molyneux, 1977).

Applying these points in turn to Lesotho, we find the following. First, although essential units of production *(ntlo* and *lelapa)*[2] were established largely on real or fictive kinship, there is much evidence that among the Sotho-Tswana peoples of the southern highveld there had long existed a larger unit of production, residence, and political allegiance: the chief's ward. This embraced within it the village and hamlet, organized on social principles transcending kinship (Ashton, 1946; Legassick, 1969). Chiefdoms were dominated by ruling lineages which had elevated themselves into aristocracies, and whose history of expansion, incorporation,. and fission is chronicled in oral tradition.

Second, while control over cattle was indeed the key to bride-wealth, and therefore marriage and human reproduction, it cannot be reduced to the latter. In cattle-keeping formations, analysis is complicated by the nature of cattle as a means of production (as well as representing access to means of reproduction). A lineage wealthy in cattle could multiply its size by *bohali* and *lenyalo la likhomo* (expressions for "marriage-with-cattle"), and by attaching clients to itself through *mafisa* (see above, p. 30). Indeed, it was the skillful combination of these practices as a strategy that partly accounts for Moshoeshoe's rise to power in the 1820s (Sanders, 1969; Wilson, 1969; Kuper, 1975; Kimble, 1979). Moreover, control of land—whether manifested in the annual distribution of land for cultivation, securing its return to communal usage for winter grazing, or establishing reserved grazing areas—appear to be economic powers exercised by chiefs long before the nineteenth century.[3]

Third, the ability to appropriate surplus in the Sotho chiefdoms was not restricted to the category of elders. Within lineages, the patriarchal elder or eldest son of the senior house was in a relation of dominance over others and was able both to appropriate and centralize surplus and to determine the distribution of resources to wives, brothers, uncles and children. But there had also emerged forms of tribute labor based on the relations of two distinct groups, chiefs and commoners (or subjects). Through the organization of age groups and military regiments, chiefs were able to draw on tribute labor in four major branches of activity: cattle keeping, cultivation, hunting, and military service.

Thus the view of Sotho society as "classless" is misleading not only in relation to Moshoeshoe's kingdom but also to the preceding period of development in the eighteenth century. Rather than Moshoeshoe symbolizing the initial phase of transition from the lineage to a tributary mode of production, it may well be the case that his reign expressed the historical moment at which the latter established its real domination over the former. The consolidation of chieftainship and the emergence of the state were crucial aspects of this later phase of transition. Before the period of *lifaqane*, attempts by Sotho chiefs to consolidate their position as a class were undermined by the continuous segmentation and fission of ruling lineages, due to their patrilineal organization. Junior branches were easily able to split away, taking cattle with them and settling new land, thereby weakening the bid by some royal lineages to extend their domination over a broader confederation (Legassick, 1969; Machobane, 1978; and on the Nguni, Slater, 1976). It seems then that Moshoeshoe was able to "seize the time" at a particular juncture of internal crisis and external pressure and Sotho history moved into a new phase of development.

The changes in the three areas outlined above—the organization of production, property relations, and modes of surplus appropriation—were further advanced in Moshoeshoe's period, when they were linked with the development of the state. The latter secured the consolidation of power by one aristocratic lineage, Moshoeshoe's Bakoena, which stamped its own dynastic identity as a (newly) royal lineage on the institutions of the state. The latter encompassed all spheres of social activity: economic, political, juridical, and ideological. The chief's ward, the central political unit, centred on *lekhotla* (the court, but also the council of advisors), and included two other important organizations—*pitso* (public meeting or parliament, which the chief could summon), and *lebotho* or regiment based in the chief's age set *(mophato)*.

The system of government was both hierarchical and decentralized, held together by Moshoeshoe's innovation of "placing" chiefs. At the territorial level, Moshoeshoe "placed" his own brothers and senior sons in strategically distributed regions (Phoofolo, 1981: 43–54). At the level of these regions or districts, the senior chiefs were allowed to "place" their own descendants, thereby effectively displacing and downgrading previous local political structures. Thus "placed," a chief was able to allocate land within his area of control; to demand tribute labor from the followers of subordinate chiefs, as well as from his own; to administer unoccupied land (of increasing significance as external boundaries were closed off and internal expansion became the only source of new land); to open his court to appeal from the courts of subordinate chiefs; and to call *lipitso* which all subordinates and followers were supposed to attend. With this "placing" system, Moshoeshoe attempted to resolve the problem of succession that had bedevilled Sotho chieftaincies. By deliberately creating space within certain limits for potential secessionists to organize subpolities, he also secured an institutional base for the dynastic succession (and expansion) of his own, royal, lineage.

The Sotho military regiment based in the chief's ward, while not as developed as among Mazulu, served a combination of economic, political, and ideological purposes. It was, among other things, a form of organizing tribute labor to work in the chief's fields; the nucleus of military organization; and the major determinant of a man's political identity. Attendance at *lipitso* called by *marena* (chiefs) for example, took the form of men mounted and armed in their regiments. Other important economic institutions based in the chief's ward included *maboella* and *mafisa* (mentioned above), and *matsema* (tribute labor).

The material basis of the domination of commoners by chiefs lay in the latter's effective control over the basic means of production, cattle and land. To secure access to land for cultivation, grazing, and secure residence, a commoner homestead had to enter a relationship of allegiance to the chief. This involved control by the chief over the labor-time of his adult male subject, the most important expression of which was the performance of tribute labor in various branches of activity. This gradually came to limit the capacity of commoner homesteads to organize production independently of the chieftainship.

The mobilization of male labor in activities organized by the chiefs was made possible by, and served to reinforce, the division of labor within the commoner homestead. This division was based on gender and age and increasingly tended to restrict women's productive activity to the homestead and to agricultural work. This increasing identification of female labor with individual homestead production, and male labor with the performance of public, social labor, meant that any expansion of production of the commoner homestead depended primarily on increased access to female labor, while that of the chief depended on increased mobilization of male labor time. At the same time, the process of accumulation of wealth of a chief was also dependent on his own private household, organized on patrilineal principles, hence the mobilization of women, children, and cattle.

The historical conjuncture of the *lifaqane* and the impact of settler and mercantile penetration in the following fifty years tended to strengthen the position of the chiefs as a whole in relation to control of the main means of production—cattle and land. Senior chiefs began to regard the land under their political control as their "property." Allocation of land rights became more complex, as did the procedures required to resolve disputes between chiefs and subjects, and between different fractions of the chiefly class—senior and junior, Koena and non-Koena. Resolution of particular disputes created precedents for new legal principles and practices. Control over land became simultaneously a central condition for the reproduction of the chiefs' collective power and the most important site of conflicts between chiefs. It is also important to note that in the course of interminable negotiations with the British over the boundaries of Lesotho and the Orange Free State, Moshoeshoe and his sons—as the "diplomatic" representatives of the new Sotho state—enhanced both the sovereignty of the central kingship in relation to the land and the rule of their own dynasty.

The importance of coming to grips with the development of social class and the emergence of the state in nineteenth century Lesotho is even clearer when the penetration of merchant capital in this period is considered. In Lesotho, merchant capital took three forms: traders, missionaries, and settler farmers. In the case of the latter, trade and war represented two sides of the same coin. Between the 1840s and the 1860s, Basotho fought a series of dramatic wars to defend their cattle and land, handicapped only by British attempts to prevent their acquisition of modern arms and by a series of debilitating negotiations.

The same settlers also sought to acquire the grain, labor, and cattle of Basotho through exchange, which flourished during this period. The missionaries, with their creed of the three C's—Christianity, Commerce, Civilization—encouraged the emergence of small commodity producers, and with their attack on *bohali*, polygamy, *matsema, lebollo* (initiation school), and other key institutions, sought to sever the relations between chiefs and subjects. Missionary penetration in Lesotho was one of the greatest "success" stories of evangelical endeavor of the region in this period and was a major force in stimulating commoditization. However, the principal force in this process was the Koena lineage itself, which used its command over the labor time of its male subjects and its capacity to extract a surplus product to dominate the new exchange relations and obtain commodities: cattle and guns. Despite the emergence of some forms of migrant labor, the exchange of agricultural produce remained the most significant mode of participation in the market at this time (Kimble, 1979).

Cape Colonial Rule, 1870–1883[4]

Lesotho was initially annexed by Britian in 1868 and its administration handed over to the Cape Colony without any consultation three years later (Mohapeloa, 1971; Burman, 1971). The 1870s were a major turning point for Basotho. They had been renowned for four decades as good suppliers of grain and labor to the surrounding white settlers and colonists. The demand for both commodities increased greatly with the boom generated by the discovery of diamonds in Kimberley in 1870. The rapid emergence of capitalist production in the diamond fields, with its corresponding demand for mobile or free labor, had dramatic repercussions for the supply of labor previously recruited through semi-feudal relations. In the absence of a dominant mode of production or a dominant class in southern Africa at this time, however, employers experienced a permanent shortage of labor. Wages rose steadily and guns were supplied freely to attract workers.

In this critical decade between the discovery of diamonds and the discovery of gold, and before the influx of imperial capital, there was no clear shift of orientation in the fragmented apparatuses of the colonial adminstrations established under the hegemony of merchant capital. The immediate concern of the (Cape) colonial administration in Basutoland was to foster commoditization and monetization. However, these same conditions of mercantile penetration ensured that large numbers of adult male Basotho began to sell their labor-power as a commodity on a regular basis, although only in exchange for wages which would secure access to certain commodities. Broadly speaking, the key stimulus to labor migration during the 1870s stemmed from the Koena lineage's strategy to reproduce its dominance in the new context of colonial rule, although clearly other forces were also at work. The other major economic development of the 1870s was the dramatic increase in production of agricultural commodities—wheat, maize, sorghum, wool, and mohair. This was part of a more generalized commoditization of production, in which the further development of a home market and the imposition of money taxation were also important factors. Of greatest significance, however, was the intensification of surplus extraction by the chiefs and the increasing realization of this surplus through exchange, as chiefs sought to expand their accumulation and their consumption of imported commodities.

The changes of the 1870s had important social and political effects in three areas. First, formal colonial rule threatened the coherence of the institutions of the pre-colonial state and the solidity of chiefs as a class. For example, the Cape administration assumed powers of allocating land and controlling the conditions of expansion of merchant capital and attempted to restrict the chiefs' ability to appropriate surplus. The rule of magistrates and the imposition of Cape colonial law seriously threatened the powers of king, chief, and patriarch alike.

Second, and somewhat ironically, colonial rule served to expand the activities of the precolonial state apparatuses it was supposed to replace, both "new" functions like tax collections and "traditional" ones like the work of *makhotla* (the courts). Chiefs' households expanded with a growing convergence of private and public activities centered on them. Chiefs were also affected by the pressures of commoditization and monetary calculation became central to their economic organization in the 1870s.

Finally, commoner households in general experienced increased pressure on the labor time of their members, directly from the chiefs' demands for male tribute labor and indirectly from colonial taxation. At the same time, it now becomes harder to generalize about commoner households due to the emergence of a distinct group of monogamous Christians and because some smaller households were being marginalized through the "simple reproduction squeeze" (Bernstein, 1979). The growing heterogeneity of homesteads was manifested in differences in household composition, access to means of production, and economic behavior.

In assessing the political implications of the socio-economic changes of the 1870s it is important to note limitations to the domination of the Bakoena under Moshoeshoe: It had existed for only a generation before colonial rule; the problem of segmentation had been contained rather than definitively resolved; central political authority was still vulnerable in the face of dynastic politics generated by conflicts between older and younger brothers in lineages (the 1890s saw a resurgence of such dynastic politics; see Phoofolo, 1981). At one level, the advent of colonial rule strengthened the individual positions of the senior chiefs, whose capacity to extract a surplus from their followers was enhanced by the increased penetration of merchant capital (promoted by the colonial administration, as noted above). The multifunctional post of magistrate was designed ultimately to replace the office of senior chief, but in practice the colonial administration was forced to operate through the chiefs. Interestingly, the establishment of (initially) four magistrates' administrative districts acknowledged the previous four principal wards of Moshoeshoe's senior sons. Chiefs were used to collect taxes and as police, and the colonial administration was for the most part forced to accommodate itself to the power of the chiefs, including the manning of their courts.[5]

At another level, however, the strength of the chiefs as a collective political force declined considerably, particularly through the weakening of its central focus in the kingship. Moshoeshoe's oldest son and successor, Letsie I, was reduced to the status of *primus inter pares,* and he was often overshadowed by his stronger brothers, Molapo and Masupha.

The period following Moshoeshoe's kingdom was therefore contradictory in political terms, as illustrated by the Gun War *(Ntoa ea Lithunya)* of 1880–1881 and the civil war of 1881–1883. The first was an uprising against the Cape administration occasioned by the policy of "Disarmament," a direct attack on the chief's powers of military organization. The entire senior hierarchy of the chieftainship threw its weight against the colonial government (Ajulu, 1979). In the civil war that followed, however, the energies of the senior chiefs were turned inwards to a dynastic struggle exacerbated by the effects of colonial rule and mercantile penetration.

BRITISH COLONIAL RULE, 1884–1930[6]

Following the civil war, the Cape Colony handed back the government of Basutoland to Britain with legislative and executive powers vested in the British High Commissioner. According to one historian, the implicit admission of defeat by the Cape administration meant that "the chiefs had won" (Burman, 1981: 181). In one sense, elaborated below, the Bakoena chiefs were very successful in establishing their place in the subsequent British colonial state. On the other hand, the chiefs were not able to defeat imperialism and the next eighty years of colonial rule were to transform completely the economic and political character of the kingdom.[7] Before analyzing the political articulation of the colonial state, it is necessary to first outline the historical conjuncture in southern Africa as a whole.

Gold and Migrant Labor

What follows is a highly compressed account of a complex historical period, which is the object of much current debate and controversy (see, among others, Legassick, 1980; Legassick and Wolpe, 1976; Bundy, 1979; Morris, 1980; Marks and Atmore, 1980; Marks and Rathbone, 1982; Levy, 1982). The discovery of the rich gold reefs of the Rand in the mid-1880s set in motion what has been described as the era of segregation in South Africa (Wolpe, 1980b). In the age of high imperialism, the mechanisms of primitive accumulation of capital were dominant in the subcontinent. It was not until the emergence of a viable manufacturing sector and the emergence of capitalist agriculture that the capitalist mode of production began to reproduce itself on an expanded basis. Indeed it was not until the 1910s that gold captial was in a position to assert its organized strength against the predominantly black working class it had brought into being.

During the period 1880–1920, moreover, primitive accumulation did not predominantly take the form of expulsion of the direct producers from the soil. Although a surplus population was generated on the land (through, among other things, the decline of various branches of production, the development of the home market for imported commodities, and the gradual reduction of total land resources available to non-capitalist modes), this surplus population tended to remain on the land in a "latent" form, still organized around non-capitalist production units.

> The extent to which the agricultural surplus population actually passed over into an urban or manufacturing proletariat was inhibited by the specific conditions under which it was formed. In the white (agricultural) sector, this was because the institution of capitalist relations . . . took the form of a labor-tenancy relationship. In the Native Reserve sectors, this was because of the preservation . . . of forms of non-capitalist relations of production. [Legassick and Wolpe, 1976: 99]

To explain this preservation, a broad historical perspective is necessary.

By the last quarter of the nineteenth century, in part as a result of the previous penetration of merchant capital, gold mining capital and the colonial power, Britain, were faced with the existence of strong non-capitalist ruling classes in both the settler and African social formations. These ruling classes premised their domination on the maintenance of a unity between the direct producers and the means of production. On the one hand, the white settler farmers secured their labor supply and surplus extraction through the labor tenancy system (Morris, 1980). On the other hand, within many of the African kingdoms in close proximity to the new gold reefs (Batswana, Bapeli, Basotho, Maswazi) comparable structural situations existed. For different reasons, capital and the colonial power were forced to proceed differently in relation to these dominant classes. Fierce wars were necessary in both cases, and in this respect the Basotho Gun War could be set alongside Isandhlwana (1879), and perhaps Majuba (1881) and the Anglo-Boer War (1899–1902). In all these instances the military and political strength of Britain, was put to a severe test. But the outcomes involved very different kinds of political arrangements, and at this point any analogy between Afrikaner and African experiences becomes meaningless.

From the viewpoint of the demand for labor, one critical outcome of this period of struggle was the creation of conditions of industrial capitalist production on the basis of a migrant labor force, the most distinctive characteristic of which was that it was neither separated from access to means of production *nor* from the relations of exploitation entailed by this non-separation. In short, the political compromise illustrated by the establishment of the new colonial state in Basutoland, guaranteed a certain continuity to the class relations of Moshoeshoe's kingdom.

One effect of this was that the aggregate bargaining power of the early migrants from many of the African kingdoms proximate to the gold mines—a power demonstrated in their selective capacity to evade certain levels of wages, lengths of contract, and even conditions of work—was relatively favorable during the years 1890–1900. In the following decade, mining capital found itself further frustrated by migrants from these societies. In the years following the South African war, the labor markets of the subcontinent were unsettled, disrupted by the high rates paid by military and construction employment and by conditions of work on white farms. But during this decade, mining capital was able to secure a labor supply at low wage levels by access to an "artificial reserve army of labor" beyond the geographical confines of South Africa (Legassick and Declerq, 1978).

Between 1910 and 1920 conditions of labor supply began to change for mining capital. On one side, recruiting mechanisms were tightened up, competition between mines was more or less eliminated with the institution of the maximum average wage, and general conditions improved with the establishment of a viable unitary state structure. On the other side, mining capital was now in a position to enforce lower wage levels and longer contracts on its now expanding reserve army of labor in the very African kingdoms whose inhabitants had earlier demonstrated a relative independence. The debilitating effects of land shortage, deepening commoditization, and the development of a territorial division of labor in the subcontinent which exposed African agricultural commodity producers to competition with subsidized white capitalist farmers, all combined to reduce the value of the rural bargaining power of African producers. By the 1920s and 1930s, mining capital was able to secure a cheap labor supply in a form which had effectively deprived the latter of its muscle: migrancy.

From this vantage point, it indeed looked as though thirty years earlier Africans had been conceded "the vestiges of 'rural bargaining power' at the expense of prohibiting them from acquiring urban bargaining power" (Legassick, 1980: 267). The pendulum of class struggle had for the time being swung firmly against the migrant proletariat (although see O'Meara, 1975).

In the case of Lesotho, this pattern is very clear, and the period was marked by intensive struggles of the emergent migrant proletariat against capital. In the 1890s, although Basotho sold their labor power on a greater scale than they had done in the previous 20 years, they did so to some extent "on their own terms." One clear example was the difficulty experienced by gold mining in securing any Basotho workers at all, since the latter preferred the higher wages and marginally better conditions on the diamond mines. By the early 1900s, Basotho were still rejecting the contract lengths offered on the gold mines. Not only did they reject the six-month contract in favor of three months, but in many cases they chose to go for one month at a time, a preference which the gold mines made some moves to accommodate.

Basotho also disliked the interference of recruitment with their free movement. Their penchant (well into the 1900s and 1910s) for what contemporaries considered a kind of "freelance" or "hawking" of labor power was reflected in their opposition to signing contracts before departure, to the chiefs acting as recruiters, or even to taking passes specifically for "laboring purposes." Once at work, there is evidence that Basotho could demonstrate a high degree of independence, walking out, refusing to do work other than that they had agreed to do, demanding advance payment of wages and complaining of conditions (Kimble, 1981). In my view, this high degree of independence manifested by Basotho migrants is not so much indicative of "worker consciousness" (Van Onselen, 1978), as a demonstration that Sotho homesteads were still viable economic units. The question is how the recruitment strategies of mining captial articulated with social forces in Basutoland, to generate a particular kind of migrant labor forces.

By the 1920s mining capital was in a much stronger position, while conditions inside Basutoland had changed dramatically under the impact of colonialism. By the middle of the second decade of the twentieth century, concentration of stock and people in the lowlands had created serious problems of erosion, soil exhaustion, and ecological imbalance. Younger men were having to wait longer for their first plots of land, which were also smaller and more fragmented. Marginalized elements had nothing more than residence rights, garden plots, and possibly grazing rights (maybe for stock held on *mafisa*).

For others, arable land for production was not scarce but they were subject to competition from white farmers, lack of assistance from the colonial administration, and political opposition from a debilitated chieftainship. The most effective commodity producers during this period were those engaged in the production of wool and mohair. The mountains had proved a viable area for rearing sheep and goats, and there was little competition inside South Africa for what was basically an international export. But even the full development of this branch of commodity production was made difficult under the conditions of early colonial rule (as we shall see below), and it was never a possibility for the majority.

In general, by the 1920s for those households sending migrant workers to the mines, higher wages would have been imperative to maintain previous standards of living and to cope with higher taxes. In conditions of the strength of mining capital and virtually fixed low wage rates, the growing dependence of such households on migrant wage labor was indicated by the increase in the average length of contracts. For the most marginalized there was a growing tendency to abandon the land. In Basutoland shortfalls in tax revenues were increasingly attributed to the prolonged absence of Basotho in the towns of South Africa.

During the 1920s the Union of South Africa began to develop legislative and administrative means to inhibit urbanization of Africans. This was not possible, however, without the development of appropriate political mechanisms to retain the growing latent surplus population in the rural areas. The key agent acting to restrict Basotho workers to a cyclical migration was the colonial state, whose particular articulation between the chiefs and administration generated its own kind of political and economic logic. This logic was indeed in the broader interests of capital and of imperialism, but it is important to specify the character of the struggles that determined the precise mechanisms involved. I shall suggest how a particular articulation was established in the genesis of the colonial state in Basutoland, and then illustrate its effects in the two key areas of the courts and taxation. On this basis it is possible to demonstrate why the return of migrant workers gradually became imperative for both parties in the colonial state.

The Establishment of Colonial Sovereignty

The imposition of British rule in 1884 created a new framework for the construction of a colonial state premised on an explicit, if unequal, alliance between colonial administration and chieftainship.

The Regulations of 1884 quite clearly returned various key spheres of judicial and administrative powers to the latter—in particular, their right to hold courts and determine land allocation (Basutoland Government, 1909: 76–83). In the 1880s British colonial policy, itself a product of past strategy as well as present conjuncture, changed direction in southern Africa. While its basic political calculations were now guided by the need to foster conditions for the successful investment of mining capital, and to ensure a profitable spin-off to the local "supportive" mercantile and (later) agricultural classes, a number of constraints operated.

Gladstonian principles of self-sufficiency for the colonies and the failure of a "native policy" based on principles of Cape liberalism and integration (particularly for those African societies which retained their territorial and social integrity under the boom conditions of the 1870s) dictated a certain "minimalism." Although Basutoland was considered one of the most productive African kingdoms, the British government was unwilling to spend any extra time or money devising a solution for what had proved a difficult territory to govern and one which (as Rhodes crudely put it) would "still be there for us," whatever happened.

Rhodes spoke for the Cape government which would later form part of the Union of South Africa. The Act of Union in 1910 included a clause empowering the British Crown, in specified conditions, to transfer Basutoland, Bechuanaland, and Swaziland to the Union. While the early years of colonial administration were marked by a repeated acknowledgment of the "provisional" character of British rule, this was not the same as "non-intervention" or "laissez faire" (Prim, 1935: 49, 76; Hailey, 1953: 67, 80). These formative years saw a selective restructuring of the chieftainship and intervention in its activities by colonial officials. Rather than the continuation of Moshoeshoe's project of "nation-building" by his son Letsie (king 1870-1891) and grandson Lerotholi (king 1891-1905), in "partnership" with the British Resident Commissioner, a qualitatively new process was set in motion: the construction of a *colonial state*. As the anti-colonial organization *Lekhotla la Bafo* was later to argue, this involved "a deprivation of the chiefs' authority over their people in the country of their birth," ultimately leading the chiefs to "become the agents and tools of their own ruin" (LNA, S3/22/2/4, 1930).

The immediate political aim of Clarke and Lagden, the astute Resident Commissioners between 1884 and 1903, was to establish a way of working with the senior chiefs and particularly the king (whom they renamed "Paramount Chief"), above all to avoid confrontation with the chiefs as a class. To this end, they manipulated dynastic politics and fractional struggles amongst the chiefs, intervened selectively in "placing" and in land disputes and provided strategic assistance to bolster the power of the "Paramount" while ensuring that he did not "forget from whom his real power derived" (CAR, 1898-9: 47). This policy was put to the test in 1898 by the "uprising" of Masupha, Lerotholi's uncle and most serious pole of opposition to his rule, as well as the most consistent opponent of colonial rule among the senior chiefs (Mohapeloa, 1966; Burman, 1981).

The defeat of Masupha was a watershed in Sotho political history, which in my view has not been adequately assessed (though see Phoofolo, 1981). It signified a change in British colonial rule which dug in for a longer, if still temporary, stay. At the same time it represented a critical moment in the relationship of the senior house of Moshoeshoe (Lerotholi's faction) and the colonial administration, which henceforth was institutionalized in the political structures and practices of the colonial state. Both parties had good reason to obliterate the threat represented by Masupha and had thus activated the alliance in their own immediate interests. As a result, the political future of the "sons of Moshoeshoe" (the political grouping of his most senior descendants) was tied in with the colonial administration. Similarly, the latter was locked into an embrace with the chieftainship and found its room for maneuver more restricted in practice than the constitutional latitude of the 1884 Regulations suggested.

Construction of the Colonial State

Bearing in mind that there was a constant interplay and discrepancy between constitutional position and political practice, one of the purposes of the colonial administration in incorporating the chiefs in the state was to make use of their powers of government. The decentralized Sotho chieftainship was an effective means of accounting for every homestead and individual in the territory. This "almost complete control of the people" (CAR, 1893-1894: 20) was the heart of the matter for colonial power. The identification of a man (and through him his dependents) for purposes of taxation, judicial fines, labor contract, or census, was constituted through his district, chief, "headman," and—if necessary—his father. Immigration and residence could be controlled through the "useful principle that no one can be permitted to reside on the land of a chief to whom he refuses allegiance" (CAR, 1898-1899: 47), or, for that matter, to whom he refused to pay (colonial) taxes. Yet by locking into the complex structures of Sotho political domination, the colonial administration was entering into competition with the chiefs on their own terrain. The question for both the dominant and subordinate partners in the colonial state was how to make use of and yet neutralize the other. This was the nub of the political articulation, although clearly the balance of power lay in the hands of the British.

The constitution and functioning of the courts, and the content and operation of the law, were of utmost importance to both chiefs and colonial officials. In pre-colonial Lesotho, *lekhotla* was the central site of government and administration, and under Moshoeshoe *makhotla* were the embodiment of political sovereignty and hierarchy, through which hereditary chiefs had increasingly become the authoritative exponents of *melao* (laws). The capacity to enforce, or overturn, judgements on subordinates was a central aspect of the chiefs' powers of coercion. Cape colonial rule had challenged this juridico-political structure, beginning with the key post of magistrate, and had thereby consolidated the chiefs' opposition, later expressed in the Gun War. The 1884 Regulations establishing British rule, however, abandoned substantive changes to family law codes and recognized the administration of native law in the chiefs' courts (Basutoland Government, 1909: 76-83). At the same time, sovereignty was to reside in the colonial administration, and the 1884 Regulations endowed the Resident Commissioner with formal powers to appoint chiefs, to recognize and regulate their courts, and to provide for appeals from chiefs' to commissioners' courts.

> It shall be lawful for any Native Chief in the said territory, appointed by the Resident Commissioner, to adjudicate upon and try such cases, criminal or civil, and to exercise jurisdiction in such a manner and within such limits, as may be defined by any rules established by the authority of the Resident Commissioner [Basutoland Government, 1909: 77].

Precisely how these activities were to be carried out was left open. The practices of the first Resident Commissioners, who were primarily concerned with manipulating dynastic politics rather than institutionalizing the 1884 Regulations, continued into the early twentieth century. The mechanisms deployed by the administration to restructure the chieftainship within the colonial state bore very little relation to the constitutional formulae. The problems this raised were not confronted by the colonial administration until later, by which time the colonial state was a reality and the chieftainship proved a far tougher nut to crack than expected (Hailey, 1953).

The principal means used by colonial officials to try to control chiefs were these: (1) intervention in disputes over administrative land boundaries between chiefs; (2) creation of the Basutoland National Council and the constitution of *Melao oa Lerotholi* (Laws of Lerotholi; Poulter, 1972); (3) manipulation of payment to chiefs of tax percentages and "allowances." Intervention in all three spheres was essential to establishing the dominance of the colonial administration. Inasmuch as each form of intervention effectively recognized and in some cases consolidated the political power of chiefs, it also involved contradictions for the colonial administration.

First, concerning the land question (which can only be touched on here), colonial officials were aware from an early date that boundary disputes between chiefs had major political significance, particularly as settlement, cultivation and grazing expanded into previously little populated districts. Although these bitter and manifold disputes appeared to colonial officials to have the benefit of "completely localizing tribal attention" (CAR, 1895–1896: 6), the administration was drawn into judgments, particularly in cases involving arms and bloodshed which became more frequent in the early twentieth century. Despite this increasing involvement in dynastic and district politics, the colonial administration was never able to alter fundamentally the "placing" system. In effect it continually made political interventions rather than devising an alternative structure of government. The persistence of "placing" meant that one of the principal mechanisms of reproduction of the chiefly hierarchy (and hence of its courts) remained intact. The consequent multiplication of courts, fostered by "placing," was recognized as a problem by colonial officials in the 1920s:

> It was never the intention of either the Basuto themselves or the Government that the entire male offspring of a chief should each be called a chief, have his caretaking and his court . . . the country is filling up with so-called chiefs who have their courts [LNA, S3/6/1/5, 1926].

Second, the formation of the Basutoland National Council in 1903 ushered in a new phase of the country's political history (Mohapeloa, 1977). It consisted of ninety-five representatives appointed by the *Morena ea Moholo* (the king or Paramount Chief) and five by the Resident Commissioner, " with the purpose of taking (the chiefs) into partnership and giving them an interest in affairs" (Pim, 1935: 20). The Colonial Office was anxious that the Council should alter the system of government, and that its powers should be strictly limited to questions of "native" concern and "internal affairs":

> We cannot keep Basutoland for ever as a native reserve, and when the time comes for opening it to European enterprise, a full fledged native Parliament may be awkward, if its functions and proceedings are not strictly limited [Colonial Office minute quoted in Mohapeloa, 1977: 12].

However, given the balance of political power in the local colonial state, the unusual fluidity of institutional definition, and the perspective of impermanence, the council (BNC) quickly became an important site of struggle over the political relations at the heart of that state, and a locus of definition or constitution of these relations.

This is exemplified most clearly in the establishment of *Melao oa Lerotholi*, illustrating political articulation at work. *Melao* were proposed and drawn up at the initial meeting of the BNC in the recognition that "things had changed" since the days of Moshoeshoe, and in an attempt to record precisely how they had changed. The eighteen laws finally accepted covered an extremely wide range: rights of succession, procedures of economic, judicial and political administration by the chieftainship; civil and family law; and operation of the courts. In many respects, these laws had an extremely uncertain status (Poulter, 1972), but in practice they represented the most significant constitutional intervention in the internal dynamics of the chieftainship of the entire period under consideration (Hailey, 1953: 62). Although in strictly colonial terms *Melao* were regarded merely as guidelines for "checking and controlling what were considered to be arbitrary and rapacious decisions of courts of native chiefs" (CAR, 1903–4: 12), they were to become a crucial point of reference and a constitutive moment for the hereditary chieftainship in colonial conditions.

The consequence of this codification for relations between Basotho people and their chiefs were to be profound. In the view of Philip Molise, a commoner advisor to Lerotholi, "now the chiefs were bound to obey their laws even though they did not know what they had let themselves in for" (BNC, 25 July 1903). Yet chiefs were no longer "bound" *ka batho* (by the people). They were now being "bound" by the colonial state. At the same time, the colonial administration had also "let itself in for" a competing definition of control and sovereignty in a sphere where, according to the 1884 Regulations, it was designed to reign supreme. The very existence of the BNC as a forum where amendments to these laws were made, details of "customary law" were refined for the benefit of the colonial courts, and indeed where the chiefs were implicated in virtually every administrative and fiscal move by the administration, illustrated the limits and contradictions of the colonial state.

Third, the colonial administration sought to control the chiefs through manipulating payment of tax percentages and "allowances." The payment of a percentage (in the range of 6–10%) of tax collected to the senior chiefs and their most important subordinates was a practice begun under Cape colonial rule, representing both a recognition by the administration of the key role played by the chiefs in this activity and a means of control over their pursuit of it. By giving each chief a vested interest in the collection of tax (payment of which had become the effective condition for access to land), the colonial administration was tying pre-colonial to colonial tribute, and implicating the chiefs further in promoting commoditization (penetration of merchant capital and securing labor for industrial capital).

More concretely, this combination of forms of appropriation of surplus in the office of the chief continued a process begun in the 1870s, whereby the chiefs' political and economic calculations in relation to their subjects began to change. There was now an incentive to multiply the tax-paying productive units of their followers (through encouraging immigration and fragmentation); and, with pressure on the allocation of arable land, to replace non-taxpaying units (such as widows) with new tax-paying units (bachelor migrants). This was only one aspect of fundamental changes taking place at the heart of the chief's household and political ward. The senior chiefs, faced with ever-increasing needs for cash, actively sought to entrench these percentages (and other gratuities) as political rights inherent in the recognition of the chieftainship by the colonial administration. Thus, for example, the Paramount might request that the administration effectively "recognize" the placing of a new chief by granting him a small tax percentage, or discipline subordinates who refused to "recognize" the tax collectors of their seniors; or a particular chief might demand that he or his son "inherit" the colonial gratuity paid to his father or himself.

Although these payments provided one of the most effective and "legitimate" (i.e., politically accepted by Basotho chiefs) means that the colonial administration could deploy to control the politics of the chieftainship, it was again more a mechanism of negotiation than of systematic control. As with the other mechanisms discussed above, this area was marked by the political struggles of the 1880s and 1890s.

In 1900, the Resident Commissioner Lagden had admitted that there were problems involved in any attempt to systematize the payment of allowances and gratuities,

> The matter is complicated in that certain incongruities crept in 1884 [sic] due to political legacies left by the Basuto war and the various rulers who held intermittent control and the original scale had but a meagre relation to the amount of tax actually paid [LNA, S3/29/8/8a, 1918].

Lagden had suggested "a gradual reduction by time and a fixing of our attention upon those who are responsible and competent to carry out orders" (LNA, S3/29/8/8a, 1918). However, the system of payment had continued to be complicated and determined by political maneuvers of individual officials, such that two decades later the administration found itself fighting a rearguard battle to establish that "What is given by Government to a chief is a present and cannot be looked upon as an inheritance like cattle to which his son may succeed" (LNA, S3/5/1/18b, 1925), and even to ensure that allowances were used for the "political and disciplinary purposes" for which they had been intended (LNA S3/5/1/18a, 1925).

The role of colonial taxation generally in promoting commoditization—whether manifested in agricultural production or the formation of wage labor—has been well demonstrated. Less attention has been paid to its effects on the organization of production and social relations, and in this case on the political relationships constituting the colonial state. The rest of this section discusses how taxation policy was located in the wider concerns and calculations of the colonial administration, and how the chiefs became involved in a widening of the tax net that, in turn, led inexorably to the promotion of migrant wage labor (with an equal emphasis on its return).

Colonial Taxation, Commodity Production, and Migrant Labor

For the colonial administration, taxation of Basotho was a *sine qua non* of colonial rule. There is no doubt that at the broader level of colonial and imperial strategy, the decades following the Anglo-Boer war had opened up a deeper committent to the "cause of the gold mining industry" (Levy, 1982: 133). The post-war Milner administration recognized that a prosperous mining industry was the basis for reconstruction and expansion of the entire subcontinent (Levy, 1982: 132–40). Political and administrative institutions developed during the earlier period of hegemony of merchant capital were adapted to suit the new demands of the now dominant mining capital, but their adaptation was not straightforward. The colonial state in Basutoland took specific steps to align itself more closely with the requirements of the mining industry, such as legislation to facilitate and regulate recruitment; while through its entry into the Customs Union, it became locked into a set of arrangements which benefited the fledgling manufacturing industry in the Union. Yet it would be mistaken to view the colonial administration in Basutoland after 1902 as a single-minded "instrument" for turning the country into a labor reserve for the mining industry. The pursuit of this strategic aim was necessarily mediated by the structures, institutions and political relations through which the state itself was constituted.

The state in Basutoland promoted labor migration in order to bring money from wages into its territory: encouraging the formation of labor power as a commodity was the specific form in which the state mediated "the function of capital." As well as encouraging the recruitment of labor for the mines, railway construction, and farms of South Africa, its reliance on taxation led the colonial administration to promote trade, and then selected areas of commodity production within Basutoland. With "successful" promotion of migrant labor to the extent that its earnings became the major source of Basotho "purchasing power," taxation, and investment in commodity production, the colonial state—both officials and chiefs—became just as concerned to secure the return of migrants.

By the time of the Anglo-Boer war the administration recognized that Basutoland would continue to

> supply the sinews of agriculture in the Orange Free State, . . . railway works, coal mining, the diamond mines at Jagersfontein and Kimberley, the gold mines of the Transvaal, . . . and a large proportion of domestic servants in the neighbouring territories [CAR, 1898–9: 7–8].

On one hand, it was argued, Basotho had increasing wants "which they must supply by labor if they cannot supply them from their grain"; on the other hand, any major increase in this supply would await the widespread "shortage of gardens" (Transvaal, 1903: 224; CAR, 1901–2: 9). The supply of migrant labor was assessed by the colonial administration in the light of its preoccupation with increasing direct and indirect taxation. The new Resident Commissioner Stoley made the following assessment:

> With respect to the agricultural industry, it is possible that the limit of production has been reached, and it is unlikely that higher prices for

grain and stock will be obtained in the future. . . . The quality of the produce, particularly with reference to horses, mohair and wool, may be improved, and efforts in this direction are among the most interesting of future administrative plans. . . . Nor is it reasonable to expect that the native laborers will be able to add to the wealth of the country by larger future earnings. The demand for laborers is great, but the wages offered are reduced. The laborer, however, if denied the opportunity for spending his earnings in drink, and if afforded the facilities for remitting his money to his home, ought to continue a good customer to the Basutoland trader [CAR, 1901–2: 5].

From the turn of the century, then, the colonial administration began to move, albeit in a desultory way, towards a concept of "development expenditure," which was strictly circumscribed by both the structural and political relationships which constituted the colonial state. Despite encouragement from the white trading community, which sought to take advantage of the promising climatic and soil conditions in Basutoland and rising prices in the Union, the colonial administration did not have high expectations for wheat cultivation as a stable commodity. It was favorable to distribution of wheat seed on the basis of advance credit, but remained skeptical in the light of the "element of uncertainty as to the realization of a revenue, largely dependent upon the success or failure of a season's crops" (CAR, 1903–4: 6), and turned its attention to the development of livestock production, particularly of sheep and goats.

There were important limits to such "development expenditure." First and most important, there was virtually no "welfare" component involved. Colonial expenditure on health was minimal, while (European type) education was handled by the missionary societies. Second, the administration was tied to certain clear patterns of expenditure and accounting. Administrative and coercive apparatuses featured highest on the agenda for expenditure, while the adminstration loaned large sums of money to colonial infrastructural development schemes elsewhere in the subcontinent. Any investment in agricultural development in Basutoland was accorded very low priority and any increase in expenditure had to be covered by a fresh extraction of surplus from Basotho. Third, the colonial administration did not act to improve the terms of trade to the advantage of Basotho commodity producers, either inside or outside Basutoland. For example, the development of transport was determined by the needs of white traders. Fourth, the administration was bounded by its class alliances, both with the chiefs inside the colonial state, and with the European traders. The clearest example of this can be seen in its ambivalent relationship with the emergent petty bourgeoisie.

It is not possible to do justice here to the process of class formation taking place in colonial Basutoland, a process that reflected the complexity of articulation of diverse social relations. But one development of the late nineteenth and early twentieth century was the emergence of a petty bourgeoisie whose distinctive characteristic was that it was building a basis for accumulation outside the tributary relations of exploitation which characterised the chiefly class. The primary location of this social group was in retail and other services (such as canteens, small butcheries, taxi-services) which developed more or less in pace with the government reserves, or camps, in the territory. Entry to these activities necessitated access to some means of production or small capital, since facilities for credit for Basotho were highly restricted, and often "straddling" employment in the colonial state was involved (Cowen, 1977). Alongside this group we must place the successful entrepreneurs in wool and mohair farming, some of whom lived on the lowlands, and hired shepherds to keep their flocks in the mountains. Yet others were the less specialized but successful commodity producers based in the mission stations which had protected and fostered them since the nineteenth century.[8]

What these petty bourgeois strata had in common was a desire to divorce themselves from the relations of personal and political dependence on their chiefs, and thereby to gain control over their own labor-time and that of their dependents and hired wage-laborers. Yet the colonial administration was only prepared to give this group limited political support in its struggles to carve out an economic niche. This was because they did not wish to encourage competition with the organized white traders, because they feared arousing the opposition of the chiefs, and because they recognized the political significance of an emergent petty bourgeois nationalism for the Union, where it was seen as "an agency for the creation of unrest and disorder" (LNA, S3/22/1/2, 1922).

Given its reluctance to facilitate the emergence of a class of Basotho based in commodity production, the colonial administration was left with its alliance with a class (the chiefs) reluctant to place its powers over the mobilization of labor at the disposal of the regime where it could perceive no economic or political gain. For example, repeated exhortations from colonial officials for the chiefs to call *matsema* to eliminate the fast spreading "burrweed" (which severely diminished both the quality of the sheep pasture and that of the wool product) were frustrated. As one colonial official reported with exasperation in 1912:

> The apathy of the Basuto chiefs is largely accountable for the spread of noxious weeds in the territory. . . . Although tenacious of their right to call out their followers to cultivate their lands, they do not like to exert their authority by ordering men out on any work of public utility [LNA, S3/25/1/29, 1911].

Such labor, he continued, they apparently believed should be paid for by the colonial administration, which promoted such schemes, since burrweed was "a matter solely affecting sheep owners, and [they] would leave it to such persons in their own interest to eradicate burrweed."

A further problem with colonial development schemes was that they were designed to reach (and did reach) only a minority of Basotho tax-payers. The colonial administration gradually became increasingly aware of a degree of specialization taking place between different branches of production, both regionally and in class terms. The rich wool men, for example, were rapidly identified as beneficiaries of the dipping and other anti-scab measures, and, as soon as it became clear that they were making gains from the post-war inflation in commodity prices, the administration attempted to tap this through an indirect export tax aimed specifically at the wool producers (LNA S3/6/1/4, 1923). Wheat production was only regularly successful in the southern districts of Mafeteng and Mohales Hoek; while cattle and horses were exported to some degree from the Qacha's Nek district.

Meanwhile, in the view of the administration, a class of laborers was beginning to emerge who could only meet their tax and other cash needs through labor migration, predominantly to the mines. The administration thus accompanied its minimalist development schemes with continual attempts to extend the tax net, raise the level of tax, and promote conditions for recruitment and remittance of wages. From an early date, colonial reports noted with alarm the degree to which Basotho laborers were tending to "spend a larger proportion of their earnings outside Basutoland," bringing back with them "newly purchased articles" (e.g., CAR, 1903–1904: 6; 1905–1906: 4; 1906–1907: 4). This alarmed traders and colonial administration alike. By 1913, according to one of the leading white traders of the country, the "spending power of the people in this Territory is derived chiefly from three sources of supply, viz: agriculture, stock raising, and labor; and probably the greatest of these is labor" (LNA, S3/25/1/30, 1913).

To locate and successfully tap the "spending power" of Basotho, the colonial administration constantly sought to improve methods of collection and extend the tax net. There was a gradual shift in emphasis from "hut tax" (i.e., taxation based on the principle of occupation of land by married men) to "poll tax" (i.e., tax of the individual adult, to tax of unmarried young men). A practice had developed whereby a family would send a younger member out of the household to work in order to earn tax money, among other things. The colonial administration, frustrated by the possibility of witnessing an ever-increasing cash resource beyond the tax net, sought to impose personal tax responsibilities on these "bachelors." This later proved to be a major point of controversy between colonial administration and chiefs, the latter in this instance representing the interests of partriarchal heads of households seeking to retain control over their sons' labor-time and surplus product.

Several years after the imposition of "poll" tax, the administration sought to lower the minimum age-limit for tax payment to "catch" all the young men who worked in the mines (i.e., to conjoin tax payment formally to wage labor). The chiefs thoroughly opposed this suggestion. The implications of permitting adult responsibility for their labor, earnings, and tax payments to unmarried men of 18 were too ghastly to contemplate. A juvenile age threshold would have the effect of driving all young men of that age, otherwise engaged in production at their fathers' homesteads, out to labor. As Philip Molise lucidly stated the problem in 1916:

[T]here are boys of 21 who look after things here (i.e. herd stock) and who never go out to the mines to work. . . . [M]ost of the boys of 18, 19 and so on look after their father's stock at the mountains. There are some boys of these ages who run away to the mines. I would say let these boys be made to pay and not those who look after the cattle of their fathers . . . [W]e cannot understand why our boys should be made to pay as if the Government was poor. . . . Until we hear that . . . Basutoland is bankrupt we see no reason why our children should be made to pay. . . . If our boys are compelled to pay then they will leave our cattle at the mountains to go to Johannesburg [BNC, 28 August 1916].

The issue of age was left unresolved, but the attention of the chiefs and councillors on the BNC, under prodding from the administration, turned increasingly to the problem of how to increase tax revenue. In the 1918 BNC session, for example, two years after successfully rejecting the imposition of a tax threshold at 18 years, the chiefs made their own suggestions, acknowledging that "tax is a crucial matter for the maintenance of the chieftainship." Some suggested that the administration should organize road parties; others that migrants should be forced to remit tax money; others that land should be taken away from widows and given to potential tax-paying bachelors (BNC, 31 August 1918).

Payment of tax had become of great political as well as economic importance to the chieftainship. We have already seen how tax percentages had been absorbed in the chief's accounting, and to some extent in their internal political calculations. The collection of the tax, the rights to exercise coercion against those in arrears or late in paying, became a jealously guarded power. Any attempt to introduce change by the administration was resisted. Thus, as evidence of increasing abuse and slackness on the part of the chiefs began to reach the ears of the administration, the latter was forced to recognize, as with so many of the other areas of its relationship with the chiefs, that in order radically to reorganize this department, which had become invested with such political significance, it would be necessary to restructure the chieftainship itself.

It is an extremely interesting demonstration of the process of articulation to see how the Koena Paramount Chief incorporated one of the key institutions of colonial domination—tax—into his own construction of the past and present relationship between chiefs and administration. Thus, in 1920, the Paramount Chief insisted on his "right to inform the chiefs myself about the day of tax collection," in the following terms:

> [T]his does not begin in my days, it has been the procedure of my father and grandfather, who were before me. As you know, . . . of all works, this of tax is the one which binds me, as it is the work which united me with the Government, it having been the work given to Moshesh by the Government so that it might be in his "power . . . [W]hat will be left for me if I should no longer inform the Basuto about tax and the day for its opening . . . [A]lthough this (new) day has been so well appointed, . . . it did not mean to divest me of so great a right of mine under the Government of the King [LNA, S3/29/8/8c, 1920].

Thus within the colonial state, both chiefs and colonial administrators were led inexorably to recognize the necessity of increasing tax payments and of ensuring its satisfactory collection. There was a limit on simply increasing direct taxation, as long as the principle of undifferentiated tax remained, since it was recognized that many Basotho simply could not pay the increasing amounts. Moreover, there was absolutely no guarantee, as time wore on, that those driven out to work in order to fulfil their tax requirements would either make their tax payments, or return to Basutoland at all.

In 1916, during the lengthy discussions about the age threshold for taxation, various BNC speakers referred to "young men who go to the mines and never pay their tax since most of them stay there for two or three years"; while others referred to long-standing absentees as having been "mere children when they left Basutoland," but now were "men who ought to pay" (BNC, 29 August 1916). It transpired that many young men on finishing their contracts moved away from the mines to seek other jobs in the growing urban areas of the Union, some keeping families both in Basutoland and at the mines or locations. Some attributed this to the 1911 registration of bachelors, but all agreed that it was a growing tendency (BNC, 1910, 1916, 1918). When accused of inefficiency in tax collection in their districts, the chiefs protested that this was due to the growing absenteeism of registered tax payers, and to the lack of means to enforce payment of tax from migrant laborers. The problem was thus centrally defined as how to ensure the remittance of migrants' wages.

In the 1920s methods for deferring workers' pay and taxes (developed by the central recruiting agency of the South African Chamber of Mines, the NRC, which faced similar problems in many South African territories) were taken up by both parties in the colonial state. Wary of criticism from bodies like the recently established International Labor Organization (concerning tied wages, forced labor, and so on), and after a series of exposures of British practices in their other African colonies, the colonial administration in Basutoland was reluctant to enforce deferred payment of wages and passed the responsibility to the chiefs. The latter, less obliged to consider their international "image," recommended the legal enforcement of deferred payment for every migrant worker recruited by the mines (BNC, 29 September 1928). The outcome was the posting of a Basutoland government official on the Reef with the function of tax collection, and promotion of remittances by workers to relatives at home.

In sum, this is how the logic of migrant labor developed. Initially, workers had been encouraged to go out simply to return with money for tax payments. The question then became one of ensuring the remittance of wages, the payment of taxes, and the return of the migrants themselves, in order to sustain their relatives, the chieftainship, and the colonial state itself. The chiefs, through their close economic and political articulation with the colonial administration, had become active agents of this process.

Political Impasse

The analysis so far has tried to demonstrate that the imposition of colonial domination in the era of segregation entailed real struggle at the level of the political. The architect of the colonial state was indisputably the British colonial power. The broader political and economic imperatives of colonial rule were established beyond the boundaries of Basutoland, and the incorporation of local ruling classes into the heart of the colonial state was a well-tested strategy in the history of the British empire. It may be asked, then, how significant this struggle really was.

My answer is this: Political domination is necessarily contradictory and its contradictions are intensified in the era of imperialism. First, domination is a process, not an act; once established, it has to be continually reproduced. Second, domination can take subtle forms, and British colonial imperialism often succeeded in constructing the consent of sections of the dominated. It is extremely important to elucidate in some historical detail the manifold contradictions set in motion by colonial domination, and their consequences for both rulers and ruled. While the effects of struggle in Basutoland may not, in themselves, have weighed very much in the scales of the British empire, as the history of the colonial period is reconstructed the significance of its contradictions and struggles for the present conjuncture in southern Africa should become clearer.

In the case of Basutoland, I have argued that the construction of the colonial state affected both social forces involved—the chiefs and the colonial administration. For the former, it was a question of substantial transformation. For the latter, it was a question of mediating the wider interests of capital and colonialism through local interests and social relations. The process resulted in a kind of seamless web, a complicated embrace from which it was difficult to escape. In this section, I shall demonstrate how the colonial state entered a phase of ossification, and how the hereditary chieftainship originally established by Moshoeshoe became the central focus of political struggle and the symbol of Basotho national identity.

The period following the first world war ushered in a decade of economic difficulty in southern Africa. After a short post-war boom, with the rocketing prices for certain export commodities (including wool and mohair) and inflation in imported manufactured goods, the 1920s saw a sequence of falling prices, droughts, and political unrest in the Union. In Basutoland, these economic trends were compounded by the incapacity of the colonial state to increase the proportion of its income from customs revenue, or to secure alternative means of employment for migrants when, for example, the gold or diamond mines closed up. It was precisely at this time that the colonial administration wanted to reorganize aspects of political and economic policy in the territory, and confronted some of the contradictions and obstacles which were firmly entrenched in the structures of the colonial state.

Taking the chieftainship first, it is clear that by the early 1920s a degree of political involution had occurred. One of the weaknesses of Moshoeshoe's system of "placing," which did not emerge until the limits of internal territorial expansion had been reached, was that it had incorporated rather than fundamentally altered the dynamic of political expansion within the patrilineal chieftainship. The problem lay in the tendency for every chief, once placed, to place in turn his own adult sons in positions of political authority beneath him. Hamnett (1975: 29) has summed up the "profoundly ambiguous" development of the chieftainship after Moshoeshoe's death. He points to the "non-repetitive," "once-for-all" establishment of the cardinal segments of Moshoeshoe's lineage (the dynasties of his senior sons) which left untouched the problem of "internal segmentation within each of the cardinal lineages, as they divide into subordinate lineages nested within the major lineage that generates them. In other words, there was the problem of what to do with junior sons." The problem was provisionally resolved by creating new wards and jurisdictions "within and subordinate to existing chieftainships," but "clearly this process could not go on for ever":

> [T]he time was reached, more quickly in some parts of the country than in others, when a jurisdictional plenum had been achieved. . . . Wherever and whenever this point was reached, the problem of younger sons reasserted itself [Hamnett, 1975: 31].

By the 1930s the chieftainship structure, according to Hamnett, was characterized by a "proliferation of jurisdictions" and a "multiplicity of wards" (Hamnett, 1975: 31–35). This process of political involution, contained within the parameters of the colonial state, had reached a point of serious impasse. The intrepid Labane Chokobane, a spokesman in the BNC for the Basutoland Progressive Association, dared to raise the question of whether every chief should have the right to make all of his sons into chiefs in turn. He was silenced by the king's representative for raising a dangerous question, which threatened the fundamental principles of birthright, succession and royalty, and the subject was dropped from discussion (BNC, 29 September 1928). Yet this was to be one of the areas ultimately affected by the colonial "reforms" some ten to fifteen years later (Hailey, 1953: 81–88).

The most critical manifestation of involution was in the operation of the courts, since every chief had the right to hold a court, and indeed, saw this as a major source of income as well as a key locus of authority. The problem of multiplication of courts was only one aspect of the problem, however. There is clear evidence that there were numerous problems with the operation of the courts, in terms of the number of cases mounting up, the increasing tendency of Basotho to take their cases on appeal from one court to another, and the question of whether justice was being done according to the Laws of Lerotholi. One of the most debilitating effects of colonial rule, as noted earlier, was to strengthen the sectional interests of the chiefs at the expense of Sotho society. This was evident in matters of economic organization, too, such that chiefs lost interest in maintaining the necessary ecological balance, and became more concerned with the numbers of their followers, control of pastures for their own herds, and so on. Another problem was that the apparatuses of the chieftainship were beginning to prove inadequate to cope with the tremendous increase in administration entailed by the developments of the previous thirty years. Although the colonial administrators exaggerated the "abuses" of power, there is evidence from several sources that corruption and inefficiency were increasing.

With their articulation in the colonial state, chiefs had become extremely jealous of all areas of administrative, judicial, executive and economic activity which they had managed to hang on to. They were well aware of the implications of giving up any of these powers and prerogatives. As early as 1913, when the idea of appointing helpers to the king's court to speed up business was proposed in the BNC, the question immediately arose: who would pay these helpers? If the administration financed them, then by right some of the court fines would belong to the administration. "Let us take care," pointed out one speaker, "lest we take bread out of the mouth of the Paramount Chief" (BNC, 18 August 1913). It was clear that the chiefs would not be able to get this kind of assistance for nothing, yet neither could they contemplate formally employing others in the pursuit of their political offices, since this would jeopardize the elementary principle of service from followers and subordinates on which the whole edifice of chieftainship was based. Yet Basotho demands for improvement in the administration of justice began to mount in the following decades.

From the perspective of the colonial administration, it was just as difficult to try to change the chieftainship as to make it "work." It is instructive to contrast the pessimism and hostility expressed by the assistant commissioners in their annual conferences of the 1920s with the smug satisfaction expressed, for example, by the Resident Commissioners in the 1890s and early 1900s, when the chiefs were considered to be the "most efficient instrument it is possible to conceive for the control of a native population" (CAR, 1903–1904). By the 1920s, chiefs were seen as a serious political obstacle to colonial rule, whether through their disregard (or manipulation) of the police, their apparent laxity in tax collection, their maladministration of justice, or their refusal to implement development schemes. Yet basic reforms presented acute political problems. On one hand there was the ever-present danger of "causing serious dissatisfaction" (LNA, S3/29/8/8b, 1919). On the other hand, measures of reform could be effectively blocked.

Throughout the 1920s, a serious struggle developed between chiefs and administration over the reform of the chief's courts. The issue was sparked off by a series of denunciations of Sotho courts in the South African press, giving the High Commissioner a pretext to pressure the BNC for reform. The first response of the BNC was to introduce some amendments to the Law of Lerotholi (passed in 1922), since in its view this was indisputably an area of concern for the chieftainship alone, a position which the administration appeared to endorse. Five years later, the administration was still impatient for results, and came to the conclusion that a more dramatic restructuring of the entire chieftainship was required. The outcome was the Native Authority Proclamation, designed to regulate Sotho courts and alter the powers and duties of chiefs, which was itself influenced by the 1927 Native Administration Act in South Africa (Simons and Simons, 1983: 345–60).

The proceedings of the 1929 BNC, at which the draft proclamation was presented for discussion, clearly expressed the impasse of the colonial state. Introducing the proposed legislation, the High Commissioner's written address emphasized that he had

> no desire to deprive the Paramount Chief or any of the Basuto Chiefs
> of their rights. . . . On the contrary, the Government wishes to strength-

en and preserve the Chiefs' powers and functions . . . by adding to the powers of the Native Courts . . . authority and prestige [BNC, 17 October 1929].

The BNC was not impressed. The Resident Commissioner was told in no uncertain terms that he should not make "native laws," nor appoint chiefs, rather his role was to "advise and confirm the chiefs of Basutoland who are appointed by God, by birth, and who were confirmed by Queen Victoria. . . . Give advice, this is what you were sent here for by the Imperial Government."

Several senior chiefs simply refused to discuss the proposed proclamation, one arguing that "I don't call these regulations, the Government today is asking us to make a new treaty" (BNC, 17 October 1929).[9] The political importance of the issue drew the King himself to the BNC chamber the next day to ask "Is there any doubt that there is a wish to deprive the Paramount Chief and Chiefs? Where do I come in? Why should people be ordered without reference to me?" (BNC 18 October 1929). Unable to clarify the status of the BNC, the chiefs, or the 1868 Treaty, the Resident Commissioner was forced rapidly onto the defensive and a revolutionary new development took place. It was proposed that a large sub-committee of the BNC, composed of 25 senior chiefs or their representatives, 10 other less senior chiefs, and effectively one government nominee (Chokobane, the lone vocal supporter of the proclamation on the BNC), should hold consultations and discussions on the proposed legislation. Five days later, the committee reported back to the council, with the emphatic conclusions that

as they have been appointed as coming from all corners of Basutoland, they called *pitsos* in order to find out the feelings of the people with regard to the little book (published proposals). . . . We have found through letters and reports, . . . that the Basuto nation throughout unanimously fear the enacting of the proposed proclamation, and the nation desires that the book of the Laws of . . . Lerotholi should be confirmed (enforced), and caused to be respected and made use of by the courts of Chiefs in Basutoland [BNC, 23 October 1929].

The administration was soundly defeated. On reading these debates five years later, Special Commissioner Pim concluded, with absurd overstatement, that there was "no rule, either direct or indirect by the British government!" (Pim, 1935: 49). Pim concluded that Basutoland was a "Nation . . . ruled by its Chiefs," in which the British administration "can merely proffer advice." In his view, the Basotho received "protection without control," and were "obsessed by the idea of their absolute independence" (Pim, 1935: 49).

Pim had been called in as a Special Commissioner to Basutoland to survey the problems faced by various administrations, make a critical assessment of past policies, and suggest necessary measures for what has been described as the "fatal transformation of the [British] colonial state" in the 1930s (Lonsdale, 1981). The broader effects of the depression of the 1930s on the colonies cannot be discussed here, but in the case of Basutoland, the British government concluded that drastic changes in the chieftainship were a precondition for any effective reform of the colonial state. The outcome was a series of changes introduced between 1938 and 1946 (delayed by the outbreak of the war) which, amongst other things, put "chiefly office on a statutory basis," limiting the recognition of chiefs to a gazette drawn up through consultation between the senior chiefs and the colonial administration (Hamnett, 1975: 35-6).

Pim's observations on the nature of the colonial state were clearly wrong. The above discussion demonstrates that his position (uncritically assumed by later writers) that the chieftainship was virtually untouched by British rule, or that the colonial administration practiced a policy of non-interference in the years before the Second World War, is seriously misleading. What it does is to obscure the *colonial* character of the articulation of the state in the period considered here. At the same time, this analysis has tried to show the danger of *reducing* the dynamics and contradictions of the colonial state, and the political struggles they gave rise to, to the "functions" of the state for imperialism (thereby characterizing the chiefs as mere "tools" of imperialism). This recognition is particularly important in the case of Basutoland which, from the colonial perspective, was a "natural" territorial acquisition for the Union of South Africa. The tenacity of the hereditary chieftainship in this account is the object of my concluding comments.

CONCLUSION

What was it that enabled this chieftainship to construct around itself a discourse of "independence" and sovereignty while it was so clearly articulated in the colonial state? Here I can only indicate two elements of an adequate answer. First, the chiefs had come to symbolize a vital political and ideological component of the political discourse of Lesotho's "special relationship" with Great Britain, as the quotations at the beginning of the essay demonstrate. Second, the material basis of colonial Basutoland during the period 1890-1930 was that the majority of the people were still organized around non-capitalist relations of production and dependent on the chieftainship.

To take the first point. Other historians of southern Africa have observed the tremendous importance attached by many African leaders and progressives during the colonial era to *imperial* (i.e., British) direct control over affairs as opposed to what were seen as local *colonial* and *settler* interests. It has been suggested that this was a legacy of the period when Cape liberalism dominated the politics of the subcontinent (Willan, 1982: 241-2) although clearly it reflected political reality in the years leading up to the Union. Basotho, it must be remembered, considered themselves as having never been conquered, and as having defeated, moreover, both the Orange Free State and the Cape Colony through diplomatic and military means. As reconstructed by the sons of Moshoeshoe following British re-annexation of Basutoland in 1884, the significant moment in the "special relationship" was the treaty of 1868. That Basutoland had been annexed, de-annexed, and re-annexed, did not change this as far as Moshoeshoe's successors were concerned. Throughout the period 1890-1930, with the assistance of the organized political forum of the BNC, and the formal enshrinement of the principles of operation of the hereditary chieftainship in the Laws of Lerotholi (1903 and 1922), the political history of Basutoland became centrally focused around the complex of hereditary chieftainship-land-Sotho law (Hamnett, 1975: 107), a complex which was entrenched in the Schedule to the Act of Union in 1910.

The colonial administration never succeeded in devising workable institutional structures consistent with the 1884 Regulations, and became enmeshed with this complex for administrative, fiscal, juridical and other purposes, with the result that it was increasingly unable to change the terms of the initial relationship. Thus, although prescribing the most fundamental changes to the shape of the colonial state in 1935, Commissioner Pim stated with typical colonial arrogance:

> The Nation, is still, taken as a whole, very strongly attached to the institution of chieftainship and there is certainly nothing which can take its place at the present time. That devotion to the institution should be taken advantage of to develop a real system of "indirect rule" and to meet the growing discontent with the conduct of individual Chiefs and sub-Chiefs. The task will be an exceedingly difficult one as the Basuto are fanatically attached to their independence and deeply suspicious of anything which can be represented as an attack, direct or indirect, on that independence, more especially if it has any relation to their land [Pim, 1935: 76-77].

The second reason is more complex, and relates both to the reality of the popular experience of the chieftainship and to the evolution of a particular version of anti-colonial politics. Despite increasing evidence of struggle against the ossification of the chieftainship described above, I would suggest that for Basotho this generally represented a struggle over the limits of the chief's power rather than opposition to the class character of that power. In conditions of the articulation of modes of production, and of the particular character of commoditization and penetration of capitalism in Lesotho in the nineteenth and early twentieth centuries, the majority of the people were still organized in non-capitalist relations of production centered on the economic and political organism of the chief's household/ward (although this had undergone transformation as a result of articulation).

The chiefly class, the chiefly enterprise, the apparatuses and institutions of the chieftainship, were all a reality under colonial domination. The practice of migrant labor, moreover, emerged out of this context and did not, at least initially, involve expulsion of direct producers from the land. Migrant workers entered relations of capitalist production at the point of production, but retained their position within the (restricted) pre-capitalist mode in Basutoland (see Wolpe, 1980a, 1983, for the concept of extended and restricted modes of production, and their articulation). Once expulsion began to take place, with movement of Basotho migrants into urban residence or permanent wage employment in the Union, there was, as shown above, a concerted strategy by both chiefs and colonial officials to foster the return of these migrants and to lay the foundations for a new phase of labor migration.

The development of the two major political organizations independent of the chiefs during this period is instructive. The Basutoland Progressive Association (BPA) was representative of a certain section of the economically most successful petty bourgeoisie. Under colonial conditions this social group was isolated within the Sotho social formation, frustrated in its development as an objective social stratum by the colonial administration, and unable to find allies within either the dominant (chiefly) class, or the dominated (commoner-migrant) classes. It remained dependent on its benefactor, the colonial administration, for both economic expansion and political support.

The more radical organization, *Lekhotla la Bafo* (LLB) was initially established by petty-bourgeois elements, but its political trajectory was entirely different from that of BPA. Infused with an anti-colonial content from the beginning, its educated representatives were ejected rapidly from the major political forum, the BNC, and it attempted to develop a political base amongst the more fundamentally alienated social forces in the country—the marginalized, women, landless, and poorer migrants—while retaining links with the less successful petty bourgeoisie and lower ranks of the chieftainship. Attentive to political developments amongst nationalist and leftist forces in Union politics, the LLB developed a more sophisticated political line, and began to interpret the hereditary chieftainship as a crucial ally in the struggle against incorporation in the Union (Edgar, 1982).

By 1929, then, some of the potential class opponents of the chiefs rallied behind them in opposition to the Native Authority Proclamation. Subsequently, the LLB became one of the leading defenders of the chieftainship-land-Sotho law complex, actively constructing this as the symbol of the political integrity of the nation. The interpretation of the politics of the LLB is a matter of current historical debate (Ladu-Gore, 1981; Edgar, 1982; Weisfelder, 1974), but I would suggest that, in retrospect, this most important political manifestation of "clinging to the chiefs" led to their fetishization in what might otherwise have become a more radical opposition to colonial rule.

The symbolic complex of hereditary chieftainship-land-Sotho law thus became the ideological key to the political struggles during the early colonial period, with different social forces struggling to infuse these symbols with different content. In as much as the new British colonial administration confirmed this complex in its actions after 1884, it too entered the arena of struggle, attempting to give its own definition to these symbols and thereby was forced to remain on a restricted political terrain. It was the task of the colonial power, in the decade of the "fatal transformation of the colonial state," to attempt to reconstruct this terrain.

NOTES

1. This section is based on Kimble (1979).

2. *Ntlo* and *lelapa* are both words for "house," the former emphasizing descent, property, identity and status, the latter residence and consumption (see Phoofolo, 1980).

3. These powers, it may be suggested, express a form of property relation neither properly communal nor fully private, approximating that described by Marx as "Germanic" (Marx, 1973: 477; see Slater, 1976: 77ff).

4. The sources used for this section are given more fully in Kimble, 1979, 1982.

5. The "slackening of the chiefs' influence and the preference of the people for Cape rule" is overestimated by Burman (1981: 75–90), possibly as a result of her uncritical use of colonial sources for the period. But see also Phoofolo (1980).

6. This section draws on my current Ph.D. research on "Migrant Labor and Colonial Rule in Basutoland, 1890–1930." The years 1885 to 1890 were not marked by any developments significant for the present analysis.

7. The position that re-annexation of Basutoland by the British enabled the political legacy of Moshoeshoe to be fulfilled is the kind of myth that serves the apologetics of colonialism. Its influential formulation was by Pim (1935); it was subsequently reproduced by Hailey (1953), and adopted uncritically by Spence (1964), Thompson (1975), and Sanders (1975).

8. Many of these activities were also undertaken by senior and junior chiefs but, in economic terms, tended to remain secondary to their continuing appropriation through tributary relations of production. In political terms, the potential conflict with the colonial administration over these activities remained insignificant relative to struggles over the powers and prerogatives of the chieftainship. Common economic interests in the development of commodity production and circulation, however, did provide a basis for alliance between some "radical" chiefs and the political organizations of the petty bourgeoisie (see pp. 64-65 below).

9. This refers to the *pitso* held in 1868 at which Basotho formally accepted British sovereignty and the first colonial regulations (Sanders, 1975: 304–5). The colonial administration, of course, considered this treaty to have been superseded by the Regulations of 1884, but even Pim observed the tremendous significance Basotho attached to the treaty.

REFERENCES

AJULU, R. (1979). "The Gun war in Basutoland, 1880–1: some aspects of the destruction of the 'natural economy' and the orgins of articulation." B.A. dissertation, National University of Lesotho.

ASHTON, E. H. (1946). The Social Structure of the Southern Sotho Ward. Cape Town: School of African Studies.

Basutoland Government (1909). High Commissioners' Proclamations and Notices to June 20th 1909. Cape Town: Argus.

BERMAN, J. and J. LONSDALE. (1979). "Coping with the contradictions: the development of the colonial state in Kenya, 1895–1914." Journal of African History 20: 487–505.

BERNSTEIN, H. (1979). "African peasantries: a theoretical framework." Journal of Peasant Studies 6(4): 421–443.

BNC [Basutoland National Council] Proceedings of Sessions, 1903; 1910; 1913; 1916; 1918; 1928; 1929. London: Public Records Office.

BUNDY, C. (1979). The Rise and Fall of the South African Peasantry. London: Heinemann.

BURMAN, S. (1981). Chiefdom Politics and Alien Law: Basutoland Under Cape Rule. 1871–84. New York: African Publishing Co.

Colonial Annual Reports, Basutoland. 1893–4; 1895–6; 1898–9; 1901–2; 1903–4; 1905–6; 1906–7. London: House of Commons (Sessional Papers).

COWEN, M. (1977). "Some problems of capital and class in Kenya." Nairobi: Institute of Development Studies.

DUPRE, G. and P.-P. REY. (1980). "Reflections on the relevance of a theory of the history of exchange," in Wolpe (ed.), The Articulation of Modes of Production. London: Routledge & Kegan Paul.

EDGAR, R. (1982). "Josiel Lefela, Lekhotla la Bafo, and the creation of an ideology of rural protest, 1919–1930." Presented to the Conference on Southern Africa in the Comparative Study of Race, Class and Nationalism, New York, September.

HAILEY, LORD (1953). Native Administration in the British African Territories. Part V: The High Commission Territories. London: HMSO.

HAMNETT, I. (1975). Chieftainship and Legitimacy: An Anthropological Study of Executive Law in Lesotho. London: Routledge & Kegan Paul.

JONES, G.I. (1951). Report on Basutoland Medicine Murder. London: HMSO. Cmnd. 8209.

KIMBLE, J. (1982). "Labour migration in Basutoland, c. 1870–1885." In S. Marks and R. Rathbone (eds.), Industrialisation and social change in South Africa: African Class Formation, Culture and Consciousness, 1870–1930. London: Longman.

———(1981). "Aspects of the penetration of capitalism into colonial Basutoland, c. 1890–1930." In Class formation and class struggle. Selected proceedings of the 4th Annual Conference of the Southern African Universities Social Science Conference, National University of Lesotho.

———(1980). "Concepts in transition. Labour migration in southern Africa, c. 1890–1910, with reference to Basutoland." Presented to Peasants Seminar, University of London, November.

———(1979). "Towards an understanding of the political economy of Lesotho: the origins of commodity production and migrant labour, 1830–c. 1885." M.A. dissertation. National University of Lesotho.

KUPER, A. (1975). "The social structure of the Sotho-speaking peoples of southern Africa." Africa, 45(1): 67–81; 45(2): 139–49.

LADU-GORE (1981). "British imperialism and the struggle for peace in Lesotho: the historical significance of the Lekhotla la Bafo." Presented to the 4th Annual Conference of the Southern African Universities Social Science Conference, National University of Lesotho (June).

LEGASSICK, M. (1980). "South Africa: capital accumulation and violence." In H. Wolpe (ed.), The Articulation of Modes of Production. London: Routledge & Kegan Paul.

———(1969). "The Sotho-Tswana peoples before 1800." In L. Thompson (ed.), African societies in southern Africa. London: Heinemann.

———and F. DECLERQ (1978). "Capitalism and migrant labour in southern Africa: the origins and nature of the system." Presented to Labour Migration Seminar, University of London, June.

———and H. WOLPE. (1976). "The Bantustans and capital accumulation in South Africa." Review of African Political Economy, 7: 87-107.

Lesotho National Archives. Letter Books and Files.

S3/5/1/18a. Resident Commissioner to High Commissioner. 29 April 1925.
S3/5/1/18b. Resident Commissioner to S. Maama. 9 May 1925.
S3/6/1/4. Minutes of Assistant Commissioners' Conference. November 1923.
S3/6/1/5. Minutes of Assistant Commissioners' Conference. April 1926.
S3/22/1/2. High Commissioner to Resident Commissioner. 28 November 1922.
S3/22/2/4. Lekhotla la Bafo papers.
S3/25/1/29. Annual Reports. Mafeteng. 1911-2.
S3/25/1/30. Annual Reports. Hobson Report. 1912-3.
S3/29/8/8a. Resident Commissioner to High Commissioner. 9 December 1918.
S3/29/8/8b. High Commissioner to Resident Commissioner. 21 May 1919.
S3/29/8/8c. Paramount Chief to High Commissioner. 9 November 1920.

LEVY, N. (1982). The Foundations of the South African Cheap Labour System. London: Routledge & Kegan Paul.

LONSDALE, J. (1981). "States and social processes in Africa: a historiographical survey." African Studies Review 24(2): 139–225.

MACHOBANE, L.B.J. (1978). "Mohlomi: doctor, traveller and sage." Mohlomi 2: 5–27.

MAMDANI, M. (1976). Politics and Class Formation in Uganda. London: Heinemann.

MARKS, S. and A. ATMORE. [eds.] (1980). Economy and society in preindustrial South Africa. London: Longman.

————and R. RATHBONE. [eds.] (1982). Industrialisation and Social Change in South Africa: African Class Formation, Culture and Consciousness, 1870-1930. London: Longman.

MARX, K. (1974). Capital, Vol. 3. Harmondsworth: Penguin.

————(1973). Grundrisse. Harmondsworth: Penguin.

MEILLASSOUX, C. (1981). Maidens, Meal and Money. London: Cambridge University Press.

————(1979). "Historical modalities of the exploitation and over-exploitation of labour." Critique of Anthropology 4(13–4): 7–16.

MOFOKA, S. (1980). "The theory of the social position of women in Lesotho." Mohlomi seminar paper, National University of Lesotho.

MOHAPELOA, J.M. (1977). "Indirect rule and progress towards self-rule and independence: the case of Lesotho." Presented at International Conference on Southern African History, National University of Lesotho, June.

————(1971). Government by Proxy: Ten Years of Cape Colony Rule in Lesotho. 1871–1881. Morija: Morija Printing Press.

————(1966). "The essential Masupha." Lesotho Notes and Records 5: 7–17.

MOLYNEUX, M. (1977). "Androcentrism in Marxist anthropology." Critique of Anthropology, 3(9–10): 55–82.

MORRIS, M. (1980). "The development of capitalism in South African agriculture: class struggle in the countryside." In H. Wolpe (ed.), The Articulation of Modes of Production. London: Routledge & Kegan Paul.

O'MEARA, D. (1975). "The 1946 African mine workers' strike and the political economy of South Africa." Journal of Commonwealth and Comparative Politics 13(2): 146–73.

OMVEDT, G. (1980). "Migration in colonial India: the articulation of feudalism and capitalism by the colonial state." Journal of Peasant Studies 7(2): 185–211.

PHOOFOLO, P. (1981). "The Basotho social formation and the rinderpest epizootic of 1897." Ph.D. dissertation, Northwestern University.

————(1980). "Kea Nyala! Kea Nyala! Husbands and wives in nineteenth-century Lesotho." Mohlomi seminar paper. National University of Lesotho, June.

PIM, A. (1935). Financial and Economic Position of Basutoland. London: HMSO, Cmnd. 4907.

POULTER, S. (1972). "The place of the Laws of Lerotholi in the legal system of Lesotho." African Affairs 21(283): 144–62.

REY, P.-P. (1979). "Class contradiction in lineage societies." Critique of Anthropology 4(13–4): 41–60.

RUGEGE, S. (1980). "The struggle for state power in Lesotho, 1950-1970." (unpublished)

SANDERS, P. (1975). Moshoeshoe: Chief of the Sotho. London: Heinemann.

————(1969). "Sekonyela and Moshweshwe [sic]: failure and success in the aftermath of the Difaqane." Journal of African History 10(3): 439–55.

SANTHO, S. (1981). "South Africa and the captive economies. Lesotho: the role of the post-colonial state." Lumumba Society Symposium, National University of Lesotho, January.

SAYCE, R.U. (1924). "Ethno-geographical essay on Basutoland." Geographical Teacher 12: 266–88.

SHEDDICK, V. (1954). Land Tenure in Basutoland. London: HMSO.

SIMONS, H.J. and R.E. SIMONS. (1983). Class and colour in South Africa, 1850–1950. London: International Defence and Aid Fund.

SLATER, H. (1976). "Transitions in the political economy of south east Africa before 1840." Ph.D. dissertation, University of Sussex.

SPENCE, J.E. (1964). "British policy towards the High Commission Territories." Journal of Modern African Studies. 2(2): 221–46.

TEMU, A. and B. SWAI. (1981). Historians and Africanist History. London: Zed Press.

TERRAY, E. (1979). "On exploitation: elements of an autocritique." Critique of Anthropology 4(13–4): 29–39.

THOMPSON, L. (1975). Survival in Two Worlds: Moshoeshoe of Lesotho, 1786-1870. Oxford: Clarendon Press.

TRANSVAAL (1903). Report of the Transvaal Labour Commission, together with minority report, minutes of proceedings and evidence. Johannesburg.

TURNER, S. (1978). "Sesotho farming: the conditions and prospects of agriculture in the lowlands and foothills of Lesotho." Ph.D. dissertation, University of London.

VAN ONSELEN, C. (1978). "Worker consciousness in black miners: Southern Rhodesia, 1900-1920." In I.R. Phimister and C. Van Onselen, Studies in the History of African Mine Labour in Colonial Zimbabwe. Harare: Mambo Press.

WEISFELDER, R.F. (1977). "The Basotho monarchy," in R. Lemarchaud (ed.) African Kingships in Perspective: Political Change and Modernisation in Monarchical Settings. London: Frank Cass.

———(1974). "Early voices of protest in Basutoland: the Progressive Association and Lekhotla la Bafo." African Studies Review 17(2): 397–409.

WILLAN, B. (1982). "An African in Kimberley: Sol. T. Plaatje, 1894-8," in S. Marks and R. Rathbone (eds.), Industrialisation and Social Change in South Africa: African Class Formation, Culture and Consciousness, 1870-1930. London: Longman.

WOLPE, H. (1983). "The articulation of modes and forms of production." Presented to Karl Marx Centennial International Seminar, University of Burdwan, March.

———(1980a). "Introduction," in H. Wolpe (ed.), The Articulation of Modes of Production. London: Routledge & Kegan Paul.

———(1980b). "Capitalism and cheap labour power in South Africa: from segregation to Apartheid," in H. Wolpe (ed.), The Articulation of Modes of Production. London: Routledge & Kegan Paul.

2

NEO-COLONIALISM, CAPITALISM, AND THE STATE IN NIGERIA

BJÖRN BECKMAN

A DEPENDENT NEO-COLONIAL SOCIETY

The Oil Glut and the Crisis of The Nigerian State

As this is written (in September 1982), the Nigerian state faces a serious fiscal crisis, as international recession has caught up with the oil producers. During 1981, Nigerian oil sales dropped by more than half, wrecking the fiscal basis of an expansion program, which had just gathered momentum after the somewhat cautious years immediately preceding and following the return to civilian rule in 1979.[1] Expectations had risen high. There were rewards and prizes to be collected by those who were on the winning side. Much had to be spent to secure a return to power in 1983. Import controls were relaxed, major wage concessions granted, and foreign grains flooded the markets to contain food shortages. Contracts were signed for the construction of the new federal capital, steel works, dams, irrigation schemes and universities, to mention only some of the most conspicuous projects. Negotiations for

Author's Note: Parts I and III of this chapter were presented in different versions to a Conference of the Nordic Association of Political Scientists, Turku, August 1981 under the titles "Oil, state expenditure and class formation in Nigeria" and "Whose State? State and capitalist development in Nigeria." The latter was also published in *The Review of African Political Economy* 23 (1982). Both have been revised as components of the essay for this volume.

other giant investment, including a liquefied natural gas plant, were
actively pursued.

With the oil glut, the floor dropped under this expansion, although
it was allowed to roll on for some time, quickly exhausting once
impressive reserves, before the brakes were finally pulled. By early
1982 the state found it difficult to honor current commitments,
including the maintenance of public services, payment of teachers'
salaries and contractors' dues, not to speak of the unpaid bills
accumulated as a result of internal transactions within the public sector, electricity bills, and so forth. Development projects ground to a
halt. As sharp restrictions were imposed on imports and state expenditure, private and public companies alike were laying off workers at
a high rate, both as a result of the down-turn of economic activity
and because of the shortage of imported raw materials, spares, and
the like.[2]

Compared with the long term stagnation and decline faced by most
African economies, the current Nigerian crisis could be considered
light, although it is certainly not taken lightly by the mass of
retrenched workers and by those who find schools without teachers,
clinics without drugs, real wages dropping and prices soaring in this
import dependent economy. International financiers have been less
disturbed as they consider Nigeria "underborrowed" and are willing
to provide credits for the continuous flow of commodities. It is therefore quite possible that the Nigerian state will "overcome" the immediate crisis, as it shifts to an increasing reliance on foreign borrowing,
while simultaneously accommodating itself to a lower level of oil
earnings.[3] Nigeria is as yet far from the point where it is threatened
by international bankruptcy as in the case of Mexico. Still, this is a
direction in which Nigeria may well be heading. A growing portion of
oil revenue is absorbed by the current costs of the public sector, leaving a diminishing margin for investments. Much of these can be
financed by borrowing but returns are unlikely to meet capital costs.
Debt-servicing will therefore eat deeper and deeper into oil revenues.
In due course Nigeria would be ripe for IMF and World Bank "reha-
bilitation" and "restructuring" exercises. The pattern from elsewhere
repeats itself with depressing monotony.

Neo-Colonial Dependence: A Restatement
of Some Basic Traits

The primary purpose of this chapter is to draw attention to aspects
of the neo-colonial economy which dependency analysis tends to

ignore. There is a need, however, to first summarize the broad agreement which exists among radical critics of Nigeria, Marxists or non-Marxists, about certain basic characteristics of the neo-colonial order as it persists. From there we can proceed to pinpoint the limitations of that perspective.

1. The first feature, of course, is the extreme dependence on export earnings from a small number of primary commodities. The replacement of peasant export crops with petroleum has in the Nigerian case reinforced this pattern, leaving the economy exposed to fluctuations in the world economy and dependent on a small group of transnationals which dominate the international oil business irrespective of the degree of nationalization of their local subsidiaries.

2. Foreign companies dominate the advanced sectors of the economy as can be easily verified by looking at a Nigerian business directory (ICON, 1982).[4] The list is topped by a number of former colonial trading companies which have transformed themselves into commercial and industrial conglomerates. The principal ones are subsidiaries of leading transnationals such as Unilever (UAC) and Lonrho (John Holt). "Indigenization" has led to the transfer of shares and directorships to Nigerians but nobody doubts that the functioning of these firms is primarily determined by their role as subsidiaries of foreign companies, replicating and promoting products and production controlled by the latter. Dynamic sectors which have particularly flourished during the years of high petroleum earnings such as construction are dominated by a small group of large foreign firms (Julius Berger, Dumez, Impresit) despite the proliferation of minor Nigerian companies. The oil companies themselves are of course high up on the list.

3. Irrespective of ownership and degrees of direct and indirect involvement by foreign capital, production in the advanced sectors is totally dependent on the importation of goods and services. Much industrial production consists of crude forms of assembly, mixing and packaging (Forrest, 1982; Ekuerhare, 1980). Even more genuine industrial processes depend on imports for raw materials, components, spare parts, management, and maintenance, not to speak of basic product design and technology. Rates of local value added are very low but, even so, they exaggerate the real local contribution as overheads and labor costs are heavily subsidized through monopolistic pricing, protection, and direct subsidies. Most major so-called manufacturers in the country have little interest in changing this situation as much of their profits arise from their function as market-

ing outlets for products either produced or supplied by their foreign principals.

4. The extraverted nature of the economy is also demonstrated in the manner in which external solutions are sought to problems of agricultural production. Food scarcity has been met by a sharp increase in food imports. Agricultural strategies are either based on a massive importation of fertilisers or on capital intensive irrigation schemes. Consumption patterns which cannot be supported from domestic productive resources (e.g. of wheat) are effectively entrenched, undercutting the market for domestic food producers and making Nigeria heavily dependent on continued and expanded food imports (Andrae and Beckman, 1981).

5. The fluctuations of oil earnings and the way in which they are tied to import intensive development programs and new consumption patterns combine to push Nigeria rapidly into a dependence on international banks. This is undercutting the degree of leverage provided initially by oil. Future oil earnings are increasingly mortgaged.[5]

6. The various aspects of dependency combine to distort the development of the productive forces and, in particular, obstruct an effective mobilization and utilization of domestic resources. Surplus is siphoned off by foreign companies as profits, fees, and other payments. A small section of the population is profiting disproportionately from this dependent development, and imports are also disproportionately geared to satisfy the needs of this narrow stratum. The economy is underdeveloped not because it is not growing—it does, quite fast at times—but because of these distortions and blockages placed in the way of the development of national resources for national purposes. The root cause lies in Nigeria's mode of incorporation, economically, politically, ideologically, in a subordinated position, into a world economy dominated by transnational corporations. Imperialism refers to the structures of economic, political, and military power within the world capitalist system which generate and maintain dependence and external domination.

7. Domestically, it is the alliance between the dominant foreign interests and the collaborating elements in the public and private sector—partners, agents and other dependents—which secures the reproduction of the local political conditions necessary for the maintenance of this dependent neo-colonial order.

The above picture of neo-colonial dependence in Nigeria seems as valid in 1982 as it was in 1972 or 1962, with minor revisions. If anything, dependence has deepened (Ola Oni, 1982; Osoba, 1978). The range of primary exports has narrowed simultaneously as their share in GDP has risen sharply. In 1962, foreign firms were present only in a few sectors, and their operations were on a modest scale. Their presence has been greatly inflated in both respects. With the expansion and differentiation of their activities, foreign firms are more deeply entrenched than ever. The complex network of connections with Nigerians in the private and public sector have made them more, not less, powerful. A lower level of net inflow of foreign private capital in recent years reflects primarily the success of foreign firms in financing their expansion from local sources.

The sectors of the economy which depend for their survival on a constant inflow of imported inputs are more numerous than ever. The economy and the state are therefore even more vulnerable than before to disturbances in the capacity of the country to pay for such imports. At independence, Nigeria was virtually self-sufficient in food. Now food dependence is a major problem. External indebtedness has begun to build up at a high rate. The current fiscal crisis not only confirms the persistence of neo-colonial dependence, but exposes the new and serious dimensions which have been added.

Dependence and Class Formation

After two decades of independence, Nigeria, it seems, is as dependent and foreign dominated as ever. There may be problems at the level of concepts and measurements when it comes to "operationalizing" such an analysis as to catch the substantive dynamics towards greater or lesser dependence and domination.[6] This is not the problem here, however. I am fully satisfied that when radicals in Nigeria speak of continued or deepening dependence and foreign domination, they speak of realities which cannot be brushed aside with reference to the vagueness of the concepts involved. I am also convinced that this state of affairs has serious consequences for the economy, leading to blockages and obstructions in the development of productive forces, as well as to particular modes of appropriating value (Andrae and Beckman, 1981). To explore the mechanisms of these obstructions and distortions is a vital task of social science. The current critique of dependency theories should not lead to the abandoning of such enquiries but to theoretically and methodologically more thorough ones. Politically, dependency analysis is clearly important in providing support for strategies aiming at strengthening national productive capacity, sectoral integration, raising levels of value added, regional economic cooperation, and so forth.

The problem with dependency analysis, however, at least as it has developed in the Nigerian context, is the tendency to reduce contradictions in neo-colonial society to the national dimension, paying little attention to the dynamics of class formation. On the one hand, we meet the nation and the people, on the other imperialism (foreign capital) and its domestic lackeys. While this formula may be politically useful, it may be so for too many different (and opposed) reasons. At the radical end, it may mean the smashing of the neo-colonial state, wholesale confrontation with the domestic bourgeoisie, the compradors, and a radical breach with international capital (Ola Oni and Onimode, 1975; Osoba, 1978; Usman, 1979; Madunagu, 1982). At the less radical end, the formula may merely be evoked in support of the Murtalas against the Gowons, the Ayidas against the Asiodus, or whoever is considered more or less nationally progressive in a given situation, and in support of some tightening of the Nigerian Enterprises Promotion Decrees.[7]

The class analysis of the dependency perspective tends to focus on factional divisions within the bourgeoisie rather than on the contradictions between capital and labor, including peasant labor, within dependent neo-colonial production (Beckman, 1980). The primary concern is with the comprador character of the domestic bourgeoisie and the weakness or non-existence of a national bourgeoisie proper. Simultaneously, however, much hope is placed on patriotic elements in the bureaucracy and within the armed forces as possible sources of support for more nationalist policies. The distinction between compradors and patriots therefore tends to become one of ideology rather than objective divisions.[8] But what happens when former compradors take to nationalizations, indigenization and the construction of integrated steel works? Have they changed their minds and thereby stopped being compradors or are they merely engaged in a more sophisticated imperialist strategy for dominating the economy?

The second part of this essay summarizes how oil money, as spent by the Nigerian state, has resulted in major changes at the level of production and class formation. It argues that the Nigerian state is busily promoting capitalist development in close cooperation with foreign capital as well as a growing class of Nigerian capitalists.

What kind of state is this? The third and major section of this essay discusses the nature of the state which presides over, administers, and promotes this dependent, neo-colonial capitalist development. Using the case of the indigenization of foreign firms, I discuss whether or not the Nigerian state fits the pattern of a neo-colonial state serving foreign economic interests or if it should rather be seen as an organ of a domestic bourgeoisie which rises under its protective umbrella. My argument is that it combines both roles and that the distinction between them is subordinated to its more fundamental role as an organ of capital in general vis-à-vis labor, as well as vis-à-vis pre-capitalist relations of production.

Each phase in the process of integration in the capitalist world economy throws up its own constellation of social and political forces, setting the stage for subsequent phases, altering the preconditions for strategies for continued subordination as well as for resistance and collaboration. Each phase generates its own internal dynamics, capitalism from below as well as capitalism from above. Dependence and foreign domination provide parameters within which these processes take place. In themselves they cannot indicate the contradictions to which social processes give rise. Contradictions are primarily generated in the processes of production. This is where social relations are translated into social and political forces, into classes and class organizations.

To conclude I summarize my understanding of the nature of contradictions, especially in the relationship between national and class struggles.

OIL, STATE EXPENDITURE, AND CLASS FORMATION

Before Oil and Civil War[9]

The Nigerian colonial economy was built on the production of cash crops for export by peasants, the principal crops being cocoa in the West, palm produce in the East, groundnuts and, to a lesser degree, cotton in the North. In addition, extractive industries, tin mining and timber, were operated by foreign capital. A small number of foreign commercial firms dominated the import-export trade. At a lower level, a broad stratum of indigenous traders, transporters and related service producers emerged. Until the last decade of colonial rule, there was hardly any large-scale industry, although petty commodity producers multiplied in manufacturing.

Reliance on peasant production spared colonial capital the need to confront directly existing social relations of production. Political pressures (e.g., taxation) and commercial incentives redirected production within existing structures. Commercialization of land and labor developed gradually. Family units on independent holdings remained dominant although their participation in the world market changed the internal logic of production and reproduction.

At the level of the state, this mode of subordinating peasant production had its corresponding political form. Existing power relations were manipulated for the purpose of controlling the peasantry politically. While traditional authority was occasionally mere fabrication, one may still speak of an element of alliance with pre-capitalist ruling classes, whose members were transformed into petty bureaucrats in the colonial system. On the whole, however, bourgeois class rule in colonial Nigeria had no domestic class base. Aspiring indigenous commercial and professional groups were kept out of political influence until the decolonization phase. They were treated as either essentially irrelevant or potentially dangerous to the current mode of appropriating peasant surplus labor.

The colonial state apparatus was limited in size and scope. The commercial form of incorporating peasant production required little direct state involvement. Apart from basic investments in ports, roads and railways, and the enforcement of law and order, there was little investment in public services, either economic or social. Colonial education and health services were largely handled by Christian missions. No effort was made to build an African bureaucratic class until decolonization was unexpectedly placed on the agenda after the second world war.

No significant change took place in the local economic base of the state during the period of decolonization (1945–1960). It remained based on peasant export production. There was a shift, however, in the manner in which the surplus from peasant production was disposed of. In the context of the British war economy and post-war metropolitan reconstruction the colonial government intervened in the produce trade, establishing state export monopolies and withholding surplus from the producers (although some "kulak" accumulation occurred). The post-war boom in primary commodities provided an exceptionally favorable world market situation for this transformation.

The global context included the changing balance between imperialist powers, the universal rise of anti-colonial movements, and the growing influence of the socialist bloc. Nigerian nationalism was distinctly bourgeois in its ideological orientation but, unlike India, there was no class of Nigerian capitalists to challenge the hegemony of colonial capital. Nationalism could be easily accommodated in the decolonization exercise. The colonial bureaucracy was indigenized, and the political forms of parliamentary democracy introduced.

Under the influence of the new political arrangement, state activity increased dramatically. Export earnings from peasant agriculture were redirected to finance an expansion of public services, including the central administrative functions of the state itself. The number of wage earners in the economy (insignificant up to then), as well as the number of petty producers servicing this class, rose fast. Towns and urban centers expanded. While much of the public services were diffused regionally, the primary effect was a general centralization of commodity earnings in the urban political centers. The country provided a sufficiently distinct home market for a modest level of import-substituting manufacturing, also encouraged by the new rules for imperialist competition (the termination of colonial territorial monopoly). The state offered subsidies and incentives to foreign capital to undertake such investments. Participation by private Nigerian capital was not seriously considered. Nigerian "entrepreneurship" was instead to be encouraged in various small-scale schemes. Public investment institutions (regional development corporations) reflected this balance of forces.

The consolidation of Nigerian control over the state apparatus after Independence did not bring about any significant shift in this pattern before the collapse of the First Republic (1966). However, individual Nigerian bureaucrats, politicians, and businesspersons, in alliance with sections of foreign business, were now in a better position to accumulate wealth, strengthening the foundations of a domestic bourgeoisie.

Politically, this aspiring bourgeoisie was divided among itself on regional and tribal lines. A weak federal structure with strong regional governments reflected partly an intentionally divisive colonial mode of administration. More fundamentally, however, it corresponded to the regionalization of the economic base of the state itself, each region drawing on a distinct type of peasant production.

The early collapse of the First Republic (the military coups and civil war of the 1966–1970 period) can be understood in terms of the disintegration of this regional economic base and the rise of petroleum as a powerful centralizing force.

The coming of independence coincided with a decline in the world market prices for Nigeria's major exports. To protect its earnings the state, through the state marketing monopolies, raised the effective rate of surplus appropriated from the peasants. This was particularly harmful to the producers as costs of production were also rising. The threatening fiscal crisis placed the question of what would happen to the new source of revenue, petroleum, at the center of political struggle.

It was only by the mid-1960s that the production of oil began to have a notable impact on public finance. The question of control over oil-producing territory (mainly the delta of the River Niger and the continental shelf), and the method for dividing the revenue, were crucial issues in the ongoing struggle between centralizing and separatist tendencies. The military defeat of secessionist Biafra placed oil firmly under the political control of the federal government. The war effort led to a radical strengthening of central state power and its means of enforcing "national unity." Nationalist tendencies in the leadership were also encouraged by the vacillating or hostile maneuvers of leading Western governments and oil companies over the secession issue.

The federal war effort also stimulated the growth of business transactions. Contracts to supply the rapidly expanding federal army with food, equipment, housing, and so on, became an important means of business and accumulation, and a source of domestic bourgeois class formation. On the other hand, massive recruitment into the armed forces added greatly to the uprooting of peasants and the expansion of the wage earning class. The rate of import-substituting industrialization was stepped up behind the protective barriers of the war economy.

The Rise of the Oil State[10]

Oil and civil war laid a new foundation for the contemporary Nigerian state. Oil replaced peasant export crops as the dynamic basis for Nigeria's incorporation in the world market. Foreign private investment in the oil industry became the leading source of accumulation. Once restraints imposed by war were removed, production accelerated, averaging some two million barrels per day towards the end of the 1970s. (The oil glut brought it down to well below one million in late 1981, recovering to around one and a half in 1982.) The dramatic rise in oil prices from 1973, as well as the growing share of company income kept by the government (partly through increased state ownership, partly through raised taxation) have combined to raise, within a decade, the import capacity of the economy and the spending capcity of the government by over ten times. It is via state expenditure that oil has its impact. The direct contribution of oil operations in terms of employment and related economic activity is limited.

The share directly contributed by oil to federal revenue has risen from one quarter to well over three-quarters during the 1970s, much of the remainder depending on oil as well—for example, taxes on imports funded by oil revenues, (Forrest, 1979) The decline in revenue from peasant exports has continued not only in relative but also in absolute terms. Peasant resistance to taxation and state marketing is one cause. The growth of the domestic food market (untaxed and uncontrolled) is another. Prices have swung in favor of the domestic market at the same time as the competitiveness of peasant export production has declined in world market terms (illustrated, for example, by the relative fortunes of West African and North American vegetable oil production). Well over half of federal revenue is spent by the federal government, the rest being allocated to state governments which depend on such allocations for 90 per cent of their revenue. The material basis of regional state power has been eliminated. Old regional state institutions have been drastically weakened relative to the federal center through the successive dismantling of the old state structure. From four states during the First Republic, the number was increased to 12 in 1967 and to 19 in 1976 (Yahaya, 1978). The clamor for new states continues.

Much of oil revenue has gone to pay for the costs of new state apparatuses, and much so-called development expenditure has been for the infrastructural investments demanded by such expansion: offices, residential areas, electricity, water supplies, roads, airports, and the like. The multiplication of local government headquarters similarly generated a spate of physical investments. To crown it all, a new federal capital in the center of the country (Abuja) is planned to absorb a sizeable portion of federal investment funds throughout the 1980s.

The program for the civilian bureaucracy is matched by the accommodation of a quarter million strong armed forces inherited from the civil war with its expensive officers' corps. The common soldiers constitute an important section of the new proletariat, often living under particularly oppressive conditions. With the return to civilian rule (1979), politicians have reentered the scene as conspicuous consumers of public funds and services.

The expansion of the institutions and cadres of the state itself, administrative, military, and political, is the number one field in which oil money has been sunk. The location of these institutions are the primary growth centers of the Nigerian economy, generating directly and indirectly a wide variety of economic activities. The leading productive boom sector has therefore been the construction industry, with a multitude of foreign and indigenous contractors, builders and suppliers. The production of building materials and other inputs has correspondingly been a key manufacturing sector, ranging from small local furniture workshops to transnational firms producing aluminum, glass and other sophisticated building materials. The state itself has made major investments in the cement industry. The current establishment of a number of steel rolling mills are primarily linked to the needs of the construction industry. The much delayed Ajaokuta Steel Complex and the completed Delta Steel Works will supply the rolling mills with their raw materials. The construction industry is a big employer of temporary labor, contributing to the growth of a large, mobile and unstable working class, moving from one construction site to another in search of employment.

Another basis for the construction industry and a second major area of public investment has been in communications, especially the federal trunk roads and harbor development programs. Here foreign controlled (though partly indigenized) construction companies have dominated with advanced technology, while indigenous firms often undertake sub-contracting (e.g., for the supply of gravel).

Road construction has speeded up the economic integration of the Nigerian territory and reduced barriers against the movements of commodities and people. But it is movements between main centers and along a limited number of main access routes which are primarily facilitated, downgrading in relative terms access outside these areas. Uneven development takes on new dimensions, leading to new cleavages in the distribution of economic opportunities as well as in the pattern of outside penetration.

Domestic petrol prices have been kept low and the state has made heavy investments in distribution. Pipelines have been extended from the coast to the far northern corners of the country. Fleets of state and privately owned tankers ply the new trunk roads to feed the rapidly growing stock of private and public vehicles. The number of vehicles registered annually rose from 30,000 to 400,000 during the 1970s (Central Bank, 1980). There have been major investments in car assembling, replacing gradually the massive importation of vehicles which accounted for almost one-fifth of total imports in 1976. Transport has been a major field for domestic commercial capital since the colonial days, from the small transporter with his single pick-up to the owners of fleets of ten-tonners. Many of the leading Nigerian capitalists of today have their origin in large-scale transporting. It continues to be a strategic area of accumulation for the domestic bourgeoisie. Its work force is large but fragmented. Most drivers are employed on a rental basis having to pay a fixed amount per day to the owner.

Education and Class Formation

Education was already given high priority in public expenditure during the First Republic, especially in the South. The 1970s witnessed a massive diffusion of educational institutions at all levels throughout the country, including universities (17 by 1982), polytechnics, teacher training colleges, and secondary schools, all making a major economic impact (physical structures, feeding, maintenance, wages) in their dispersed locations. The number of university students grew from 14,000 in 1970 to 53,000 in 1978 (Central Bank, 1980). The number of secondary school students was approaching one million in 1978 and primary school students well over ten million, although attempts to introduce Universal Primary Education have run into major financial problems and, in some areas, local resistance. In view of the even higher rate of public sector expansion in general there has been no major problem so far in absorbing the high output of graduates and secondary school leavers. There is a big difference in this respect, however, between different parts of the country, which have developed very unevenly in terms of formal Western education. Regional (ethnic) constraints in the job market, especially in the public sector (through so-called positive discrimination in favor of people from less developed areas), are therefore causing growing difficulties even for higher school leavers in search of relevant employment in some of the southern states. On the other hand, the more advanced business sector in those parts allows simultaneously for graduates and others to be recruited into managerial positions.

The growth of a trained professional class in the business sector (state and private) is an important aspect of present capitalist transformation. Unlike the original, largely uneducated Nigerian business class (which still dominates the scene), the new generation is more easily integrated with, and adopts the class outlook of, international capital. It is also important to stress the growing sophistication in the training of this new class. Many go to business schools in the United States. The teaching of management sciences spreads fast not only through the formal higher school system, but also through a variety of public and private bodies run by firms of business consultants, often with foreign partners. The manner in which so much business in Nigeria originates in the upper echelons of public bureaucracy also puts a special premium on higher education as a means of access, not least in the arrangement of deals between international firms and government officials.

Public investment in education at the lower end has no lesser significance for class formation, when a rising number of low-level school leavers are separated from the traditional skills and productive activities of the peasantry and made available to the nonagricultural labor market. Education is the major basis for recruitment and promotion, not only in public services but also in the advanced sectors of industry.

The primary schools serve as key institutions for socializing wage labor. But only a minority of the school leavers are actually absorbed into formal employment on leaving school. A majority spend years in the reserve army of unemployed, part-employed or temporarily employed, or more or less marginally self-employed, peddling occasional goods and services. While working class in aspiration and education, their actual class environments are more those of petty commodity producers, the lumpenproletariat and the outcasts.

The Expanding Domestic Market

In every place where new public institutions have sprung up, there has been a diffusion of subsidiary economic activities of a longer term character than one-off investments and passing construction booms. The regular salaries and wages of the employees, the feeding of students, and the servicing and maintenance of vehicles and equipment, and the like, have generated a demand for local supply of goods and services. The proliferation of petrol pumps, beer parlors, coca-cola stands, bakeries, roadside mechanics, hotels, tailors, taxies, pharmacies, and so on, is clearly linked to the spending power of stable sources of wage incomes at the local level.

All these activities, in turn, have their own supply lines which link them to the wider economy. They also expand jointly the local market for food and other rural produce (fire wood, rural crafts), increasing rural earnings and demand for urban produced commodities and services.

State expenditure at all levels generated a massive increase in demand for all sorts of goods from cement to champagne. Much of it has been met by the more than ten-fold increase in the value of imports during the 1970s. During the first half of the 1970s few restrictions were imposed on this flood in the wake of the civil war. Pent-up demand was further inflated by large general wage increases. While major bottlenecks developed in the country's physical capacity to import at this rate, as witnessed by the famous cement scandal (Turner, 1976), it was at first well within the limit of oil earnings. Up to 1975 there was even a rapid build up of a balance-of-payment surplus. A minor deficit in 1976, however, was followed by a big drop in 1978. The late years of the last decade and the early years of the 1980s were marked by government attempts to put a brake on imports, including various control measures (e.g., pre-consignment inspection). Sharp cuts were also made in federal allocations to state governments and other public institutions, adding to a general slowing down of economic activity, especially in construction. After the return to civilian rule in 1979, imports were again allowed to expand, culminating in 1981. The oil glut punctured this expansion and import restrictions were again imposed in 1982.

Heavy import dependence in all leading lines of the economy and the large overall size of the import business have important implications for Nigeria's position in the world economy. Nigeria is now a major field for competitive struggles between the world's leading industrial exporters, a position enhanced by international recession. Strategies for capturing the Nigerian market are thus a key factor in structuring their relations to the domestic ruling class and its state institutions. Similarly, the handling of this massive flow of imports, state and private, has become a key basis for accumulation and class formation.

Major foreign controlled commercial houses like the United Africa Company, Paterson Zochonis, SCOA, CFAO, UTC, and John Holt, continue to maintain a strategic lead in the import trade, despite their public relations attempts to portray themselves as essentially manufacturing firms. They have successfully survived attempts to indigenize trading. Nigerians also buy eargerly into such leading former colonial firms, which often offer the most attractive shares traded in the Nigerian capital market. But big and small Nigerian importers also flourish on their own, as well as in partnership with foreign suppliers or overseas agents. Big Nigerian businesspersons often establish subsidiaries abroad through which they maintain their supply lines. The federal government participates in the general import business through the National Supply Company (NNSC), albeit under constant attack from the private business sector. A Presidential Task Force for the importation of rice caused major havoc in 1981–1982, as politicians, bureaucrats and businesspersons struggled among themselves to get the largest possible share of this lucrative business. Various state governments have also at times set up their own supply companies, operating as importers of scarce commodities in their own right.

Banks play a crucial role in administering the import business. Participation in its finance has been a major source of accumulation for international bank capital, especially with the decline in productive investment in metropolitan markets. With its balance of payment deficits of the late 1970s Nigeria entered the international finance market on a significant scale. Foreign borrowing was sharply stepped up in 1981–1982 with the new payments crisis. It is likely to become a major aspect of the country's deeper integration in the world capitalist system. Nigeria is not as yet borrowing "up to her capacity."

Manufacturing Industry

Incomes generated by state expenditure not only led to massive imports, but also sustained a significant expansion of domestic manufacturing (Forrest, 1982). Employment in officially recorded enterprises grew from some 70,000 before the civil war to a quarter million by the mid-1970s. The share of manufacturing in national income, however, is still less than ten percent and is dominated by light consumer goods industries. The recorded sector grew by an average of some 12 percent per annum over the 1970s, which was about twice the growth in national income in real terms. Textiles have been a leading line, claiming virtual self-sufficiency in the late 1970s, with a quarter of the total manufacturing labor force, and using mostly domestically produced cotton. By 1982, the industry faced a serious crisis due to undercutting by illegal imports. On the whole, the pattern does not vary much from other Third World countries going through a phase of early industrialization. Beer, soft drinks, cigarettes, and detergents, are conspicuous growth industries. A wide variety of processed foods, electronic equipment, pharmaceuticals, cosmetics, and household wares is now marketed as made in Nigeria, often, however, after very crude processes of mere assembling and packaging.

The size of the domestic market has broadened greatly the range of consumer goods which are produced domestically. It has also allowed for a modest increase in the production of components and other intermediary goods. Heavy investments in vehicle assembling have strong linkages to other productive sectors (transport, construction, agriculture) apart from the subsidized market for private cars (such as official car loans). Vehicle assembly has a particularly low domestic value added, but the government is pushing for more domestically produced inputs. As in the case of the construction goods industry mentioned above, vehicle assembling is expected to provide a major market for domestically produced steel. The capital goods industry, on the other hand, is still marginal. State investment in the machine tools industry is presently undertaken in partnership with an Indian firm.

Much industrial production takes place outside the officially recorded sector, including small-scale industries such as cement block making, stone crushing, food grinding, baking, garments, wood processing, printing and so on. It is likely that these activities exceed by far the recorded sector in terms of total employment, with important implications for the structure and organization of the working class. The workers in this sector are rarely unionized. They do not benefit from minimum wage agreements and have little job or income security.

The state takes an active part in manufacturing, from support schemes for some of the small-scale industries (provision of credit, extension services) to heavy direct investments in "strategic" industries such as petroleum refineries, steel works, and cement. Through federal and non-federal investment institutions the state is a major partner in all leading sectors of large-scale industry (Forrest, 1980). Some of these partnerships date from the time of the regional development corporations of the First Republic. Most have been brought about by legislation in the 1970s requiring foreign firms to sell either 60 or 40 percent of their shares to domestic interests, state or private, the proportion depending on the size and complexity of the enterprise (Collins, 1977; Hoogvelt, 1979; Biersteker, 1980). Numerous smaller firms have passed over to private Nigerian hands and private Nigerians also hold a significant part of the equity in larger firms. But in most of the latter it is the state which has become the principal domestic partner.

Agriculture: Decline or Expansion?

Despite the dramatic increase in the non-agricultural population, a majority of the Nigerian people is still employed in agriculture. The prevailing official picture of Nigerian agriculture is one of stagnation and decline, with all hope pinned to massive public development programs. The evidence called upon in support of this picture includes rising domestic food prices (rising faster than consumer prices in general), and the sharp increases in food imports (rice, wheat, sugar, and milk, in particular). Reference is also made to the decline in traditional agricultural exports. There is an outflow of people, and young people in particular, from rural areas to the towns which may also be taken as evidence of rural decline.

There is a danger that this picture of stagnation and decline conceals one of the major, dynamic changes in the development of Nigerian capitalism: a dramatic increase in the commercialization of agriculture oriented toward the domestic food market and the consequent radical broadening of the rural market for manufactured goods (Beckman, 1982c). The rise in food prices has provided a powerful incentive to commercial expansion and the restructuring of production, including class relations in the countryside. Stagnation or decline in per capita production of food is compatible with a major increase in production for the market. The fact that this increase has not been able to keep up with a growth in the non-agricultural population of perhaps ten percent per annum during the past decade should not cause surprise. The rise in imported food, again, is also motivated by changes in consumption patterns away from commodities traditionally produced in the country.

While it is possible that a majority of rural communities have not been pulled into this new commercial transformation, what is significantly new in Nigerian agriculture is not stagnation but *expansion*. This expansion is spearheaded by those areas which in the past were restructured for commodity production. Where land and labor had already been drawn into production for the market producers have responded more easily to the new signals. The decline in the production of old cash crops can therefore not be taken as evidence of stagnation. The rapid growth of the domestic food market also stimulates the development of commercial production in areas which had not been suitable for the old export crops. The spread of consumption items such as bicycles, transistor radios, corrugated steel roofing, cement block buildings, and motorcycles bear witness to this transformation. This is not, of course, the same as a general rise in the material conditions of the people. It is a process involving rural producers very unevenly, depending both on preexisting resource endowment (land, labor, capital) and the differentiating dynamic of the process itself. We witness the rise of new holdings as well as the alienation of old, consolidation and expansion as well as proletarianization and marginalization. For that portion of the rural population which already depended on buying food, the new situation may well be catastrophic.

This is the context in which the state has decided to intervene on a large scale (Forrest, 1981; Beckman, 1982c; Wallace, 1980). It has done so most conspicuously through the irrigation schemes under the River Basin Development Authorities, which encompass the whole of the country. Three schemes in the far north (Sokoto, Kano, and Borno), primarily devoted to wheat production, have so far taken most resources. They are highly capital intensive, covering rather small populations which are extensively "reorganized" (subordinated to capital) to match the advanced technologies. The Savannah Sugar Complex is another investment of well over one-half billion naira (over $700 million) based on irrigated agriculture and using wage labor rather than reorganized peasant production. The role of foreign capital varies from part ownership (Savannah) and management to that of building contractors and suppliers.

A very different strategy is pursued by the state in cooperation with the World Bank in the integrated rural development schemes which began on a pilot basis in three select areas in the north in 1975 and are presently planned to cover most of the country. The Bank lends somewhat less than half the project costs ("foreign exchange costs") and controls management of the schemes. Fertilizers, improved seeds, mechanization and other farm services, are provided partly on a credit basis within the project areas, with emphasis on the so-called progressive farmers. Farm Service Centers are established with stores and extension staff. These schemes accelerate the commercial transformation of agriculture, with greater encouragement to capitalist farming than existed in the colonial period. With its own command system, anxious to bypass the Nigerian ministerial organization, the Bank operates a characteristically neo-colonial organization. Nigerian state capital is brought under the control of international "public" finance capital. While many large-scale capitalist farmers are established and supported under the schemes, the primary beneficiaries seem to be the upper-middle peasantry, whose expanded holdings increasingly rely on hired labor and commercial inputs (Beckmann, 1982c).

The Nigerian Agricultural and Cooperative Bank is more explicitly involved in large-scale capitalist farming, lending to private and state companies and corporations. Through Central Bank regulations, the state is also pushing commercial banks to get involved in financing capitalist agriculture. The state prescribes the number of rural branches banks must open as well as the minimum they must lend to agriculture, backed by state guarantees. State-operated tractor hiring units and financial support for cooperative organizations are other ways in which the state intervenes directly in agrarian relations. Allocations of land for capitalist farming (mostly for urban based entrepreneurs) is administered under the new Land Use Decree, nominally introduced to protect the interests of the landless. As in the past, the state plays a leading role in the marketing of certain major cash crops (primarily cocoa and cotton, while palm oil and groundnuts largely escape state trading). Investments in direct state-owned production schemes are growing and foreign partnerships in this field are actively courted. A special joint commission has been set up with the United States government to handle such cooperation. Brazilian partnership has been invited in the livestock sector to facilitate the transition to modern ranching.

Capitalist Class Formation
in a Neocolonial Society

Oil feeds the state; the state feeds its employees and its contractors; the contractors feed their employees and their sub-contractors, and so on. The domestic market expands; imports increase but so does domestic production. What happens when the oil is finished? What is happening right now as oil revenue slumps? Critics of the neocolonial economy point to its extreme vulnerability, its dependence. Oil gluts cause havoc, and further havoc will ensue as oil reserves are depleted. There is no evidence that the modern production structures which have proliferated in the past decade have led to a reduced dependence on oil. We do not know how much oil is left. Known reserves may last a couple of decades at the current rate of extraction. But new areas remain to be explored and the explorers probably know more than they tell.

In any case oil money is likely to continue to flow in great quantities for a considerable time to come. It will continue to sustain and lubricate production and markets, irrespective of whatever self-sustaining productive circuits exist or develop alongside oil. But the former do exist: producers of food, cotton, textiles, cement, steel, basic housing and transport will feed each other even when oil disappears, surrounded by craftspersons, traders, and other producers of private and public services.

Nigeria has entered a volatile phase of capitalist transformation. It feeds on oil but not oil alone. Oil money prepares the way for and reinforces the developing internal markets and productive circuits which are sustained by the activities of Nigerian workers and peasants, not just by oil. It could be argued, on the other hand, that oil chokes domestic production which is undercut by imports (Andrae and Beckman, 1981). Important domestic skills in agriculture, food processing, clothing, and construction are killed off. This is true and it is a serious problem. It should not obscure, however, the upsurge of economic activity stimulated by oil and the spread of new skills by which it is accompanied.

This is not an attempt to establish a "balance sheet" for capitalism. The social value of such activities and skills, new or old, is not considered here. We are concerned with changes in the structure and organization of production. These changes are accompanied by new patterns of control over means of production and over the appropriation of values produced. The pattern is neocolonial and dependent. More fundamentally, however, it is capitalist.

The contradictions of capitalist development originate both in Nigeria's dependence on production for the world market and in the internal organization of production. Crisis and recession in the world economy have drastic consequences for the entire Nigerian economy. The manner in which individuals are affected, however, depends on their position within the domestic political economy. Capitalists and workers may have a common interest in protecting themselves against international recession. But the solutions they seek involve the primary contradiction between the two classes. Protecting wages and employment is not the same as protecting profits as the one is likely to be at the expense of the other. Similarly, the state and primary producers may be equally exposed to falling commodity prices but are likely to confront each other in a struggle over the division of a shrinking surplus.

The external contradictions, arising out of Nigeria's dependent neo-colonial position, manifest themselves only in a concrete class context. National contradictions translate themselves into those of class. To the ruling class "austerity" may be a "national" issue. To peasants and workers it is more a matter of class struggle. They may be urged to accept lower producer prices and wages in the "national interest," but this will be unacceptable to them as long as the manner in which surplus is appropriated in the society is unacceptable.

To focus on the development of classes therefore does not mean abandoning the national issues which are the central concern of the dependency problematic. Class analysis of a neo-colony must take into account the manner in which the organization of production and class formation are structured by dependence and external subordination. The question of national emancipation in turn cannot be divorced from the concrete class content of the strategies by which it is pursued.

It is to this dialectic of national and class contradictions that I turn in the last major section of this chapter, in discussing the class character of the Nigerian state and the relevance of indigenization policies for understanding it. Before doing so let me summarize the main features observed in this section:

(1) The leading role of state expenditure and state capital in capitalist development and class formation. (2) The close involvement of international capital, state and private, in all sectors of the Nigerian economy. (3) The operations of the state and of international capital are closely geared to the rise of a broad Nigerian domestic bourgeoisie, state and private. (4) The process of capitalist transformation is supported from below by petty commodity producers responding to these developments. (5) Despite the low proportion of Nigerians employed in large-scale manufacturing industry, perhaps over one-third of the population is now made up of workers, nonagricultural petty commodity producers and classes other than the peasantry. (6) The large home market for agricultural produce is a major basis for capitalist transformation and adds significantly to the expansion of the home market for industry.

THE CLASS CHARACTER OF THE NIGERIAN STATE

The discussion so far has sought to demonstrate that in Nigeria continued and deepening neocolonial dependence goes hand in hand with a dynamic process of capitalist transformation and class formation. The dynamism does not reduce dependence and subordination. On the contrary, more areas, sectors, and people are incorporated. The state plays a crucial role in this dependent capitalist development. How can we locate and explain the functioning of the Nigerian state within these parameters of external domination and domestic class formation?

Within a historical materialist perspective the state is understood as a category of class power. The process of state formation is in itself part of the process of class formation. The contradictions which exist at the level of production are expected to manifest themselves in the class character of the state. Class forces which dominate at the level of production can therefore be expected to structure the exercise of state power. One may thus speak of the state as an organ of the ruling class without either adhering to an "instrumentalist" or a "functionalist" view of the state, that is, without seeing governments either as "executive committees of the ruling class" or what they do as necessarily "functional" from the point of view of the interests of the ruling class. What we do expect, however, is to find some basic correspondence between the manner in which state power is formed and wielded and the logic of economic power relations at the level of production.

How do we, from such a theoretical perspective, locate the Nigerian state within the parameters of neocolonial dependence and capitalist class formation? A neocolonial society should be expected to have a neocolonial state pursuing neocolonialist development strategies. But if this is so, how do we explain the policies of successive Nigerian governments to expand the sphere of national control in the economy, including nationalizations of oil companies and banks as well as the general program for "indigenizing" foreign enterprises? Is not the state putting all sorts of pressures on firms to raise levels of value added and to strengthen internal linkages between industrial sectors?

Which class forces control the Nigerian state? Is it the agents of international capital and foreign domination, or does the state serve as a platform for national class forces arising in opposition to the former? Let us examine both propositions, using the policy of "indigenization" as a test case.

The State as an Organ of International Capital

A strong case exists for arguing that the Nigerian state is an organ of international capital. This is a common radical position and inspires much of the current critique of the state from a national bourgeois as well as from a socialist perspective (Osoba, 1978; Ola Oni and Onimode, 1975; Turner, 1980). In fact, it serves as a meeting ground where such different and ultimately opposed political forces seek to establish a united front. The position is often argued within the context of a theory of neocolonialism, which emphasizes continuity with colonial domination and sees independence as largely formal. Real control over the economy remains with foreign capital and nationalist leaders are coopted by imperialism, inheriting a state imposed by imperialism for its own purposes. The nature of the state itself therefore does not change fundamentally: The nationalists never really challenged the pervasive domination of the economy by imperialism and were left to administer the state on behalf of foreign capital.

According to the perspective of neocolonialism, the contemporary Nigerian state can therefore be described as a comprador state: State institutions and officials operate as agents of imperialism. The real ruling class remains the bourgeoisie of the metropolitan countries. It is not that the indigenous businessmen and bureaucrats merely masquerade as a national bourgeoisie. They are allowed to play this role by their foreign paymaster. In fact, they are performing a vital ideological function as their nationalistic rhetoric conceals the true class nature of the state. When they travel to international conferences attacking imperialism and clamoring for a new international order, they simultaneously take the opportunity to check their international bank accounts which are regularly replenished by foreign friends. Corruption is not the failure to play the game according to the rules of the official ethic. It is a normal means whereby foreign firms compensate politicians and bureaucrats for their agency services. The methods are numerous. Cooperating ministers may be allowed, for example, to exercise patronage within the domain of the foreign firms. They nominate their own candidates to board memberships and management posts and when they themselves retire they will be taken care of appropriately.

There is ample evidence to support this view of the Nigerian state as a neocolonial, comprador state, acting as an organ of international capital in its continued exploitation and oppression of the Nigerian people. The continuous factional rivalries of Nigerian politics, military and civilian, ensure that the corrupt transactions with foreign capital are repeatedly (although selectively) exposed and documented. Nor does radical Nigerian opinion need to wait to be informed by official commissions of inquiry or by documents released by one or other warring faction. Much information about the forms, crude or subtle, in which international firms tie local leaders to themselves, is common talk.[11] Moreover, with partnership increasingly becoming the official policy, and the prevailing institutional framework for the relationship between the state and foreign capital, there is less need for secrecy. It often requires little ingenuity to expose the shallowness of such partnership arrangements in so many cases where state participation means little more than the collection of fat allowances for state representatives on boards with little control over, or even information on, actual operations.

The Case of the "Indigenization"
of Foreign Enterprises

The policy of "indigenization" (Collins 1977; Hoogvelt 1980; Biersteker 1980; Ake 1981) can be seen as the institutionalization of this sham partnership. Under the cover of a smokescreen of nationalist ideology, foreign capital in Nigeria is now more securely entrenched than ever. The smaller firms which were totally taken over by Nigerians did not constitute much of a sacrifice for international capital. They mostly belonged to Lebanese anyway, who have their own mysterious ways (including double citizenship) of surviving in business. They certainly do not represent any of the major sectors of interest of international capital. For the latter it was a question of whether to have a 60 percent or 40 percent local partnership. There were certainly risks involved; that the new part owners would meddle in the business, pushing their nephews on to management, discriminating in favor of their own kin or home area in employment, and the like. But these "risks" were also opportunities. The exchange of favors could be more open. There was no longer any need to send messengers through ministerial backdoors; business could now be settled between official partners. A big bonus, of course, was the handsome addition to the capital stock brought along by the local partner. There was no need to hand over existing assets as firms could expand through new issues of equity. Remember how foreign firms elsewhere are anxious to finance their expansion by mopping up domestic savings (while retaining, of course, their right to remit profits).

"Indigenization" has meant that a significant amount of the oil earnings of the Nigerian government has been recycled into financing the expansion of firms that, for all practical purposes, remain firmly under the control of international capital. This is a plausible radical interpretation of what has happened. It has nothing to do with whether or not this was an effect intended by those technocrats and politicians who were pushing the idea. They may in fact have been in good faith and inspired by the most laudable national sentiments. But neither is it primarily a question of cheating somebody.

It has been argued that the Nigerian government was outwitted by cunning foreigners. It is also claimed that the policy was subverted by unpatriotic Nigerian individuals (officials and private businesspersons) who colluded with the foreigners (Akeredolu-Ale 1976; Nigerian

Economic Society 1974; Biersteker 1980). From this persepctive it is not the state itself which is neocolonial or comprador but certain elements within the state or the local bourgeoisie. The state is too weak or inefficient to enforce its patriotic intentions. The political implications are that if the patriotic elements could be reinforced and the unpatriotic ones weeded out, things would be alright.

While this could add to the bite of the indigenization policies, it would hardly transform their subordination to the extended penetration by international capital. Certainly, there was a lot of maneuvering and dodging by foreign firms seeking to have it both ways before settling for the new form of partnership. Why shouldn't they? It is a question of profit maximization. There is nothing which is so good that it cannot be better. The officials of the Nigerian Enterprises Promotion Board are undoubtedly justified in their concern with the evasiveness and unpartnerlike behavior of some of the foreign firms. The acrimonies on both sides, however, should not be misread as an expression of any fundamental antagonism. They should not be allowed to obscure the basic logic of a transformation essentially in the interest of foreign capital, and tightening rather than loosening its grip on the Nigerian economy.

Problems of the "Neocolonial" Model of the State

It may be easy to support this radical interpretation of the Nigerian state on theoretical grounds. In addition, a wealth of documentation can be marshalled in support of the claim that the Nigerian political economy is dominated by international capital. It seems therefore also a plausible materialist position to assume that this domination is reflected at the level of the state. From such a position it is logical to identify the international bourgeoisie as the real ruling class, in the Marxist sense of the term. Backed by such theoretical assumptions and empirical evidence, it is possible to make sense of indigenization policies and other seemingly "nationalist" features in the recent operations of the Nigerian state. They can be seen as objectively integrated into the logic of imperialist domination. They either spring from the requirements of international capital, are restructured to fit such needs, or are neutralized so as to be compatible with them.

The problem with such an approach is not that the conclusions are necessarily false. On the contrary, I believe that it makes good sense to assert that the Nigerian state is a product of imperialism and that it continues to serve the interests of international capital.

The problem is that the very generality of this explanatory model may fail to motivate useful theoretical work and concrete studies which allow use to see the specific economic and political forms of imperialist domination and how they link up with class struggle. If every aspect of the state is reduced to the needs of imperialism, very little may actually be explained, unless, of course, such conclusions are arrived at through an analysis of the ways in which imperialism is articulated at all levels of the social formation. The supremacy of international capital may well be confirmed by such analysis but this would require an evaluation of the forces over which it dominates. To say that it ultimately comes out on top should not allow us to ignore the strength and organization of the forces which it incorporates, co-opts or subdues. That strength will surely be decisive for the strategies chosen by international capital in each new phase. The danger of a simple neocolonial model of the state is that it denies domestic social forces their own dynamics.

How then are we to take account of the existence and rapid expansion of a large domestic bourgeoisie? How does it affect the material determination of the state? Is it compatible with a general theory of imperialist domination? I believe it is. But it requires a more developed understanding of what that domination means than is implicit in the radical position outline above. Before we arrive at that, let me outline a second "explanatory model" of the Nigerian state which takes as its point of departure the growth of the Nigerian bourgeoisie.

The State as an Organ of the Domestic Bourgeoisie

The colonial state systematically obstructed the growth of a powerful domestic bourgeoisie. It sanctioned the monopolistic practices of the colonial commercial firms in their struggle to eliminate native competition in the all important export-import business. Politically, it allied itself with aristocratic elements, blocking demands for democratic political representation from the budding new "middle class." Colonial economic policies in the decolonization phase centered on the restructuring of the colonial monopoly firms to ensure their access to markets after independence. Under growing nationalist pressures, however, colonial regional development corporations were gradually geared to support Nigerian entrepreneurs, although at a very humble level. With the succession of bourgeois nationalists to state power, the resources of the state were increasingly used to promote their interests as an aspiring bourgeoisie. The methods used varied, and involved intense sectional competition. The activities of state development corporations were greatly expanded, resulting in a wide range of enterprises either sponsored or owned by the state. In the latter case it was normally stated that such enterprises in due course would be transferred into private Nigerian hands. The state thus took on the role of caretaker for the budding bourgeoisie. At first, all major investments were left to foreign firms but Nigerian state institutions increasingly involved themselves in large-scale productive and commercial operations. While the economic contribution of such enterprises was frequently dissipated through corruption and misappropriation, they were significant in providing a source of "primitive accumulation" by an incipient capitalist class in society at large. They also generated a growing cadre of Nigerian administrators and managers engaged in state capitalist enterprises. Others acquired similar experiences while serving with foreign firms. The marketing boards controlling the exports of peasant produce promoted Nigerian "licensed buying agents" as another important contribution to bourgeois class formation under state monoply protection.

The strength of the state as a national bourgeois class institution was greatly enhanced by the defeat of the separatists in the civil war and the rise of the oil economy after it. I have outlined above how federal and non-federal state expenditure, sector by sector, contributed to bourgeois class formation. State funds were systematically used to sponsor Nigerian firms, often in competition with foreign ones. Despite the continued dominance of the latter in, for example, large-scale construction, it may be more significant, from the perspective of the class character of the state, to note the steadily growing proportion of contracts now handled by Nigerian firms. We can also note that these contracts have grown steadily in size and complexity.

The state itself has expanded its participation in all major sectors of the economy, often at the expense of foreign capital. Oil and banking may be mentioned as particularly strategic. There is still much complaint about the inefficiency of state supervision of the oil companies but national control has certainly been enhanced. Similarly, the Central Bank's direction of commercial bank operations has been tightened up. The state pushes ahead with strategic investments in the steel industry with Soviet partners, having failed to obtain Western support.

Generally, oil wealth has greatly enhanced Nigeria's bargaining position in the international economy. It can make demands and impose restrictions on the operations of foreign firms. The Nigerian market is very valuable, international competition is intense, and concessions by international capital to the national economic aspirations of the Nigerian state are necessary. We need only record the way Nigeria nationalized BP to put effective pressure on Britain in the Zimbabwean independence negotiations. Nationalism is a powerful political force in Nigeria. This is the context in which we can return to the question of Nigeria's policies of indigenizing foreign enterprises.

Indigenization Reconsidered

"Indigenization" offered a focal point for national self-assertion by the domestic bourgeoisie. It had consolidated its position in the course of the Civil War, and oil provided funds and bargaining power to back up sweeping claims for the takeover, in whole or in part, of the assets of foreign firms. It was an accelerating process. Timidity and fumbling in the design and implementation of the first Decree (1972) subsequently generated fresh agitation, resulting in the revised Decree of 1977. Demands were drastically stepped up, this time for Nigerian majority ownership in most enterprises except the largest and technically most complex ones. It is true that in many cases the transfer of shares gave little effective control, but this in turn has generated a spate of fresh demands for tightening restrictions on foreign management ("expatriate quotas") and closer inspection by the Enterprises Promotion Board, including tougher reprisals against defaulting firms. The growing competence and business experience of those representing the Nigerian partners, state or private, must also be taken into account. The ability of the foreign partners to play tricks on the local ones was likely to diminish. "Competence," of course, does not prevent people from being bought. But combined with the latent threat of erratic nationalist outbursts, limits were thus set to the possibility of manipulations. If foreign firms are to survive in Nigeria, they must come to terms with the aspirations of the domestic bourgeoisie, inside and outside of the state apparatuses.

The muted response of international firms to the successive waves of nationalizations—protests, if any, were timid—should not, therefore, be mistaken for complacency or as proof that nothing of significance really happened. The challenge was real. Strong reactions from individual firms or from their home governments might have seriously endangered access to this strategic Third World market for a long time to come.

The nationalist flavor of indigenization should not be equated with patriotism or commitment to throw off foreign domination in any more fundamental sense. The Nigerian bourgeoisie, for its own class reasons, wanted a bigger share of the profitable foreign controlled business operations going on in its territory. It wanted to be admitted on an equal basis to the exploitation of Nigerian resources and labor, rather than to chase out foreign capital. In fact, influential sections of the Nigerian bourgeoisie are seriously concerned that indigenization policies have unduly frightened foreign capital, thereby undercutting the range of partnership which they wish to pursue for their own purposes. The 1977 Decree has recently been revised in order to permit foreign majority ownership in agricultural ventures.

To sum up: The rising domestic bourgeoisie is emancipating itself in and through the state, either in the form of state support for private capital or through direct state participation in production and exchange. The indigenization exercise is an example of both.

Problems of the "Domestic Bourgeoisie" Model of the State

There is much evidence to support the proposition that the Nigerian state operates as an organ of the rising domestic bourgeoisie. How is this compatible with the similarly plausible argument that it serves international capital? If, as we have already agreed, foreign capital continues to dominate directly or indirectly in the major sectors of the economy, how can we explain that the domestic bourgeoisie seems to be using the state successfully to strengthen its position relative to that of foreign capital? Is the tail wagging the dog? The neocolonial model of explanation has a ready answer: It is an optical illusion. Foreign capital dominates as before, and it is only the form of domination which changes. The domestic bourgeoisie, whether state or private, is used by foreign capital for its own purposes. The "national" character of this class and its state institutions is even necessary in order to maintain this illusion, under the cover of which foreign capital continues to undertake its exploits.

How can this riddle of who uses whom, who depends on whom, be solved in a way which is both consistent with the two sets of evidence which we have surveyed and which also makes sense theoretically? Is it the "interdependence" or "mutual dependence" which liberal development theorists have put forward as an answer to the radical view of dependence and underdevelopment?

To be able to solve the problem of how state power reflects the relative influence of various class segments, Nigerian and non-Nigerian, we must first ask more questions about the relationship of the

Nigerian state to the internationalized processes of capitalist production, realization and accumulation. The capitalist state is not above sectional contradictions. Still, its mode of functioning and the role of such sectional influences can only be understood if we take as the point of departure *the unity of capital vis-à-vis social forces which are opposed to it,* either within the process of capital accumulation itself or in its confrontation with pre-capitalist or non-capitalist social relations of production, where the latter are gradually transformed and subordinated. Let us therefore outline a third perspective on the class determination of the Nigerian state: *the state as the organ of capital in general.*

The Nigerian State as an Organ of Capital in General

While the Nigerian state serves as an organ both for the penetration of international capital and for the emancipation of the domestic bourgeoisie, it cannot be reduced to either. Nor is it possible to comprehend the significance of either of the two aspects, without examining such activities of the Nigerian state for which the distinction foreign/domestic is not relevant. *The primary role of the Nigerian state is to establish, maintain, protect and expand the conditions of capitalist accumulation in general, without which neither foreign nor Nigerian capital can prosper.*

When a section of the lumpenproletariat of Kano stones the luxury cars and mansions of the propertied classes, inspired by a confused yet revolutionary opposition to the new order (Federal Government Report, 1981), it is bourgeois property and bourgeois class rule in general which need to be defended. The massive shooting without trial of prisoners taken in this class war performs the same crude function as the bloody punitive expeditions by which the British state imposed its domination in the interest of colonial capitalism.

The establishment and maintenance of "law and order" is the crucial role of any state, and the content and practice of law and order is defined by the class character of the state. The particular form of repression demonstrated in the "Maitasine rebellion," suggests the unconsolidated nature of the capitalist state and the partial manner in which production has as yet been subordinated to capital. The need to dispatch senior police officers to Thailand and other places in order to study "modern methods" of riot control (as reported in the public inquiry) are signs of the way this class warfare is being stepped up.

But violent repression is only one aspect of law and order. More generally, it is a question of establishing and enforcing the complex pattern of rules which are necessary for capitalist accumulation. Bourgeois property relations must, on the one hand, be liberated from the bonds imposed by pre-capitalist relations of production. They must be protected, on the other hand, from challenges from within, that is, from the very forces which emerge within the new mode of production. The Land Use Decree of 1978 may be taken as an example of the former. Private and state property in land is protected against the claims of traditional owners, at the same time as the law facilitates the appropriation of land for "commercial" use. Under the decree large areas of land are currently being taken over by the emerging bourgeoisie.

Legislation relating to the organization and control of labor is the prime example of the second type. The regulation of the rights of labor to organize and the restrictions imposed on such rights are fundamental to the operations of any capitalist society. The Nigerian state has struggled hard, largely unsuccessfully, to establish its control over the organization of the working class. When unions in the mid-1970s were dangerously close to success in forming a united organization under radical leadership, the state stepped in, purged the leadership, and set up a new organization with state support, financed from deductions of union fees by employers. The state failed, however, to prevent the radical elements from gaining an upper hand in the new organization. Employers refused to adhere to the check-off system, and attempts to establish unions in individual companies were resisted by the employers with impunity. On the other hand, the right to unionize is still a fiction for a large section of the Nigerian working class. Shopfloor activists are sacked at will, and unions are banned from participating in politics.

The question of "law and order" extends to the whole sphere of state rules and sanctions, relating to the regulation of money, banking, and trading in a capitalist society, including the protection of equity capital, the enforcement of the laws of contract, and so on, which we do not need to go into here.

The regulation of the procedures by which such rules are decided and altered, however, is the essence of bourgeois state formation itself. Civil war, military dictatorship, and the elaborate constitutional regulation of the transition to civilian rule in Nigeria are all successive stages in this process, reflecting the changing conditions of accumulation. The process shows *the transition from a regionally fragmented state structure based on the appropriation of surplus from peasant production, to a centralized state system based on the petroleum industry, and a growing domestic market for agriculture and industry.* The new constitution (1978), with its division of functions between numerous institutions and office holders, is also an elaborate attempt to regulate the sectional competition of the bourgeoisie in such a way as to ensure the hegemony of the federal center.

The massive direct investments by the state in the extraction, processing and distribution of petroleum, in steel, cement, transport equipment, trunk roads, telecommunications, power generation, and ports and airports cannot be reduced either to the sectional aspirations of the Nigerian bourgeoisie (although these may affect the physical location of plants and roads), or to any division between foreign and Nigerian capital. It is a question of laying the physical foundations of a particular type of development based on accumulation within a world market context. The state undertakes these investments not because they are in any way unwanted by private capital, local or foreign, but because only the state itself is prepared to guarantee the profits of the private investors who struggle between themselves to participate as contractors, suppliers, and managers. In the meantime, new productive forces are created which facilitate the expanded reproduction of capital.

Labor power must also be produced and reproduced on the scale and higher levels required by accumulation. We have noted the rapid expansion of both general and specialized education and its role in the recruitment of wage labor from below, the structuring and disciplining of labor (advance by "qualification"), and the creation of a managerial class. Typically, the "food and shelter" programs of successive Nigerian regimes are firmly oriented towards the minority of Nigerians who earn salaries and wages. The World Bank is presently deeply involved in both fields, seeking to generate a commercial food surplus (rather than raising the general level of food consumption among the masses), and to provide "modern housing" for those on fixed wages (rather than raising the housing standard of the mass of urban and rural poor). Finally, in the sphere of ideology, state control over mass media as well as over education is used for the purpose of creating the ideological orientation necessary to support the bourgeois state and protect international accumulation.

The repressive, regulative, productive, reproductive, and ideological activities of the state indicated briefly above cannot be understood in terms of the requirements of any particular segments of capital, domestic or foreign. The fact that foreign construction firms profit more from the big trunk road contracts, while Nigerian firms make more money from the smaller ones, has important consequences for accumulation and capitalist development (e.g., in the way profits are invested). This is of secondary importance, however, to the fact that these roads, big or small, Nigerian-built or foreign-built, themselves feed into a particular mode of accumulation in society at large which is decisive in determining the class character of the state.

Indigenization: The Third Approach

In an attempt to determine the class character of the Nigerian state, the "national" divisions between foreign and Nigerian capital are not decisive. We need to place such secondary contradictions in the context of the basic problems facing capital in general, that is, in its relation to social forces opposed to capital or obstructing capital. It does not mean that secondary contradictions do not matter. On the contrary, they can occasionally disrupt and wreck capitalist accumulation and the operations of the capitalist state. Similarly, they may divide and paralyze social and political forces opposed to capital. Secondary contradictions are therefore intentionally manipulated by the ruling class for the purpose of managing and controlling primary ones. This is the context, for example, in which ruling class manipulation of regional, ethnical, and religious contradictions should be understood in contemporary Nigerian politics (Nnoli, 1980; Toyo, 1980).

Secondary contradictions within the capitalist class on national, sectional, and sectoral lines may threaten accumulation in so far as they undermine the capacity to face primary problems of subordinating labor or precapitalist social forces. The policy of indigenization is an attempt to regulate competition between international firms and the rising Nigerian bourgeoisie. The need for this does not arise from the intensity of that competition as such. In fact, competition may be much more intense between sections of foreign capital (on sectoral and national lines) and between sections of Nigerian capital with different foreign alliances. We need to look elsewhere, to *the role of indigenization in the consolidation of bourgeois class rule and the management of primary contradictions.*

In the framework of this approach, indigenization contributed to the consolidation of the Nigerian ruling class by encouraging closer partnership between Nigerian and foreign capital. It bolstered the "national authenticity" of the Nigerian state which was very much in doubt because of its place in international accumulation. This authenticity was officially asserted by subjecting international capital to the regulative powers of the state. Simultaneously, indigenization enhanced the national credentials of the foreign companies. ("Why do you attack us? We are Nigerian now.") The scope for attacking capital on an anti-foreign platform was reduced, weakening the links between anti-imperialist and anti-capitalist agitation in the working class. It also diverted petty-bourgeois nationalist aspirations from potentially threatening alliances with popular anti-imperialist and anti-capitalist social forces. More generally, indigenization served to strengthen the domestic social and political basis of international accumulation in Nigeria. The advantages and disadvantages experienced by individual firms, foreign and Nigerian, in the course of the indigenization exercise, should not distract from its wider usefulness in the development of capitalism in Nigeria.

CONCLUSIONS: IMPERIALISM AND CLASS STRUGGLE

In the third part of this chapter, I have shown three things. First, that the state serves as an organ of foreign capital in Nigeria as it expands its operations and entrenches itself more deeply. Second, I have shown how the state is simultaneously engaged in building a domestic bourgeoisie. Third, I have suggested that the most significant role performed by the state in support of capitalist development cannot be reduced to the interests of such sections of capital, Nigerian or foreign. Instead, it needs to be seen in the light of the interests of *capital in general.*

Does neocolonial dependence matter if the state, the domestic bourgeoisie, and international capital are all busily engaged in building capitalism in Nigeria? Clearly much can be done to strengthen the bargaining power of the state in dealing with foreign capital, exposing the manipulations of the oil companies, the fictitious manufacturing of the industrialists, the fraudulent internal transfers of transnational corporations which dodge taxation and inflate contracts, and so on. There is similarly a greater scope for pushing international manufacturers into linking up with domestic production and with each other, using stick as well as carrot. Such a national struggle would necessarily involve confrontation with those "comprador" elements within the bureaucracy and in political office, who profit from allowing the dodgers and the manipulators to have their way. It would equally involve confrontation with their domestic allies in the private sector.

But the advancement of the domestic productive structure opens up new economic opportunities, new scope for manipulations and profiteering by nationals and foreigners alike, and the confrontation would not necessarily be antagonistic. New bureaucrats, perhaps equally corrupt, will make their careers from promoting the capital goods sector and agro-based industrialization, in alliance with the same old transnationals or with their hungry competitors waiting around the corner.

The expanded economic and social basis of capitalist state power in Nigeria has raised the capacity and competence of the domestic bourgeoisie inside and outside of the state apparatus, to advance its own interests in its dealings with international capital. Its bargaining power—as well as its managerial, technical, and professional competence—are enchanced in the handling of businesses and complex organizations, state and private, and also in its ability to provide political protection for capital through legislative, repressive, and ideological means. Its strength is partly due to the ability to generate its own class basis by providing support, officially or unofficially, for bourgeois class formation. It is a process in which international capital itself is closely involved in coaching and monitoring its domestic partners. The ultimate power of the domestic bourgeoisie lies in the manner in which it can use state power to regulate the access of international capital to "its" territory (Beckman, 1981a).

But as the bourgeoisie emancipates itself it faces crises and contradictions specific to the dependent, neo-colonial situation in which it is located. (Beckman, 1982b). Export instability destabilizes the state and undermines its ability to exercise, control, and reproduce legitimacy for itself, as well as for the domestic ruling class and its international allies. Import dependent industrialization grinds to a halt and the working classes resist or revolt as imported essential consumer goods disappear from the markets and real wages collapse. The full depth of the agrarian crisis is exposed as the capacity to import food in large quantities is curtailed.

The guardians of international capital, the IMF and the World Bank, will no doubt come to the aid of the threatened Nigerian state. International consortia will be formed to secure new credits (with appropriate conditions attached). International consultants will be parachuted into crisis-ridden ministries and state corporations to perform great feats of crisis management. But the balance of order and anarchy in the international capitalist system is fragile. Foreign capitalists will fall over each other in trying to cash in on the crisis, including orgies of wreckless lending linked to the desperate export promotion policies of equally crisis-ridden advanced industrial countries. The transfer of assets abroad by whatever means, foul or fair, may again become the principal preoccupation of worried businesspersons, foreigners and nationals alike.

As domestic protests gain in strength, the international friends of the Nigerian state are also likely to assist in crisis management with their peculiar blend of food aid and security advisers, seemingly contributing to greater stability while in practice further undermining the ability of the state to respond to the situation through effective policies rather than repression. The crisis generates strong pressures in the direction of the militarization of state power as well as more repressive domestic policies generally. These may similarly serve to consolidate state power in the short run while simultaneously contributing to the ideological bankruptcy and illegitimacy of state and ruling class alike.

The scenario is ambiguous. On the one hand, we see significant advances in bourgeois class and state formation and we can show that international capital is actively involved in a non-antagonistic manner. The emancipation of the domestic bourgeoisie and the capitalist state goes hand in hand with the penetration by international capital. The process is linked to significant advances in the industrial sector, producing for an expanded domestic market with roots in the commercial transformation of agriculture as well as in advances based on the non-agricultural petty commodity sector.

On the other hand, we see a process full of contradictions which tends to destabilize the state and push it into strategies of self-preservation which are counter-productive. Its closer incorporation into the world capitalist economy which petroleum has brought serves simultaneously as a source of emancipation and subordination for the Nigerian bourgeoisie. The state becomes an arena of intense factional infighting, engaging a wide spectrum of divisions on sectoral, national, regional, and other sectional lines, each group seeking access and control. Bureaucratic, military, and political fiefholders struggle to defend their own channels of patronage and appropriation. Private business interests, foreign and national, use all means at their disposal to make money flow their way.

There is no necessary incompatibility between these two aspects of capitalist state and class formation in Nigeria. As I have argued elsewhere, the anarchic conditions of factional struggles may well provide excellent conditions for capitalist accumulation, at least for those who learn to operate the system ruthlessly and efficiently on its own terms (Beckman, 1977). The stakes are high and failure may be severely punished. But the ability of operators, national and international, to find their feet in conditions of crisis and major upheaval seems quite impressive, judging from the Nigerian experience.

But things may turn sour for the international class alliance which presently runs Nigeria. The sectional manipulations of bureaucratic and political fiefholders may once again backfire and pull the country into violent turmoil. The looting of public coffers may develop to a point where the self-reproductive capacity of the economic and political system is exhausted. Reckless economic policies may destroy markets, push petty producers to retreat into subsistence production, and send the bourgeoisie scrambling for the safety of their properties in London and Rio de Janeiro.

The scenario is ambiguous but it is not without its logic. It is *the logic of internationally subordinated, state monopoly capitalism*. It is a system which to an extreme degree depends on production for the world market and where the mode of incorporation at that level is crucial for domestic class and state formation. Its subordination is neocolonial as it is not merely an effect of the uneven development of productive forces at the world level, but of the distinctive manner in which colonialism has structured the preconditions for integration. It is state capitalist because of the strategic role of state capital in generating the conditions for capitalist accumulation and class formation. It is monopolistic in the sense that the accumulation of capital, state and private, foreign and domestic, is strategically dependent on the monopolistic conditions created by the state. It is the combination of these features which simultaneously makes the state so powerful and so vulnerable.

It is also the logic of imperialism. The essence of imperialism, as I understand it, is the enforcement of monopoly profits by political and military means. Colonialism was monopoly by direct territorial conquest. The contemporary form is a transnational alliance of international capital backed at both ends by the power of the state. Imperialism needs domestically rooted bourgeois class forces in order to establish the appropriate material and political conditions for its profits. The domestic bourgeoisie, on the other hand, uses the alliance with international capital to buttress its class rule and accumulation. Jointly, the two parties cooperate to hold back popular pressures for social and democratic reform. As a consequence, capitalism in the Third World tends to take on a particularly oppressive, backward, and predatory character. Struggles against imperialism are therefore inseparably linked to domestic class struggles.

Imperialism contributes to the prolonged suffering and oppression of the peoples of the Third World *not so much by obstructing capitalist development but by promoting specific forms of capitalist development.* These forms are determined by the class alliances which flourish under its hegemony and by the kind of state which such alliances sustain. The struggle against imperialism is the struggle against such alliances and states. There is no other social basis for the struggle than in the concrete contradictions generated by this particular form of capitalist development. It is rooted in the concrete experiences of resistance and organization developed by those classes which confront capital and the state.

The resistance to internationally subordinated, state monopoly capital comes from the workers who are brought into direct confrontation with the state as the principal owner of large-scale capital in its partnership with private capital, foreign and domestic. It also comes from all those workers whose efforts to organize in defense of their interests are suppressed by the state or by capital with the backing or tacit support of the state. Resistance comes from the peasants whose land is invaded and whose labor is appropriated by the state in cooperation with international capital and a rising rural bourgeoisie, but also from those peasants and urban petty-commodity producers whose access to basic inputs as well as market outlets are monopolized by the same forces. Also, small Nigerian capitalist find that their conditions of survival are constantly circumscribed and threatened by state monopolistic arrangements.

This resistance is taking form in concrete struggles, from the militant actions of the Peugeot and Dunlop workers to the armed rebellion of the peasants at the Sokoto-Rima Basin Development Scheme (Oculi, 1980). The populist politics of Kano and the PRP (People's Redemption Party) demonstrates the confluence of anti-feudal and anti-monopolistic social forces. The resistance is also evidenced in the fight by students and intellectuals against growing political repression (Usman, 1982b).

The state provides the unity and cohesion of the international alliance of monopolistic forces which are presently imposing themselves vigorously and brutally on the Nigerian people. Nigeria is waiting for the political organizations which will give similar unity and cohesion to the emerging alliance of anti-monopolistic and anti-imperialist social forces, whose resistance is as yet scattered and fragmented.

NOTES

1. For the official view of the crisis, see the Presidential address on the 1982 Budget Proposals, Dec. 1981, also in *New Nigerian* 21 Dec. 1981, and the Presidential Address on the State of the Economy, April 1982, also in *Sunday New Nigerian* 11 April 1982. Successive crisis policy measures are reported in the weekly *West Africa*, including the drastic Economic Stabilization Order of June, 1982. The deteriorating external payments situation can be followed in the Monthly, Half-Yearly, and Annual Reports of the Central Bank of Nigeria. These also gives indices of consumer prices, industrial production, and other indicators. For the business view of the crisis, see official statements by the Manufacturers' Association of Nigeria in their *Industry News* (e.g., 1 July 1982), the Association of Chambers of Commerce, Industry, Mines, and Agriculture (e.g., Address by National President, "The Nigerian Economy; An Appraisal," *Financial Punch* 7 June 1982). See also major company reports such as the UAC Chairman's Address, Annual General Meeting 12 April 1982; Usman 1982a, and Ola Oni 1982 (also in *New Nigerian* 28 May 1982).

2. Labor retrenchments are reported erratically in the business and labor columns of the major Nigerian newspapers. For an attempt to bring together this scattered information, see the labor reports in the *Sunday Triumph* (Kano).

3. This optimistic view seems to be taken by the international business community as reflected in the columns of *West Africa*, and the annual survey of the Nigerian economy in the *Financial Times* of London.

4. For the top 50 list (according to turnover), see *Business Times* 21 Sept. 1984. The top ten are: UAC, PZ, SCOA, Mobil, CFAO, UTC, John Holt, Total, Food Specialities (Nestle), and RT Briscoe.

5. The federal public debt is reported by the Central Bank. In addition, state governments have recently engaged in heavy international borrowing, mostly on a suppliers' credit basis. Also individual state corporations have built up their own foreign debts. The total public debt is not known.

6. Much justified criticism has been directed against the ideological character of some of the key concepts of the dependency school, including the concept of development itself (Phillips 1977; Brewer 1980).

7. The government of General Murtala is often considered to have been more nationalistic than that of General Gowon. Senior bureaucrats such as A. Ayida and P.C. Asiodu have been associated with "tougher" or "softer" lines vis-à-vis international capital. The proceedings of the annual conferences of the Nigerian Economic Society is rich in evidence of these more moderate divisions (e.g., over indigenization policies). See also Akeredolu-Ale, 1976.

8. For an attempt to distinguish between the compradors and the more nationalistic technocrats, see Turner, 1980.

9. On the colonial and early post-colonial political economy (up to the mid-1970s), see Williams, 1976b and Aina, 1981.

10. For general surveys of the Nigerian economy in the 1970s, see Rimmer in Kirk-Greene and Rimmer, 1980, Financial Times, 1980, and Olaloku, 1970. The various writings of Tom Forrest add up to the most comprehensive picture. For official figures, see Central Bank reports. A handy summary of these is provided in Central Bank, 1980.

11. For a list of some of the more famous public scandals of this type, see Osoba, 1978 (including the "Scania Bus Scandal in which some crooked businessmen in Sweden and Nigeria ripped off the Lagos Municipal Transport Service"). The UPN (Unity Party of Nigeria) and NPN (National Party of Nigeria) party press (e.g., *Daily Sketch* and *National Concorde*) excel in disseminating information about the shady deals of the businessmen-cum-politicians of the opposite camp.

REFERENCES

AINA, T.A. (1982). "The state, industrial policy and industrial transformation: the Nigerian experience and its problems, 1946-1979." Presented to Nigerian Political Science Association, Jos.

———(1981). "Class structure and the economic development process in Nigeria: an examiniation of the differential place and role of social classes in the development process 1945-1975." Presented to Nigerian Political Science Association, Kano.

AKE, C. (1981). A Political Economy of Africa, London: Longmans.

AKEREDOLU-ALE, E.O. (1976). "Private foreign investment and the underdevelopment of indigenous entrepreneurship in Nigeria" in G. Williams (ed.), Nigeria: Economy and Society. London: Rex Collings.

ANDRAE, G. and B. BECKMAN (1981). "The wheat trap: bread and underdevelopment in Nigeria: project proposal and outline." Stockholm: Department of Human Geography.

BECKMAN, B. (1982a). "Whose state: state and capitalist development in Nigeria." Review of African Political Economy 23.

———(1982b). "Capitalist state formation in the third world." Presented to Nordic Seminar on Problems of Class Analysis, Uppsala (AKUT 19).

———(1982c). "Public investment and agrarian transformation in northern Nigeria." Presented to Workshop on State and Agriculture in Nigeria, Berkeley.

———(1981a). "Ghana, 1951-78: the agrarian basis of the post-colonial state" in J. Heyer, P. Roberts and G. Williams (eds.), Rural Development in Tropical Africa. London: Macmillan.

———(1981b). "Imperialism and the 'national bourgeoisie'." Review of African Political Economy 22.

———**(1980). "Imperialism and capitalist transformation: critique of a Kenyan debate."** Review of African Political Economy 19.

———(1977). Review of G. Williams (ed.), Nigeria: Economy and Society, in Review of African Political Economy 10.

BIERSTEKER, T.J. (1980). "Indigenization and the Nigerian bourgeoisie: dependent development in an African context." Presented to Conference on the African Bourgeoisie, Dakar.

BREWER, A (1980). Marxist Theories of Imperialism: A Critical Survey. London: Routledge & Kegan Paul.

Central Bank of Nigeria, Annual, Half-Yearly, and Monthly Reports. Lagos.

——— Economic and Financial Review. Lagos.   .

———(1980) Nigeria's Principal Economic and Financial Indicators 1970–1978. Lagos.

COLLINS, P. (1977). "Public policy and the development of indigenous capitalism: the Nigerian case." Journal of Commonwealth and Comparative Politics 15(2).

———TURNER, T. and WILLIAMS, G. (1976). "Capitalism and the Coup," in G. Williams (ed.), Nigeria: Economy and Society. London: Rex Collings.

EKUERHARE, B.U. (1980). "The impact and lessons of Nigeria's industrial policy under the military government, 1966–1979," Nigerian Economic Society, The Nigerian economy under the military. Proceedings of the 1980 Annual Conference.

Federal Government of Nigeria (1981). Report of the Kano Disturbances Tribunal of Inquiry. Lagos.

———(1978). Land Use Decree. Lagos.

———(1977). Nigerian Enterprises Promotion Decree. Lagos.

———(1972). Nigerian Enterprises Promotion Decree. Lagos.

Financial Times (1980). "Nigeria: twenty years of independence," 29–30/9. London; also: Ibadan: Spectrum Books, 1981.

FORREST, T. (1982). "Recent developments in Nigerian industrialisation," in M. Fransman (ed.), Industry and accumulation in Africa. London: Heinemann.

———(1981). "Agricultural policies in Nigeria." In J. Heyer, P. Roberts and G. Williams (eds.), Rural Development in Tropical Africa. London: Macmillan.

———(1980). "State capital in Nigeria." Presented to Conference on the African Bourgeoisie, Dakar.

———(1979). "Federal state and capitalist transformation of Nigeria." Department of Economics, Ahmadu Bello University, Zaria.

HOOGVELT, A. (1980). "Indigenisation and foreign capital: industrialisation in Nigeria." Review of African Political Economy 14.

ICON (1982). ICON Nigeria Company Handbook and Guide to Operating Business in Nigeria. Lagos: Jikonzult Management Services.

KIRK-GREENE, A. and D. RIMMER (1981). Nigeria since 1970: A Political and Economic Outline. London: Hodder and Stoughton.

MADUNAGU, E. (1982). Problems of Socialism: The Nigerian Challenge. London: Zed Press.

Nigerian Economic Society, Proceedings of Annual Conference (1974). Nigeria's Indigenisation Policy. Proceedings of a Symposium. Ibadan.

NNOLI, O. (1980). Ethnic Politics in Nigeria. Enugu: Fourth Dimension.

OCULI, O. (1980). "The political economy of planning the Bakolori irrigation project 1974–1980." Centre for Social and Economic Research, Zaria (seminar paper).

OLALOKU, F.A. [ed.] (1979). Structure of the Nigerian Economy. London: Macmillan.

OLA ONI (1982). "The present economic crisis and the way out." New Nigerian 16/4. Kaduna.

——— and ONIMODE, B. (1975). Economic Development of Nigeria: The Socialist Alternative. Ibadan: The Nigerian Academy of Arts, Sciences and Technology.

OSOBA, S. (1978). "The deepening crisis of the Nigerian national bourgeoisie." Review of African Political Economy 13.

PHILLIPS, A. (1977). "The concept of 'development.'" Review of African Political Economy 8.

TOYO. E. (1980). "National interest and structural contradictions in the Nigerian economy." Department of Economics, University of Calabar.

TURNER. T. (1980). "Nigeria: imperialism, oil technology and the comprador state." In P. Nore and T. Turner (eds.), Oil and Class Struggle. London: Zed Press.

———(1976). "The Nigerian cement racket." Oberlin, Ohio.

USMAN, Y.B. [ed.] (1982a). Political repression in Nigeria. Kano. Bala Mohammed Memorial Committee.

———(1982b). Who Is Responsible? The Nigerian Workers and the Current Economic Crisis. Kaduna: The Governor's Office.

———(1979). For the Liberation of Nigeria. London: New Beacon Books.

WALLACE. T. (1980). "Agricultural projects and land in northern Nigeria." Review of African Political Economy 17.

WILLIAMS G. [ed.] (1976a). Nigeria: Economy and Society. London: Rex Collings.

———(1976b). "Nigeria: a political economy," in G. Williams (ed.) Nigeria: Economy and Society. London: Rex Collings.

World Bank (1981). Accelerated development in Sub-Saharan Africa. Washington.

YAHAYA, A.D. (1978). "The creation of states," in K. Panter-Brick (ed.) Soldiers and Oil: The Political Transformation of Nigeria. London: Frank Cass.

3

POLITICS, METHOD, AND
EVIDENCE IN THE "KENYA DEBATE"

GAVIN KITCHING

The materialist doctrine that men are products of circumstances and upbringing, and that, therefore, changed men are products of other circumstances and changed upbringing, forgets that it is men that change circumstances and that the educator himself needs educating. Hence, this doctrine necessarily arrives at dividing society into two parts, of which one is superior to society (in Robert Owen for example) [Marx, *Third Thesis on Feuerback*].

In general, academic debates, and especially those (usually the most important and long-lived) with political implications, tend to end in a whimper rather than a bang. They usually dribble to an end with the participants exhausted or bored, and with an implicit agreement either that the data that would provide conclusive vindication for one side or the other do not exist or cannot be found (this happens frequently in historical debates), or a general realization that what is at stake are fundamental differences in epistemological or methodological standpoints which "the data" in themselves will not

Author's Note: Essential background texts for the Kenya debate are Leys (1975), Swainson (1977 and 1980), Langdon (1977 and 1980a) and Kaplinsky [ed.] (1978). The debate itself however, can be said to be composed of Leys (1978, 1979, and 1980), Langdon (1980), Kaplinsky (1980) and Henley (1980). A recent outsider's view of the debate is Beckman (1980). The essential background to the Nairobi agrarian debate is Leys (1971) and the published part of the debate is composed of Mukaru Ng'ang'a (1981) Anyang' Nyongo (1981), Njonjo (1981), Gutto (1981) and Cowen (1981). See also the latest contribution by Cowen in a review article (1982).

resolve and which the participants are too ill-equipped (or too tired) to address. In the case of a debate about contemporary trends, in which prognoses about the future play an important part, there may even be an implicit agreement to fall silent and to let new evidence accumulate for twenty years or so. When this happens the original participants (even if they are still alive and thinking) have usually got other fish to fry. The above flippant but I think accurate generalizations apply to every debate of this sort I have encountered—to the "rise" (fall) of the gentry debate in English seventeenth-century economic history, to the debate on the nature and causes of the transition from feudalism to capitalism, to the "standard of living" controversy of nineteenth-century British economic history.

Despite its short duration and its very small number of contributors (see author's note above), the Kenya debate is already marked by that mutual weariness and exasperation which usually precedes a general withdrawal from the fray. This increasingly exasperated tone derives in turn from the shift, which occurred very early in the debate, from disputation about facts and data, to a much more open-ended and inconclusive discussion of the *relative significance and importance* of different facts.

I shall argue throughout this chapter that this open-endedness and indeterminacy, which is rapidly leading to a dialogue of the deaf, can only be resolved by an explicit focusing of the debate upon the *political implications* of the various positions within it. So far this has not happened, and, in fact, the political implications of the various positions have been left implicit or dealt with as asides in occasional paragraphs. It is unclear why this is. Partly perhaps it stems from a fear (commonplace in academic-political debates of this sort) that if political issues and postions become the primary concern, the debate will simply degenerate into personalized polemics. Partly too, it may spring from the difficulties which Kenyan participants in the debate experience when explicitly political views appear in print. I will argue, however, that the main reason for this general reticence is that all the contributors to the debate are uneasy and somewhat confused about the political positions they occupy, and thus have "something to hide" politically. Instead of treating these political difficulties and confusions as a product of a distinctly difficult and confusing political conjuncture in East Africa (and indeed in Africa as a whole) and thereby using them to illuminate that conjuncture more clearly, nearly all participants tend to treat them idealistically as lacunae or contradictions in their own political ideologies, not to be made public until they have been privately resolved. I shall argue that these contradictions inhere in reality, and not in some inadequate intellectual appropriation of it. It follows therefore that they are not resolvable "privately," i.e., by the formulation of a more "adequate" theory, and that even "academic" debates about theory and methodology will remain indeterminate until those political contradictions and confusions are openly stated and expressed.

This latter point—about the relationship between the lack of political clarity and explicitness in the debate and its theoretical quality— can be simply asserted here, since in a sense it is the aim of the *whole* of what follows to demonstrate it. It may be put thus: Without an explication of the political implications of the various positions which are in conflict in the "Kenya debate," it is just not logically possible to derive *criteria of significance or importance* to assign to the different "facts" (in many cases, as we shall see, the same "facts") which are in dispute. Moreover, without both the use of such explicit criteria and the construction of explicit arguments to defend different criteria (which arguments will necessarily be political) there is simply no way of ending or even reducing the factual indeterminancy and mutual incomprehension which marks the debate at the moment.

THE HISTORY AND STRUCTURE OF THE DEBATE

The Kenya debate began with Colin Leys's revision of his own original and very influential thesis on Kenya which appeared as *Underdevelopment in Kenya* (1975). The revision was published three years later as "Capital Accumulation, Class Formation and Dependency: The Significance of the Kenyan Case" (Leys, 1978). This rather peculiar origin of the debate is important in two respects. In the first place, Leys's revision was much more of the methodology and underlying assumptions of his original views than of the empirical material which had supported them. This is significant because, as I shall argue, Raphael Kaplinsky and Steven Langdon (Leys's principal antagonists in the debate) have often seemed not fully to appreciate this point and have attempted to reply to "revisionist Leys" using very much the same *kind* of empirical evidence, and indeed very much the same kind of methodology as he had himself employed in *Underdevelopment in Kenya.* Second, the original research and writing of both Kaplinsky and Langdon on Kenya had been very much influenced by the approach and the findings of Leys's original book. Thus they found themselves in the situation of acolytes betrayed by their teacher. Their efforts have been bent therefore to maintaining the views of Leys "mark 1975" against those of Leys "mark 1978" and indeed attempting to get a revision of the revision.

It is therefore important to look carefully at the structure of *Underdevelopment in Kenya* in order to understand precisely what Leys was revising. The first point to note about the book is the relatively short time span with which it is concerned. Its sub-title is "The Political Economy of Neo-Colonialism 1964–1971," and indeed with the exception of a brief second chapter significantly titled "The Colonial Economy and the Transition to Neo-Colonialism in Kenya" the book is entirely concerned with trends in this eight-year period.

This simple fact is highly significant, as we shall see, but for the moment I will briefly summarize Leys's 1975 sketch of Kenyan history prior to his real starting point in 1964. It can be reduced to nine sequential steps of argument and chronology.

(1) "Significant" Kenyan history starts with land alienation to Europeans. This is because (2) the alienation of vast areas of land to settlers plus the concomitant restriction of Africans to reserves, produces (3) the monopolization of marketed export and domestic agricultural production by settler capital, and the reduction of Africans to subsistence producers and cheap labor for the farms and plantations. All this is facilitated and aided by (4) the role of the colonial state, which acts very largely as a source of cheap finance and subsidized infrastructure for the settlers and as their principal labor recruiter. This system (5) only comes to an end with the Mau-Mau uprising from which follows (6) the land consolidation and resettlement schemes. The latter however are (7) considered mainly as a device for successful counter-insurgency and de-radicalization of the independence movement. This device is (8) seen as eminently successful in sacrificing the interests of an outmoded settler capital to those of a new manufacturing and finance capital developed in Kenya after 1945. Thus we arrive conveniently at the gateway to (9) "neocolonialism" (1964-71).

One of the prime factors leading Leys to revise this original thesis was the influence of Michael Cowen's longer-term historical work on Central Province which had unearthed a much more deeply rooted process of "indigenous" capital accumulation and class formation among African people in this part of Kenya. This threw into doubt two central props in the original Leys thesis. The first was the view that the history of African peasant agriculture prior to the Swynnerton plan[1] had been a largely one-dimensional story of marginalization, impov-

erishment, and subordination to settler capitalism (the thesis pio-
neered by van Zwanenberg [1975] and Brett [1973] upon whose work
Leys's second chapter draws heavily). The second prop (the logical
concomitant of the first) was that the commoditization of peasant
agricultural output and thus the formal subordination of peasant
producers to international forms of capital was a process totally post-
dating the 1950s. It could therefore be safely treated entirely within
the context of a discussion of post-Swynnerton land consolidation
and registration and of African land settlement schemes in the Rift
Valley (which is what occurs in the third chapter of Leys, 1975, under
the title "Continuity and Change in Agriculture"). Cowen's work on
wattle production (1975 and 1979), in particular blew a large hole in
this latter assumption. But this was not all. Cowen's work also demonstrated that in the pre-Emergency period in particular, the process
of differentiation and accumulation within the peasant sector had
been closely interlinked to a process of differentiation of the off-farm
wage labor force, and to various forms of accumulation in non-agricultural trade and petty-commodity production. Cowen used the concept of "straddling" to characterize the central mechanism in this early
accumulation process.

It is clear that Leys came to feel (though unfortunately he did not
make this explicit in his revision, and has not really done so since)
that this much "richer" and "more eventful" African economic history
of the pre-Emergency period, plus the very subtle and complex process
which Cowen believed had affected peasant agriculture in the post-
Swynnerton period (I shall come to this shortly), threw not only these
two central props but, in fact, the whole argument of *Underdevelopment in Kenya* into doubt. For the central assumption upon which
that argument rested was that the prime movers in *all* events and
phenomena of any significance in the African political economy of
Kenya had always been essentially *external* to that political economy.
That is, to put it somewhat crudely, anything of note which had
happened to Africans had always been *done to them* from outside, at
first by white settlers and the colonial state—Leys's original account,
again following van Zwanenberg and Brett, simply treats the latter as an
agency of the former—later by multinational capital and a few rich
African "compradors" and "politicians" who were seen, unproblematically, as the agents or accomplices of multinational capital.

Given this assumption, Leys's history of Kenya could then be heavily front-loaded toward the present, because the nearer one approached
the present the more had been "done" to Africans (i.e., the greater had

been the variety of these external forces and the greater their impact). Thus the history of Kenya becomes, as it were, more "interesting" and more significant with each movement toward the present, and this implicitly justifies the structure of a book in which about forty pages are devoted to the entire period prior to 1964, and 235 pages to the eight years between 1964 and 1971.

However, it becomes clear that the problem with Leys's original treatment of history went even deeper than this. For his 1975 view of Kenya did not simply give greater weight to "external" as against "internal" causes and processes, it also had a firm view of the consequences of those causes, and this view very much determined the way both Kenya's past and its "present" (i.e., the period 1964-1971) was understood. Putting it simply, Leys's "1975" view was that the predominant consequence of the impact of colonialism and neocolonialism upon Kenya had been the continuing exploitation and suppression of the bulk of its African population. The aim of the whole analysis is to show that behind the apparent discontinuities of later Kenyan history—the coming of independence, the replacement of settler capital by multinational manufacturing and finance capital (and some African capital), by the apparent agrarian revolution around land consolidation and settlement and peasant-produced export crops—there lay a much more profound continuity. This continuity consisted in the poverty of the bulk of the country's African people and a structurally unchanged pattern of exploitation, inequality and drain of resources to the exterior, even if in the post-independence period the mechanisms and beneficiaries of these processes had changed somewhat. As a result of all this, in Leys's 1975 account we find the following:

(1) No consideration of precolonial trends in the African economy and thus the question of the relevance of any of these to postcolonial developments cannot even be posed. (2) The treatment of the impact of the settler presence on African agriculture is completely one-dimensional or uni-directional (i.e., it is treated as an unmitigated disaster) and the contradictory nature of this relation, particularly in the 1930s, is not explored (see Kitching, 1980: 57-107). (3) The treatment of the colonial state is similarly one-dimensional and fails to engage either with the contradictory impact of some of its "support" for settler agriculture or the pressures of other colonial interest groups (especially plantation capital, missionary groups and metropolitan economic and political interests) upon the colonial state (Kitching, 1980: 57-199, and Lonsdale and Berman, 1979). Also the settler interest itself is treated as homogeneous, a profoundly problematic assumption (see Redley, 1976). (4)

Finally, the Swynnerton and post-Swynnerton changes in peasant production are only treated from a political perspective which Leys takes from Wasserman[2] and, except for some rapid remarks on aggregate output and on the areas of land consolidated or resettled, no other dimensions of these very wide-ranging changes are considered.

The last point implies a more general absence within Leys's 1975 account—the lack of *any treatment of peasant agriculture in Kenya as a system of production*. That is, in all his treatment of agriculture in Kenya (including Leys, 1971) early Leys never considers peasant producers in their *active* role as producers. At most they are occupants of various-sized plots of land, receivers of varying incomes, and producers, *in the aggregate*, of volumes of aggregate output. But the actual, disaggregated social and material *processes* by which they produce and consume, their labor processes on and off the farm, their material relations of production which determine what and how they produce, these never figure in the analysis at all. It is perhaps this absence, this silence, above all others which is both symptom and cause of the early Leys's conception of peasants as passive objects rather than active agents of the historical processes, as the "done to," rather than the "doers." And this absence extends to his analysis of the 1964-1971 period, as well as his treatment of the earlier period.

All this explains then the importance of Cowen's work in Leys's revision of his original thesis. For Leys, as it were, "discovered" these absences in his own work by seeing them "present" in Cowen's. Their discovery in turn led Leys to what in fact is the central point of his revisionist thesis: *A proper historically-based political economy of Kenya, and of Africa in general must result in a much less deterministic conception of historical process than does the dependency perspective.* Or to put it another way, the prime failing of the dependency perspective is not this or that empirical finding or trend which it may identify, but the unidimensional "closure" of historical processes which follow from its highly "externalist" and overdetermining conception of colonialism and imperialism. He wishes to assert against this, in his revisionist position, the old but still profound aphorism of Marx that Kenyan peasants, like all other "men," *make their own history*, though not (given the reality of colonialism and imperialism) in circumstances of their own choosing. He wants, in short, to conceive colonialism and imperialism as at most *constraining contexts* within which African people are *actively* struggling, against each other, against nature, and against imperialism itself (some of them, sometimes). He believes that, in contradistinction to this, dependency or underdevelopment theory treats colonialism and imperialism as quasi-omnipotent prime movers in comparison with whose massive, over-determining (and generally harmful) effects, the activities, wishes, and goals of the colonized and imperialized are but puny things. The latter can therefore be treated as essentially passive objects of externally determined historical processes.

This point, would, however, have come across more powerfully and sooner in the Kenya debate were it not for two circumstances. In the first place Leys failed to make it as central and as powerful in his original revision as he should have done, and mixed it up with a number of empirical assertions about "indigenous" capitalism in Kenya, about the nature and role of the state there, and about economic trends within the contemporary Kenyan economy. These latter, somewhat unfortunately, then became the prime focus of Langdon and Kaplnsky's replies. In the second place, Langdon and Kaplinsky themselves were not perhaps best placed, given their own professional backgrounds, to really understand either the thrust or force of this revision. Neither of them had, or has, any experience of doing "long-period" historical research either in Kenya or anywhere else and both of them operate with the conventional development economist's methodological tool kit. That is, they both work primarily by taking *short period* time series out of national accounts data and inferring present and likely future trends from them.

This in turn means that Leys's remarks about history and the "ahis-toricity" of dependency theory, both in his original *Socialist Register* piece (1978) and (somewhat more insistently) in later contributions (1979, 1980) went, for the most part, straight over their heads. They concentrated instead upon identifying empirically testable "hypotheses" about *contemporary* trends in Kenya to which Leys could be seen or be construed to be committed, so that they could then "test" them using the tools and data with which they were familiar.

Leys's response to this, an ambiguous mixture of assertion that Langdon and Kaplinsky were (are) not seeing the central point, with a willingness to challenge some of their empirical data, or their interpretations of them, has not helped clarity. It has left the impression that these issues concerning empirical trends *may be* the central point, or at least that they are close enough to the central point to warrant reply. Langdon and Kaplinsky's continued ignoring of the agricultural dimension to the whole question, and in particular their apparent failure to read Cowen's material (or, perhaps, to understand it) has also not helped the issues to come clearly into focus.

We must now turn to Langdon and Kaplinsky's replies and consider these in their own right. For in my view they do demonstrate precisely those characteristics of "externalism" and historical "closure" which Leys is so worried about, though again this is as much demonstrated by what they do *not* do, by what they do *not* consider (by the substantive and methodological absences in their work) as by what they do say.

Langdon and Kaplinsky assimilated Leys's auto-critique as essentially the substitution of an "optimistic" assessment of the prospects for capitalism in Kenya for the "pessimistic" thesis of his original book. They therefore responded to this thesis by trying to turn it into better defined empirical "hypotheses," or propositions which could then be tested and refuted. Thus Langdon for example, in his most lengthy contribution to the debate (1980) sees the center of Leys's revisionist position as an assertion that Kenya "is a country undergoing a comparatively rapid transition to capitalist relations of production, due in large part to the political strength of an indigenous class of capital" (1980: 4). Langdon then breaks this down into a two part proposition about the post-independence state in Kenya—(1) "the state is controlled by an indigenous Kenyan bourgeoisie," and (2) a proposition that capitalism in Kenya is "fundamentally transforming the social relations of production." He then offers a counter view of the class composition and control of the state, and a refutation of the "transformatory" hypothesis about Kenyan capitalism. I shall return to the question of the state later, for in my view it has been an area of the Kenya debate which has been as arid and indeterminate as it has been central, and it will be necessary to demonstrate this.

Considering the second part of Langdon's refutation, we should note the methodology of its construction, for it is both revealing and typical of the approach adopted by him and Kaplinsky.[3] Langdon has Leys committed to the view that capitalism in Kenya is fundamentally "transforming" the "social relations of production." But in itself, he clearly feels, this is just a phrase, it could mean anything or nothing, so it needs more precise definition before it can be meaningfully addressed. In this search for tighter definition, he turns for help, somewhat oddly perhaps, to Karl Polanyi.

In his detailed analysis of capitalist transformation in Western Europe, Karl Polanyi concentrates above all on the emergence of national labour markets in the framework of which the vast majority of the population must sell its labour power, for a wage, in order to live.

Although such social change was not the sole defining characteristic of capitalism, this growth of wage employment was at the heart of the new capitalist relations of production that emerged in Western Europe. In analysing capitalist transformation in Kenya, then, it is essential to focus on the growth of wage employment in the country [1980: 14].

Hence we get, via Karl Polanyi, from transformed social relations of production to the growth of wage employment—that is, from what Langdon would undoubtedly see as the vague and abstract to the concrete and testable. When the testable is tested, Langdon is able to suggest both that the rate of growth of such employment is low, and that if current population and labor force growth rates in Kenya continue it will take several hundred years (anything from 201 years to 604!) before the number of Kenyans employed outside enumerated wage employment starts to fall.

Of course, in this tranformation of the abstract into the concrete and testable, a very great deal has disappeared, spirited away under the authority of Polanyi. To put it at its simplest, this procedure effectively removes any concept of development under capitalism which *does not, of necessity, entail the universalization of the capital/wage-labor relationship.* That is, as a *historical* proposition about Kenya (a proposition addressing, say, the period from 1918 to 1980) one might simply wish to say that there has been a long-term (but not smooth or linear) increase in the volume and value of the output of all commodities over this period, and a sustained (but again not smooth or linear) growth in per capita income. This increased volume and value of commodity production and rise in per capita income has been accompanied by a rise in both the volume and value productivity of labor and land in agriculture and of total output, output per worker and per capita earnings in manufacture and other major sectors (see Kitching, 1980; Cowen, 1976). Insofar as this long-term historical process has occurred under the auspices of both national and international forms of merchant, finance and industrial capital, then it has been *the development of commodity production under capitalism.* It has *not* involved the universalization of the capital/wage relationship, but it has involved the growth of the importance of this relationship in some sectors (e.g., manufacturing) and an actual diminution of its role in some others (e.g., agriculture) since World War II. This conflicting trend in the development of the capital/wage relationship is one of the most important characteristics of capitalism in Kenya, and a source of its predominant contradiction, as Cowen in particular has always stressed (see below).

If it is a *historical* proposition of this sort which Leys is essentially concerned to establish, and if his concept of the development of capitalism in Kenya is of this broader and more multi-dimensional form (which I think it is, though Leys might have been clearer on the matter), then of course Langdon's critique, focused on "wage employment" is largely beside the point.

But Langdon is not finished yet. Having used a model derived from Frances Stewart to show that the growth of the Kenyan proletariat is going to be mighty slow, he suddenly narrows the scope of his argument even further. Having moved from capitalism to wage employment in one bound, another leap takes us to this proposition:

> Import reliance for inputs to the industrial sector can be examined from a similar perspective. A marked decrease in the import share of goods used by Kenyan industry would suggest growing linkage effects to the rest of the economy, and an increased impact on social and economic transformation throughout the country (1980: 17–18).

So "social and economic transformation throughout the country" is now to be understood as "growing linkage effects" to the rest of the economy from *manufacturing enterprises* based in Kenya. Of course he finds precious little evidence of such growing linkages. The employment linkage, he has already indicated, is small because of the highly capital-intensive nature of manufacturing enterprises in Kenya, particularly those (the vast majority) which are subsidiaries of multinational companies. This is especially so if they are simply producing products developed originally for metropolitan markets in Europe and North America. Similarly such subsidiaries usually prefer to use imported material inputs, even if local alternatives are available, so the backward linkages (as they are called) to local producers who might supply such inputs (and thus increase their output, income and employment generation) are small (Langdon, 1980: 18–24).

No doubt this is largely true, but as a critique of revisionist Leys, it is once again beside the point, for clearly when one speaks of the transformation of the social relations of production by capitalism in Kenya one does not mean only or even primarily the growth of backward and forward linkages from manufacturing industry to the rest of the local economy. This may, it is true, become significant at a certain stage in the continuing historical process of capitalist development, but considered historically as a long-period process in Kenya, several other phenomena are far more significant, because they are essential prerequisites of the very emergence of manufacturing industry. These

include, for example: (1) Changes in the output mix and cropping
pattern in peasant agriculture, changes which are both the cause and
effect of (2) A commoditization of an increasing proportion of that
output. This leads to (3) An increased monetization of exchange relationships, a monetization also aided by (4) The emergence of a partially
proletarianized wage labor force both on farms and plantations and in
urban areas, an emergence which in turn requires (5) Changes in the
sexual division of labor in peasant agriculture and an intensification of
that labor both by an expansion of the working day, and improved hoes,
ploughs, and crop varieties. (See Kitching [1980: Parts 1 and 2] where
there is an attempt to validate the thesis schematically outlined here in
empirical detail.)

To repeat, such changes are the essential prerequisite for the penetration of transnational industrial capital. Reducing the discussion of
"social and economic transformation" under capitalism to the analysis
of a short period in which such transnational industrial capital is
already present (so that one can then focus entirely on its future
prospects), is rather like trying to write a history of science entirely
around the question of fast-breeder nuclear reactors: It may produce
a rather gloomy view of the future but an awful lot is taken as given.

Further elements in Langdon's critique are concerned with the
profitability of transnational subsidiaries in Kenya vis-à-vis indigenous manufacturing enterprises, and with the "independence" or otherwise of the indigenous Kenyan capitalists whom both Leys and
Swainson (1980) had given as examples of an indigenous bourgeoisie
emerging in partial autonomy from, and in opposition to, multinational capital. But here, as in Kaplinsky and indeed in Leys and
Swainson, the issue is posed in such a way as simply to be unresolv-
able on the currently available evidence. Both sides in the debate concur that all these indigenous Kenyan capitalists have been heavily
dependent upon various types of state support in their growth to
prominence, and that many (though not all of them) began their
careers as managerial employees of multinationals in Kenya and
maintain close links with such capital even when branching out into
independent or semi-independent ventures. Thus the evidence (whether
on GEMA holdings, or Karume's Tiger Shoes, or JK Industries or
Udi Gecaga and Lonhro) can be read both ways: to support either an
"indigenous," "independent" bourgeoisie thesis (Swanson, Leys) or a
modified "comprador" thesis (Langdon, Kaplinsky). Or at least it can
be read that way, *so long as the prime focus of concern is the likely*

future prospects of these African capitalists, i.e., so long as the central issue is whether or not they form the nucleus of a new, independent "national bourgeoisie."

The issue, however, is simply not determinable by reference to short-period profitability trends, or by reference to formal statistics on ownership of capital or multiple directorships, which Langdon and Kaplinsky in particular have used. There are two reasons for this. First, as Henley (1980) points out in his reply to Kaplinsky, evidence on shareholding is itself a very partial guide to crucial issues of control and accumulation. In any case what is required in assessing the possible or likely trajectories of indigenous Kenyan capitalists is evidence of dynamic process, rather than the comparative statics which are all that can be derived from time-series statistics. That is, one needs both longer-period histories of capital accumulation by Kenyans (of the sort provided, for example, by Swainson) and for the contemporary period "participant observation" studies of Kenyan capitalists "in action." Researchers would need to be with Udi Gecaga in the numerous boardrooms which he frequents, tap his phone calls (especially the business ones), ransack his files, listen to his barroom plots and his bedroom conversations—in short, plumb the dynamics of his relationship with multinational capital (alias Tiny Rowland in this case), the state (i.e., a thickly interwoven network of politicians and senior government officials), and the wider Kenyan economy. For it is through these day-to-day processes that Gecaga struggles to maximize profits and minimize losses, chooses some investments and has others blocked off, "allies" (in some deals) with multinational capital and "struggles" (in others) against it, or more complicatedly, tries to maneuver the terms of *all* his alliances to his own advantage, and struggles against particular parts or actions of multinational capital and "indigenous capital."

It is the aggregate *outcome* of *activities* like these, of Gecaga, of Njenga Karume, of Justus Kalinga and of many others who are like them (or who would be like them) that together with changes in the international capitalist conjunctures which confront Kenyan capitalists (as they confront Marxist analysts) as "constraints" within which they have to act, will determine the future of capitalism in Kenya. To make even a better guess about that future, one would have to have access to, *be in on,* those activities, "in on them" to the full extent that these men themselves are. But such access is not available to social scientists (*qua* social scientists) Marxist or otherwise. Since, therefore, we do not have access to the processes and activities which are forming the future, the only second best is to record it later, as history, as past events, related to us in a no doubt censored fashion "in tranquility," by such men looking back, or as old files deposited (again no doubt with both delibrate and unintended censorship) in public archives. This is the *only* valid "second best" available. Trying to "read off" such dynamics (or lack of them) from published profit figures, or published statistics on shareholding is not even a second best, *it is just an epistemological error*. It is the wrong kind of knowledge which, however much we may probe, is not knowledge of the *dynamics* of capitalism in Kenya and cannot be made such. It is at most the form of appearance of an underlying process and a frozen form at that. It is rather like trying to infer the likely result of a football match from half a dozen snapshots of the action taken after ten minutes of the first half.

This point applies *a fortiori* to that part of the debate which is concerned with the role of the Kenyan state. Broadly, the choice currently on offer is between (1) a view of the Kenyan state as a locus of class struggle and a struggle between foreign and national capital in which, certainly at certain moments, the nascent national bourgeoisie has been dominant and has successfully used state power against foreign capital; and (2) a conception which sees foreign capital in alliance with the auxiliary Kenyan bourgeoisie still in control of the state, but with this control constantly under challenge from a lower tier of "technocrats" and "middle-level officers" in the Central Bank and "in most ministries and parastatals" who articulate a "nationalist" ideology and practice in opposition to this supreme power block (Kaplinsky, 1980: 31,39; Landgon, 1980: 7,9). At the moment there is simply no way of choosing between these two conceptions, or of any other conception, because the same small amount of empirical evidence available is adduced in support of both conceptions.

Thus, for example, Swainson sees the very existence of the Capital Issues Committee (CIC) of the Kenyan Treasury and the New Projects Committee of the Ministry of Commerce and Industry as signs that the Kenyan state is intervening, moderately effectively, to control the activities of multinational capital and to support the movement of indigenous capital into manufacturing. Langdon (1977: 41–55; 1980: 185-193, 209-211) and Kaplinsky (1978, 1980) are much less impressed by the effectiveness of these institutions, and more important (in the context being discussed here), see them as reflecting much more the attitudes and activities of Cowen's "intendant class" which "owes it social character to its training ... acquired in western educational institutions or local institutions heavily influenced by western standards" (Langdon, 1980: 9). This "class," occupying middle-level positions in several ministries and in the Central Bank, acts upon the basis of a Fabian social reformist ethic acquired through its training, and also (one could hypothesize) upon the basis of a "dependency" conception of Kenya's economic position in the world, also acquired, perhaps from Western radicals, in the course of this same training. This ideological stance sets this class or stratum in opposition to the dominant power block of representatives of African capital closely allied to the multinationals. Such institutions as the CIC and the New Projects Committee, therefore, far from being instruments of the indigenous bourgeoisie or acting in their interests (Leys, Swainson), are in fact institutions representing, rather weakly and ineffectively, the nationalist economic policies of this subordinate stratum within the state.

Now how would one choose between these two interpretations of state institutions and activities? First, one would have to be able to observe these institutions in action. Their mere existence in and of itself tells one nothing; questions of their effectiveness and of the actual use of their powers in particular instances are clearly central. The problem however, is that, *given the amount and type of information about such cases to which academics can gain access* these examples nearly always turn out to be readable in at least two different ways, depending upon the very theoretical positions of which they are supposed to be proof or disproof. For example, there are several cases in which the CIC appears to have taken a tough line with multinational capital (see for example Swainson, 1977: 53; 1980: 210), but others in which it has failed to prevent actions by multinational capital to which it was opposed (Langdon in Kaplinsky, 1978: 179). To evaluate the two theoretical perspectives from these apparently contradictory examples one would have to know very precisely what pressures were brought upon the CIC in the various cases, *who* articulated those pressures and how, *who* dominated the CIC decision making in particular cases, and the motives and interests of all the parties concerned. In short, one would need very much the same kind of information about the real processes of state decision making which I hypothesized one would need about Udi Gecaga in order to decide whether he is best to be categorized as a representative of an "independent," "indigenous" captal in formation, or a mere "comprador" with a few side interests of his own.

But surely, it will be said, if one cannot get access to this kind of information, if one cannot bug the telephone switchboards of the Central Bank and the ICDC, if one cannot plant cameras and microphones in a hundred offices and a thousand bedrooms, surely one can at least *infer* from outcomes. Surely, for example, if the CIC refuses Brook Bond of Kenya permission to take over a coffee factory in Limuru which shortly thereafter became the property of a group made up of Udi Gecaga and two African directors of the Kenya Tea Development Authority, this shows that the CIC operates in the interests of indigenous capital (Swainson, 1977: 53). Or if the Central Bank of Kenya's attempt to insist that General Motors pay a with-holding tax on service fees was defeated by an alliance of GM and the Industrial and Commercial Development Corporation (ICDC), this shows that the ICDC acts on behalf of multinational capital against the nationalist intendant class within the Central Bank (Kaplinsky, 1980: 100).

One only needs to present these cases in this way for it to be obvious that no such inference can be made in either case. In the former case, for example, one might have been dealing with a situation in which the forces within the CIC determining the initial refusal of permission to Brook Bond were Kaplinsky's nationalist techno-crats, who, in an issue which was relatively marginal to Brook Bond, and in which, perhaps, its political alliances had not been well pre-pared or activated, were given bureaucratic "space" to indulge their nationalist preferences and to exclude a multinational from some national assets. Once this decision was made however, Gecaga gets wind of it (a drunken "intendant" a little too boastful at a party?) and steps in sharply to make a national take-over bid with help from a few friends strategically located within the Kenya Tea Development Authority.

In the second case too, one can imagine a situation in which a fiercely nationalist group of intendants within the ICDC are deter-mined to increase the amount of local vehicle manufacture in Kenya. As a first stage in this process, the cooperation of multinational capi-tal is necessary, and it is recognized that there will be some short term foreign exchange costs to be borne, especially from service fees and the importation of parts and equipment in what will initially be a purely assembly operation. At a later stage, however, they intend to insist upon local manufacture of a wider and wider range of compo-nents and intermediate goods, and to extend state control of the equity of these subsidiaries so as to force this diversification. They have just succeeded in getting General Motors on the hook with a joint venture assembly agreement when a group of over-zealous com-rades in the Central Bank threaten to abort the whole process by some understandable (but in this case, mistaken) zeal about withholding taxes. It then becomes necessary to ring up a few friends over there in the CB, perhaps throw a party or two, and remind some key figures in the CB of the previous ICDC cooperation in their own business ventures, and the nationalist alliance is firmly sealed once again. The boys in CB see the nationalist force of the venture with GM and quietly step aside. Intendants victorious. Perhaps the flippant tone will be resented, but it is almost invited by the vacuity and ambiguity of the examples which are continually thrown about in this area of the debate. Perhaps the ultimate example here is the Fiat-Gema deal which has been advanced as a prime example of: (1) the movement of indigenous capital into manufacturing (Leys, 1978), (2) the capitulation of indigenous capital to a multinational (Langdon, 1980), and (3) the weakness of indigenous capital within the state as compared with transnational capital (Kaplinsky, 1980).

The point, then, is that on *both* sides in the Kenya debate a great deal of dubious inference from highly partial information is being dignified as theory(ies) of the state and made to stand in place of the sort of knowledge of political processes and struggles which academics do not have *and cannot get*. My own guess, for what it is worth, is that every businessman in Kenya and every state official from a lower-middle level upward could be categorized as a "national bourgeois" from some points of view, with reference to some of his/her activities and aspirations, and as a "comprador" from others. They enter into conjunctural alliances around particular struggles and issues which could be categorized as in the interests of transnational capital sometimes in some respects, and as hostile to those interests and nationalist in thrust at other times and in other respects. Such alliances at times give parts of the state apparatus (the ICDC, the CIC, the Central Bank) one coloration and at times another. Similarly "transnational capital" (or particular representatives of particular parts of it) is in there too, making alliances, trying to use people who are trying to use it, at times succeeding, at times failing wholly or partly.

In short, it is all very complex and shifting, and a great deal of it social scientists never see and can not see. That "knowledge is power" is not merely a cliché. It is a true and powerful insight, well appreciated by all parties in the battle for access to and use of state power in Kenya. On all sides, that is hidden which it is in one's interest to hide, *and* that is revealed which it is in one's interests to reveal, or whose revelation may damage an adversary. In this situation, social scientists sit around like starving sparrows, picking up crumbs of information where they fall, sometimes at first hand, more usually at second or third hand (from newspapers and other media).

What am I saying then? That no theory of the state is possible for contemporary Kenya, that it requires that we know what we cannot know, and that in the absence of that knowledge, all is rather pretentiously dressed conjecture? Yes, but there is also something more. In the current state of knowledge, and of capitalist development in Kenya, there is only a *negative* statement one can make about the State, a negative statement which is nonetheless important and significant. It is in fact a two-fold negative proposition that (1) the State is *not* an agency of any single force in Kenya (i.e., it is *not* the agency of multinational capital or of indigenous capital, or of any "fraction" of either form of capital), it is rather *a continual site of struggle* among all these forces, a struggle whose outcome is not foreclosed, and which continually results in contradictory policy outcomes; and (2) the state is not an "it,"—that is, it is not a unity, for the struggle outlined above has, as one of its effects the fracturing of the State, and indeed of particular state institutions, into contending forces which themselves enter into conjunctural alliances and oppositions. The State in Kenya is a mess, in short, and it is so because it is embedded in a society and economy undergoing continual conflicts between nascent forms of national capital, different fractions of transnational capital, and (in partial overlap with the above) between different social strata, ethnic and regional groupings, and so forth, within the indigenous population. This complexity is not reducible to a "last instance" hegemony of national or transnational capital because in the current historical movement (where a "moment" may be 50 years or more in duration), *the question of that hegemony is precisely one of the central issues which are at stake.* Its resolution is on the historical agenda: It is not yet resolved and may be resolved in historically unprecedented ways.

In my view these essentially negative propositions about the state, the only propositions which are appropriate in an historical moment of intense struggle for the State, in themselves constitute a *coup de grace* for a certain sort of dependency theory, which depends for its central political force on a "last instance" formulation of the state as the "agency" of multinational capital. At the moment the anti-dependency position need only assert that the above position does *not* hold, at least in Kenya. It is unnecessary to go further.

THE KENYA DEBATE CONTINUED:
THE "AGRARIAN QUESTION"

As we have already seen, Colin Leys's revision of his 1975 book was primarily influenced by Michael Cowen's work, which means that it was primarily influenced by work on agriculture. Indeed, those sections of the 1978 article which attempt to validate a concept of indigenous capital accumulation within Kenya are primarily concerned with *accumulation in agriculture and livestock production* in the pre-colonial, colonial and post-colonial period (Leys, 1978: 246–254). The sections on the "highly significant contemporary movement of African capital into manufacturing production" (Leys, 1978: 254) represent in fact a rather brief addendum to the discussion, relying heavily on Swainson (1977). They are very tentative in nature, suggesting nascent tendencies at most. The subsequent concentration of the debate on tendencies within Kenyan *manufacturing* has not therefore been helpful in clarifying the issues at stake.

It might seem therefore that a more recent development of the debate to embrace the "agrarian question" directly would be more likely to address those major theoretical and political issues. However, to date the published contributions to the Kenyan agrarian debate have also been rather disappointing, principally because once again the central political implications involved are tacitly assumed rather than explicitly enunciated, or where they do appear this is as the occasional aside, rather than as a central focus.

Two contributions by Ng'ang'a and Anyang' Nyongo in particular are in the worst and most arid traditions of "academic Marxism" in which a Chayanovian-derived theory of "the peasantry" (Ng'ang'a 1981) is derided for its failure to make use of an Althusserian "mode of production"/"articulation" apparatus (Anyang' Nyongo 1981), without it ever being clear on either side what precisely either concept is being used to explain or what would be at stake (apart from perhaps, and rather ironically, a naively positivist "descriptive accuracy"), in the adoption of one mode of conceptualization rather than the other. The debate really becomes interesting only in the exchanges between Njonjo (1981), Gutto (1981), and Cowen (1981). However, even here, for want of an explicit intellectual and political history to the debate, the political issues at stake do not emerge as clearly as they might. I shall attempt to provide such a context in what follows.

Originally, it can be said, the adoption of a "dependency" perspective on Africa (and indeed on the Third World as a whole), was frequently accompanied by an essentially populist conception of the peasantry. This is, the "primary contradiction" within dependent, neocolonial states in Africa was conceived as that between the "needs" and "welfare" of "the people" in general and a narrow stratum of "compradors" who in alliance with imperialism and multinational capital had betrayed "the people" for their own enrichment. The primary goal of revolutionary struggle, therefore, was for the overthrow of this comprador or auxiliary bourgeoisie and for the installation of "socialism" which would bring "real development," the "real fruits of independence" to "the people." In this conception of "the people," "the peasants" had a predominant weight reflecting their actual numerical predominance in many Third World societies, though occasionally reference might also be made to a "worker/peasant alliance" against imperialism where an agricultural or non-agricultural proletariat of any size was also present.[4]

As was the case, for example, in some early Narodnik formulations in nineteenth century Russia (Kitching, 1982; Walicki, 1969; Mendel, 1961), enthusiasts for this particular position were understandably not very enthusiastic about research (whether Marxist or otherwise) which demonstrated growing inequalities within the peasantry, or which purported to identify an emergent class of rich peasants or *kulaks* engaged in accumulation and exploitation of poor peasants or the landless. In some cases such research was explicitly denounced as an attempt to "divide the people" and to weaken the unity of the anti-imperialist struggle, an issue which was also one of the primary areas of dispute between Marxists and other Tanzanian radicals in the early years after independence. (See the seminal contribution to this debate by Saul, 1973.)

Leys (1971) represented an interesting variant of this populist dependency position, in that it uses an essentially Chayanovian concept of "peasant economy" and society to assert the existence of a process of "peasantization" in Kenya. In this process small-scale petty commodity production in agriculture, primarily using family labor, is seen to be expanding within Kenya's rural areas, and by dint of the high density settlement schemes in the Rift Valley, is actually colonizing and "re-peasantising" the large farm areas of the former "White Highlands." This "peasantization" of Kenya serves as the foundation of an essentially populist, clientist politics in which peasants are mobilized for the political support of a small ruling elite, but only in exchange for the latter endorsing and encouraging through the state the *de facto* hegemony of the "peasant mode of production." The process of peasantization is thus seen as both a symptom of the fundamentally undynamic and non-transformatory nature of capitalism in Kenya, and as a principle impediment to such dynamism, in that it represents an actual reversal of such tendencies toward proletarianization of labor power as had been present in colonial Kenya, and indeed places a block in the way of sustained capital accumulation through exploitation of wage labor. Leys also makes liberal use of Chayanovian concepts of "demographic cycles" in the "peasant economy" to deny that any lasting process of class differentiation is occurring. On the contrary, he sees peasantization as not merely the quantitative expansion of peasant smallholdings and peasant produced agricultural output, but as a broadly egalitarian process which gives a real material foundation to an essentially undifferentiated concept of "the people" in Kenya, upon which all populist politics is based.

When this particular conception of trends within Kenyan agriculture was subsequently allied to a wider dependency perspective on historical and contemporary developments in Kenya, (Leys, 1975; pp. 118-121 above) a more or less coherent theoretical and political position emerged, which, as I have suggested, greatly influenced Kenyan radicals of all persuasions. It is an index of how both material developments and theoretical positions in Kenya have changed since even the mid-1970s, that in the recent number of *The Review of African Political Economy* (1981) devoted to the agrarian question in Kenya, only one of the contributors, S.B.O. Gutto, occupies a position even vaguely resembling Leys's 1971 position.

For the rest of the contributors it is simply axiomatic that there is some class differentiation of the Kenyan peasantry. They all agree that a great deal of recent empirical evidence has shown Leys's original formulations of "peasantization" to be untenable, at least in their pure form.

This empirically induced shift poses considerable political problems, for the political merit of Leys's original position from a *dependista* point of view, was that it provided a materialist support for the *dependista's* essential project, a popular mass struggle against imperialism and its handful of local "agents" in control of the neocolonial state. If one wants to maintain that project there are two ways of responding to the "threat" posed to the popular anti-imperialist alliance by growing evidence of increased differentiation of the peasantry. One may (1) Attempt to downplay the scale and significance of these differences among the peasantry, to state that they are "exaggerated" or that they are spatially and statistically "atypical" (this is broadly Gutto's position); or (2) One may go to "the other extreme." That is, one may see such differentiation as occurring at such speed and on such a scale that the peasantry has essentially dissolved, or is well on the road to dissolution, and, some pure "appearances" to the contrary, is already proletarianized or half-proletarianized. This then provides a materialist foundation for a *new* revolutionary force (an industrial and agricultural proletariat), perhaps focused initially around the trade union movement.

This is broadly Njonjo's position, a position very reminiscent of that taken up by Lenin in *The Development of Capitalism in Russia*. Lenin's positions in that work were aimed at refuting both the "Narodniks" like V.P. Vorontsov and N. Danielson who, as Lenin saw it, downplayed the contradictions within the peasantry and the extent of peasant class differentiation and proletarianization, *and* the Mensheviks, who recognized them, but thought that the whole process was at an early stage of development and had to go much further (as had the development of capitalism in general) before revolution and socialism could come on to the "historical agenda" in Russia. Similarly, Njonjo in his contribution is hostile to "self-appointed friends of the peasantry" (which is how he categorizes Ng'ang'a), but also to Cowen's work, because the latter appears to downplay or deny the reality and speed of the proletarianization of the Kenyan peasantry.

In fact Cowen "gets it" from both sides in this debate. For Gutto he has been a principal, in fact *the* principal, source of conceptions of indigenous capital accumulation and class differentiation within the Kenyan peasantry (which is certainly true as we have seen, as far as Cowen's impact on Leys's revisionist theses is concerned). But Cowen's theoretical revolution, as Gutto sees it, is based on an analysis of some entirely exceptional and untypical parts of the Kenyan countryside. For Njonjo on the other hand, Cowen's principal fault is that he insists upon holding up some marginal and untypical statistics about the increasingly equal distribution of income from coffee, tea, and milk sales in some sub-locations in Nyeri district, against the much more obvious and significant trends to increasing inequality, and "disguised" proletarianization among the peasantry. The latter Njonjo derives both from his own empirical work on African owned large farms in the Rift Valley (1977) and from a different reading of the official statistics and surveys of peasant agriculture (1981). For Gutto, Cowen is a Menshevik lauding and exaggerating the impact of capitalism on the Kenyan peasantry; for Njongo he is a neo-Narodnik playing down the significance and scale of that impact and the "contradictions" it is generating.

The best way of clarifying these issues is therefore to present and analyze Cowen's argument concerning the development of capitalism in Kenya. As we have seen, this argument, and the detailed empirical work which sustains it, has been enormously influential in the Kenya debate, stimulating Leys's original revision and now providing the locus for the whole discussion of the agrarian question, and indeed for a growing volume of new empirical work on Kenyan agriculture. Since it is still not all that well known or understood, in part because much of it is still unpublished, and in part because of its author's somewhat opaque style, laying out this central structure may both aid subsequent contributions and open up some key theoretical issues.

Cowen's work really divides into halves, each with a rather different thrust, and each in fact relating to different periods of Kenyan history. The first half (1972, 1974a, 1974b) which particularly influenced Leys's reformulations, consists of an oral and archival-based history of agricultural developments in a small area of Central Province. The whole thrust of this work, on precolonial patterns of accumulation, on the role of the *athomi* or *asomi*[5] in land accumulation and consolidation and in agricultural commodity production in the pre-Swynnerton period (with its central focus on the straddling process), radically undermined earlier conceptions of the Kikuyu peasantry as a uniformly impoverished mass of subsistence farmers forcibly subordinated to settler labor demands.

The second half of Cowen's work, however (1974a, 1975, 1976, 1977), beginning with some insights from his work on wattle, concerned the impact of rapidly expanded peasant commodity production in Central Province in the Swynnerton and post-Swynnerton periods. The central finding here was that the "indigenous" process of *athomi* accumulation of land and other assets which had distinguished the earlier period (say 1918 to 1955 or so) was *to a degree undermined* by these later developments, developments which occurred very much under the auspices, and at the behest of, certain fractions of international merchant and finance capital. Cowen's latest work (1980a) has traced this expansion of peasant commodity production for international markets, not only in Kenya but elsewhere, to the post-1945 crisis of British capitalism.

This undermining derived from the fact that a wider range of middle and small holdings could yield much increased cash incomes for their incumbents, thereby decreasing pressures for the total proletarianization of labor power and/or for the sale of land to *athomi*. Moreover, the *athomi* partly encouraged this generalized expansion of peasant production because there were profits to be made in trading these commodities. Earlier restrictions placed upon peasant export production both by the colonial state, and (in the case of wattle) by a multinational firm, had threatened to cut them out of such opportunities for accumulation in trade. In leading a "populist" campaign to "universalize" the production of coffee, tea, milk, pyrethrum, and the like (which had not been intended in Swynnerton's original "yeoman farmer" schemes) the *athomi* increased their short-term opportunities for gaining an increased share of the surplus product *in circulation* at the cost of a longer-term partial blockage on accumulation *in production* within the agricultural section. However, they managed subsequently to escape this blockage, partially by movement into the large-farm sector in the Rift Valley, and by entry into larger scale commerce and manufacturing through using state institutions to "force" such entry. Sometimes this was done in cooperation with international finance capital and industrial capital in Kenya, sometimes in partial opposition to it.

According to Cowen, however, the current limits to capitalist accumulation and development in Kenya (limits faced by both indigenous and multinational capital) derive from this increased scope and depth of peasant petty commodity production for domestic and export markets. These limits take a contradictory form. On the one hand, the greatly increased income from both middle and small landholdings raises household living standards (the value of labor power), and allows wages paid to the partially proletarianized labor in manufacturing, commerce and agriculture to be much below the value of labor power. This is the "subsidy" to capital familiar from work on South African capitalism (Wolpe, 1972). It allows for increased profits and enhanced accumulation in *individual* capitalist enterprise.

However, the same low wages provide no incentive to raise labor productivity massively (i.e., to increase relative surplus value) and, more important, incomes and productivity in peasant commodity production rise only slowly, thereby restricting the growth of the domestic market for manufactures. Together with an only slowly growing domestic market for food (for only some peasants have entirely substituted non-edible cash crops for food production), this slowly growing domestic demand places restrictions on the *universalization* of capitalist relations of production. In particular *the univer-*

salization of the capital/wage relationship is made very problematic. If "indigenous" or transnational manufacturing capital in Kenya is to increase massively the *mass* of surplus value overall (rather than the rate of surplus value in individual enterprises and sectors), then it must break through the barrier posed by the viability of peasant production on medium and small holdings. This viability, however, was created, and continues to be supported by others sections of both indigenous and foreign capital engaged in the trading, processing and marketing of peasant-produced commodities. Whether such a "break-through" will occur is not known; it will be determined in struggles at both the national and international levels.[6]

This is an extremely sophisticated and modulated argument. It does not assert *either* a classical *dependista* "blockage" or "stagnation-ist" position, or an inevitable process of continued capitalist development in Kenya. The difficulty, in fact impossibility, of situating Cowen's position in either of the conventional alternatives also explains why it can be attacked from both! Its "first half" exploded a number of central *dependista* positions, while its "second half" employs a properly sophisticated notion of "contradiction"[7] to indicate both the potentialities and limits of capitalist development in Kenya. These, moreover, are not simply ineluctable "givens" but products and objects of struggle and human praxis, whether by indigenous Kenyan capitalists, "middle peasants," or representatives of different forms of multinational capital.

The position has another theoretical implication of enormous importance. Cowen's attempt to demonstrate that certain forms or fractions of "international capital" (Forestal, Brook Bond Leibig, British, German and American finance capital) have been responsible for the "resurrection" of peasant commodity production in Kenya (a "resurrection" which in turn places definite limits upon the possibilities for multinational manufacturing capital) throws into doubt the application of any simple-minded "capital logic" approach to the question of capitalist development at the periphery. For such constradictions indicate that there is no *single* "capital logic" the results or consequences of which can be "read off from" some simple organizing premises such as, for example, the drive for the maximum "valorization" of "capital in general" (see Fröbel, Heinrichs, and Kreye, 1980). Or more precisely, it suggests that even if "capital in general" is obedient to some "fundamental laws" (such as the drive to offset declining profitability in the long term), the consequences of such a logic for particular capitalist economies can be very different. They depend upon the balance of particular sectors of production within those economies, and the implications of that logic for sectors with (for example) very different organic compositions of capital.

The subtlety and fecundity of Cowen's formulations does not mean that their truth has been unambiguously demonstrated. Two areas in particular remain problematic and open to empirical investigation. They are (1) the generalizability of Cowen's Central Province finding that "middle peasants" have been the prime beneficiaries of the post-Swynnerton expansion of peasant commodity production, and (2)—closely related to the first area—the question of whether pauperization and proletarianization of poor peasants may be proceeding much faster and more dramatically in other rural areas of Kenya, away from the "commercial heartlands" of Central Province. Cowen (1981: 64-66) himself has presented some evidence on South Margoli in support of the second hypothesis, but has argued, *contra* Njonjo, that where this is happening it is because capitalist penetration has been much *less* profound than in Central Province. Therefore it certainly cannot be taken as evidence that the "inevitable" consequence of capitalist penetration of peasant agriculture is growing differentiation or inevitable pauperization or proletarianization.

The most obvious comment on all this is that it is in these areas that further empirical work needs to be done, and is indeed beginning to be done (Kongstad and Mönsted, 1980; Carlsen, 1980; Cooper, 1980; Bager 1980; see also the review by Cowen, 1982). Even in the case of Central Province there are alternative ways of reading the available evidence to that provided by Cowen (Kitching, 1980: 342–344), but the point is that once Cowen's argument has been clarified and the theoretical import of particular empirical propositions made clear, these *are* questions which to a degree are empirically resolvable. Although, as the very structure of Cowen's argument also makes clear, even if they are resolved they will not (and if correctly posed theoretically they should not), suggest the "inevitability" of *any* outcome in the continuing process of struggle which characterizes capitalist development in Kenya, as anywhere else.

I wish now to pull together the various strands in this discussion of the Kenya debate and to stress again some central points as a prelude to a more explicit discussion of the hidden politics of the debate in the final part of this chapter. The Kenya debate began with a revision of an orginal thesis put forward by Leys (1971, 1975). This revision was interpreted by Langdon and Kaplinsky as the substitution of an "optimistic" prognosis of the possibilities for capitalist development in Kenya, for the original highly "pessimistic" thesis. They attempted to reduce it to some more specific and "testable" empirical "hypotheses" about the prospects for the development of manufacturing industry in Kenya, and in doing so, I have argued, they in fact evacuated its central content. This content was nothing less than a complete reconceptualization of the *long term* historical process of capitalist development in Kenya. It involved rejecting essentially "omnipotent" or "overdetermining" and "externalist" conceptualizations of colonialism, imperialism, and multinational capital and substituting for them altogether more "open" conceptualizations. These allow greater space for the active role of the African people of Kenya in testing and indeed redrawing the boundaries or limits placed upon their activity by the colonial and post-colonial context. An essential part of those "open" conceptualizations is a much more sophisticated understanding of the *contradictions* inherent in the actions of settler capital in colonial Kenya, the colonial state, and (in a later period) of the post-colonial state and of multinational capital. A refusal to treat any of these phenomena as "monoliths" with a uniform set of functions, objectives, or consequences, is perhaps the single most important strand in the opening up of that "space" for African initiative, and for according an important role to struggles *among* African people in the trajectory of capitalist development in Kenya.

This reconceptualization was not a product of some Althusserian "theoretical practice" upon concepts. On the contrary, it derived from Leys's appropriation of the theoretical implications of Cowen's detailed empirical work, especially concerning the *agricultural sector.*

It was unfortunate that Leys himself, both in the original revision and in subsequent contributions to the debate, did not give due prominence to this aspect of his thesis but continued to give at least limited credence to Langdon and Kaplinsky's very narrow understanding of it by entering into a (somewhat half-hearted) contesting of their empirical propositions. This led to some very confused and necessarily indeterminate disputes over a small number of episodes and trends within contemporary Kenyan economic history, in which contending "theories of the state" and of the relative strengths of "indigenous" versus "transnational" capital have been erected on flimsy and highly ambiguous evidence. I have suggested that this flimsiness and ambiguity could only be avoided by totally different epistemological procedures, by a totally different *kind of* knowledge to that which both sides use, but a kind of knowledge that is not and cannot be available to academics *qua* academics.

I have also examined the more recent extensions of the debate into a central (and in my view much more appropriate) concern with the agrarian question. At the same time, I attempted to demonstrate that in this area too, an apparent unwillingness to draw out and make explicit the political implications of the various positions adopted has made the debate to date both more confused and arid than it should be. I have suggested, however, that essentially the same basic political positions were at stake in this area as in the better-known debate about manufacturing, but that Cowen's work and Leys's revision has now shifted the ground in the agricultural debate very markedly. In particular, Njonjo's adoption of a Leninist position on the rapid though "disguised" proletarianization of the Kenyan peasantry now confronts Cowen's more complex and modulated position, with the older "populist" position set out in Leys's 1971 article (and reduced in Gutto's work to a highly qualified shadow). However, the thrust of Njonjo's position is to *reconstitute* the older populist conception of the Kenyan "people" in unified struggle against a comprador-imperialism alliance in a conception of a mass Kenyan "proletariat" *playing essentially the same role* but this time in struggle against both indigenous and foreign capital. I indicated my preference for Cowen's formulations but stressed that they are by no means invulnerable from empirical attack and that this is an area in which more research needs to be done and is being done.

This particular understanding of the genesis and primary thrust of Leys's 1978 revision has an implication which has been underlying my argument and should now be made explicit. *It is simply unnecessary from the point of view of the Leys/Cowen position to challenge many of the empirical propositions put forward by Langdon and Kaplinsky.* It clearly is the case, for example, that the Kenyan economy will face increasingly severe debt and balance of payments problems in the immediate future, as it is also likely to face impediments in increasing manufactured exports or in expanding employment in manufacturing. Since the Leys/Cowen position does *not* entail a vision of a smooth, non-contradictory upward trajectory of capitalist development in Kenya it is *not* required to rebut any and all pieces of empirical evidence which suggest that such a trajectory is unlikely. It only needs to assert (as Leys himself has now clearly realised) that the implicit postulation of such a trajectory upon which some (not all) dependency positions depend for their "critiques" is itself idealist, and shows a distinctly naive and un-Marxist understanding of capitalism, and that capitalist development is *of necessity* both episodic ("conjunctural") and unstable, a thing of spurts and pauses, booms and slumps. In fact even a conventional exponent of "trade cycle" and "business cycle" theory has no difficulty in demonstrating this (see, for example, Simkin, 1951). What *must* be challenged, though, is the methodology employed by Langdon and

Kaplinsky, in particular their development economists' addiction to short time series data, and, above all, their highly deterministic and *mechanically materialist* conception of transnational capital. To put it at its simplest, the underlying thrust of all the arguments advanced by Langdon and Kaplinsky is that only such developments are possible in Kenya which "transnational capital" (conceived as a monolith) will "allow." Indigenous capital can move into those sections of manufacturing which are "not profitable enough" for multinational capital, employment in manufacturing will increase if multinational capital changes its production technology but will not if it does not. Economic growth in Kenya may continue if the world system surmounts its current crisis or if there is massive industrial relocation (by "multinational capital") to Kenya, but will not if these things do not occur. Even Langdon's scenario for a technocrat-led "redistributionist" strategy has to postulate an "economic crisis" in Kenya as a necessary prerequisite, a crisis deriving largely from *externally induced* balance of payments crises and the failure of Kenya's manufacturing export strategy (Langdon, 1980: 57-58).

It cannot be said too strongly in response to this that transnational capital is *not* a monolith with a single overdetermining goal or objective (after what has been said above, support for this assertion is, I trust, unnecessary here), and that it is *not* a question of what this (falsely) postulated monolith will "allow" but what Africans in Kenya can *obtain.* This *will be determined in activity,* in the struggles of some peasants against others, of workers against bosses, of sections of "indigenous capital" against sections of transnational capital (and perhaps in alliance with other sections). Above all, at the moment, much is to be obtained through victory in the struggle for the Kenyan state and for the resources and powers of which it disposes. Of course particular conjunctures will favor some forces and disfavor others, but once the monolithic conception of multinational captial is abandoned and a more detailed research into its many forms and branches is undertaken, it is by no means certain that the current world crisis will have *only* deleterious consequences for capitalist development in Kenya.

POLITICS AND THEORY

With this last point, we come to the political heart of the matter, the concern of this final section. It may be expressed as a puzzle. In general, or at least until quite recently, dependency theory in Africa was advocated by men and women who were socialists, radicals, or revolutionaries (at least in self-image) of one form or another. That is to say, it was advocated by people who were dedicated to struggle *against* imperialism, *against* inequality and poverty, for "real" independence and socialism. And yet it was premised upon a vision of "the enemy," of imperialism, of multinational capital, which endowed "it" with apparently all conquering power, total clarity and unanimity of purpose, and almost omnipotent causal potency. Now logically a commitment to such a conception of the enemy, of the opposing forces, should be productive of simple fatalism and hopelessness. After all if imperialism really is like that, the only thing to do is give up, "lie back and enjoy it," throw down one's puny arms and bow to superior force, insight and power.

One therefore concludes that most of the advocates, at least of the crudest forms of dependency theory, did (or do) not, in fact, believe what they were saying, or perhaps it is a question, in this case as in some previous historical cases, that the postulation of omnipotence to the enemy is a psychological and emotional prerequisite of sallying forth bravely to meet him. It is almost as if David had to exaggerate Goliath's strength and size, *and* his own weakness and slightness, in order to get up the courage (or perhaps the desperation) to go out and slay him. Perhaps too, the sense of outrage and injustice which derives from the image of such an "unfair" contest helps to build revolutionary determination (perhaps!).

But the puzzle does not end there. Logically too, a theory of a totally all-powerful and omnipotent imperialism should preclude the practical construction of any alternative state of affairs. But once again it is simply an empirical observation that the vast majority of radicals in Africa who espoused dependency perspectives, did believe very passionately that an alternative was possible and worth struggling for. How many political tracts, having painted a formidable and gloomy picture of all the inequities perpetrated by imperialism in Africa in the past and in the present, would end nonetheless with a rallying cry to the "peasants and workers" to rise up and throw off the oppressor as a prerequisite for the creation of "real development" under socialism?

And it is here that the genuine "crisis" of radicalism in contemporary Africa lies. For as the Kenya debate clearly demonstrates (as much by certain reticences and silences in the positions of *all* the contributors as by anything that they do say), *there is now a widespread loss of faith and belief that any alternative to capitalism in Africa is practically available.* The cause of this "crisis of radical belief" is not hard to discern. It lies in the widely recognized (but rarely publicly acknowledged) fact that *all* of the various "socialist" experiments and regimes in black Africa to date have at best had ambiguous results for the welfare of the peasants and workers who live under them, and at worst have been an unambiguous disaster.

In the case of Kenya in particular, the experience of Tanzania in the 1970s and the gradual seepage across the border of information on that experience, has thrown all radical thinkers and activists there into a greater or lesser confusion. For again, it is simply a biographical fact that many of those radicals in Kenya who espoused dependency critiques of the Kenyan state and economy also had a distinctly soft spot for the alternative being created by their southern neighbor. Tanzania played a role for many Kenyan radicals rather like that played by the Soviet Union in the political struggles of Communists in western Europe in the inter-war period. It appeared to show, in reality and not merely in theory, that an alternative to "dependent," "neocolonial" capitalism was available and functioning. And sharply increased doubt about that has also had rather the same effect in Kenya as the 1956 revelations about Stalinism had on western Communism in the post-war period—that is, loss of morale, direction, and certainty.

I do not have the space here to discuss the Tanzanian experience nor any of its political implications (see the piece by Gibbon and Neocosmos in this collection). I simply want, by way of conclusion to this chapter, to say that the future of socialism in Africa may well depend upon the response of radicals to the experience of these first socialist states in black Africa, upon the way those experiences are assimilated and understood. Quite obviously, if there is an unwillingness to face up to some of the harsh realities of the situation, a determination to bury one's head in the sand in some spurious "solidarity" with such regimes, then *nothing* will be learned, because there will be no *desire* to learn anything.

It seems more likely however (and in my view this would be just as disastrous) that those experiences will simply be *assimilated into the dependency perspective* as just one more proof of its correctness, i.e., it will be asserted that the experiments in Ghana or Tanzania (or Mozambique or Angola?) failed because "imperialism" was too strong for them, because in the unequal battle with the "world system" and "multinational capital" they succumbed, perhaps sold out by their "compradors" and "bureaucratic bourgeoisies."[8] It is clear from the way that I have stated this position, that I do *not* agree with it, and that certainly in the Tanzanian case I believe that there were many other more important factors at work which cannot, except by stretching these concepts till they are devoid of all meaning, be laid at the door of "imperialism" or "multinational capital" or "compradors." I believe that in the Tanzanian case certainly this failure has much more to do with the historically formed behavior of the Tanzanian ruling class, and in particular with its apparent *total unwillingness or inability to abide by the most elementary rules of accumulation*. But that is another story.

To return to the Kenyan situation, and to other situations in black Africa where radicals and socialists confront capitalist systems at work, there is now, in my view, a sharply increased danger that in the crisis of faith which I perceive, a continued allegiance to the dependency position will play straight into the hands of the most conservative groups in those societies. Because, of course, such groups are perfectly willing to make use of anit-imperialist slogans provided that they coexist with a realization (explicit or tacit) that no total alternative to the existing system is possible, that is, provided that anti-imperialism is understood as winning more space for local capitalists in national and international markets, or getting better terms in government deals with Hitachi, Ford, or the World Bank. There exists a real danger that on the Left, as well as on the Right, the "fatalism" and "hopelessness" that I suggested ought logically to follow from the "omnipotent" conception of imperialism found in dependency theory, will *in fact* begin to manifest itself. Getting the best possible deal out of "imperialism" so conceived will come to seem the only "practicable" option; "the enemy" will indeed be perceived as too strong for any other possibility.

And it is for this reason that Björn Beckman's recent attempts to "transcend" the Kenya debate, and in particular to challenge its unproblematic coupling of the "national bourgeoisie" with "progress," and of "imperialism" with "retardation," while insightful and powerful in many specifics respects, still seems to me not to grasp fully the essential *political* problem with the dependency perspective. In a recent piece dealing with that perspective in Nigeria, he writes:

> Neither the new study of imperialism (as the internationalization of capital) nor the new interest in accumulation and class formation in the periphery provide what underdevelopment theory seems to offer third world radicals: a theoretical platform for the combined struggle against imperialism and the domestic ruling class. The platform itself may have been undermined, its deficiencies exposed, but many will cling to it, as long as the alternatives offered seem to be unable to address themselves to the strategic issues at stake [1981: 10].

This may be true but the crucial point surely is not to have a theory which identifies an enemy to struggle *against* (very much, in the spirit, I have suggested, of Sisyphus's struggle with the stone), but a theory which can help one struggle *for* a better and workable *alternative*. The basic requirement of such a theory is that it be constructed round concepts of imperialism, multinational capital, the world system, colonialism and the like, that provide space to incorporate what is, I submit, factually the case. Namely, that *what Africans do matters*: What they did in the past *actively shaped* colonialism and imperialism, importantly affecting its impact upon Nigeria, Kenya, Tanganyika, and that what they *do* in the present, the *way* that they struggle against local and international capital, the *way* that they appropriate and learn from the experiences of socialism in Africa (and indeed the *way* they *behaved* in Tanzania, Mozambique, and the rest) are molding the present and will mold the future.

Meanwhile we will finish this article by simply noting the way that the various contributions to the Kenya debate have responded to the "crisis of faith" which I have identified above. Cowen and Leys seem to have responded (though thcy are rather demure about saying so in print) by essentially endorsing the present state of affairs in Kenya as the best practically and politically available at the moment (though the future is not foreclosed). It is impossible even to infer what alternatives, if any, some of the African contributors owe their allegiance to, although Njonjo, at least, seems to be wedded to some concept of an imminent "proletarian revolution" focused around an agrarian and industrial working class seen as already half completed. Langdon and Kaplinsky, if they ever did owe any allegiance to any of the "African socialist" alternatives currently on offer have abandoned them, and now explicitly advocate reformist solutions within capitalism. This, as I stated earlier, is a perfectly honorable position, but in the light of the quotation at the head of this chapter, it is entirely predictable that the mechanically materialist conception of historical and social processes that they share with all dependency theorists has culminated in a vision of "liberation from above" by some enlightened class of "intendants" (Langdon, 1980: 8, 9, 57–58; Kaplinsky, 1980).

Finally, so as not to fudge where I have accused others of fudging, I should state my own position. I believe that a socialist alternative to capitalism in Africa *can* be constructed by a sophisticated socialist movement created among the working classes of Africa as they *slowly* expand through time. A prerequisite of such a construction, however, is an abandonment of mechanical materialism and wholehearted embracing of a conception of historical process which places an important, indeed primary (though not exclusive, or purely voluntarist) stress upon the *activities* and *beliefs* of Africans (including African socialists). Part of this change would involve an appropriation of the socialist experience in Africa to date which acknowledges and learns from the mistakes made *by Africans* in those experiences.

I believe, however, that the formation of a sophisticated socialist working class in Africa will take a long time and that a prolonged period of struggle against a developing capitalism there is one of the important prerequisites of its creation. To that extent I am "happy" to see continued capitalist development in black Africa (though this may or may not occur). Only in such ways can liberation be won by African workers *from below* rather than "granted" to them from above (a prospect I consider unlikely in any case). But before all this, there is a block in the road of socialist construction in Africa which must be removed and removed entirely—this is dependency theory. For the construction of socialism requires activity born out of a realistically informed *hope*, not out of a desperate hopelessness, a hopelessness that is totally unjustified by history.

NOTES

1. R.J.M. Swynnerton's *A Plan to Intensify the Development of African Agriculture* (1954), known conventionally as "the Swynnerton Plan" is often regarded as the beginning of the colonial government's attempt to commercialize and individualize African peasant farming in Kenya. However, many of Swynnerton's ideas had earlier roots (see Sorrenson, 1967), although they were taken up with a new urgency from the mid-fifties onwards as a response to the Mau-Mau rebellion.

2. Wasserman (1976). Leys's other major source for this discussion is Sorrenson (1967), which also treats land consolidation and registration in Central Province very much from the "political point" of view, i.e., as a tool for counter-insurgency after Mau-Mau.

3. I have chosen Langdon's paper to exemplify the particular and very narrow way in which Leys's revision has been assimilated. I might equally well have chosen Kaplinsky's work and especially his 1980 article, where Ley's position is reduced to five "hypotheses" for "testing." Since the arguments advanced in that piece overlap markedly with those advanced by Langdon, and since, more importantly, the kind of evidence presented, and the kind of methodology used to refute these five hypotheses are identical to those in Langdon, I have not felt it necessary to deal with Kaplinsky's contribution separately. Except where explicitly stated, points made here with respect to Langdon's paper may be taken to refer to Kaplinsky's piece as well.

4. Although this position has a long history in Comintern resolutions adopted from 1926 onwards, one of its first modern academic formulations was in Worsley (1964).

5. *Athomi* or *Asomi* is the collective noun from the Bantu verb to read, meaning literally "the readers" or "those who read" and was used in Central Province, Machakos and elsewhere in Kenya to refer (originally) to mission educated families.

6. This argument is found scattered through Cowen's papers and articles, see especially 1977. A useful summary of it is in Cowen, 1981: 69–73.

7. I say a "properly sophisticated" concept because in a great deal of vulgar Marxism, something only counts as a "contradiction" of capitalism if it is, or can be presented as, leading to the economic breakdown and/or the political overthrow of capitalism. Njonjo (1981) occasionally falls into this usage.

8. In the case of Tanzania the beginnings of such an assimilation can already be found, in Shivji (1976) and von Freyhold (1979).

REFERENCES

ANYANG' NYONGO P. (1981). "What the Friends of the Peasants' are and how they pose the question of the peasantry." Review of African Political Economy 20: 17–26.

BAGER, T. (1980). Marketing Cooperatives and Peasants in Kenya. Uppsala: Scandinavian Institute of African Studies.

BECKMAN, B. (1981). "Imperialism and the national bourgeoisie." Review of African Political Economy 22: 5–19.

———(1980). "Imperialism and capitalist transformation: critique of a Kenyan debate." Review of African Political Economy 19: 48–62.

BRETT, E.A. (1973). Colonialism and Underdevelopment in East Africa: The Politics of Economic Change 1919–39. London: Heinemann.

CARLSEN, J. (1980). Economic and Social Transformation in Rural Kenya. Uppsala: Scandinavian Institute of African Studies.

COOPER, F. (1980). From Slaves to Squatters: Plantation Labour and Agriculture in Zanzibar and Coastal Kenya 1890-1925. New Haven, CT: Yale Univ. Press.

COWEN, M.P. (1982). "Some recent East African peasant studies." Journal of Peasant Studies 18(1).

———(1981). "The agrarian problem: notes on the Nairobi discussion." Review of African Political Economy 20: 57–73.

———(1980a). "The British state and agrarian accumulation in Kenya after 1945." Swansea: University College of Swansea Centre for Development Studies.

———(1980b). "The commercialisation of food production in Kenya's Central Province after 1945." Swansea: University College of Swansea Centre for Development Studies.

———(1979). Capital and Household Production: The Case of Wattle in Kenya's Central Province 1903–1964. Ph.D. dissertation, University of Cambridge.

———(1976). "Notes on capital, class and household production." Nairobi. (mimeo)

———(1975). "Wattle production in the Central Province: capital and household commodity production 1903–1964." Nairobi. (mimeo)

———(1974a). "Patterns of cattle ownership and dairy production 1900–1965." Nairobi. (mimeo)

———(1974b). "Concentration of sales and assets: dairy cattle and tea in Magutu 1964–1971." Nairobi: University of Nairobi Institute of Development Studies Working Paper 146.

————(1972). "Differentiation in a Kenyan location." Nairobi: East African Social Council Conference paper.

————and K. KINYANJUI (1977). "Some problems of class formation in Kenya." Nairobi: University of Nairobi Institute of Development Studies. (unpublished)

COWEN, M.P. and P. NEWMAN (1976). "Real wages in central Kenya 1924–1974." Nairobi. (mimeo)

COWEN, M.P. and F. MURAGE (1974). "Notes on agricultural wage labour in a Kenyan location," pp. 39–59 in Development Trends in Kenya. Edinburgh: University of Edinburgh Centre of African Studies.

FREYHOLD, M. von (1979). Ujamaa Villages in Tanzania: Analysis of a Social Experiment. London: Heinemann.

FROBEL, F., J. HEINRICHS, and O. KREYE (1980). The New International Division of Labour: Structural Unemployment in Industrialised Countries and Industrialisation in Developing Countries. Cambridge: Cambridge University Press.

GUTTO, S.R.O. (1981). "Law, rangelands, the peasantry and social classes in Kenya." Review of African Political Economy 20: 41–46.

HENLEY, J.S. (1980). "Capitalist accumulation in Kenya—straw man rule OK." Review of African Political Economy 17: 105–108.

KAPLINSKY, R. (1980). "Capitalist accumulation in their periphery—the Kenyan case re-examined." Review of African Politicial Economy 17: 83–105.

————[ed.] (1978). Readings on the Multinational Corporation in Kenya. Oxford: Oxford University Press.

KITCHING, G. (1982). Development and Underdevelopment in Historical Perspective: Populism, Nationalism and Industrialisation. London: Methuen.

————(1980). Class and Economic Change in Kenya: The Making of an African Petite-Bourgeoisie 1905–1970. New Haven: Yale University Press.

KONGSTAD P. and M. MONSTED (1980). Family, Labour and Trade in Western Kenya. Uppsala: Scandinavian Institute of African Studies.

LANGDON, S. (1980a). Multinational Corporations in the Political Economy of Kenya. London: Macmillan.

————(1980b). "Industry and capitalism in Kenya: Contributions to a debate." Presented to Conference on the African Bourgeoisie, Dakar.

————(1977). "The state and capitalism in Kenya." Review of African Political Economy 8: 90–98.

LEYS, C. (1980). "What does dependency explain?" Review of African Political Economy 17: 108–113.

————(1978). "Capital accumulation, class formation and dependency: the significance of the Kenyan case." Socialist Register: 241–266.

————(1975). Underdevelopment in Kenya: The Political Economy of Neo-Colonialism 1964-1971. London: Heinemann.

————(1971). "Politics in Kenya: The development of peasant society." British Journal of Political Science 1 (1): 307-337.

————and J. BORGES (1979). "State capitalism in Kenya." Presented to the Annual Meeting of the Candadian Political Science Association, Saskatoon.

LONSDALE, J. and B. BERMAN (1979). "Coping with contradictions: the development of the colonial state in Kenya 1895–1914." Journal of African History 20: 487–505.

MENDEL, A.P. (1961). Dilemmas of Progress in Tsarist Russia: Legal Marxism and Legal Populism. Cambridge, MA: Harvard University Press.

NG'ANGA MUKARA D. (1981). "What is happening to the Kenyan peasantry?" Review of African Political Economy 20: 7–16.

NJONJO, A.L. (1981). "The Kenya peasantry: a re-assessment." Review of African Political Economy 20: 27–40.

———(1977). The Africanisation of the White Highlands: A Study in Agrarian Class Struggle in Kenya 1950–1975. Ph.D. dissertation, Princeton University, Princeton, NJ.

REDLEY, M.G. (1976). The Politics of a Predicament: The White Community in Kenya 1918–1932. Ph.D. dissertation, University of Cambridge.

SAUL, J. (1973). "Who is the immediate enemy?" in L. Cliffe and J. Saul (eds.), Socialism in Tanzania: An Interdisciplinary Reader. Volume 2: Policies. Dar es Salaam, Tanzania: East African Publishing House.

SHIVJI, I.G. (1976). Class Struggles in Tanzania. London: Heinemann.

SIMKIN, C.G.F. (1951). The Instability of a Dependent Economy: Economic Fluctuations in New Zealand 1840–1914. Oxford: Oxford University Press.

SORRENSON, M.P.K. (1967). Land Reform in the Kikuyu Country: A Study in Government Policy. Oxford: Oxford University Press.

SWAINSON, N. (1980). The Development of Corporate Capitalism in Kenya 1918–1977. London: Heinemann.

———(1977). "The rise of a national bourgeoisie in Kenya." Review of African Political Economy 8: 39–55.

WALICKI, A. (1969). The Controversy over Capitalism: Studies in the Social Philosophy of the Russian Populists. Oxford: Clarendon.

WASSERMAN, G. (1976). Politics of Decolonisation: Kenya Europeans and the Land Issue 1960–65. Princeton, NJ: Princeton University Press.

WOLPE, H. (1972). "Capitalism and cheap labour power in South Africa." Economy and Society 1(4): 425–456.

WORSLEY, P. (1964). The Third World. London: Weidenfeld & Nicolson.

ZWANENBERG, R.M.A. van (1975). Colonial Capitalism in Kenya 1919–1939. Nairobi: East African Publishing House.

4

SOME PROBLEMS IN THE POLITICAL ECONOMY OF "AFRICAN SOCIALISM"

PETER GIBBON and MICHAEL NEOCOSMOS

Since the
late 1950s a number of regimes in newly independent African countries
have described themselves as being or becoming "African socialist." At
first these declarations were met with enthusiasm by European left-wing
intellectuals, among others. Later this enthusiasm waned (at least for
those countries which first struck out along this road). Disillusion
concentrated on two issues in particular. First, no regime in Africa
succeeded in disengaging itself from the capitalist world economy and
its financial institutions, or even appeared to pursue this option
seriously. Second, little or no substantial positive changes could be
detected in the operation of these countries' state machines, which
tended to remain highly bureaucratic and distant from the populace. By
the first half of the 1970s a kind of consensus emerged amongst left-wing
students of "African socialism." It was commonly agreed that, in the
broadest sense of these terms, the African socialist countries remained
capitalist (or capitalist dominated) economies or states.

Digesting this fact took some time. The trauma of a break with an
ill-conceived faith in a particular variant of "African socialism," or in

Authors' Note: We have benefited from the comments of the editors, M.P. Cowen, and K.J. Havnevik in redrafting this paper, which was originally presented to the 1983 British Sociological Association Conference in Cardiff. Responsibility for the main arguments and position, mistakes, and errors rests entirely with the authors themselves.

one of its prophets, may have played some part in this, though only for a minority. Most European publicists of "African socialism" soon established a rewarding cycle of discovery, militant commendation, and creeping doubt (never articulated into a critique), followed by migration to the next land of promise. More important, however, were certain apparent theoretical problems entailed by accepting these views. These involved not so much reconciling captialist content with socialist forms, for there were precious few of the latter. Rather the issue was one of understanding how these countries could be spoken of as capitalist or dominated by capitalism when the vast majority of their population were peasants, and when they also lacked indigenous ruling classes of an obviously capitalist kind. Ironically it was precisely these characteristics which gave conviction to the original claim that these countries, if not actually socialist in a Marxist sense, were at least following a middle path or third way between capitalism and socialism. To summarize: In recent years the difficulties encountered by disillusioned left-wing intellectuals in understanding "African socialism" have concerned not so much the status and relation to capitalism of postcapitalist institutions and economic forms as precapitalist ones.

In the late 1970s a number of solutions to these difficulties and problems were proposed. In the economic field the two major candidates for consideration were dependency theory and articulationism.[1] By renaming precapitalist economic forms dependent capitalism or dependent development, and regarding what was denoted by these terms as effects of intrusions by metropolitan capital on an otherwise spontaneous process of endogenous economic growth, dependency theory reconciled the former with the world capitalist system. Articulationism in general proposed that these so-called precapitalist economic forms were exactly that and that their relation to world capitalism was an external one mediated either via a dialectic of preservation-dissolution or by a mechanism of unequal exchange or both.

In order to cope with the problems surrounding the "African socialist" state and the nature of its ruling class, somewhat different positions emerged. A striking feature of the latter was their tendency to cut across, rather than neatly correspond to, the solutions suggested to the problems of economic analysis. One argument advanced was that finance capital, together with local compradors, constituted the ruling-class of "African socialist" countries and that the absence of an indigenous local capitalist class was simply proof of this. A second line of approach was that associated with the notion of bureaucratic bourgeoisie, in which an indigenous capitalist class was said to be in the process of formation on the basis of, *inter alia,* a collective appropriation of state revenues. A third view sought to reconcile these accounts by maintaining that finance capital constituted the ruling-class, while the bureaucratic bourgeoisie operated as its governing-class.[2] It could be pointed out that these approaches share a tendency to be descriptive rather than explanatory, and to resolve genuine difficulties primarily by inventing new titles for already known phenomena (e.g., dependent capitalism, bureaucratic bourgeoisie, governing class). It could also be pointed out that in seeking demonstration, they tend only to embroider and illustrate with respect to the historical development of particular social formations and to present reality as the circumstantial outcome of what effectively amounts to chapters of accidents (e.g., presence or absence of settlers). There is little point in carrying this criticism further here since these positions have tended recently to fall by the wayside, and in Britain at least, to have been displaced in preeminence by the work of Henry Bernstein—not least because of the additional arguments ranged against them by Bernstein himself (e.g., Bernstein, 1976b, 1979, 1982).

The importance of Bernstein's contribution lies not only in the systematic character of these criticisms and in the extent to which his own positive formulations seem on the verge of providing a new consensus in the academic world of rural sociology (e.g., Goodman and Redclift, 1981), but also in other ways. Bernstein adds as a central question to be investigated the previously largely unacknowledged struggle between **state and peasantry under "African socialism." Most significantly, his** work provides what might be termed a 'limit case' of a particular sort of analysis: one that seeks to acknowledge the special qualities of peasant production while at the same time attempting to avoid any implication of dualism (a major error of earlier approaches) by talking only of capitalism in the economies in question. It is from a critical assessment of this limit case that at the moment any general alternative nondualist approach must begin.

This chapter commences therefore with a critical examination of the work of Henry Bernstein. It must be pointed out in advance that this examination largely concerns what are identified as implicit assumptions and general positions in his work, rather than his actual concrete pronouncements. It will be suggested that while Bernstein's critical assessments of previous positions (notably articulationism and peasantism) is correct in most respects, his work exhibits a strong tendency to the reproduction of problems similar to those it diagnoses in others. In particular, it will be argued that it fails to go far beyond the empirical **obviousness of the contradiction between peasants and the "African** socialist" state and mistakes its dominant character for the determinant or fundamental contradiction of these societies.

The wider objective of this chapter is to address in a new light some of the problems examined in the existing literature, including that of the nature and causes of the contradiction between peasants and state. A number of new arguments will be put forward with the intention of advancing the debate. In particular an effort is made to pose questions of both political economy and politics at a more abstract and general level than hitherto, as a necessary basis for more effective concrete investigation.

The first general question posed is whether the precapitalist forms evidently so common in contemporary poor countries (including "African socialist" ones) are not in reality an integral part of the capitalist mode of production itself as understood by Marx, Engels, and Lenin. This, of course, raises the problem of the definition of capitalism, which is understood here as generalized commodity production founded upon the contradictory relation between capital and wage-labor. Capital and wage-labor are two sides of the same social contradiction and among other things, individually represent functions, class places or class bases indispensible to capitalism, which need not themselves be personified in groups of capitalists or wage-laborers as such in every branch of the economy, but which explain the existence of classes at a general level (Neocosmos, 1981). The classic Marxist account of the small-holding peasantry, producing commodities in a generalized and systematic manner, in fact visualized this kind of production as a specific *combination in a single household* (of one or more individuals) of these class bases or functions.

A second question posed is whether the antagonism between peasants and the state detected by Bernstein under "African socialism" necessarily represents a conflict of a class versus class variety, as he suggests, or whether it represents a struggle over the division of social revenue between two distinct kinds of capitalist enterprise. The former of these two kinds of enterprise are characterized as petty-capitalist enterprises, a category whose concrete conditions may include not only well-to-do and middle peasants, but all systematic commodity production on the basis of personal or household labor (including poor peasant production in so far as it falls into this category). The latter are characterized as state economic enterprises, the nature of which is modified by the particular form of state in which they are situated. It hardly needs adding that very different political conclusions follow from these different assessments.

A third general question examined is that of the conditions under which the contradictory character of capitalism continuously creates anew distinctively petty-bourgeois (including peasant) forms of enterprise, that is, of *how capitalist petty commodity production is daily resurrected on a world-wide basis as an inescapable and integral part of capitalist development itself*, and not as the outcome of policy, historical accident, nor of "functional usefulness" for capital.

A fourth general question asked concerns the conditions under which contradictions between state capitalist economic enterprises and peasant capitalist enterprises in "African socialist" countries become so intense that they can appear as the determinant contradictions of these social formations. In relation to this question it is suggested that what most repays investigation are the political conditions under which these state enterprises can be effectively deregulated from the forms of internal control normally associated with large-scale capitalist enterprises and modern capitalist states. It is further suggested that the context of this deregulation is provided by the systematically contradictory character of the state under "African socialism," which itself derives from the character of its ruling class and the character of the class struggles which structure the social formation.

In other words, a new route toward solving the problem of the postcolonial state is proposed. Instead of seeking to derive the character of this state from what is functionally necessary to bring an indigenous capitalist class into being, it is suggested that it is more properly derived from an examination of the nature of locally dominant classes as they are presently constituted, together with the contradictory complex of class struggles which for classic Marxism always determined variations in state forms. These questions which are tackled throughout the last two sections of the paper, are not necessarily addressed in the strict order depicted here.

It is customary to conclude introductions of this kind with a range of caveats to the arguments which follow. In this case it needs to be stressed that this chapter may reveal a tendency to simplify certain positions and issues for both polemical and heuristic reasons, to leave certain questions half-answered and others unanswered completely, and to fall short in certain places in its standards of proof and demonstration. The reason is however, that even the minutest advance in theory is only conceivable with these drawbacks or, to be exact, these marks of struggle.

THE ERRORS OF PEASANTISM

The work of Henry Bernstein is characterized by an explicit departure from most of the existing formulations utilized in the political economy of "African socialism," and by an explicitly stated novel project. These strands of his work come together in "Notes on Capital and Peasantry"

(Bernstein, 1977). The opening remarks of this paper indicate an intention to draw a line between his own work and certain recurrent tendencies in the work of his predecessors. In particular, Bernstein identifies four misguided assumptions which any genuinely materialist investigation must necessarily reject.

(1) An error in many works to date has been the presence of peasantist assumptions: the notion that there is a distinctive peasant mode of production underlying the heterogeneous forms of peasant involvement in commodity economy. This argument is rightly criticized by Bernstein as being essentialist. In the case of peasant mode of production formulations, the essence usually designated (from Chayanov onward) has been that of a specific kind of economic calculation.

(2) Bernstein rejects the notion of articulation of modes of production, a formulation obviously closely associated with advocating the existence of a peasant mode of production. No argument is advanced in support of this rejection in Bernstein (1977), but an earlier and fuller draft (Bernstein, 1976a) contains an excellent critique of Meillassoux's concept of articulation.

(3) Bernstein argues that it is necessary to avoid unequal exchange interpretations of the exploitation of African peasantries, a position, of course, closely associated with articulationist views and, simultaneously, necessarily assuming the independence of individual commodity producers bound up with the peasant mode of production position.

(4) Finally, Bernstein identifies as a last related mistake, the tendency to understand the emergence of the present agrarian social order as an effect of a superimposition of new forms of exchange relations on pre-existing production relations, an assumption he elsewhere identifies most clearly with the work of G. Kay (Bernstein, 1976b), but which can also be seen as complementary to peasantist, articulationist and unequal exchange viewpoints. The major error of superimpositionism, like that of the other assumptions attacked here, is its adherence to a mechanical dualism. The materialist conception of social development, on the other hand, understands social relations of production and exchange as a dynamic and reproductive unity.

In passing, it may be noted that Bernstein's indication of an underlying unity of conception behind these different assumptions—previously always treated as relatively distinct, unconnected and to some extent mutually alternative—itself constitutes a notable advance. At the same time, when combined with his own project, it is this which makes his ensemble of positions a limit case, and for this reason so important. By limit case is meant a version of a basic thesis which takes to the limit the qualification of this thesis demanded by rigorous criticism. If the basic thesis (in this case the special form of peasant production) can be maintained under these circumstances, then its claim to general validity can be regarded as significantly advanced.

Bernstein's primary positive concern has been to establish generally what he has called the "dynamics of commoditization" of peasant production in conditions of the "epoch of imperialism," and the important sources and effects of variation within this process (which he has designated "differential commoditization"). His method has been to take petty commodity production in the first place as a "form" not specific to determinate modes of production, to define it and to investigate its variant conditions of change, which are considered to be explicable chiefly in relation to their historical specificities. The major argument is that rather than capitalism articulating with or being superimposed upon a separate mode of production which has remained basically the same throughout the modern period, it has entered petty commodity production, forming petty commodity producing enterprises of—in part—a new type. That is, while these enterprises have retained major continuities in their form, their content (relations with capital) is today of a new kind.

To expand: A double thesis is present in Bernstein's analysis. One side of this is that today, far from there being a duality of distinctive systems of production (tied by a relation of exchange) in sub-Saharan Africa, there is actually a common capitalist one, in which capital is (in the process of) regulating the conditions of peasant production, converting the peasant into a "wage-labor equivalent." In the absence of a strong local capital (taken as an a priori assumption) this regulation has been undertaken by the postcolonial state, driven by a variety of tensions. However, these same tensions also constitute a limit to the effectiveness of this regulation. (Bernstein does not indicate to what extent this limitation is responsible for regulation reaching only the stage of converting peasants into "wage-labor equivalents," rather than into wage-laborers proper.)

On the reverse side of the coin, the peasant is (generally) not actually dispossessed of his or her means of production, and to this extent the "forms" of production embodied in his or her enterprise are not capitalist ones. The peasant remains . . . a peasant. This view is obviously related to the notion that peasants fall short of becoming wage-laborers (except when they are actually "depeasantized").

While some objections may be made to the terminology employed here (especially to the term "wage-labor equivalent") it is hard to take exception to the basic argument. At this stage of elaboration its most noticeable feature however is ambiguity, for the extent to which one accepts that the peasant remains a peasant depends precisely upon what is meant by "peasant." To put the matter in a different way: The extent to which one accepts that the content and form of peasant production diverge in the present period hangs wholly upon what is implied by the form of peasant production, and what degree of determinacy is implicitly assumed in it. For example, if all that is being claimed in the notion of "retention of a continuity in form" is that the peasant remains an agriculturalist, then the claim that content and form diverge is unexceptional, since no degree of determinacy is usually attributed to engaging in agriculture alone. If, however, form is used as an English equivalent of the German *Weise* (as it often is), in other words to mean a mode of production in some sense, hence scientifically suggesting determinacy, the whole meaning attributable to a change in the content of peasant production is weakened.

Marx himself used form both in the sense of *Weisen* (modes), and in the sense of *Formen* (kinds) of production within a specific mode (e.g., manufacture and machine industry under capitalism). In the latter sense what is meant is the specific ways in which the fundamental contradiction of a given mode of production is embodied. *Formen* never exist independently of the contradictions which they contain, anymore than these contradictions occupy an independent existence from their expressions. In the sense of *Formen* (which will be the sense employed in this paper) one can hence speak only of capitalist forms, feudal forms and so forth, and never significantly of forms spanning modes of production, as Bernstein perhaps wishes to. These forms will not be the same, only with different "contents," between modes of production: they will necessarily be forms peculiar to given modes of production, sharing their fundamental contradiction, but expressing it in different ways. The form of capitalism and (say) feudalism may happen to share certain empirical attributes but this will be a matter of historical accident only upon which no general theory can be constructed.

To sum up the argument so far: Bernstein's claim to advancing a materialist understanding of the political economy of "African socialism" lies in an attempted departure from formulations of a dualistic /essentialist/empiricist kind, that is, from those which believe the truth about peasant economy is to be found in an examination of the practices of peasants themselves, which see any change in peasant economy as arising externally to it and which identify the initial dimension of this change as one variant or another of the "creation of a new environment" in which peasants carry on as before, but much less successfully. The major way in which he values this departure is to suggest the (partial) transformation of the peasant enterprise by capitalism. The degree of this transformation is seen as a contingent matter. It is never completed while the peasant retains his or her peasant identity. The extent to which this represents a genuine departure hinges on what is meant by peasant identity and the effectivity which this identity is granted. More significantly, the latter is also a test of the idea that dualism/essentialism/empiricism in the political economy of African socialism can be avoided while saving the category of peasant. The results of these tests can only emerge from detailed interrogation of Bernstein's arguments.

A convenient starting point is Bernstein's characterization of peasant production in sub-Saharan Africa (Bernstein, 1977). It is to be noted immediately that Bernstein desists from the assertion of an absolutely distinctive peasant "form" of production. Instead, peasant production is subsumed under the general materialist category of petty commodity production. Therefore, it is the manner in which this latter category is defined that is of consequence. Bernstein posits it in contrast to both natural economy and capitalism. With respect to the former, it differs by involving the production and purchase of exchange values, but remains similar by being characterized by a mode of calculation oriented to securing the means of subsistence, a "logic of . . . subsistence in the broad sense of simple reproduction of the production of the producers and the unit of production (descriptively the household)" (Bernstein, 1977: 62). With respect to capitalism, it tends to be characterized by the absence of a logic of accumulation (Bernstein, 1977: 63,64,67). Bernstein goes on to use the notions of "logic of subsistence" and "primacy of meeting simple reproduction needs" more or less interchangeably, sometimes even in a manner suggesting a pure subsistence model, for example: "Of course for the peasant, as for the wage-worker, there is no 'surplus-labour' insofar as all labour is expended in order to meet the costs of simple reproduction" (Bernstein, 1977: 72).

Two points may be made about the definition. One is that its content has a definite subjectivist bias. Despite claims to the contrary it tends to define petty commodity production not in terms of social relations of any sort but rather as a type of subjective calculation on the part of the individual petty commodity producer himself or herself. Conversely, since the degree of commodity production undertaken is held a priori to be variable and contingent, its contribution to the general definition of petty commodity production amounts simply to the acknowledgment that it occurs. Hence the "commodity production" element of "petty commodity production" tends to be represented in the definition as a residual (one might say superimposed) element. This manner of conceiving petty commodity production enjoys a long pedigree (both within and outside Marxism) in which A.V. Chayanov's is only the best known name.

Second, the practical effect of rendering the commodity producing element of petty commodity production residual (by dint of making its degree contingent) constitutes a slippage back toward not only a subjectivist form of analysis, but a *peasantist* form of subjectivism. Bernstein writes that under certain low degrees of commoditization (and presumably other circumstances also), within the "logic of simple reproduction," an option available to petty commodity producers is to withdraw in part or wholly from commodity production, in order to produce use values alone (Bernstein, 1981: 52,56). While this is qualified by the adjective "relative" and by quotation marks around "withdrawal" such an option is discussed as a possibility.

The point here is that if it was actually petty commodity production as such which was being discussed, rather than peasant production, it would make little sense to speak in these terms. Withdrawal to any degree is not a conceivable option, while retaining the same "production form," in any meaning at all for the petty commodity producing shoemaker or tailor. It is so only in so far as the latter have ceased to be shoemakers or tailors. This option thus only makes sense, if it makes sense at all,[3] for agriculturalists. Hence withdrawal cannot be associated with what is supposed to be covered here by the notion of the "logic of subsistence" in general, only with the *peasant* "logic of subsistence."

The preliminary conclusion can be stated that while Bernstein sets out to define "peasant identity" in a non-peasantist manner, this non-peasantism is so constructed that it tends to revert to a peasant essentialism as soon as attention is explicitly directed toward the "form of production." Moreover, a reading of the remarks regarding "withdrawal" is that this peasant essentialism is granted an independent effectiveness with respect to petty commodity production's own prospects of reproduction. (Because of his or her essential "form of calculation"— among other things—the peasant can choose to be a petty commodity producer.)

The extent to which Bernstein's work reverts to a conception of the independent effectivness of the peasant sector, can also be examined through his treatment of the concrete effects of the conversion of the peasant into a "wage-labor equivalent" as he or she becomes incorporated into capitalist production relations. The initial question here concerns the way in which the peasant/petty commodity producer is exploited: is he or she exploited in a manner which depends to a decisive degree upon being part of a sector independent of capitalism?

If one speaks of a direct regulation of peasants by monopoly capital within overall capitalist relations, then in Marxist terms this can mean one of two things. Either these peasants are employed as a form of wage-labor and are subject to capitalist exploitation in the form of surplus-value extraction based on the commodity status of labor-power; or they may be regulated as one type of capitalist enterprise by another type of capitalist enterprise, with the effect of a particular allocation of the general distribution of total surplus-value. If on the other hand, one insists that they are neither a form of wage-labor nor a particular type of capitalist enterprise but something else characterized in the first instance by the distinctiveness of their "logic of production," then evidently their relationship with monopoly capital will not be one internal to the capitalist mode of production, but to some degree or other an external one between two distinct modes of production—in short an articulation of modes of production.

The only systematic conceptualization of such a relation has been provided by the unequal exchange formulations of A. Emmanuel and S. Amin (e.g., Emmanuel, 1972). Despite the insistence that he is speaking of a transformation of the relations of production (formation of regulated wage-labor equivalents), it is a variant of this conception to which Bernstein also reverts as a consequence of maintaining the formal distinctiveness of the peasantry from capitalism.

In "Notes on Capital and Peasantry," Bernstein defines two forms of the "exploitation" of peasants by capital, both of which involve the notion of the peasants "underpaying themselves" the full cost of their production. Firstly it is argued that as petty commodity producers can on occasion[4] produce (most of) their own necessities independently, the exchange-value of the commodity they produce may fall below the full value of the cost of their reproduction during the labor-time expended on commodity production. In these circumstances use-value production thus subsidizes a part of these reproduction costs. Second, it is argued that the degree to which petty commodity producers "underpay" themselves in this respect will be determined by the general market price of whatever they produce, which will be set according to the conditions of production in branches of production (presumably in metropolitan countries) with the highest productivity of labor. Hence while an exchange of commodities for cash does take place between the peasant and the marketing enterprise, this is only a form of exploitation. Such "exploitation," it is maintained, can be intensified as the terms of trade for peasant produced commodities deteriorate (Bernstein, 1981).

These arguments regarding exploitation are by no means identical to Emmanuel's. Indeed, they are of course closer to (and in some respects duplicate) those advanced by Marx in the well-known section of *Capital* (Volume 3) on peasant land parcels. To this extent the following comments apply equally to those formulations. Both these and Emmanuel's arguments share first and foremost the notion of the intervention of an independent variable into the operation of the law of value in one or other of the branches of production between which exchange takes place.

Emmanuel's formulations are well-known. The "exploitation" of poor countries, which elsewhere he also describes as the "exploitation of simple commodity producers," occurs on the basis of their sale of a product of a relatively large number of hours in order to obtain in exchange the product of a smaller number of hours. The main explanation which Emmanuel offers for this "unequal exchange" is that while the law of value operates with respect to production in the poor countries, its operation is modified in the rich ones by disproportionately large socially/ethically/historically established "factor rewards" to labor (and capital).[5]

In the third volume of *Capital*, Marx explains a similar situation by a means which at first sight seems radically different, but whose underlying logic is very similar. In those circumstances where a peasantry is indebted to usurer's capital, the law of value may be suspended with respect to the determination of peasant returns to labor-time, since the peasant will accept any price at all for his commodities, and can do so within certain limits as a result of a subsidizing cushion of use-value production and the tolerance of lower than average subsistence levels. In this formulation and Bernstein's derivation from it, it is fully capitalist commodity production which operates "normally" and petty commodity production that does not, due to the existence of a different basis there for determining the payment of labor-power (according to criteria of "direct subsistence" [Marx] or "simple reproduction needs" [Bernstein]) which ultimately also serves as an independent variable. Whereas for Emmanuel, petty commodity producers are "rewarded normally" (in aggregate terms at least) and capitalist commodity producers are "overpaid," for Marx (and Bernstein) capitalist commodity producers are underpaid. In both cases what is postulated is the distinctiveness of the logics at work.

A distinctive logic, of course, implies an independent sector—independent of the capitalist relations of production otherwise held to embrace the peasantry generally. It is not being suggested here that Bernstein states that peasants will always remain peasants. It is being suggested that nonetheless he sees the exploitation of peasants (and therefore also ultimately their expropriation) as occurring on the basis of their remaining partly noncapitalist.

Finally, it is necessary to go to the heart of Bernstein's project. To repeat, this is presented as a study of so-called differential commoditization on the one hand, and a struggle said to arise out of attempts to step up this commoditization by increasing regulation over the peasantry, on the other. Regulation over the peasantry is seen as a process by which they become more or less subjugated and subsumed to capital. This struggle is visualized as having recently reached a decisive stage in Tanzania. What is distinctive about this approach is its claim to focus upon capitalist production relations. This focus is presumably embodied in the claim that the increased legal regulation of peasant production is a preliminary or anticipatory form of expropriation, and in the implicit statement that this corresponds to a decisive break in the nature of commoditization experienced by the peasant. At a certain stage of both control/commoditization a "direct relation" with capital is entered into.

The problem which this poses is the nature of the relation which existed prior to this decisive break in control/commoditization. By default, this relation, although characterised by a degree of commoditization, is also characterised by an absence of control. One wonders what kind of commoditization this could be. For the fact is that once peasants (or anyone else) *systematically* produce commodities they are all controlled—by definite and precise forms of capitalist regulation which act as the absolute limits of their activity. It is not even meaningful to talk of differential commoditization if this is meant to imply degrees as opposed to types. There are only two "degrees" of commoditization: systematic or generalized commodity production (which includes petty commodity production) or occasional and non-generalized commodity production, which is not effectively commodity production at all but part of a different noncapitalist mode of production. Of course peasant commodity producers may resent legal regulation, but no such regulation (short of effective expropriation) is of any fundamental significance once capitalist market regulation has been established. All petty commodity production has always lived with such legal regulation.

The point is that implicitly accompanying Bernstein's notion of a critical stage in commoditization/control, which is at the same time not proletarianization, is necessarily some notion of an effectively independent entity not yet regulated. That is, the stage of commoditization/control described by Bernstein can only be regarded as decisive if regulation from the outset by the laws of competition is ignored, if in other words, it is actually the replacement of peasantness by fully fledged commodity production which is the real subject of the discussion. To put the matter another way: if what is only now being discussed is capitalist regulation, this assumes a prior state of peasant self-regulation stretching back from colonial intervention to the 1970s. It is only an imputed change of such significance that can account for the weight Bernstein attaches to today's struggles between petty commodity producers and capital/state.

It is this fundamental ambiguity concerning the status of what went before today's changes which accounts for the equal ambiguity in Bernstein's work regarding what these changes consist of, and regarding the actual character of the "logic" of peasant enterprises. The focus upon capitalist production relations turns out to be highly misleading, since in practice it serves as a means of implicitly reintroducing a notion of peasantness distinct from capitalism.

This review of Bernstein's work has been partial and confined to the central theses of his political economy. His contribution to the discussion of the post-colonial state will only be discussed briefly toward the end of this chapter. No discussion has been offered of any of his concrete observations about Tanzanian politics and economy many of which are of the highest value. Further, it should be repeated that his work has been critically considered precisely because it embodies a genuine effort to grapple with certain theoretical problems on the basis of a rejection (formal at least) of what previously passed as the prevailing Marxist wisdom.

Nevertheless, his argument must be regarded as unsuccessful. The category of peasant has been saved but at the price of reverting to the very conceptions Bernstein set out to avoid. These conceptions come further to the fore in Bernstein (1981), with its silent insistence from the very first page that the major confrontation under "African socialism" at the phenomenal level (peasants versus state) reflects a necessarily determinant contradiction lying just beneath the surface within these phenomena themselves, and that it is the task of materialism to extract this through an interrogation of these same empirical phenomena. Via a notion of petty commodity production which is really a synonym for peasant production, the peasantry is implicitly identified by Bernstein with the location of a subjectivist logic of economic calculation. This logic is granted a considerable independent effectiveness, obliging capitalist domination of the peasantry to occur through relations of a dualistic kind (inter-sectoral exploitation). Despite the definition of peasant production as petty commodity production, the principal aspect of this relation—designated by the term commoditization—is presented as being an effective opposition to peasant production.

As far as the notion of an intrinsic contradiction between peasantry and state/capital is concerned, it can be said that this assumes: (1) that the given divisions and entities of society are merely to be accounted for in terms of their essential nature, and (2) that, moreover, there is no particular obligation for materialists to analyze the abstract determinations whereby peasantness and forms of state are structurally produced as an antagonistic unity under "African socialism."

It bears repetition that Bernstein's position seeks to uncover as the basis of reality not a general unifying system of real processes giving rise to a variety of contradictions at all societal levels, but a series of semi-empirical idealized essences (ideal types) standing in an external relation to each other, responsible for their own respective phenomenal differences and oppositions, and effectively constituting "eternities." As this procedure transforms a phenomenal contradiction into an essential one, the contradiction then comes to constitute its own conditions of existence. Like the idealized categories themselves, it becomes more or less ahistorical, suggesting that ultimately it cannot be subject to structural transformation and can only change under the impulses of either its own linear immanent development or external bludgeoning. Finally, what this means is that by endorsing a phenomenal account of reality Bernstein simply renders more profound the lived ideology of the dominant agents in social relations, in this case the state personnel of "African socialism," whose adversarial policies with respect to the peasantry are founded precisely upon a similar conception of reality. The contradiction discussed is primarily a contradiction from their viewpoint, not the viewpoint of the masses.

CAPITALISM AND PETTY COMMODITY PRODUCTION

Bernstein's contribution has been considered as a limit case, in the sense that it consciously strives to combine the notions of capitalist domination of the economy and a distinct petty commodity producing sector without falling into dualism and the empiricist and idealist errors associated with it. It is not suggested here that the tendency of his argument to revert to dualist formulations means that all such further attempts must a fortiori have this fate—though this is a possibility. What it does is to strengthen the case for a radically different approach to the relations between petty commodity production which is systematically anti-empiricist in its method. It will be argued in what follows, that notwithstanding certain unsatisfactory statements in *Capital* (Volume 3) concerning peasant land parcels, such an orientation is present in classic Marxism, and may be (re)discovered through a process of theoretical investigation. It will be suggested that according to classic Marxism, peasant petty commodity producers on the one hand, and both capitalists and proletarians on the other, are not valid polar opposites, that petty commodity producing enterprises are equally the product of capitalist relations as supposedly more capitalist forms of the labor process, and that consequently the class basis of a petty commodity producing petty bourgeoisie is constantly produced and reproduced by the contradiction between capital and wage labor. Classic Marxism occupied these positions on the basis of both a specific conception of capitalism and a specific method of explanation.

In order to overcome the dualism noted as a major flaw of Bernstein's position, it seems crucial to distinguish the phenomenal empirical entities of lived relations from the relations and contradictions which produce such phenomena. The latter are what Marx terms the essential relations or production relations of capitalist society, referring principally to the antagonistic relation or contradiction between wage-labor and capital. This contradiction is the fundamental contradiction of capitalism and it constitutes, as Sayer (1979) has pointed out, the conditions of existence of the different phenomena of capitalist society. The relationship between phenomena and their conditions of existence—the contradiction between capital and wage-labor—is not an essentialist one because the former are not expressions of the latter (hence their production must be explained), and because the latter do not exist independently of the former.

Thus although classes of wage laborers and capitalists are the effects of a relation between capital and wage-labor, such collectivities need not exist in all capitalist social formations. Even when they do exist, the wage-labor/capital contradiction of exploitation is not apparent *in* them. On the contrary, what is apparent, as Marx shows, is precisely an external relation of more or less equal exchange between these classes. The internal contradiction between wage-labor and capital which underlies the existence of these classes has to be discovered through a process of critique—that is, a process of elucidation of their conditions of existence. This process of discovery must then be used to investigate the specific conditions which give rise to the particular forms of phenomena in social formations (the particular kinds of classes and their characteristics including "principal" and secondary contradictions, the particular forms of the social division of labor, of the state, and so on). These brief points are made, not in order to provide a systematic discussion of an important epistemological question (this is undertaken at greater length in Neocosmos, 1983), but in order to make explicit a fundamental dividing-line between historical materialism and bourgeois ideologies.

To bring these remarks together: In what follows it will be understood that to suggest that a social formation is capitalist by virtue of being founded on the contradiction between wage-labor and capital is not to assert that all—or even the majority of—enterprises in this social formation will conform to a "type," in which capitalists and wage-laborers are present, and which constitutes the measure in relation to which all other forms deviate. What makes enterprises, and more generally social formations, capitalist or not, is not their supposed essential features, *but the relations which structurally and historically explain their existence.* Thus in order to show the capitalist character of African social formations it is not necessary to find sociological categories of capitalists or "potential capitalists," wage-laborers or "wage-labor equivalents." What has to be shown in order to "prove" the capitalist nature of such social formations, is that the social entities and differences which form the social division of labor in such formations are only explicable in terms of the wage-labor/capital relation.

As part of this project it is necessary first to establish at a relatively general level that petty commodity production is a product of this fundamental contradiction. This argument will follow a number of distinct steps: (1) After a preliminary definition of petty commodity production, it will be proposed that all commodity producing entities (individuals, enterprises, economic and social sectors, countries, and so on) within a social system of generalized commodity production, possess certain important characteristics which can only be understood as the product of the capital/wage labor relation. (2) The integral situation of *petty* commodity production within capitalist relations will then be examined, and in the process the nature of petty commodity production further clarified. (3) A number of indications will be provided of the conditions under which petty commodity production is systematically reproduced in the contemporary world economy.

Under present theoretical conditions (in particular the absence of a general theory of the international division of labor) it is difficult to go beyond this point. No claim is made to the effect that the classical Marxist case has been completed and found proven, nor that at the moment it can explain why the overriding concentration of petty commodity production is to be found in societies like Tanzania. The last part of this section will provide some general indications as to why peasant production really appears as a unified sector exogeneous to capitalism, and will thus provide the theoretical prequisites for a return to an examination of the concrete problem of the antagonism described by Bernstein in the context of "African socialism."

The following may serve as a preliminary definition of petty commodity production: this concept refers to a phenomenal category of commodity producers who posses the means of production necessary to produce commodities and who engage in production on the basis of unpaid household labor alone. It is assumed that such producers are capable of reproducing themselves as private producers of commodities without employing wage-labor and without selling (part of) their labor power. Although, as we have indicated earlier, different individuals or households (including poor peasants) may be engaging in commodity production in concrete social formations, at the more general and abstract level at which we are operating here, the assumption must be that such production alone is capable of reproducing labor at the level socially determined by the law of value. Three initial points should be made with reference to this definition: (1) The category is not restricted a priori to the economic realm of agriculture. This means (2) that petty commodity producers can equally be found in other economic spheres, and (3) that not all small producers in agriculture (and elsewhere) are petty commodity producers. For example, peasant families which produce part of their own conditions of existence but whose members sell part of their labor power are (for the purposes of this argument) considered as poor peasants (semi-proletarians).

As defined above the category of petty commodity producer in the realm of agriculture is restricted (as far as the peasantry is concerned) to the category of middle-peasants. In society as a whole it is restricted to what is sometimes referred to as the traditional petty bourgeoisie. No notion of subsistence or peasantness is assumed.

A further point must be noted. As our major concern in what follows will be to discuss the structural historical location of petty bourgeois production, we make no distinction between capitalized or noncapitalized petty commodity producers, between the low or high levels of technological endowment of such enterprises. Thus, our category may include, for example, both household firms of software/hardware computer manufacturers as well middle peasants. This particular difference does not constitute a specific problem to this kind of production, as such enterprises can be differentiated in concrete cases in a manner similar to that which small and large capitalists have always been differentiated (in terms of wage-labor employed, turnover, output, constant capital employed, or whatever).

Generalized commodity production, including petty commodity production, was attributed certain qualities by both classic English political economy and by Marx. Most obviously (as is frequently noted) it implies products whose only use-value for the producers is found in their exchange-value. Less obviously and most importantly it also implies that production is private (as opposed to collective) and individualized in its form, and that it is (relatively) specialized. Commodity production is private and individualized in the sense that it takes place within independent (an independence Marx calls "indifference") individualized entities (enterprises, economic sectors, countries, and so on) which look only to their private interests (bourgeois right) and which appear isolated from one another. This private nature of production makes possible, of course, the specialization of productive activity and the consequent necessary interdependence of these private producers via exchange. Marx discussed at length the contradictory nature of these producers who are constituted as both independent and interdependent entities within historically specific capitalist relations (especially in the *Grundrisse,* although similar arguments appear in *Capital,* Volume 1).

Part of the uniqueness of his contribution was to show that the private, independent, individualized forms of production which classic English political economy illustrated with reference to Robinson Crusoe were precisely social and historical forms grounded in quite specific relations:

> Private interest is itself already a socially determined interest, which can be achieved only within the conditions laid down by society and with the means provided by society; hence it is bound to the reproduc-

tion of these conditions and means. It is the interest of private persons; but its content, as well as the form and means of its realisation, is given by social conditions independent of all [Marx, 1973a: 156].

The most immediate of such conditions on which private interests are founded is a historically specific social division of labor. It is this phenomenon which makes possible specialization and hence interdependence mediated by exchange:

Exchange, when mediated by exchange value and money, supposes the all round dependence of the producers on one another, together with the total isolation of their private interests from one another, as well as a division of social labour whose unity and mutual complementarity exist in the form of a natural relation, as it were, external to the individuals and independent of them [Marx, 1973a: 158].

To come to the core of the argument: *this social division of labor is only explicable in terms of the separation of labor from its means of subsistence*—or, to use Marx's own terminology, the transformation of labor into wage-labor and the means of production into capital. This is so because it is only if labor is not in a position to produce its own conditions of existence—i.e., if it is forced to purchase the latter on a market—that generalized commodity production along with its private and specialized characteristics can exist. By the same logic as Lenin (e.g., 1972a: 228–231; 1972b: 37–43) in particular stressed, following Marx (1973a: 512; 1974a: 699; 1974b: 637), the development of the social division of labor through the creation of a wage-labor/capital relation is simultaneously the creation of a market.

Two footnotes may be added to this argument. The first is that the formation of a commodity producing peasantry is seen as constituting part of this general social division of labor, arising from the separation of labor from its means of subsistence and the constitution of the wage-labor/capital relation. Marx and Engels, Lenin and Mao all referred to the separation of industry and agriculture or town and country as an effect of the latter. Agriculture specializes in producing raw materials and food as a result of thereby being transformed "into a *commodity*-producing branch of the economy" (Lenin, 1972b: 38). In this process, specific agricultural enterprises appear whose economic function is commodity production. Whatever their other characteristics, this fundamental change means that they cannot be regarded as residues of previous modes of production any more than the capitalist bank is a left-over from the precapitalist usurer.

A second basic point is that as soon as agriculture ceases to be visualized as a self-contained domain lagging behind industry in its level of development, no particular significance need be attributed to the absence of wage-laborers as a social category in agriculture, nor to the fact that peasant farms may not be run as limited companies. Provided that commodity production in the countryside is generalized, that somewhere within the overall social formation wage-laborers and capital are present, and that all enterprises systematically engaged in commodity production (including peasant ones) are necessarily specialized, dependent on the market and subject to the same laws of competition and accumulation, then commodity producing peasants are an integral part of the capitalist mode of social production.

It is as well to recall that both Marx and Lenin stressed the capitalist nature of this form of production. Thus in Marx's case, for whom capitalism and private property were synonymous:

> Private property, as the antithesis to social collective property, exists only where the means of labor and the external conditions of labor belong to private individuals. But according as these private individuals are laborers or not laborers, private property has a different character [Marx, 1974a: 713].

Similary Lenin notes that "big capital and small independent production . . . are two forms of commodity economy," the former being commodity economy in "its most developed form," while the latter represents "its rudimentary form" (Lenin, 1972a: 200). At the same time Lenin always followed Plekhanov in maintaining that:

> The reality (small production) which the Narodniks want to raise to a higher level, by-passing capitalism, already contains capitalism with its antagonism of classes and clashes between them [Lenin, 1974: 444–445].

Having argued that the status of contemporary petty commodity producing peasants in the Third World is only intelligible in relation to the fundamental contradiction of the capitalist mode of production (of which they form an integral element) it remains to clarify the content of this integration. Since all systematic commodity production is produced by the formation of capital and wage-labor, in what particular manner is petty commodity production distinctive from other capitalist forms? As this question has generally been approached both structurally and historically by Marxists it is useful to follow the same procedures here.

A tendency present in some of Marx's own formulations—particularly in Chapter 32 of *Capital* (Vol. 1), "The Historical Tendency of Capitalist Accumulation," later incorporated into the key ideological texts of the Second International and reappearing in a great variety of guises ever since—has been to see petty commodity production as a phase of capitalism bound up with its birth and the transition from feudalism to capitalism generally. This phase is seen as partly coextensive with a "so-called Primitive Accumulation" which results *(inter alia)* in its destruction in favor of capitalist manufacture, itself a stepping stone to capitalist industrialization. A commonly found aspect of this same tendency is the view, made famous by Kautsky, of the linear proletarianization of the peasantry—at best held up by certain countervailing tendencies. Some of Lenin's texts on the agrarian question written prior to the 1905 revolution are also susceptible to a reading of this kind. Insofar as Marxists have been prepared to acknowledge petty commodity production as capitalist, it has generally been in this context.

Yet both Marx and Lenin also spoke of petty commodity production in a quite different historical light. Marx stressed repeatedly that petty commodity production is produced and reproduced during the period which he refers to as capitalist manufacture. The specifically capitalist nature of manufacture for Marx should be noted, as this form of the labor process is also founded on the underlying antagonistic relation between capital and wage-labor which it presupposes as a condition of its existence (its distinguishing feature is that it tends to be based on the extraction of absolute surplus-value and the formal subordination of labor to capital). Marx argues explicitly in Part 8 of *Capital* (Vol. 1) that petty commodity production is both destroyed and created during this period. This is because manufacture

> always rests on the handicrafts of the town and the domestic industry of the rural districts as its ultimate basis. If it destroys these in one form, in particular branches, at certain points, it calls them up again elsewhere, because it needs them for the preparation of raw materials. . . . It *produces* therefore a *new* class of small villagers who, while following the cultivation of the soil as an accessory calling, find their chief occupation in industrial labour, the products of which they sell to the manufacturers directly, or through the medium of merchants [Marx, 1974a:700, italics added].

This passage demonstrates that Marx's argument is much more complex than is usually asserted. Given that he maintains that the period of manufacture in England extended from the middle of the sixteenth to the latter third of the eighteenth century (Marx, 1974a: 318), it is wrong to read Marx as asserting a linear process of peasant proletarianization, at least during the manufacturing period. It is machinery and modern industry which, for Marx, "expropriates radically the enormous majority of the agricultural population" and "conquers for industrial capital the entire home market" (Marx, 1974a: 700–701). It is modern industry—a particular form of capitalist production—which for Marx "annihilates the peasant" (Marx, 1974a: 474), not capitalism in general.

It is only at this point in the argument that Marx gives a linear account of proletarianization and argues that after landlord resistance has been overcome, industry enters the sphere of agriculture and (due to its efficiency) finally destroys petty commodity production. This particular argument is facilitated by Marx's adherence, as we have noted, to a conception whereby the peasant is seen as producing primarily for "direct subsistence" (Marx, 1974b: 805), for peasant accumulation—the polar opposite of subsistence—is precluded by definition. Clearly this argument regarding the linear proletarianization of the peasantry as an effect of modern industry is highly problematic, to say the least, but this point notwithstanding it must be admitted that the totality of Marx's argument is much more sophisticated than is usually maintained. In fact it is only possible to read Marx's argument concerning capitalist development as one of linear proletarianization of the peasantry if capitalism is conflated with industrialism—in other words if one replaces a social relation by an essence of technology. On the other hand, if one wishes to adhere to the position which maintains that what is fundamental to capitalism as a mode of social production is a historically specific antagonistic social relation between capital and wage-labor, then it becomes apparent that such a relation need not necessarily imply that particular form of production (modern industry) which in Marx's terms is most detrimental to petty commodity production. In sum, the classic statement of capitalist development itself maintains that certain forms of capitalism actually produce petty commodity production while others destroy it.

Lenin also saw petty commodity productions as a permanent feature of capitalism which was reproduced even at its highest stage of development. Certain of his early texts can be read as embodying an immanentist notion of the economic differentiation of the peasantry in general and of the disappearance of middle peasants in particular.

However, by 1907 he clearly rejected this view in favor of one that saw differentiation as contingent on specific political and legal changes in Russia (Lenin, 1972c). In 1908 he not only rejected any assertion of linear proletarianization, but stressed the positive *re*creation of petty commodity enterprises in the industrial sector and their addition to the

> broad strata of the petty bourgeoisie, small proprietors. Capitalism arose and is constantly arising out of small production. A number of 'new middle strata' are inevitably brought into existence again and again by capitalism (appendages to the factory, work at home, small workshops scattered all over the country to meet the requirements of big industries, such as the bicycle and automobile industries, etc.) . . . . It is quite natural that this should be so and always will be so, right up to the changes in fortune that will take place in proletarian revolution [Lenin, 1972d:39].

Certain general conclusions can be derived from these arguments. What could be termed a struggle over control over the means of production occurs throughout the historical existence of capitalism between labor and capital, to the benefit of the latter. It is not the case however, that the process of the separation of labor from the immediate process of production takes place once and for all during a single period of so-called primitive accumulation, or even that it mostly takes place then with some subsequent mopping up of persisting remnants. Rather, there is a constant contradictory struggle in which some direct producers always manage to acquire access to means of reproducing themselves independently, only to be expropriated again later, and so on. This process also occurs in relation to the control of knowledge and raw materials as well as techniques of labor and tools by formal wage-laborers, in the so-called typically capitalist labor process. There is never a total monopoly by capital over the means of labor and culture (for various reasons, some of which are suggested below). For the moment, it is sufficient to note that capitalism systematically creates (in a non-functionalist manner) the space for petty commodity production.

The question nonetheless remains of why petty commodity production, relative to other capitalist forms, appears to demonstrate an inherent tendency towards instability. This question takes us back by an indirect route to that posed above: if what is distinctive about petty commodity production is not its precapitalist, historically transitory character, then what is it?

In *Theories of Surplus Value* Marx formulated a conception of the structural position of petty commodity producers under capitalism in a manner eminently more satisfactory than in *Capital* (Vol. 3). His critical emphasis in the former was not on primitivism, peasantness, impoverishment or cultivation according to a simple reproductive logic, but on *the combination in petty commodity production of the functions of both capital and wage-labor within a single individual or household.* Thus he notes that

> The independent peasant or handicraftsman is cut up into two persons. As owner of the means of production he is a capitalist, as labourer he is his own wage-labourer. As capitalist he therefore pays himself his wages and draws his profit on his capital; that is he exploits himself as wage-labourer, and pays himself in the surplus-value, the tribute that labour owes to capital [Marx, 1969: 408].

The general historical instability of capitalism is, of course, founded upon the fact that it calls into being its own inveterate enemy in the form of wage-labor, as Marx and Engels stated so clearly in the *Communist Manifesto.* The special exaggerated form of instability of the petty commodity producing enterprise under capitalism, it may be suggested, can be seen as the effect of the combination in the concentrated form of the single individual/household of the contradictory class places common to all capitalist enterprises. To go a little further: just as Marx and Engels spoke of the principle tendency of the capitalist mode of production as an ever-increasing division between the classes, so the corollary of this in the specific concentrated form of petty commodity enterprises is for the latter to tend, as individual units, to become differentiated into capitalists or wage-laborers. In *Theories of Surplus Value* Marx saw the "embourgeoisement" of petty commodity producers as a possible outcome alongside their proletarianization, and did not restrict himself to emphasing the latter. Thus

> the handicraftsman or peasant who produces with his own means of production will either gradually be transformed into a small capitalist who also exploits the labour of others, or he will suffer the loss of his means of production . . . and be transformed into a wage-laborer. This is the tendency in the form of society in which the capitalist mode of production predominates [Marx, 1969: 409].

He notes in addition that it is only because the producer possesses the means of production that he/she labors for him/herself—because he/she is a capitalist that he/she is his/her own laborer. He/she is thus a capitalist who employs him/herself—a petty bourgeois and not a "well-to-do proletarian."

A distinction can therefore be made between the fate of petty commodity production in capitalist society—which is to be reproduced continually anew—and the fate of individual petty commodity producers—which is to divide systematically into capitalists and wage-laborers. It is the confusion of these two quite different points which leads to formulations of linear proletarianization. It is not being claimed here that those formulations solve the whole problem. It must be acknowledged that at least two general issues require further clarification. One is the relation of the concentrated form of the internal contradiction between capital and wage-labor in the petty commodity producing enterprise to the level of development of the productive forces/powers of labor (including the labor process), and hence to the performance of the enterprise under the laws of competition. For example, the concentration of the functions of capitalist and wage-laborer is likely to have important effects for the regulation of the labor-process (and in different ways from those derived by Chayanov from the "labor-consumer balance").

Another general issue concerns exploitation *within* the petty commodity producing enterprise. If the head of household succeeds in accumulating, then this accumulation can only have been attained from household members (the question of patriarchy). The extent to which this means that, after all, one can speak of a place of wage-labor within the petty commodity household cannot be resolved here, although it will be briefly returned to below.

By what precise mechanisms is petty commodity production brought into being under capitalism by the wage-labor/capital contradiction and on what basis does it generally tend to be conserved in the areas where it seems to predominate such as agriculture? Repeating the qualification that there is no attempt here to provide a total explanation of the origins of its concentration in "African socialist" countries (which requires as a preliminary the formulation of a theory of the international division of labor and of regional differences) a number of examples may be indicated.

One of the principal effects of the contradiction between capital and wage-labor in the capitalist economy is the rise of the social productivity of labor as an effect of increased exploitation and hence class struggle. This tends to occur in all branches of production, but at an uneven rate as capital abandons some in favor of more profitable ones in a constant search for a greater rate of profit.(Some of the reasons for this unevenness will be discussed in a moment.) One consequence of this tendency may be to reopen once abandoned areas of production to small-scale enterprises. A useful example in Western countries is provided by the production of free-range poultry. The establishment of large-scale production in the poultry industry has had the necessary effect (given the level of development of the productive forces/powers of labor) of "sacrificing quality for quantity." In other words, the introduction of mass production into this branch of industry has altered the commodity into a different product, and has thereby created a market for free-range poultry among more well-to-do consumers. This market can however only be profitable supplied by small producers, given the present limits to what is technologically possible.

As far as "African socialist" countries are concerned, a parallel may be found here in the production in Tanzania of Makonde sculpture and wooden household artifacts for local expatriate, Western tourist and cheap-end fine art markets. Given the rise in the social productivity of labor in the production of household artifacts (ashtrays, combs, letters openers, and so forth) and of "cheap-end" fine art prints and reproductions, a market for an "authentic" alternative to these products has been created. Simultaneously, because of its very nature (impossiblity of intensifying the division of labor due to the necessity for the leading product—sculptures—to be one-off items carved by a single individual) Makonde sculpture will mainly be organized as a petty-commodity producing basis—individuals, households, or households grouped into co-operatives.

A second consequence of the combination of a rise in the social productivity of labor together with the uneven rate of its development is the creation of spaces making possible the realization of surplus-profits for petty-bourgeois enterprises. Again, a Western example will be given, followed by several from "African socialist" societies. The rise in the social productivity of labor in the distributive sector in the West is exemplified in the emergence of supermarkets. By their very nature as an enterprise, these cannot be situated on every street corner. As a result some small retailers will retain a locational advantage in relation to the market, enabling them to increase their prices without going out of business. The process amounts to the realization of a differential surplus-profit or rent which supplements their depleted profit.

In "African socialist" societies the emergence of enterprises on this basis is extremely common. A frequent occurence is that the rise of the social productivity of labor is accelerated by the creation of state or semi-state (parastatal) companies in production, distribution (transport and retail), and the provision of commerical services (e.g., clearing and forwarding in ports). For reasons which will be explored in the final section of this chapter, these enterprises often tend to function in a spasmodic and haphazard manner and produce commodities of poor quality, thereby obliging the toleration of petty-bourgeois enterprises which can again supplement their depleted profit by realizing a differential surplus profit or rent through selling or repairing what has now become a scarce product.

In some cases (e.g., those where the skills required are transmitted on a hereditary basis as a result of custom) it is difficult to conceive of enterprises of any other but a petty-bourgeois kind. In others, for example transport (taxis, buses, and so on) the dominant populist ideology serves to deflect medium and large-scale capital as a matter of political policy. More significantly though, *the very conditions which allow these enterprises to appear in the first place tend to restrict their development* (unavailability of tools, unreliable raw material supply, and the like) and thereby to confine them to a petty-bourgeois level. What is perhaps of greatest interest, however, is that a large number of these activities are inconceivable except in relation to the development of capitalism generally in these societies. Crafts like bicycle, radio and engine repairs cannot possibly be regarded as leftovers from precapitalist modes of production or the activities of captured precapitalist artisans, while the extent of others like coconut oil manufacture, grain milling, salt production and jaggery boiling result from meeting needs which can no longer be satisfied in ways which existed prior to capitalist conquest.

A further characteristic which helps to explain the continued reemergence of petty-bourgeois enterprises through the capitalist economy, including the "African socialist" societies is the cheapening of industrial commodities which can serve as means of production to the petty commodity producer. A common occurrence in "African socialist" countries is to find products imported or manufactured locally on an industrial scale for high income groups recycled in various ways: tires into sandals, insecticide spray cans into kerosene lamps, cups, oil cans, ladles and so on. (For a detailed description of the informal sector in Dar es Salaam, see ILO, 1981.)

In relation to agriculture it is impossible at this stage to make more than a few extremely general statements. The first is the obvious one that a place was initially created for systematic commodity production in sub-saharan Africa by the imposition of taxes and the capitalization of a basic infrastructure (such as roads, railheads, and docks) by the colonial capitalist state. Of course this is not to say that this was the primary function of the colonial capitalist state, or even anything about its motivations. Subsequently, petty commodity production has continued to be regenerated in this manner, not least as a result of international financial institutions and international agribusiness finding higher rates of profit in the further capitalization of the infrastructure than in other forms of capital export politically acceptable in these countries.

In addition, in *Capital,* Marx gives reasons why petty commodity production should prevail more in agriculture than elsewhere, reasons which are based on the general character of the contradictions of capitalism. One such argument concerns capitalist landed property which, through its extraction of rent, restricts the development of the productive powers/forces of labor in agriculture (Neocosmos, 1981). Since "African socialist" countries contain no direct equivalent to capitalist landed property in the shape of a class of landlords, this argument is not immediately applicable.[6] On the other hand, *Capital* (Vol. 1) also contains the argument that within capitalism generally the greater degree of concentration (though not necessarily in greater numbers) of wage-laborers and thereby class struggle in industrial enterprises, obliges capitalists in this sector to introduce machinery and to develop more complex and sophisticated forms of cooperation in order to compensate for the increased price of labor-power attained through class struggle. The absence of this concentration in agriculture means that this sector tends to develop at a slower rate than industry and to rely more on non-industrial forms of enterprise. Also the fact that most technological development is geared primarily to industrial labor-processes means, at the same time, that the control of nature in agriculture is "less developed."

In any event, the reproduction of petty commodity production in agriculture is strongly related to its reproduction outside agriculture. While petty commodity production implies specialization within the capitalist economy generally, it does not imply as Kautsky believed an absolute specialization into a pure agriculturalist (Kautsky, 1976: 4). It should be borne in mind that a very significant proportion of agriculturalists in "African socialist" societies belong to one and the same households as the majority of petty-bourgeois craftsmen and craftswomen.[7]

This last remark may serve to redirect attention to some aspects of Bernstein's account of the contradiction between peasants and capital/state in Tanzania. If, to return to the point of departure, what is really meant by the term peasant is a petty commodity producer sharing the same basic economic attributes as a watch-repairer or a blacksmith, then how is it that he or she appears as part of a homogeneous unit differentiated from and ranged against other social forces under African socialism? The answer to this question which has been rejected throughout is that this is due to his/her possessing a peasant quality or peasantness (including any notion of a logic specific to the peasant or any other kind of petty commodity producer). A different sort of answer now has to be constructed. This will contain both some abstract general remarks and a discussion of the conjuncture in Tanzania.

Five general suggestions may be made about why petty commodity production in agriculture tends to appear as a homogeneous peasant production. As with the rest of the argument, these suggestions derive from the analysis of the nature and development of capitalist relations advanced above.

First, this apparent homogeneity is founded on the existence of a distinct entity of "agriculture" or "the countryside." The latter is only formed through the separation from it of one section of industry after another, a process that for Marx constituted the foundation of the division of labor (Marx, 1974a: 333). It is a necessary effect of the underlying antagonistic relation between capital and wage-labor which it presupposes. "The contradiction between town and country can only exist within the framework of private property" (Marx and Engels, 1974a: 64). What Marx, Engels, Lenin, and Mao all saw as the dominance of industry over agriculture (or town over country) is of course premised on this antagonism, thus:

> The predominance of the town over the countryside (economically, politically, intellectually, and in all other respects) is a universal and inevitable thing in all countries where there is commodity production and capitalism [Lenin, 1972a: 229].

It should be reasonably apparent how the existence of a unitary entity of "agriculture" and its opposition to other such entities such as "industry," has the effect on the one hand of homogenizing class antagonisms, while on the other dividing up classes between sectors (which can then be said to obey their own specific laws or logics). This process operates in a manner identical to that by which entities such as "nations," "countries" and so on homogenize "their" social constituents while dividing "their" classes from those of others. The parallel with countries or economies is abundantly apparent in those conceptions which speak of terms of trade (an external, not a constitutive relation) between agriculture and industry and thereby replace antagonistic class relations by eternal conceptions of a conflict between sectors of buyers and sellers. This is but an effect of remaining within the terrain prescribed by bourgeois forms. What these conceptions make possible is the false identification of "the proletarian" with industry and its opposition to "the peasant," a supposedly typical rural phenomenon.

Moreover, from a phenomenal observation of the domination of the town (or industry) over the countryside (or agriculture) it is no major theoretical step to assert the dominance of the state or capital over a unified peasantry. The theoretical premise is already there in the phenomena produced by capitalist relations; all the argument requires in order to make it possible are some further circumstances, such as the absence of a class of landlords (a fact which further homogenizes the agricultural sector) and the juridical ownership by the state of large capitalist enterprises (e.g., parastatals).

The second phenomenal foundation of a unified peasantry is the individualization produced as part of the production of a social division of labor and detailed above. The private nature and production of Robinson Crusoe-like producers (typified for agriculture by Proudhon's "colonus"—see Marx, 1976b: 197, 206) who are both individualized and independent, makes possible the phenomenal existence of societies and sectors as seemingly additions of independent individual producers. Agriculture as a unity is thus produced in such a manner that it really seems to be populated by "peasants" or "farmers," so many individual versions of the typical "peasant" or "farmer."

Third, antagonisms between buyers and sellers (individualized owners and non-owners of commodities) are systematically presented by capitalist production relations as much more central or more fundamental than class antagonisms. At best, class contradictions appear as subsumed under such relations, as mere accidental and eternal "conflicts" between "owners of different factors of production" (labor, capital and land). In other words class struggles at best appear as accidental market conflicts between independent buyers and sellers of such "factors" (Marx, 1974b: chap. 48; 1972: Addenda; Sayer, 1979: chap. 3). This means both that the fundamentally antagonistic nature of the class struggle is not immediately evident, and that classes in the Marxist sense are, of course, not simply given by capitalist relations, but need to be constituted through a specific political practice. Thus it is not difficult to see how conflicts between sociologically additive groups of individualized owners of different commodities (individuals, enterprises, or more generally agents) seem to form the dominant antagonistic interests under capitalist relations. The phenomenal dominance of one such antagonism by no means alters the terms of the analysis.

Fourth, the homogeneity of "agriculture" is paralleled by that of "industry" where similar processes operate to make possible the production of a "typically industrial" enterprise and "typically industrial" classes. Despite the fact that wage-laborers may be produced within a "rural sector" (as they are constantly being separated from their means of production), their migration to the towns or to areas of large scale argicultural enterprises, contributes to make possible the conception of wage-labor as a "typically industrial" or "industrial and plantation" phenomenon. Moreover, the more rapid *(not the initial)* development of the productive forces/powers of labor and expansion of capitalist relations under the influence of industrial processes in urban areas produced by the monopolizing and concentrating effects of such relations, means of course that agriculture seems to lag behind and to be "backward" in relation to industry. As, in addition, industry (also as an effect of capitalist relations) seems to possess a life of its own so that it appears to beget its own expansion (Neocosmos, 1982: chap. 5), and profit seems to arise out of technology to the extent that "capital consists of products and these bring in profit" like pear trees bring in pears (Marx, 1972: 485), then the "backwardness" of agriculture appears even more "evident." This seeming self-reproduction of "industry" of course can only contribute to supporting the externality of its relations with "agriculture."

Finally, the phenomenal similarity between genuinely pre-capitalist labor-processes and those capitalist labor-processes where the formal subordination of labor through the extraction of absolute surplus-value predominates (Marx, 1974a: chap. 10, sect. 2), also contributes to the phenomenal production of a "backward" and unified "peasantry" by capitalist relations.

All these phenomena contribute to supporting the formation of an apparently distinct and unitary "peasantry," "external" to capital. As these phenomena are the products of fundamental capitalist relations, their maintenance only serves to reproduce such relations. Conversely, it may be concluded that a transformation of capitalist relations necessarily requires the alteration of these phenomenal unities, separations and divisions, and the construction and constitution of new forms for the emancipation of the masses.

CLASS AND STATE IN AFRICAN SOCIALISM

"Notes on State and Peasantry in Tanzania" (Bernstein, 1981) begins with a discussion of a series of measures undertaken by the Tanzanian government in the period between the Arusha Declaration (1967) and the early 1980s. An underlying argument of the paper is that as capital could not take hold of peasant household enterprises in its own name—due to the presence of restrictions on land alienation, the "absence of natural economy," and so on—it has been obliged to act through the Tanzanian state. This, "the only systematic set of social relations at the territorial level" (Bernstein, 1981: 53), can act as capital's surrogate throught the mechanism of increasingly obliging peasant enterprises to submit to legal regulation. It is this which creates, from the side of the Tanzanian state, the contradiction between state and peasantry. Bernstein roots the tendency of the state to form a strategy of this kind in a dual origin. From one side it is said to represent an effort by the state personnel, conceived as a ruling class whose formation has taken place outside capitalist enterprise, itself to engage in a collective form of accumulation.[8] From the other, since it implies the expansion of state political and economic activities, and to this extent of the state personnel too, it represents an extension of the social and political base of this ruling class.

This argument is presented by Bernstein in a nuanced manner stressing the struggles involved, and it is never implied that the Tanzanian "ruling class" will automatically succeed in these ventures. Nonetheless, it follows certain familiar lines of argument, long established in the so-called "post-colonial state" debate, in its characterization of these "ruling classes" and the significance of state forms under "African socialism." The introduction to this paper situated the emergence of these positions in relation to the problem of attempting to understand the reproduction of a capitalist dominated economy and a non-popular state in the absence of a readily identifiable capitalist ruling class. A number of solutions to it were mentioned, and Bernstein's argument can be seen ultimately as a variant of that which has become the mainstream.

This position, first popularized with respect to Tanzania by I. Shivji (1976) and extended in various forms particularly by Raikes

(1978) and Boesen (1979) organizes itself in the first instance around the "difficulty" of categorizing the senior state personnel in Tanzania, who are deemed worthy of such attention precisely because of the absence of any other sociologically identifiable group (e.g., large capitalist farmers) simultaneously enjoying economic privileges and an effective monopoly of political influence. The same empirical sociological bias that has identified this group as significant cannot provide any direct clue as to its class identity, however, precisely since it also tends to understand the latter in purely empiricist terms.

In other words, the state bureaucracy is discovered as the dominant social group to which however no clear sociological class label can be satisfactorily attached. They legally own no capital, hence cannot be capitalists; they are not small traders or producers, hence cannot be petty-bourgeois, and so on. The problem of categorization is "resolved" by Raikes (1978)—through the expedient of simply calling them a "state class"! Shivji's own argument takes the form of squaring the circle—the crisis for sociologists of the group's identity is transposed by Shivji into a crisis for the group of its identity. The group is called a bureaucratic bourgeoisie by virture of an imputed trajectory of becoming bourgeois through the imputed simultaneous extension and collective approportion of state property. Thus it seeks to substantiate its status-dominance into a property dominance on the basis of a series of political measures, thus closing the gap between what it is and what it should be according to sociology.

John Saul indicated the major problem of Shivji's analysis quite soon after its dissemination in a contribution still worth reading (Saul, 1974). Saul argued that Shivji's position embodied a teleology; the bureaucratic bourgeoisie were defined in a solely immanentist manner according to what it was imputed that they intended to become. No evidence was adduced for this intention other than the concrete acts supposedly expressive of this motive, and no explanation was provided for the basis of this intention. Indeed such an explanation is in principle impossible, since it effectively would assume bourgeois behavior in a pre- (i.e., non-)bourgeois class.

This is apart from criticism of the speculative character of the assumption that state policy embodied a necessary planned cohesion, in other words took the form of a strategy. It is also apart from the fact that within the terms of empirical sociology (which provides the parameter of the whole debate) the class identity of the bureaucratic bourgeoisie has still not really been solved. How can this group be called bourgeois empirically when on the whole it was the state which was accumulating and not the state personnel as individuals (except in a haphazard way)?

Bernstein's use of "state/capital" shares some of these problems and reflects a similar logic to the notion of "bureaucratic bourgeoisie." State and capital are seen as teleologically fulfilling each other's destinies by closing the gaps between potentiality and actuality in bourgeois class formation, political homogenization, and capitalist economic domination (Bernstein, 1981: 53–54). Again it must be stressed that there is much of value and interest in Shivji and Bernstein's contributions in this area (particularly Bernstein's account of the weakness of the state), but it seems that an alternative approach to the problem is also worth considering. It was suggested at the beginning of this paper that rather than talking about a contradiction between "peasants" generally and "state/capital," it was more rewarding to speak of one between particular kinds of peasants (namely those mainly middle peasants who live primarily from systematically producing commodities under capitalist conditions) and state capitalist economic enterprises of a particular variety. It has been argued that these peasants, namely petty-bourgeois capitalist enterprises, can be seen as produced and reproduced by capitalist relations and as acquiring a distinctive and homogeneous appearance as a result of these same relations.

The general economic space for state economic enterprises in all capitalist countries is also produced by the contradiction between capital and wage-labor in a very direct manner. The class struggle generates unevenness in economic development and specialization between and within national entities which are themselves also aspects of the division of labor. Simultaneously this also constitutes pressures to moderate the effects of the international division of labor and in particular the internationalization of capital, quite apart from additional political pressures also arising out of the class struggle for the renovation of public services, defence of given levels of employment within national economies, and so on, favoring the formation/preservation of state economic enterprises. This is only the briefest indication of some of the origins of these enterprises.

In addition it can be argued that the specificity of particular state economic enterprises, from one capitalist country to another, is also rooted in the capital/wage-labor contradiction, insofar as the operation of these enterprises is not a purely economic matter but also depends upon the state form. In *Origins of the Family, Private Property and the State,* Engels advanced the theory that the state is synonymous with the class struggle, that all class societies possess states, and that the form of the class struggle will determine the form of the state. This general theory represented a summing up of observations by Marx in his works on French politics from 1848 to 1870 and by Engels in his writings on Germany. In these works, different forms of state (democratic republic, constitutional monarchy, Bonapartist and/ or Bismarckian dictatorship) were differentiated and explained in relation to the content and degree of intensity of these societies' primary contradictions, together with its relation to secondary contradictions.

To illustrate concretely a few of the implications of this approach, a state economic venture such as the British Steel Corporation may be considered. Created in a space produced by the internationalization of the division of labor and of capital, as well as the increasing relative unprofitability for individual private capitals to invest in production of means of production, especially where enterprises in this field have long gestation periods; created also by political pressure to prevent a technical-scientific "loss" to the "national economy," the British Steel Corporation operates in a manner which directly reflects the particular character of the British State. It is not expected to be profitable—otherwise it would be denationalized—but it is expected to operate according to most of the criteria under which other enterprises in the same economy would make profits (manning levels are an obvious example, calculation of product cost an obvious exception). It might even be said that the norm of regulation applied to most state economic enterprises in Britain is one constructed to minimize as much as possible the imputed consequences of their state ownership.

This type of regulation of the British Steel Corporation is possible because the British state is a bourgeois one in which the class struggle is relatively highly developed, and hence in which the state has acquired a high degree of centralization, simplification and rationalization in its functions. The "perfection of the state machine" (Lenin) in such societies is also associated with a relative autonomy of state officials from individual private interests and a generally clear internalization of bourgeois class practices. All these enable the British Steel Corporation to be operated not merely as a de facto private enterprise subject to most of the effects of the law of competition, but also for this conformity to be relatively stringently enforced.

Under "African socialism" the same *principles* of determination of the character of state economic enterprises hold. At the same time, it is not surprising that their *forms of operation* are very different from those in the case sketched above. For while the space for such enterprises under "African socialism" is as great, if not far greater, the specification of its state forms exert a significantly novel type of modification in their regulation. In what follows, discussion will concentrate mainly upon the example of Tanzania.

At the level of global ecomomy and politics, the capital/wage-labor contradiction can be seen as responsible for the very creation of this state in the particular form it takes. It is an obvious fact, which nevertheless bears repetition, that world imperialism emerged from World War II in a severely weakened form and with several severe strategic losses (such as eastern Europe, China, North Korea).

Having already felt the debilitating effect and seen the potentially dangerous results of struggles for colonial freedom in Asia, it approached the appearance of independence movements in Africa with a previously absent sense of caution and an appreciation of the need for flexibility. Obviously destined in the long-term to become unviable for white rule, black Africa might nevertheless be constrained from falling into explicitly anti-capitalist hands provided a political adjustment could be made to incipient anticolonial forces. In particular, the global contradiction between wage-labor and capital generated a preferred solution of passing state power into the hands of inexperienced petty-bourgeois anticolonial leaders prior to the consolidation of their leadership (or of an alternative more radical leadership) in the development of popular mass anti-imperialist struggles.

This solution not only preempted the development of mass forces which would identify with the side of labor, but also created what were in effect a range of dependent semi-client petty-bourgeois ruling classes; this tendency can be regarded as over-determined by inter-imperialist rivalries, which formed the immediate background in the late 1950s and early 1960s to British willingess to pass power to "immature" political forces in many of its colonies. The notion of "Commonwealth" embodied the ideal not of a federation of the free former colonies but a set of serial relations between the British state and apprentice clients.

Tanzania, together with certain other "African socialist" states, was constituted as a petty-bourgeois state in the first instance on the basis of the ruling class which it emerged with. By ruling class here is meant the class whose practices are embodied in the state apparatus. By petty bourgeoisie is meant not a once-and-for-all given sociological status group of former middle-peasants, school-teachers, minor government officials, and so forth (although these social origins are not without importance) but a group of persons corresponding to or associated with economic ideological and political practices of a certain kind.

This is no place to embark upon a general exposition of a theory of class including the concept of practice, but several points are made by way of a preliminary clarification.

(1) Marx, Engels, Lenin, and Mao all approached the question of class primarily from what has been called a "relational" rather than a "gradational" angle, that is they saw the meaning of class not in terms of rungs on a ladder but in terms of oppositions of a systematic kind. One class is precisely what another class is not, rather than all classes conforming to different amounts of a single measure (occupation, income and so on).

(2) None of them approached class in a purely economic manner. Part of the notion of class formation, opposition and antagonism is that of political and ideological differentiation—in Mao's case one could say the overdetermining moment.

(3) It has already been demonstrated that capitalism reproduces class spaces or places on the one hand and actual phenomenal forms of a unitary and distinctive kind not corresponding to the spaces and places on the other (e.g., urban/rural dwellers, industrial workers/ agricultural laborers, urban craftsmen and women peasants, men/ women, mental/manual, young/old, black/white, regional, national and ethnic differences, and so on). Two points are worth noting here. First, as has already been remarked, "classes" are produced phenomenally as groups of owners (and hence as buyers and sellers) of specific conditions of production ("capital," "land" and "labor") and hence with "about the same relation to each other as lawyer's fees, red beets and music" (Marx, 1974b: 814). In other words class *relations* are not simply evident at the phenomenal level, where what seems to prevail is accidental conflict rather than structural struggle. Second, the various unities of the division of labor enumerated above cut across classes in such a way that classes are never just given "in the round," so to speak, even as "economic" entities.

(4) Class formation, therefore, is not simply given, but is brought about as a combination of economic, political and ideological transformations, creating overdetermined social forces occupying the different spaces or places which a mode of production entails. Marx and Engels were wrestling with precisely this issue in their somewhat Hegelian formulations concerning the distinction between classes "in"

and "for" themselves. It is not simply a question here of providing a consciousness for an otherwise economically unified category, in the manner of historicist interpretation, but rather one of constituting or forging an economic, ideological and political unity via an undercutting of the unities of the division of labor. Class formation is thus a multi-dimensional, uneven and contingent process.

(5) This process of transformation and class constitution always involves and may be overdetermined by the acquisition of a distinctive form of political or ideological identity represented materially in determinate practices—that is, regularly constituted sets of activities in the context of historically specific social relations.

(6) These practices which are constitutive of classes break with and cut across the interests (as they spontaneously present themselves) of the phenomenal unities of the division of labor described in (3 above) and polarize around structural contradictions in politics and ideology which are constituted independently of, and are irreducible to, economic contradictions. They may also polarize around political and ideological positions which combine both elements of a given structural contradiction (e.g., a petty-bourgeois position).

(7) In capitalist societies, the classes of bourgeoisie and proletariat come into existence through the acquisition of practices whose contradictory relations correspond to either side of the contradiction between capital and wage-labor. The class of the petty bourgeoisie comes into existence through the acquisition of practices whose contradictory unity corresponds to the unity of the same two elements, in a similar manner to that which, as we have seen, the economic category of petty commodity production (or for that matter similarly situated economic groups such as the "middle strata") combines capital and wage-labor in one unstable entity. A class may come into existence embracing only a tiny proportion of those occupying a "corresponding" economic function, and including many occupying economic functions other than those "corresponding" to the practices around which they become organised. In addition, the relation between practices of already constituted classes may lead to the further differentiation of sets of practices to a degree where one could speak of the formation of a new class. (The national bourgeoisie, constituted as an effect of the relation between the practices of monopoly capitalism and the practices of the proletariat, is a possible example.)

(8) In the case of the proletariat, the constitutive practices referred to are those which amplify and develop collective forms of activity and experience and uproot individual and private ones. (A communist

party plays a decisive role in this respect.) In the case of the petty bourgeoisie, the distinctive practices implied are ones which in Marx's terms "do not get beyond the limits which" petty commodity producers and shop-keepers "do not get beyond in life," in other words which do not get beyond the contradictory unity, problems and solutions embodied in petty commodity production (Marx, 1973b: 120). These practices tend to combine collective with highly individualized and privatized practices. (The secret societies of peasants or handicraftsmen of nineteenth century Europe and Asia is one example with analogues in contemporary Africa.)

In Tanzania, the petty bourgeoisie became the ruling-class not because the country was an overwhelmingly peasant one, not simply through the wish of British imperialism that it should do so, but because it was constituted around certain distinctive practices—of a petty bourgeois kind—in advance of other social classes and to which persons occupying economic functions of other than a petty-bourgeois kind became absorbed. The history of these practices remains to be written, despite the provision of valuable raw materials; in this case they were not of a secret society type. Clearly, their development was related to the specific nature of the growth of capitalism in Tanganyika, the character of the colonial state there, and the dominant diffused popular ideologies. It would be premature to attempt to go beyond this.

In any event, since independence it has been practices of a petty-bourgeois class character which have dominated the state apparatuses. To a considerable extent, policies have been pursued aimed at creating a utopia of a classless, petty-bourgeois character. Simultaneously the necessary internal contradictions of petty-bourgeois practices generally have come to the fore. Alongside such synthetic petty-bourgeois policies as *ujamaa* has been the disintegration of the dominant political practices generally into an unstable equilibrium of bourgeois and proletarian elements, pursued in a contradictory manner.

Tanzania has witnessed a regime which has combined the reactionary and the progressive, the bureaucratic and the popular, the statist and the anarchist, the modernist and the nativist, the consumerist and the ascetic, the cynical and the idealist, the aggressive and the timid, the grandiose and the apathetic—in short, which has been characterized by a systematic inability to develop, implement, and sustain consistent policies and means of monitoring them, and a tendency instead to seek a quick victory for African socialism in bombarding the population with ever-new commands, institutions and campaigns.

Moreover, it has had as well a tendency to vacillate between the principal class forces, local and international. Hence the character of the policies of the Tanzanian state has also been dependent to a large degree upon short-run contradictions between the petty-bourgeois ruling class, international imperatives and the emerging domestic proletariat. The extent to which—for example—reactionary, bureaucratic, statist, modernist, dispositions prevailed at any given moment over those that were progressive, popular, etc.—or vice versa—within this equilibrium, depended conjuncturally on the one hand upon the state of diplomatic relations with particular imperialist powers and on the other upon the level of combativity of the local working class. The petty-bourgeois character of these class practices may be seen as the most obvious "logic" of the famous Tanzanian policy of "villagization" (by which is meant here not merely the movement of the rural population into nucleated villages, but also the other rural development policies with which it has been associated).

The content and history of this policy and its predominance as a rural development policy over the classical alternatives of "waging on the strong" and popular forms of poor peasant co-operativism, in Tanzania and elsewhere, has been well documented and requires no further description (Bernstein, 1981; Coulson 1982). The fact that villagization represented one of the few conceivable middle paths between these two lines has tended to be overlooked, however. Instead, commentators have tended to discover a continuous, unitary logic for this policy either in its authoritarianism (the post-colonial state simply inherits the characteristics of the colonial state through the socialization of its state personnel) or in its imputed economic consequences (desired creation of a surplus to sustain an expanding bureaucracy). Villagization actually expresses both a conviction that a popular form of poor peasant cooperativism is desirable in a long-term sense, and that the peasants themselves are incapable of either recognising this or—even if they did—of bringing it to fruition. Simultaneously, it expresses a conviction that this cooperativism can be created *ab initio,* but that the peasants are inadequate to this task. It is this specifically petty-bourgeois way of combining an identification with and a fear of the masses which gives villagization its own characteristically contradictory nature, explaining the poles between which villagization policy in Tanzania has vacillated, and which—together with references to the general conjuncture—explains which pole was in the ascendency at which time (1967-1971, alliance between petty bourgeoisie and proletariat, identification with masses, ujamaa villagization; 1971-1975, contradiction between petty bourgeoisie and proletariat, fear of masses, enforced villagization).

Here the question of the peasant-state/capital contradiction may be approached once again. Just as it is incorrect to suggest that the primacy of villagization in the field of rural development policy has created socialism in African socialist countries and Tanzania in particular, so it is also incorrect to claim, as Suzanne Mueller (1980) has, that it has retarded capitalism. What it has tended to do (in combination with the practices of state economic enterprises on which see below) is to restrict the development of capitalism in smallholder agriculture, or at least in those sectors of smallholder agriculture where the state has a monopoly marketing position. (Evidence exists for the development of capitalist poultry and pig farming around Dar es Salaam, for example.)

Marx wrote in *Capital* of "the law that the independent development of merchant's capital is inversely proportional to the degree of development of (industrial) capitalist production" (Marx, 1974b: 328), while Lenin (1972b: 184) added "and vice-versa." This law plays an important part in the explanation of the further unification of one side of the contradiction which Bernstein and others have described. Not only does the capital/wage-labor relation as such give rise generally, through the division of labor, to a more or less unified peasant mass but the specifically petty-bourgeois rural development policy of villagization gives rise to real predominance of middle-peasant interests in village agriculture. This occurs by obliging "kulak" development to take place outside of this sphere (e.g., transport) and thereby simultaneously masks the exploitation of poor peasants, who usually have to migrate at least temporarily in order to maintain their livelihood.

The policy of villagization has given rise to the reality of a politically unified middle peasantry in other ways as well as in Tanzania. Most obviously, the physical concentration of mainly middle-peasants in villages, however undemocratic their political structures, facilitates a pooling and exchange of grievances and experiences, and the formation of common experiences of struggle in a manner generally inconceivable without the existence of a popular peasant movement.

Finally, a third way in which villagization has given rise to the political phenomenon of a unified middle peasantry has been through the solidarity spontaneously generated among villagers by the predominantly arbitrary, bureaucratic, and authoritarian manner of this policy's implementation and enforcement since around 1971. Almost without exception, studies carried out in Tanzanian villages in this period, even those like von Freyhold's (1979) initially motivated by a search for internal class divisions, have found that the advantages to all of presenting a united face against external authority has led not only to the suppression of explicit antagonisms toward local African merchant capitalists, but also usually leads to these very figures being adopted as leaders by villagers on the strength of their potential bargaining-power and prestige vis-à-vis local state personnel. These causes are to a degree mutually reinforcing, of course, since the latter is itself only conceivable on a stable basis in a situation where there is little or no direct exploitation between different peasant heads of household within agriculture. This is of course not to say that there is no actual differentiation withn Tanzanian villages, only that such differentiation has not generally been articulated along class lines.

All this is to approach the question of the Tanzanian state, its policies and its enterprises only via one route, the character of its ruling class. Also necessary is an approach via another—the character of the class struggle in Tanzanian society and its effects upon state forms, in particular the form of regulation of state economic enterprises.

Whereas most African colonial states to an extent resembled the capitalist states of industrialized Europe with respect to the characteristics of the bourgeois state, since they corresponded to an explicit (national-democratic) class struggle, albeit of a rather episodic form, between imperialism and a small white elite on the one hand and the black masses on the other, the post-colonial petty-bourgeois state ceased to do so. The first consequence of state power passing into the hands of black petty bourgeoisies was to relax internal class contradictions and class struggles. Where the petty-bourgeois leadership was itself badly fragmented, the result was a factional, intra-petty-bourgeois struggle, sometimes with the factions acting as direct or indirect proxies of different imperialist powers. Where the petty-bourgeois leadership was relatively cohesive, as in Tanzania, it meant that class contradictions and struggles might diminish almost to vanishing point.

This tendency was reinforced by the fact that independence for these states did not completely solve the national question, which was a regional as well as a local issue (for example, the maintenance of white racist power to the south). To this degree internal class division was further retarded by a continuing national popular solidarity. As a result, tendencies toward centralization, simplification, rationalization and autonomy of personnel from private interests all relaxed.

The post-colonial state acquired a tendency to disunity, duplication of functions, formlessness, autonomy of branches rather than autonomy of the entire apparatus, subjection to personal influence, and so on.

What this account of the "African socialist" state and its ruling class enables to be clarified, which has previously remained unclarified, is how a particular rural development policy might emerge on the one hand, and how a particular form of state economic enterprise might emerge on the other, with the effect that a severe antagonism develops between middle-peasants and state marketing agencies.

A useful starting-point here is the particular modification effect exercised by the presence of an incoherent petty-bourgeois state over the character of large-scale state economic enterprises. This modification effect can be examined with respect both to relations between state enterprises and other public bodies, and the internal organization of these enterprises.

Externally speaking, there is a combination of an (apparently) overwhelming "public sector" of state capitalist enterprises and an almost complete absence of centralized coordination of and control over them. The general disunity, duplication of function, formlessness, autonomy of branches, and so forth, characteristic of state organization generally under "African socialism" (though not exclusive to it) is represented in a particularly clear fashion in the public sector of the economy. It is of interest that two otherwise quite opposed recent analyses of the Tanzanian "macro-economy"—those of the World Bank (1977) and the ILO (1979)—converged precisely on this point.

Both pointed out the extremely low level of coordination between annual budget and plan, foreign exchange budget, annual financial and credit plan, money and credit policy controls of the Board of Trade and the National Bank of Commerce, wage policy, crop price policy, parastatal monitoring and the so-called Basic Industrial Strategy. The World Bank report in particular focused upon the extremely high degree of independence enjoyed by parastatals. The latter "often appear to effectively initiate and decide on major . . . investments without appropriate screening" (World Bank, 1977: 68). Parastatals have a great deal of freedom in negotiating their own deals with transnational companies. No effective yardsticks exist for measuring their performance or for holding them to particular targets. The relation between parastatals and the Treasury is effectively that the latter subsidizes whatever losses the former make. Most important of all, the general convention of setting prices for parastatal products was observed to be a cost-plus procedure, permitting the "ratification of all types of cost increase" (World Bank, 1977: 107).

Confirmation of these tendencies seems to be provided in almost every report commissioned to examine particular branches of Tanzanian state and parastatal activity. One such recent report (IDS, 1981) noted in relation to agricultural development policy that owing to constant inter-ministerial reorganization there had been "an effective loss of control on the part of Kilimo (Ministry of Agriculture) of its field staff. . . . The central Kilimo staff in Dar es Salaam now have very little direct authority over the planning and implementation of agricultural development" (IDS, 1981: 70). A separate Ministry of Livestock Development had been created, while authority over villages remained located in the Prime Minister's Office. Authority over some aspects of decision making in agriculture has also been devolved to parastatals only loosely answerable to the Ministry of Agriculture and with only accidental relations with each other. In addition the three planning units in the agricultural sector, while again formally under Kilimo, operated autonomously and duplicated each other.

Turning to the crop-buying parastatals in particular, a further recent report has claimed that

> The parastatals dealing with tea and tobacco have been unable to organise adequate extension services. Reports of the Marketing Development Bureau on parastatals consistently cite instances of lack of financial control, absence of budgeting. overspending on manpower and staff travel and delayed preparation of annual accounts. The parastatals are also unable to maintain their vehicle fleets: 90 percent of Tobacco Authority Land Rovers, over 30 percent of Coffee Authority trucks and 40 percent of Sisal Authority tractors are apparently off the road [World Bank, 1981: 12-13].

With respect to crop parastatal price setting the situation is of special interest. Whereas industrial parastatals can pass on cost increases of all kinds in the form of raising consumer prices, this is not possible for the crop buying parastatal since the price at which it retails its final product is determined outside its control, at the level of the world market. The result is not a greater discipline in incurring operational and non-operational costs, but a residual approach to calculating producer prices (which then generally seem to be ratified by the Marketing Development Bureau of the Ministry of Agriculture and confirmed by the Cabinet).[9]

According to Frank Ellis (1979, 1980a), since the inception of state monopoly marketing enterprises, official price policy has approached the questions of cost formation and producer price levels by regarding the producer price

> as a residual obtained by first subtracting all other costs of the marketing authority from estimated gross sales proceeds at exportation. This approach appears to involve the largely uncritical acceptance of marketing cost projections presented by the crop authority itself and represents a significant shift away from growers in the relative weight attached to different claims on the marketing margin [Ellis, 1980a: 1-2].

Corresponding to the effective absence of controls over parastatals by other state agencies is also an effective absence of internal control within parastal agencies. No effective mechanisms exist for corrective action based on audited accounts with respect to the different branches of a parastatal. Different cost components are not routinely subjected to prior annual limits on expenditure, determined by up-to-date information on relevant prices and operating coefficients. No rigorous substantiation is required from departments of their individual budgets or increases in them. In the Tanzanian Cashewnut Authority, Ellis even found that accounting of increased costs was actually performed on a post-hoc basis from received monthly bank statements (Ellis, 1980a: 34).

A further consequence of this high degree of internal incoherence is that individual managers with these enterprises can themselves act as enterprises rather than as bearers of a particular structure. Or rather, the structure which individual managers within the enterprise bear is one which lends itself to a high degree of individual disposal of state property. This may be used for individual monetary enrichment on a greater or lesser scale, and/or to expansion of the payroll to include relatives and friends. Equally significantly, little relation exists between this ability and any need to maintain alongside it normal capitalist levels of "efficiency."

Just as villagization reflects a simultaneous identification with and fear of the masses, so the form of the Tanzanian public sector represents again not simply a lack of control and autonomy stemming from the petty-bourgeois character of the state but also a certain petty-bourgeois political position with respect to socialism. The World Bank referred to the effect of this on investment decisions as follows:

> The present system . . . is one where investments are neither guided by a rational framework of market signals, nor by a tightly articulated cen-

tral plan. . . . The outcomes are more the result of bureaucratic interactions between parastatals, parent ministries, the Treasury and aid donnors [World Bank, 1977: 136].

One does not have to share the World Bank's identification of socialism with the plan and capitalism with the "rational market" to accept the general sense of the diagnosis. The reason for the incoherent character of the public sector is exactly the same as the reason for the incoherence of villagization: the strategy of seeking to create "non-capitalist" institutions which are simultaneously divorced from the masses.

As for the concrete effects on the relations between parastatal enterprises and mainly middle-peasant enterprises, the following can be said. What Bernstein calls the simple reproduction squeeze—that is, the most intense form of the contradication between these sets of enterprises—can be seen as the outcome of four aspects of parastatal enterprises:

(1) The consumer goods peasants necessarily have to purchase in order to reproduce themselves and the industrial goods they have to purchase to renew their means of labor are priced on a cost-plus basis which makes them unduly expensive.

(2) These commodities are in any event not obtainable on a regular basis due to the inability of parastatal enterprises to organize their distribution properly.

(3) The money incomes of peasants deriving from the sale of cash crops appear to have declined steadily in real terms, as a result of the producer pricing of cash-crops on a cost-residual basis.

(4) Even if they produce increased quantities of these cash crops peasants cannot be sure that they will be collected or paid for, again as a result of the inability of parastatals to organize properly those aspects of its operation.

Of these aspects of parastatal operation the third is the most important and the most serious in its effects. Ellis (1980b) found that smallholder peasants' terms of trade fell by 25 percent between the years 1969–1970 and 1978–1979. This fall was concentrated in export crops.

In the case of one particular crop, cashewnuts, Ellis's research showed that the unit producer prices as a proportion of the unit export price fell from 69.5 percent in 1970–1971 to 29.7 percent in 1980–1981. The major proportion of cost increases accounting for this decline was in the area of administrative costs of the Cashewnut Authority of Tanzania, which rose by 452 percent gross in the period 1973–1974 to 1978–1979 alone, while throughput of cashews fell catastrophically in the same period. After allowing for bad debts, debt and loan servicing, and so forth, it was found that underlying real administrative costs rose continuously over the decade at a compound rate of 13.7 percent per annum (Ellis, 1980a).

It is important to note that the major response by mainly middle peasants in some traditional cashew growing areas at least has not been to intensify cashew production (which has fallen drastically), nor to revert to "subsistence" (an impossibility, since even the production of use values requires a cash income to purchase certain inputs), but rather to engage in producing charcoal. This is a commodity outside the control of parastatal agencies, the price of which was rising relatively steeply, and the marketing structure of which was characterized by immediate returns, efficient collection and an absence of coercion (Havnevik, 1983: 85).

This fact above shows that under "African socialism" there is no determinant contradiction between "peasants" and capital. "Peasants," urban charcoal merchants and the private transporters acting as their intermediaries maintain relatively good relations, characterized by peasant satisfaction with returns to labor, forms of marketing and so on.

The real contradiction lies only between middle and poor peasant enterprises and the parastatal capitalist enterprises, which are in a position to systematically "cheat" the former out of a part of the revenue realised from cash crops. This "cheatint" is a consequence of the petty-bourgeois forms of organization of both the state generally and state economic enterprises in particular which make possible "mismanagement," individual managerial enrichment, and so on. (The effect of this "cheating" on peasant incomes is then intensified by other political-financial measures of the ruling class, such as a very high international exchange rate for the Tanzanian shilling.)

All this amounts to the fact that the contradiction between peasants and state/capital under African socialism is not a fundamental one between two distinctive sorts of entities. Rather, while extremely severe, it is a conjunctural one concerning forms of exchange between two different kinds of capitalist enterprise. State capitalist economic enterprises constitute the principal aspect of this contradiction by virtue of their modification as enterprises by the general character of the state. Though exchange generally is a necessary product of capitalist relations, the particular character of state economic enterprises in Tanzania is not. It is a matter of a given balance of class forces within a certain capitalist society, which finds expression in a specific state form.

Even within the context of this state form, other sorts of relations between these enterprises are conceivable (though unlikely). It is even possible to conceive of a situation where, given the existing types of enterprise, the peasants' share of the final price relations to state enterprises might fall without any loss of real income if market prices are buoyant.[10] "Cheating" as a matter of fact takes place with respect to the relations described, and this fact is explicable by them. Nonetheless the point remains that no general theory can be constructed on the basis of this "cheating."

CONCLUSION:
SOME POLITICAL IMPLICATIONS

A number of political points may be made in conclusion. The first involves a return to the question of the bureaucratic bourgeoisie. Leaving aside the theoretical problems identified with this concept, it should be pointed out that the general disorganization and disarticulation of state economic activity under "African socialism" casts doubt on the notion that a collective form of capitalist appropriation is taking place. At "best," what is occurring is the enrichment of a small number of individuals who invest their capital anyway in other non-state operations. These individuals in no sense can be regarded as constitutive of a new capitalist ruling class, any more than the individual capitalists who survived the state expropriations of the sixties and seventies collectively constitute a class. In any event, any broadening of enrichment to a wider number of individuals, even if they become capitalists, depends entirely upon the state retaining the fundamentally petty-bourgeois character described. This is not to say that there is no bourgeoisie becoming differentiated (in the sense of being formed and not of splitting up) under African socialism. Actually, the key to the problem is to recover the relational sense of the concept of the bourgeoisie rather than to discover a new status group with a particular income or life-style.

Bourgeoisies are only differentiated in relation to a struggle against other classes and their practices. A bourgeoisie exists in Tanzania insofar as there is a coherent internal critique from a bourgeois perspective (i.e., along the lines of the World Bank) of the petty-bourgeois character of the state and of parastatal enterprises. A bourgeoisie exists in Tanzania insofar as there is a group of state employees and others (their social position is not particularly relevant) who understand the Tanzanian economic crisis as a product of state irrationality and who see solutions to it in either economic liberalization (the rational market solution advocated by the rightwing of the Tanzanian ruling class) *or* the tightly controlled central plan (a "great change" solution sometimes heard advocated in "left wing" Tanzanian circles).

A second political point refers to prospects for proletarian solution, or, more properly a popular national democratic solution in "African socialist" regimes. This is not a matter of extending state property and imposing a "great change" from above (including a plan). It is a matter of identifying specific class alliances and their conditions of existence. In the debate which arose in the University of Dar es Salaam over Shivji's book (Shivji, 1976), one group of contributors put forward the view that a section of the Tanzanian ruling class was progressive and could be won over to national democratic or, rather, New Democratic politics. However, the relation between the section of this class and the proletariat was not specified. In fact, the question of political factions within the Tanzanian ruling class is not particularly significant, since both the ideology of its left section (in so far as it still exists) is predominantly statist and offers no opening towards the masses, and because the more important issue in any case is the political alignment of the petty bourgeoisie generally (from middle peasantry to state personnel). This petty bourgeoisie could only be detached from its existing practices on the basis of being drawn into political activity with the proletariat.

Membership of the petty bourgeoisie is itself never empirically self-evident, but to a large degree is constructed on the basis of particular political and ideological forms. It must be mentioned nonetheless that there seem strong reasons to regard at least two sections of the peasantry as economically occupying the position of wage-labor. First those petty commodity producers who cannot reproduce themselves except through wage-labor as well as household agriculture, and second those within the peasant household (women and children) whose labor-power may generate a degree of accumulation. This is not to argue that there is a ready-made proletariat comprising wage-workers, poor peasants, women and children, but rather to indicate a site where further investigation is of the utmost importance.

Returning to the question of an alliance between the proletariat and petty bourgeoisie, specification of its conditions is clearly even more problematical. However, one inescapable precondition of any progress has to be designated here. No political advance at all can be made in the absence of basic democratic rights for the proletariat to transform its existing subterranean forms of organization into open and independent ones.

A final political issue refers back to the point of departure of this argument: the notion advanced by Bernstein and others of a determinative contradiction between peasantry and state/capital. The political weakness of this formulation can now be gauged. Its principal defect is that it understands class antagonisms under "African socialism" from the viewpoint on the one hand of mainly middle peasant heads of households, whose own position with respect to the exploitation of labor-power is highly problematical, and on the other of the state personnel, with all the characteristics described. It must be stressed that from the viewpoint of these two sections of the petty bourgeoisie the only possible solutions to the contradiction are bourgeois (i.e., one or other of those mentioned above). To take appearances as reality, to take the empirically obvious as the underlying truth ultimately always implies seeing the world and the solution to its problems through the ideology of the bourgeoisie. It is only from the viewpoint of the masses that the truth can be discovered. In the contemporary world dominated by the imperialist phase of capitalism, this means starting from the determinant character of the capital/wage-labor contradiction. It is only around one or other of these poles that forces can be gathered to prolong the existence of capitalism or to transform it, and only within the context of capitalism that class struggles generally—wherever they occur—can be understood.

NOTES

1. A third position claimed to find a widespread tendency towards incipient capitalism in a well-differentiated rich peasantry in these countries. This position seems in the meantime to have become empirically discredited.

2. This review does not examine the solutions to these questions proposed by intellectuals associated with the Communist Party of the Soviet Union. For a critical account of these, and some of their Western versions, see Kelemen (1982).

3. With respect to the issue of whether it makes sense at all, a number of considerations come into play. First and most obvious, "withdrawal" must mean ceasing to be a petty commodity producer, since it means producing no commodities. Hence it is difficult to maintain its consistency with any logic associated with any form of commodity production. Second, there is the question of whether petty commodity production empirically

ever does revert to natural economy. Those who have maintained this with respect to Tanzania (e.g., Hyden, 1980; Ellis, 1982: 277) offer no real evidence. Such evidence as there is appears to point in the other direction. See below and more generally Havnevik (1983: 109-24).

4. Bernstein attempts to indicate the conditions of these occasions.

5. The fact that Emmanuel sees the law of value operating "normally" in poor countries does not imply that he believes money wages there to be at a "normal" level.

6. The question of the particular forms of possession of land in these societies may still be pertinent, however.

7. A survey by Havnevik (1983) of Rufiji district, Coast Region, Tanzania, found that about six out of every ten economically active persons regularly divided labor between craft activity and agriculture. Part of this district enjoyed good access to markets and raw material supplies in Dar es Salaam. Nevertheless, the major markets and raw material sources were local ones, and the combination of crafts and agriculture was significant even in the areas of the district with the worst communication with Dar es Salaam.

8. It could be argued that the very recent (March 1983) decision by the Tanzanian government to create private property in land poses a major empirical difficulty for this argument, in addition to the theoretical difficulties explored here.

9. Considerable dispute exists over the role of the Marketing Development Bureau (MDB) in Tanzania. The MDB is a group of FAO-selected expatriates, financed by the World Bank and responsible to the Ministry of Agriculture and the Cabinet. The task of the MDB is to construct initial price recommendations which may then be modified after discussion in relevant parastatals. Ellis and the World Bank's own reports (especially World Bank, 1981a) imply that this process has had a largely ritual status. A recent study (IDS, 1981: 44-5) suggests a more serious content in this task, but a consistent pattern of overruling. Payer (1982: 20) following R.H. Green, has argued, however, that its role was a major one, that it worked hand in glove with the World Bank, and that the latter chose to scapegoat it. Clearly there is more at stake in this debate than a simple evaluation of the role of the MDB.

10. This has been the case with the privately marketed commodity of charcoal. See Havnevik (1983: 85).

REFERENCES

BERNSTEIN, H. (1982). "Industrialisation, development and dependency," in H. Alavi and T. Shanin (eds.), An Introduction to the Sociology of "Developing" Societies. London: Macmillan

———(1981). "Notes on state and peasantry in Tanzania." Review of African Political Economy 21 (May-September): 44-62.

———(1979). "Sociology of underdevelopment vs. sociology of development?" in D. Lehman (ed.), Development Theory: Four Critical Studies. London: Cass.

———(1977). "Notes on capital and peasantry." Review of African Political Economy 10 (September-December): 60-73.

———(1976a). "Capital and peasantry in the epoch of imperialism." University of Dar es Salaam, Economic Research Bureau.

————(1976b). "Underdevelopment and the law of value: a critique of Kay." Review of African Political Economy 6 (May–August): 51–64.

BOESEN, J. (1979). "Tanzania: from ujamaa to villagization," in B. Mwansasu and C. Pratt (eds.), Towards Socialism in Tanzania. Dar es Salaam: Tanzania Publishing House.

COULSON, A. (1982). Tanzania: A Political Economy. Oxford: Clarendon Press.

EMMANUEL, A. (1972). Unequal Exchange. London: New Left Books.

ELLIS, F. (1982). "Agricultural price policy in Tanzania." World Development 10(4): 263–283.

————(1980a). "Marketing costs and the processing of cashewnuts in Tanzania: an analysis of the marketing margin and the potential level of the producer price." University of Dar es Salaam, Economic Research Bureau.

————(1980b). "Agricultural pricing policy in Tanzania 1970–1979: implications for agricultural output, rural incomes and crop marketing costs." Seminar on Development, Employment and Equity, Dar es Salaam. (unpublished)

————(1979). "A preliminary analysis of the decline of Tanzania cashewnut production 1974–1979." University of Dar es Salaam, Economic Research Bureau.

GOODMAN, D. and M. REDCLIFT. (1981). From Peasant to Proletarian. Oxford: Basil Blackwell.

HAVNEVIK, K. (1983). Analysis of Rural Production and Incomes, Rufiji District, Tanzania. Bergen: Chr. Michelsen Inst.

HYDEN, G. (1980). Beyond Ujamaa in Tanzania. London: Heinemann.

Institute for Development Studies (1981). Smallholder Food Production in Tanzania. Brighton: Author.

International Labour Organisation (1979). Towards Self-Reliance: Development, Employment and Equity Issues. Addis Ababa: Author.

————(1981). Basic Needs in Danger: A Basic Needs-Oriented Development Strategy for Tanzania. ILO Technical Supplements. Addis Ababa: Author.

KAUTSKY, K. (1976). (Summary of) The Agrarian Question. Economy and Society 5(1): 2-49.

KELEMEN, P. (1982). "Critique of 'The Ethiopian Revolution'" in J. Savile and R. Miliband (eds.), The Socialist Register. London: Merlin Press.

LENIN, V. I. (1972a). A Characterisation of Economic Romanticism. Collected Works 2. Moscow: Progress.

————(1972b). The Development of Capitalism in Russia. Collected Works 3. Moscow: Progress.

————(1972c). The Agrarian Programme of Social Democracy in the First Russian Revolution 1905–1907. Collected Works 13. Moscow: Progress.

————(1972d). Marxism and Revisionism. Collected Works 15. Moscow: Progress.

————(1976). The Economic Content of Narodnism. Collected Works 1. Moscow: Progress.

MARX, K. (1974a). Capital, Volume 1. London: Lawrence and Wishart.

————(1974b). Capital, Volume 3. London: Lawrence and Wishart.

————(1973a). Grundrisse. Hammondsworth: Penguin.

————(1973b). "The Eighteenth Brumaire of Louis Bonaparte," in K. Marx and F. Engels, Selected Works in One Volume. London: Lawrence and Wishart.

————(1972). Theories of Surplus Value, Part 3. Moscow: Progress.

————(1969). Theories of Surplus Value, Part 1. Moscow: Progress.

——and ENGELS, F. (1976a). The German Ideology. Collected Works Volume 5. London: Lawrence and Wishart.

——(1976b). The Poverty of Philosophy. Collected Works 6. London: Lawrence and Wishart.

MUELLER, S. (1980). "Retarded capitalism in Tanzania," pp. 203–226 in J. Savile and R. Miliband (eds.), The Socialist Register. London: Merlin Press.

NEOCOSMOS, M. (1982). Agrarian Reform and the Development of Capitalism in Agriculture. Ph.D. thesis, University of Bradford.

——(1981). "Marx's third class: the theorisation of a class of landlords under capitalism." Presented at the British Sociological Association Annual Conference, Aberystwyth.

PAYER, C. (1982). "Tanzania and the World Bank." DERAP Working Paper A285. Bergen: Chr. Michelson Institute.

RAIKES, P. (1978). "Rural differentiation and class formation in Tanzania." Journal of Peasant Studies 5(3).

SAUL, J. (1974). "The State in post-colonial societies: Tanzania," in J. Savile and R. Miliband (eds.), The Socialist Register. London: Merlin Press.

SAYER, D. (1979). Marx's Method. Hassocks: Harvester.

SHIVJI, I. (1976). Class Struggles in Tanzania. New York: Monthly Review Press.

Von FREYHOLD, M. (1979). Ujamaa Villages in Tanzania. London: Heinemann.

World Bank (1981). Economic Memorandum on Tanzania 3086-TA. Washington, DC.

——(1977). Tanzania: Basic Economic Report (Main Report) 1616-TA. Washington, DC.

5

ECONOMIE POLITIQUE DE LA GUINEE (1958-1981)

ALAIN COURNANEL

On peut
dater les débuts de la mise en valeur coloniale de la Guinée des années
1948–1950, alors que l'on envisageait de substituer à la seule activité
de traite une économie résolument orientée (partout où cela paraissait
concevable) vers l'exploitation minière, secondairement vers l'industrie. En effet, les richesses minières et les potentialités énergétiques de
l'Afrique conduisaient à envisager non seulement l'extraction de
matières premières, mais la réalisation de processus de transformation
sur place (Pré, 1951 et Moussa, 1957). La Guinée faisait précisément
partie de ces pays appelés à prendre une importance considérable
dans le cadre d'une stratégie qui visait alors à constituer une "Eura-
frique française" puissante. La mise en valeur de la Guinée devait être
axée vers la production de deux métaux essentiels, le fer et l'aluminium, dont les Etats-Unis et le Commonwealth avaient grand besoin.
La France parvenant à satisfaire ses besoins, les demandes non satis-
faites du reste de l'Europe et de l'Amérique du Nord conduisaient à
réunir des capitaux européens et américains pour constituer une
société internationale, opération qui rapporterait des devises à la zone
Franc à un moment où sa balance était déséquilibrée.
  Pour les firmes multinationales, cet attrait subit pour les gisements
guineéns dont l'existence était déjà connus avant la Seconde Guerre

Author's Note: This chapter was written and sent to press before the death of
President Sékou Touré on March 26, 1984, and consequently does not refer to
subsequent changes which have taken place since that date.

mondiale, s'expliquait par des raisons de coût, mais aussi par le mouvement général de concentration dans l'industrie de l'aluminium. Les premiers plans quadriennaux en Afrique occidentale française (A.O.F.) démarrent en 1948. Des capitaux publics viendront s'ajouter au premier flux de capitaux privés qui s'investit alors dans l'industrie minière. Ces investissements favorisèrent naturellement l'implantation d'entreprises privées d'importance secondaire.

A partir du second Plan quadriennal français (1953), des projets beaucoup plus grandioses sont envisagés: barrages, production accrue de bauxite, mais aussi production d'alumine, d'aluminium, d'acier. Dans l'attente de ces réalisations, de nouvelles enterprises se créent, attirées par un marché intérieur dont l'extension résultait de l'arrivée massive d'Européens, de la croissance du nombre des salariés guinéens, et des hausses généralisées de salaires. L'embryon d'industrie né de cette conjoncture était orienté soit vers le marché extérieur (trois entreprises), soit vers le marché intérieur (huilerie, savonnerie, fabrique de limonades, etc.), en tout une dizaine d'entreprises de taille réduite si l'on ne tient pas compte des entreprises de travaux publics, de transports, de services, qui étaient évidemment les plus nombreuses. Les entreprises minières importantes (les Bauxites de Kassa et la Minière de Conakry pour le fer) sont exclues de ce décompte, ainsi que les deux sociétés (beaucoup plus artisanales) qui exploitaient le diamant.

Durant ces dix dernières années de colonisation, 42 milliards de F C.F.A. étaient investis, la masse monétaire septuplait, le produit intérieur et le nombre de salariés doublaient, le salaire minimum interprofessionnel garanti, S.M.I.G. avait presque quadruplé.

Pour les grands projets mentionnés plus haut, les investissements nécessaires devaient atteindre 115 milliards de F C.F.A.[1], chiffre énorme quand on sait que le budget du territoire n'atteignait pas 5 milliards, et que son produit intérieur brut n'atteindra 39 milliards qu'en 1959. Ces réalisations supposaient une intégration véritablement complète dans le système capitaliste international. A Fria, le capital était souscrit par de puissants groupes: Péchiney en France était la troisième sur les 500 premières grandes enterprises. Ugine était étroitement associée à Péchiney par un réseau de participations. Olin Mathieson, contrôlé par Rockefeller et la Chase Manhattan Bank, était également un groupe puissant produisant une gamme très étendue de biens parmi lesquels les métaux non ferreux ne représentaient que 12% de son chiffre d'affaires. Le groupe suisse, par participation personnelle, était lié à de très grosses affaires (Nestlé-Société de Banque Suisse-Crédit Commercial de France). La production était limitée par les achats des membres du consortium. Ce qui permettait d'écrire: "En ce sens, Fria est bien dominé par la conjoncture très américaine" (Bell, 1963). L'Etat français participait aussi au financement du projet.

En 1958, l'économie guinéenne se présentait de la façon suivante: l'agriculture vivrière était régie par le mode de production marchand simple, et le secteur agricole produisant pour l'exportation par le mode de production capitaliste ou par une combinaison des deux (avec domination du mode de production capitaliste). Le secteur industriel quasi-inexistant était évidemment régi par des rapports de production de type capitaliste. Néanmoins l'essentiel du surplus d'origine agricole était accaparé par le capital commercial colonial dont les intérêts s'opposaient donc aussi bien à ceux des petits producteurs qu'à ceux du capitalisme agraire et du petit capital commercial guinéen dont il freinait la croissance. En outre, une fraction du capital étranger était investie dans l'industrie minière et semblait devoir rapidement supplanter le capital commercial traditionnellement dominant.

L'impérialisme français exploitait le prolétariat toujours embryonnaire et une fraction de la paysannerie (celle qui était réduite à la rémunération de sa force de travail, en dépit du maintien formel de la propriété paysanne). La nouvelle stratégie de l'impérialisme entendait s'orienter vers une exploitation beaucoup plus intense à travers la croissance du secteur industriel et minier.

Durant cette dernière décennie du régime colonial, la croissance économique avait accompagné une lutte politique serrée. Les modifications politiques et sociales intervenues sur le continent africain rendaient nécessaires des modifications profondes du système colonial. La loi-cadre Defferre allait apporter sur le plan institutionnel un début de "solution," solution rendue plausible par l'évolution du Rassemblement démocratique africain (R.D.A.) depuis 1950-1951. Dans cette perspective, la montée au pouvoir du Parti démocratique de Guinée (P.D.G.) dans le cadre de l'autonomie interne, ne compromettait absolument pas les projets économiques envisagés par le capitalisme international.

Le début de mise en valeur s'était accompagné de la croissance d'une catégorie intermédiaire d'employés et fonctionnaires africains, mieux rémunérée mais d'autant plus consciente de sa subordination et des obstacles opposés à sa promotion. Son rôle effectif de plus en plus important et sa capacité théorique en feront l'élément moteur de la lutte contre la colonisation. Dans le cadre du système des rapports de production introduit par la colonisation, cette catégorie constituait une fraction de la petite bourgeoisie. Non-producteurs, petits employés ou cadres subalternes (plus rarement moyens), ils contribuaient à la reproduction des rapports de production dans la mesure où celle-ci est assurée pour une part par le fonctionnement des appareils d'Etat (Althusser, 1970: 16), en même temps qu'ils luttaient contre ces rapports de production (Bettelheim, 1970: 57 et suite) et la division en classes qu'ils impliquaient.

Au moment de l'autonomie puis de l'indépendance, si la bourgeoisie africaine classique dans un tel contexte (planteurs, transporteurs, commerçants) restait embryonnaire, par contre une fraction extrêmement importante de cette classe venait de se former: celle qui après avoir constitué les couches subalternes de l'appareil bureaucratique, partageait maintenant le contrôle de l'appareil territorial avec la bureaucratie coloniale. Cette fraction de la bourgeoisie s'était donnée une base populaire à partir des organisations de masse (partis, syndicats) qui s'étaient développées à travers la lutte contre la colonisation. Elle était désormais associée au contrôle et au fonctionnement de l'appareil d'Etat. Jouant un rôle dans les rapports d'exploitation, elle avait pour perspective réelle (nous ne voulons pas dire consciente) l'indépendance politique sans remise en cause des rapports de production.

C'est ce que nous tenterons de montrer en abordant successivement les stratégies économiques mises en oeuvre dans la première section, et les rapports de classe qui en constituaient le soubassement dans la seconde.

STRATEGIES DE DEVELOPPEMENT ET EVOLUTION ECONOMIQUE DEPUIS L'INDEPENDANCE

Nous distinguerons deux phases dans la stratégie guinéenne: la première correspond à une tentative pour fonder en priorité la croissance sur l'accumulation nationale, la seconde s'en remet explicitement à l'intervention du capital international. L'analyse sera menée à trois niveaux: (1) Planification et croissance; (2) Inflation et crise financière; (3) Les rapports avec le capital international.

Planification et croissance

La rupture voulue par la France, l'isolement de la Guinée en Afrique (à l'exception du Ghana), la campagne tendant à présenter ce pays comme une tête de pont du communisme, l'aide offerte par les pays socialistes, rendaient inévitable la tentative de croissance auto-centrée. Celle-ci s'appuyait sur un processus de centralisation écono-mique recommandé par des experts dont l'orientation clairement marxiste et le travail de préparation du plan impliquaient une orien-tation socialiste pour le pays. La priorité devait revenir aux investis-sements dans le secteur productif, l'accumulation nationale devait représenter 50% au moins des ressources accumulées, le taux d'ac-cumulation nationale passant en trois ans de 8 à 12% du Revenu National.

L'inspiration marxiste de la Mission de Planification dirigée par Charles Bettelheim, assisté de Jacques Charrière, était repérable à plusieurs niveaux: (a) le développement ne devait dépendre ni des lois du marché, ni de la concurrence ou du profit. Le plan était impératif; (b) les objectifs de croissance étaient fixés en fonction des conditions locales, mais en contrepoint Bettelheim rappelait constamment les performances soviétiques et chinoises; (c) Bettelheim posait de la manière suivante le problème de l'utilisation du surplus national:

> la sphère de la circulation est celle au sein de laquelle se condense la majeure partie du surplus économique qui pourrait être disponible pour l'investissement. Ce surplus prend actuellement la forme de profits commerciaux appropriés en majeure partie par le capital commer-cial étranger. De tels profits économiques représentent pour l'essentiel l'excédent de la valeur nette de la production nationale sur les revenus des producteurs; mais, pour le moment, cet excédent, au lieu de consti-tuer la base de l'accumulation nationale (source de toute croissance économique durable), sert à alimenter une accumulation extérieure au pays, d'où la constante pénurie de capital dont souffre apparemment l'économie guinéenne. Cette pénurie n'est que la contrepartie de l'éva-sion vers l'étranger d'une large fraction du surplus économique national. La mise en place d'organismes commerçants d'Etat doit mettre un terme, le plus rapidement possible, à cette déperdition de force écono-mique, afin de placer le surplus économique national tout entier au service du développement national [Bettelheim, 1959: 5].

L'idée fondamentale était donc d'éviter le blocage de la croissance en arrêtant, grâce à l'étatisation des organismes commerciaux, les transferts de valeur vers l'extérieur. Cette mesure devait en outre avoir une série d'autres effets:

- Ecarter la croissance et la domination d'une éventuelle bourgeoisie commerçante, avec "pour corollaire l'appropriation privée d'une partie du fonds d'accumulation nationale" (Bettelheim, 1959: 5).

- Permettre une diversification (rendue inévitable par l'intransigeance française) des courants commerciaux.

- Parvenir à une autonomie croissante vis-à-vis du marché international, en décrochant les prix intérieurs des prix extérieurs pour les stabiliser (Bettelheim, 1959: 2).

Toujours dans l'optique d'une transition vers le socialisme, Bettelheim soulignait encore la nécessité d'une nouvelle politique des salaires et des traitements qui rompait avec l'échelle de rémunérations léguée par la colonisation. Ce type de problématique qui situait le clivage décisif entre "population rurale" et titulaires de salaires et traitements considérés en bloc, ou qui insistait sur le blocage de la croissance du fait des tranferts de valeurs, n'était pas de nature à faciliter la compréhension du problème réel qui se posait alors, celui de la constitution et de la croissance d'une bourgeoisie d'Etat. Ce texte indiquait néanmoins les orientations fondamentales des auteurs du plan. Après une dernière note rédigée à l'intention des autorités guinéennes en octobre 1960 (trois mois après le lancement du plan), Bettelheim et Charrière cessèrent définitivement leur collaboration.

En réalité, la stratégie guinéenne s'orientait dans un premier temps vers une croissance fondée sur l'appropriation de "l'excédent de la valeur nette de la production nationale sur les revenus des producteurs", pour reprendre l'expression de Bettelheim. Cette phase mettait en mouvement un processus d'étatisation qui ouvrait la voie à une certaine autonomie économique (concrétisée par une zone monétaire spécifique, un système bancaire et commercial étatisés, l'accès à une aide publique extérieure importante consentie à des conditions financières très avantageuses) sans transformation des rapports de production, qu'il s'agisse de la place de la Guinée dans la division internationale du travail, ou du fonctionnement des rapports d'exploitation à l'intérieur de la formation sociale. Avec ces mesures de centralisation, une bourgeoisie d'Etat se constitua directement en fraction hégémonique de la classe dominante, dans la mesure où elle exerçait un contrôle absolu sur la monnaie, le secteur bancaire, plus partiel sur le secteur commercial, et possédait le monopole absolu des moyens de production dans le secteur industriel en voie de formation. D'origine petite bourgeoise, elle commence à se constituer en fraction de la bourgeoisie, lors de la phase d'autonomie interne, et devient véritablement la fraction dominante de cette bourgeoisie avec le processus de centralisation.

Choisissant, pour financer sa croissance, d'investir une fraction de la plus-value appropriée (d'origine essentiellement agricole au départ, mais avec une contribution plus importante du secteur industriel attendue par la suite), la bourgeoisie d'Etat sous-estimait gravement les difficultés de l'entreprise. En premier lieu cette politique prétendait promouvoir une croissance rapide, au moment où la bourgeoisie d'Etat refusait pour elle-même tout effort d'austérité. De plus, il se produisit simultanément, dans tous les domaines, un processus de lutte, d'interpénétration entre capital public et privé, de constitution de capitaux privés à partir du secteur d'Etat, processus qui rendait impossible l'effort d'accumulation prévu par les planificateurs.

Le Plan triennal (1960-1963) fut donc un échec (Cournanel, 1968: 432 et suite) par rapport à l'optique qui était celle de Bettelheim et de son équipe. Et s'il fut bien en définitive un "plan de transition", ce n'était certes pas dans le sens escompté. Le lancement de ce plan devait être l'occasion d'une mobilisation des travailleurs. Le Ministère du plan avait pour tâche d'orienter, coordonner l'ensemble de l'activité économique, d'assurer le financement et le respect de l'échéancier des actions prévues. L'objectif immédiat était la recherche d'un certain degré d'indépendance économique.

Aussi bien dans la phase de préparation que pendant la mise en pratique du plan, des évolutions significatives vont se produire du point de vue qui nous importe ici:

(1) En pratique, en dépit des moyens d'encadrement dont disposait le P.D.G., il n'y eut aucune véritable mobilisation des villages et régions pour la préparation du Plan. Par contre, avant même sa mise en application, le Plan connut plusieurs versions successives sous la pression de la bourgeoisie d'Etat et des plus hautes instances du Parti. La logique de ces variations était fort claire: l'augmentation du budget du plan, mais en contrepartie un poids croissant de la contribution extérieure, et une diminution de la part du secteur productif (tandis qu'augmentait très nettement le pourcentage de l'infrastructure qui s'élevait de 20 à 38%).

La bourgeoisie d'Etat entendait donc s'assurer en premier lieu une masse importante de ressources, à l'occasion d'un plan qui, de par le contexte international de l'époque, était appelé à un certain retentissement. L'accent mis sur l'infrastructure renvoyait au rôle de la bourgeoisie d'Etat comme intermédiaire entre la production agricole et le capital marchand d'une part, et les marchés extérieurs d'autre part. Cette situation favorisait d'emblée l'interpénétration avec le commerce privé et allait jouer un rôle décisif dans les fluctuations de la politique commerciale que nous évoquerons plus loin.

(2) Les tâches énormes du Ministère du plan supposaient l'existence en son sein d'organismes de gestion très étoffés, mais aussi de prérogatives particulières au niveau politique. Ces deux conditions ne seront jamais remplies. La gestion restera de façon constante marquée par l'absence de coordination au niveau central et le désordre dans l'exécution des actions. L'ordre des réalisations, établi en fonction des disponibilités financières, était bouleversé par des initiatives anarchiques dont les conséquences globales restaient inconnues. Ajoutons que l'opportunité et la rentabilité d'actions précipitamment décidées, étaient tout à fait discutables. Par ailleurs, il est établi que la rentabilité des investissements est tributaire de l'ordre dans lequel ils sont entrepris. Ce désordre, résultant d'une absence flagrante de coordination, provoquait une baisse du rendement général, contribuait à diminuer l'efficacité des sommes investies, donc à favoriser les tensions inflationnistes. D'autant que la banque centrale, pour permettre au Plan d'honorer les obligations financières imprévues qui s'imposaient à lui, devait régulièrement lui consentir des avances. Des mesures de décentralisation furent prises durant le second semestre 1961. Nous aurons l'occasion d'apprécier l'incidence de ces mesures sur le plan commercial.

Sur le plan agricole, la décentralisation était censée faciliter la réalisation du Plan. Le principe admis était que les régions ne pouvaient modifier les dimensions des actions prévues qu'en finançant le supplément des dépenses nécessaires. Dans la pratique, on aboutit aux résultats suivants: les actions régulièrement modifiées, le furent fréquemment dans un sens économiquement négatif. Souvent, les fonds destinés à financer les opérations productives furent consacrés à faire face à des dépenses de fonctionnement (qui logiquement devaient être supportées par les budgets locaux) ou à des dépenses productives mais non prévues par le plan. L'organisme du Plan, informé a posteriori, était impuissant. Tout remboursement était évidemment inconcevable, puisque des violations s'expliquaient précisément par l'incapacité des budgets régionaux à faire face aux dépenses de fonctionnement courantes. Si l'on considère un instant le rôle déterminant attribué à la croissance de l'agriculture, on voit d'emblée l'importance des détournements généralisés qui se produisirent, alors que la croissance démographique, le taux d'urbanisation, l'importance des sommes lancées dans le circuit conduisaient à une élévation rapide de la demande.

L'anarchie se manifestait principalement dans le domaine agricole puisque l'industrie était encore quasi-inexistante. Mais en dehors du secteur productif, tous les domaines où s'exerçait l'action économique de l'Etat étaient marqués par cette absence de gestion centralisée, ou même de simple coordination, et par la multiplication des initiatives désordonnées. Cependant, le vocabulaire que nous utilisons ici (désordre, anarchie) ne doit pas faire illusion. Il ne s'agit pas de faire de ces phénomènes concrets les effets d'un quelconque dysfonctionnement imputable à l'incompétence. L'anarchie n'était que la manifestation de la tendance spontanée de la bourgeoisie d'Etat à se transformer partiellement en bourgeoisie privée, de la libération de l'initiative individuelle, du relâchement, sous cette impulsion, des directives centrales.

On sait les résultats du Plan triennal: un considérable écart entre les objectifs et les réalisations, en dépit d'une dépense globale de près de 50 milliards (alors que 40 milliards environ étaient prévus). On peut évaluer la croissance du Produit intérieur brut (P.I.B.) à 20% en 4 ans. Il faut tout de même préciser que toutes les actions industrielles initialement prévues, ou décidées au cours du plan furent réalisées en majorité entre 1964 et 1967, soit durant les premières années du Plan septennal (à l'exception bien sûr de celles qui furent abandonnées). Du reste, c'est à partir de 1967 que l'on peut vraiment parler de stagnation générale en Guinée.

Le Plan septennal (1964-1971) ne représentera guère plus qu'un simulacre de planification. Suppression du Ministère du plan dont les services squelettiques (20 à 25 personnes) sont intégrés au Ministère d'Etat chargé des finances et du plan. Ce plan démarra sans qu'aucun département ministériel n'ait élaboré de projets précis, chiffrés. Un an après, le budget n'en était pas encore déterminé. Il fut à maintes reprises modifié. En mai 1968, son montant atteignant 134 milliards de francs guinéens, (F.G.)[2]: 35 milliards seulement pour l'industrie, les mines et l'agriculture réunies; 17 milliards pour l'énergie; 70 milliards pour l'infrastructure; 8 pour l'habitat, etc. La part de l'extérieur dans le financement était d'au moins 70% (les possibilités nationales d'accumulation étant manifestement surestimées), mais ces ressources extérieures n'étaient pas même certaines. Concernant la répartition des fonds alloués au secteur productif, l'agriculture recevait 12% des dépenses prévues (près de 16 milliards), l'industrie et les mines environ 15% (plus de 20 milliards).

Les proportions que nous venons de donner démentaient toutes les déclarations d'intentions sur la priorité accordée à l'industrialisation en liaison avec le développement agricole. Des statistiques de mai

1968 montrent qu'à cette époque, soit trois ans avant la fin du Plan septennal, on n'avait pas investi le cinquième des sommes prévues. En réalité, tout était éclipsé par les projets de Boké (bauxite-alumine-aluminium) revenus au premier Plan, et par les espoirs de voir se réaliser le barrage du Konkouré. Dans l'esprit des dirigeants, la future économie guinéenne devait visiblement s'articuler autour de ces deux projets. Il ne faut donc pas s'étonner si ce plan s'est achevé en 1971-1972 sans avoir fait l'objet, à notre connaissance tout au moins, de commentaires substantiels.

En 1973, la Guinée lançait son troisième plan, ce dernier devant couvrir la période 1973-1978. Son montant était fixé à 590 milliards de F.G., 59 milliards de Sylis, (Economiste du Tiers Monde, 1974: 21). Les mines, l'énergie et les transports étaient les axes essentiels du plan dont le total (en F.G. courants) rendait bien compte de l'importance du phénomène inflationniste: 42 milliards devaient être financés par l'aide extérieure, soit 70% du total.

De fait, ce plan mettait logiquement au centre de ses préoccupa-tions les réalisations minières si longtemps attendues, et en voie de réalisation principalement sous l'égide du capital international. Mais dans ces conditions, et c'était déjà le cas pour le Plan septennal, il était plus juste de parler de listes de projets ou de programmes d'investissement. Il est assez significatif que ce Plan ait décidé de con-sacrer 10 milliards environ de F.G. à l'élevage, l'agriculture et l'arti-sanat réunis (soit 5% du total), alors que par ailleurs il était question de donner une priorité absolue à la production de denrées alimen-taires. Le plan était on ne peut plus clairement subordonné à une stratégie dont la concrétisation dépendait du capital étranger.

Nous n'avons eu connaissance d'aucune information sur le déroule-ment et les résultats de ce troisième plan. Un nouveau Plan quin-quennal (1978-1983) était projeté; on semble y avoir renoncé. En 1980 enfin, la Guinée a annoncé son quatrième Plan de développe-ment (1981-1985). Son montant (Ind. et Tr. d'O.M., 1981: 16 et Marchés Tropicaux, 1980: p. 2477) atteindra 38 milliards de Sylis dont 32 seront consacrés aux investissements et 6 à l'amortissement de la dette publique. Le secteur productif recevra 59% des investisse-ments qui seront ventilés comme suit:

Agriculture, eaux et forêts	22%
Elevage et pêche	3%

Industrie	10%
Energie	9%
Mines et géologie	8%
Travaux publics	7%

L'objectif poursuivi est un taux de croissance de 5% du P.I.B. pendant la période couverte par le plan. Un élément positif est à souligner au moins au niveau des intentions: la part consacrée au secteur agricole et assimilé est beaucoup plus élevée que par le passé. A plus long terme, les responsables souhaitent parvenir à un taux de croissance de 10% en 1990 (Marchés Tropicaux, 1981b: 1862 et suite). En définitive, depuis l'Indépendance, quelle croissance la Guinée a-t-elle connue?

On peut partir d'un P.I.B. de 40 milliards de F.G. en 1959-1960. Le niveau atteint à la fin de la décennie tournait autour de 70 milliards (Amin, 1973: 398 et Cournanel, 1976: 36-37). En appliquant pour la période 1970-1977 (estimations de la Banque Mondiale) un taux de croissance de 5,4% (Hodgkinson, 1982: 473 et Ind. et Tr. d'O.M., 1981) à monnaie constante, on parvenait à un produit de 101 milliards, soit une multiplication du produit par 2,5 en 18 ans, à monnaie constante.

De 1964, première année depuis l'Indépendance où avait été établi sur place un tableau des ressources et emplois, à 1979, le produit par tête avait seulement progressé de 36% (Cournanel, 1968: 443-444). En francs courants la croissance avait été considérable, puisqu'à partir de 1977 le Produit national dépassait le milliard de dollars. Rappelons qu'en 1964 déjà, alors que le P.I.B. ne dépassait pas 55 milliards en francs constants, il était supérieur à 140 milliards en francs courants. Mais il s'agit là d'un problème sur lequel nous allons revenir dans le point suivant. Précisons pour finir qu'en 1979 l'agriculture représentait 40% du P.I.B. (42% en 1964), les mines 18,8% (5% en 1964), l'industrie de transformation 3% (29% en 1964), ce qui globalement traduisait une évolution négative du secteur productif.

Inflation et crise financière

Sur le plan commercial, la Guinée a successivement connu (de 1960 à 1980) l'étatisation-centralisation, la décentralisation-libéralisation (libéralisation signifiant ici le développement du commerce privé), puis le retour à un contrôle plus centralisé de l'Etat qui ne fera que se renforcer après 1967 quand le rationnement sera instauré, à nouveau la libéralisation à partir de 1978. Ces oscillations ont ponctué la formation de capitaux privés, l'édification de fortunes personnelles au détriment des ressources publiques.

Des calculs détaillés faits en 1960 établissaient que sur un total d'importations de 7 milliards de F C.F.A. (Cournanel, 1968: 226–227), le secteur d'Etat pouvait réaliser un profit net de 2,5 milliards. Les importations, en très rapide augmentation, atteignirent 12,3 milliards (en 1960) et 17,9 milliards (en 1961). Après un an de fonctionnement, les deux comptoirs qui constituaient l'armature du commerce d'Etat avaient pourtant réalisé moins de 2 milliards de F.G. de bénéfices. C'est la somme qu'ils versèrent au Plan.

Dans ces conditions, il fut décidé de liquider les deux comptoirs et de transformer en entreprises autonomes (contrôlées par les autorités locales), leurs succursales régionales. Parallèlement étaient créées des sociétés nationales spécialisées d'importation et d'exportation. Les comptoirs régionaux, devenus autonomes, s'endettèrent lourdement auprès des sociétés nationales commerciales. Cet endettement atteignait plus de 2,6 milliards de F.G. quand l'expérience fut arrêtée. A titre de comparaison, précisons qu'au cours des années suivantes les montants nets des bénéfices des sociétés nationales d'importation furent les suivants: 2,04 milliards en 1964, 2,39 milliards en 1965, 1,9 milliards en 1966. C'est dire l'importance des pertes subies par les ressources publiques durant la phase de décentralisation-libéralisation, mais aussi la modicité des profits des entreprises publiques dans les phases de renforcement du secteur d'Etat. Après 1964, le contrôle de l'Etat sur le secteur commercial n'est plus remis en question. Les conditions économiques ambiantes (stagnation et pénurie extrêmes à partir des années 1968–1969) expliquent que dès 1967, et surtout à partir de 1968, le rationnement ait été instauré pour les principaux produits alimentaires. Néanmoins le ravitaillement des boutiques des Comités de quartier ou de village du P.D.G. qui procèdent à la répartition, sera longtemps assuré par des commerçants privés qui feront la liaison entre les Sociétés nationales d'Etat fournissant les marchandises et les boutiques en question. On imagine les effets d'un tel système sur l'extension du marché parallèle.

Dans les années soixante dix, on allait utiliser les Pouvoirs révolutionnaires locaux (P.R.L.), dans les campagnes pour réaliser la vente directe et groupée des récoltes au réseau commercial d'Etat. Les P.R.L. assuraient également le ravitaillement des populations, aussi bien en milieu urbain que rural. A la suite des mesures prises sous prétexte de combattre l'inflation, le commerce privé va cesser à peu près toute activité à partir de 1975. Les paysans étaient contraints de livrer leurs récoltes aux magasins des P.R.L., gérés par les représentants du Parti. Les échanges se faisaient de plus en plus en nature. Les transactions étaient l'objet d'une surveillance constante de la police économique.

Au plan national, l'organisation se présentait (Horoya: 1976) ainsi: IMPORTEX (monopole des importations et des exportations)→ 4 sociétés sectorielles; COFICOM→ Enterprises nationales spécialisées. Au niveau régional, COFICOM s'articulait sur les Entreprises régionales de commerce, les Entreprises commerciales d'arrondissement, enfin les P.R.L.

Les émeutes de 1977 obligèrent le régime à reculer. Le commerce privé reprenait à partir de 1978–1979, et les agriculteurs furent autorisés à vendre eux-mêmes leurs produits sur les marchés.

Après avoir mis sur pied une monnaie et un système bancaire propres, la Guinée allait rapidement avoir recours à la création monétaire pour assurer le financement des investissements, des découverts de gestion ou des déficits administratifs courants. La Banque Centrale consentait directement aux entreprises et établissements travaillant à l'exécution du plan des crédits à long terme. Les données essentielles de la situation de la Banque Centrale en juin 1965 sont présentées dans le Tableau I.

Les chiffres avancés par Samir Amin (1971) sont encore supérieurs aux évaluations que nous présentons ici, puisqu'il évalue les crédits aux enterprises d'Etat à 41,5 milliards pour 1965 (les crédits à l'économie en Guinée coïncidant pour l'essentiel avec les crédits aux entreprises d'Etat). Toujours selon Samir Amin:

> De 1965 à 1968, les concours nets du système bancaire aux entreprises d'Etat (crédits accordés à ces entreprises moins dépôts de celles-ci) diminuent de 30 à 27 milliards. En revanche, les concours nets à l'Etat augmentent de 12 à 31 milliards. Au total, les concours nets du système monétaire à l'Etat et aux entreprises publiques augmentent de 42 à 58 milliards [Amin, 1971: 268].

En 1968, la situation des entreprises d'Etat était castastrophique. Pour la majorité, le pourcentage de la capacité de production utilisée était tel que la gestion ne pouvait être que déficitaire. Il faut égale-

TABLEAU 1

Actif	
Avoirs extérieurs nets	9,05
Créances sur l'Etat	9,36
Créances sur l'Economie	18,06
Actifs divers	2,41
	38,88
Passif	
Circulation Fiduciaire	17,93
Dépôts des Banques	9,96
Dépôts des entreprises publiques	1,11
Dépôts du secteur privé	1,80
Dépôts du gouvernement	7,08
Passifs divers	1
	38,88

SOURCE: Banque Centrale de la République de Guinée

ment considérer les détournements non seulement de fonds, mais de matériels, de moyens de production d'une façon plus générale. En tenant compte du déficit administratif courant et des pertes des entreprises d'Etat, Amin pense que chaque année 6 milliards de F.G. étaient rendus disponibles par des moyens inflationnistes, soit environ 50 milliards sur 8 ans (Amin, 1971: 268).

En 1966–1967 le cours du dollar au marché parallèle était monté à 1250 F.G. (245 au taux officiel) pour atteindre 2000 F.G. en 1971. On pouvait parfaitement appliquer ici l'analyse élaborée par Ryelandt (1970: 29) à partir du cas zaïrois:

L'écart croissant entre les taux de change officiel et parallèle stimule la fraude avec l'étranger. Ce transfert vers l'extérieur des ressources nationales peut prendre de nombreuses formes: exportations non déclarées, sous-évaluations des exportations et surévaluations des importations, réexportations frauduleuses de marchandises importées sous licence. Toutes ces pratiques aboutissent à réduire considérablement la capacité d'approvisionner le pays par les chenaux officiels et stimulent la hausse des prix intérieurs. Cependant la marge entre le cours officiel de la devise et le niveau des prix intérieurs attire de plus en plus de spéculateurs qui se l'approprient et l'exportent par le marché parallèle, où l'offre démesurée de monnaie nationale, tout à fait disproportionnée à sa demande accélère sa dépréciation. Les profits considérables procurés par cette opération, accentuent les pressions visant à obtenir des devises au cours officiel, et aggravent la désorganisation et la corruption des organismes chargés du contrôle douanier et des changes, la spéculation conquiert une place dominante sur le marché. Si les écarts de prix entretiennent et amplifient le mouvement inflatoire, en réduisant l'offre sur le marché et en orientant les revenus vers des fins spéculatives, ils le font aussi en alimentant une expansion continue des masses monétaires.

Au moment de la création du franc guinéen, la masse monétaire était d'environ 6,7 milliards. En 1963, lors de la seconde réforme monétaire, on peut l'estimer entre 18 et 22 milliards. Elle atteignait 39 milliards en 1965, 80 milliards lors de la troisième réforme monétaire de 1972, celle qui substituait le Syli au F.G. (Cournanel, 1976: 35). La masse monétaire avait alors été multipliée par 12 et le produit par à peine plus de 2.

A partir de 1975, (Marchés Tropicaux, 1981a: 1185 et Bulletin d'Afrique, 1981: 18) la Guinée essayait à nouveau de redresser la situation avec l'aide du F.M.I. et de quelques pays. Une ponction de 55% était réalisée sur la circulation monétaire. La décote du Syli sur les marchés clandestins fut réduite, 1 à 5 contre 1 à 10 en 1975. Selon M. Sékou Touré, une plus grande austérité financière aurait permis de résorber la dette du Budget Général vis-à-vis de la Banque Centrale. Un institut d'émission rattaché à la Présidence était créé. Néanmoins le redressement opéré n'était pas suffisant pour mettre un terme au commerce clandestin, à la thésaurisation et aux trafics de devises.

En avril 1981 intervenait donc la quatrième réforme avec changement de signes monétaires. Le but recherché est en particulier d'arrêter l'exportation frauduleuse d'une part importante de la production agricole. Ce qui explique les efforts entrepris parallèlement depuis 1978 pour remettre en route la faible industrie de transformation.

Sur le plan externe la Guinée était, pour la période 1959-1965, un des pays du monde ayant reçu l'aide par tête la plus élevée. Le Fonds monétaire international évaluait la dette extérieure totale à plus de 200 millions de dollars, en juin 1965, soit l'équivalent de 50 milliards de F C.F.A.

Selon d'autres évaluations (Amin, 1971: 269–270), qui concordent d'ailleurs avec les précédentes, mais couvrent une période plus longue, la Guinée aurait reçu de 1960 à 1965 plus de 45 milliards en francs constants d'aide extérieure (20 milliards de prêts à long terme des pays de l'Est et 19 milliards d'aide américaine, le reste étant fourni par l'Allemagne Fédérale, la Grande Bretagne et la B.I.R.D.) et 30 milliards de 1965 à 1968 (18 des Etats-Unis, 12 des pays socialistes).

En dépit de cette aide extérieure, la balance des paiements n'a pu être équilibrée, son déficit englobant le déficit commercial, les transferts de revenus des compagnies minières et des techniciens étrangers. Toujours selon les évaluations de Samir Amin, la dette extérieure fin 1968 s'élevait à plus de 65 milliards (elle avait atteint le P.I.B.). Le coût annuel du service de la dette s'était élevé depuis 1968–1969 à plus de 4 milliards, absorbant le tiers du revenu des exportations (Africa South of the Sahara, 1973: 400). J. Latremolière (1975: 9 et suite) évaluait la dette extérieure à 750 millions de dollars en 1975, ce qui correspondait à 154 milliards de F.G. au taux officiel (ou à 15,4 milliards de Sylis). De 1973 à 1980 la Guinée a reçu 605 millions de dollars des pays arabes, soit 10,6% de l'ensemble de leurs engagements en faveur des 41 pays africains non arabes (Jeune Afrique, 1981: 42).

En dépit d'une amélioration de la croissance (mines, agriculture) entre 1973 et 1978, la dette extérieure atteignait fin 1978 1025 millions de dollars, soit plus de 96% du P.I.B. en monnaie courante. La moitié de cette dette avait été contractée vis-à-vis des pays socialistes. Les arriérés du service de la dette atteignaient 4 milliards de Sylis, soit près de 30% des investissements réalisés entre 1973 et 1978: "La balance générale des paiements indique des déficits successifs qui atteignent 2510 millions de Sylis en 1980" (Marchés Tropicaux, 1981b: 1862). Pour la décennie 1981–1990, le rédacteur de "Marchés Tropicaux" précisait:

Compte tenu des ressources propres que la Guinée peut fournir pour ses investissements, le montant total de l'aide extérieure pour la décennie 1981–1990 s'élèverait à 37,4 milliards de Sylis, soit 1877 millions de dollars aux prix de 1980, ce qui représente une aide correspondant à 8,9% du P.I.B. annuel moyen. Ce niveau ne doit pas être considéré comme exagéré, car il reste dans les limites courantes des programmes d'aide extérieure. Mais dans cette somme le projet du Konkouré n'est pas repris; en l'incorporant, l'aide atteindrait alors 18,8% du P.I.B. En admettant que cette aide puisse être accordée, il faudrait, pour que la Guinée puisse repartir sur des bases saines, que sa dette antérieure soit reportée à 1990 et que la dette nouvelle résultant des prochains investissements ne commence pas à être exigible avant cette date.

On voit que la situation reste très préoccupante, pour ne pas dire plus, car la Guinée a jusqu'ici toujours surestimé les ressources propres qu'elle entendait consacrer à ses investissements. Pendant trop longtemps les autorités ont pratiqué une politique d'utilisation intensive et improductive de la monnaie, en sacrifiant de ce fait sa couverture extérieure.

Les rapports avec le capital international

L'indépendance politique de la Guinée fut accueillie avec hostilité par le capital privé, notamment par le capital commercial français. Quelques petites entreprises industrielles semi-artisanales, les seules qui existaient en 1958, restèrent sur place. Dans le domaine agricole, des planteurs européens, surtout français, revendirent leurs plantations à des nationaux ou à des Libanais.

L'usine de F.R.I.A. dont la réalisation avait commencé et à qui la Guinée conservait les garanties accordées avant l'indépendance, fut achevée en dépit de pressions, semble-t-il, du gouvernement français. Par contre les grands projects relatifs à Boké (aluminium-aluminebauxite), au Konkouré (barrage-usine hydroélectrique) et à la réalisation d'une aciérie, étaient abandonnés. En effet, le complexe électrométallurgique supposait un financement public (Etat français et B.I.R.D.) de 18 milliards F C.F.A. sur 29 milliards. La production d'aluminium réclamait 35 milliards d'investissements, dont 11,5 milliards de concours de l'Etat français au groupe privé français engagé dans l'opération.

La rupture politique délibérément voulue par la France après le référendum, rendait impossible la mise en chantier de ces projets, la B.I.R.D. ne souhaitant s'engager que dans la mesure où la France cautionnait l'opération. Ce désengagement et l'effet produit par le rapprochement avec les pays socialistes ouvraient une longue période de réticences du capital privé étranger.

En 1961 donc, après l'éviction du capital commercial français de ses positions dominantes, la création du franc guinéen, et pendant la période de retrait des banques françaises, se produisit la rupture avec les Bauxites du Midi. Les installations dont le gisement était déjà pratiquement épuisé, furent nationalisées, puis remises en route avec du personnel (pour les cadres techniques) en provenance des pays socialistes. La décision guinéenne fut prise à la suite notamment d'infractions à la nouvelle réglementation monétaire et bancaire. Le Code des Investissements fut promulgué le 6 avril 1962 (Revue de Dév. Econ. 1964).

Déjà son optique différait sensiblement de l'orientation dominante en 1960, car il s'agissait désormais d'attirer les capitaux privés étrangers. Le VIe Congrès, tenu en décembre 1962, et où l'on pouvait déjà tirer les principaux enseignements du Plan triennal (qui s'achevait théoriquement un semestre plus tard), marquait officiellement le terme de cette période de difficultés avec le capital privé étranger. Par ailleurs, le Congrès popularisait en Guinée la formule de la société d'économie mixte, en la présentant comme un instrument privilégié de développement, susceptible d'être utilisé dans des domaines fort divers. Dès 1963, en vertu d'un contrat conclu entre l'A.I.D. et le gouvernement, la société américaine Cecchi entreprit des études en vue d'établir un climat propice à l'investissement privé. Le premier rapport ("The Climate for Private Investment in Guinea. The Basis for Industrial Growth", Cecchi and Co., 1963) était présenté comme la plate-forme, dirons-nous, d'un livre blanc à venir sur l'investissement privé et la politique de développement en Guinée. Les auteurs considéraient que le VIe Congrès avait donné le signal d'une politique favorable à l'investissement privé, et que dans l'avenir, la majeure partie des objectifs industriels serait atteinte grâce à l'action conjuguée du capital guinéen et du capital privé étranger.

Cependant, le Code guinéen des investissements n'était pas jugé de nature à attirer suffisamment le capital privé. Les facteurs susceptibles de décourager la venue d'investisseurs étrangers étaient, selon ces mêmes auteurs, relativement nombreux en Guinée: inconvertibilité de la monnaie, déséquilibre de la balance des paiements, non adhésion aux organisations internationales, manque d'information, organisation déficiente des services publics, non rentabilité des entreprises existantes. Plus précisément, on souhaitait que la Guinée adhère aux organisations internationales, adopte une politique bancaire et fiscale susceptible de juguler l'inflation, fasse quelques aménagements au Code des Investissements (auquel on reprochait notamment d'offrir une insuffisante protection aux investissements d'une certaine envergure, d'être vague, de prévoir des avantages spéciaux dont certains pourraient bénéficier et d'autres non, de ne pas concerner les industries déjà existantes). Allant plus loin encore, on préconisait un plan d'investissement à long terme (après l'échec du Plan triennal dans le domaine industriel, précisait le rapport) et, à court terme, la création d'un Ministère du développement économique et d'un organe conseil pour les investissements privés. En 1963, comme suite semble-t-il à ces recommandations, il se produisit une reconcentration des départements économiques au sein du Ministère du développement économique et du Ministère des transports.

En octobre 1963, fut signée la convention entre Harvey Aluminium et le gouvernement guinéen. Le gouvernement américain émit des garanties d'investissement à dater de juin 1965, tandis que la B.I.R.D. octroyait en mars 1966 un prêt d'études.

La Compagnie des bauxites de Guinée (C.B.G.) fut constituée pour reprendre l'ancien projet de Boké. Le capital d'abord partagé entre la Guinée (49%) et Harvey (51%), fut ensuite redistribué entre de nouvelles parties prenantes. Harvey céda 17% de ses parts à Aluminium Company of America, Alcan Aluminium Limited (dont dépendaient les Bauxites du Midi à qui, originairement, incombait la mise en chantier du premier projet de Boké), Pechiney-Ugine, Vereinigte Aluminium Werke AG, Montecatini-Edison SPA.

L'ensemble du projet revenait à 170 millions de dollars dont 80 millions à la charge de l'Etat guinéen (le coût estimé de l'infrastructure). Ces 80 millions étaient entièrement prêtés à la Guinée (74% en devises prêtées par la B.I.R.D. au taux de 5% pendant trente ans, et 26% prêtés en F.G. par l'A.I.D., sous forme de marchandises, de manière à ne pas aggraver l'inflation). La production devait atteindre près de 9 millions de tonnes de bauxite, soit au prix moyen F.O.B. de 7 dollars la tonne de bauxite métallurgique, plus de 60 millions de dollars (Yearbook of International Statistics, 1972-1973: 430).

La participation guinéenne dans le capital était représentée par la contrevaleur du gisement. Outre la perception d'une taxe à la production (environ 4,5 millions de dollars par an) et d'un impôt sur les bénéfices, la Guinée devait percevoir 65% des bénéfices déclarés, soit un gain net de plus de 12 millions de dollars par an.

Par ailleurs l'alumine serait vendue 60 dollars la tonne. Les travaux ayant débuté avec retard, l'exportation de bauxite de Boké a commencé en 1973 avec un total encore modeste de 900 000 tonnes. (J. Latremolière, 1975: 9) estimait qu'elle atteindrait en 1975, 4,9 millions "représentant un apport supplémentaire au pays de 35 millions de dollars, soit 752 millions de Sylis" ou encore 7,5 milliards de F.G.

La période 1970–1975 paraît avoir été favorable du point de vue des accords conclus en vue de l'exploitation des ressources minières. A côté du projet de Boké tant attendu (le premier accord remonte à

1963), et recemment amputé par les partenaires américains de prolongements envisagés (usines d'alumine et d'aluminium), des accords concernant aussi la bauxite ont été conclus avec les Soviétiques (Kindia), et les Yougoslaves et Alusuisse (Tougué-Dabola) tandis qu'un projet existait avec des pays arabes pour produire de l'alumine (à Ayékoyé), et que les Roumains étudiaient la possibilité d'implanter une usine d'aluminium.

La seule production de Boké pouvait selon certains observateurs (Latremolière, 1975: 10–11) se stabiliser à 10 millions de tonnes en 1979, et faire de la Guinée le premier exportateur mondial. Comme nous le verrons, en 1980 la production de Boké n'avait pas atteint cet objectif.

De plus on prevoyait qu'en 1985, la production totale de bauxite en Guinée pourrait atteindre 25 millions de tonnes, celle d'alumine 4 millions de tonnes, la production d'aluminium restant beaucoup plus imprévisible car on sait seulement que dans les cinq années à venir la production d'aluminium dans les pays en voie de développement passerait seulement de 8 à 14% de la production mondiale, selon des "sources industrielles autorisées" (O.N.U., Conseil Econ. et Social, 1975: 7 et suite).

L'exploitation du fer devait également se faire dans le cadre d'une société d'économie mixte avec capitaux japonais, belges, suisses, yougoslaves, etc. Les prévisions étaient de 15 millions de tonnes en 1978, total appelé à doubler ensuite. Une société d'économie mixte était même créée pour la prospection et l'exploitation pétrolières. Le partenaire américain de la Guinée, Buttes Resources International, était certain de découvrir du pétrole. Par ailleurs, la société F.R.I.A. était devenue une société mixte en février 1973 (Friguia), la Guinée acquérant une part de 49% en échange de droits miniers permettant aux associés de F.R.I.A. d'exploiter de nouveaux gisements. F.R.I.A. assurait déjà en 1972, la moitié des exportations (Le Moniteur Africain, 1973: 4 et suite) guinéennes et les 3/4 de ses rentrées en devises, et la production de FRIGUIA devait passer de 700 000 à 1 100 000 tonnes d'alumine.

L'ampleur des projets miniers expliquait l'importance de l'infrastructure et des transports dans le Plan quinquennal de 1973: en principe plus de 200 milliards de F.G. (35% du budget total du plan). Cette optique ne pouvait qu'accélérer le rythme du financement d'origine étrangère. L'aide extérieure escomptée pour le Plan 1973–1978 dépassait en fait 80%. Selon le Président Touré, en 1974 la moitié de ce financement seulement était assurée (L'Economiste du Tiers Monde, 1974: 21 et suite).

Quoiqu'il en soit la concrétisation des projets envisagés en collaboration avec le capital international intervenait à un moment crucial pour la Guinée, étant donné l'absence de croissance depuis 1967, la pénurie et la crise financière. En 1974, soit plus d'un an après la dernière réforme monétaire, la Guinée achetait pour 6 millions de droits de tirage spéciaux pour faire face aux difficultés de balance des paiements entre octobre 1972 et octobre 1973. C'était la première fois que la Guinée avait recours au financement compensatoire (Marchés Tropicaux, 1974: 1075). La Guinée souhaitait mettre à profit cette conjoncture longtemps attendue.

En 1978 le secteur minier représentait 97% des exportations guinéennes (Industries et Tr. d'O.M., 1980: 286). La production de bauxite atteignait en 1980 7,6 millions de tonnes de Boké (contre 10 millions prévus pour 1979) et 2,6 millions de tonnes à Kindia. La production d'alumine, à Friguia, plafonnait à 650 000 tonnes. A l'exception de celui de Kindia, les projets mentionnés plus haut n'avaient toujours pas été réalisés, qu'il s'agisse d'alumine, d'aluminium ou de fer. Les potentialités exceptionnelles du pays sont toujours soulignées, mais la concrétisation des multiples projets ébauchés reste fort lente: F.R.I.A. (devenu Friguia) en 1973, Boké en 1973, Kindia ensuite, mais avec les Soviétiques.

Il n'en reste pas moins que les productions de Boké et Kindia représentaient un supplément de 70 millions de dollars par rapport à l'année 1972, soit plus que la moyenne des exportations guinéennes pour la période 1970–1972.

La décennie 1980–1990 verra peut-être le mouvement s'accélérer. Nous reviendrons sur ce problème en conclusion.

LUTTE DES CLASSES ET CAPITALISME D'ETAT

Bien que le développement du capitalisme en Guinée soit resté limité, les rapports de production restent bien significatifs du capitalisme d'Etat. A ce titre deux questions nous retiendront ici: la définition de la bourgeoisie d'Etat à partir des rapports de production; la lutte des classes en Guinée et le rôle du parti unique.

Rapports de production et bourgeoisie d'Etat

Nous avons vu que la Guinée s'était, dès le début, engagée dans un processus de centralisation économique alors sans exemple dans le contexte africain: étatisation du commerce extérieur et du système bancaire, création d'une zone monétaire spéciale et d'entreprises publiques dans divers domaines, étatisation de la propriété du sol. Mais l'existence de la propriété d'Etat n'implique pas, en elle-même, des rapports de production socialistes. Pas plus que le processus de centralisation économique entrepris en Guinée ne signifiait une transformation dans la nature des rapports de production hérités de la colonisation. En effet,

C'est être entièrement prisonnier de l'idéologie juridique que de penser que le capital public ne serait pas l'objet d'une appropriation (c'est-à-dire d'une monopolisation) privée (au sens du matérialisme historique, c'est-à-dire au sens d'un monopole de classe). Il n'y a donc pas de contradiction entre la reproduction des capitaux privés et la reproduction des capitaux publics, du seul fait de leur statut juridique différent. Celle-ci est à l'époque de l'Impérialisme, l'une des formes de l'appropriation privée, de l'appropriation des moyens de production par une classe, la bourgeoisie, qui se constitue dans cette appropriation même. C'est seulement dans le procès d'ensemble de l'appropriation qu'il peut y avoir des contradictions [Balibar, 1974: 162].

La fraction de la bourgeoisie guinéenne qui avait été associée au contrôle de l'appareil forgé par la métropole, va devenir une bourgeoisie d'Etat se définissant par les pratiques d'exploitation. Le contrôle (par un noyau inamovible) du parti unique et des autres appareils idéologiques d'Etat, permettait à la bourgeoisie d'Etat d'exercer en tant que classe des droits absolus sur l'ensemble des moyens de production. Les travailleurs n'étaient porteurs que de leurs forces de travail, et la séparation était effective entre travailleurs et moyens de production. La classe dominante utilisait en toute liberté, sans aucun contrôle populaire ni contrepoids, la force de travail et les moyens, produits ou objets de travail (matériel, pièces de rechange, matières premières, produits finis). Comme l'écrit Mahmoud Hussein: "Dominant le processus de production tout entier, la classe au pouvoir ne paie au producteur que le prix de leur force de travail . . . , après quoi, elle s'empare de tout le reste de la valeur nouvelle créée par cette force de travail (qui devient ainsi plus-value) et l'utilise comme bon lui semble" (Hussein, 1971: 172).[4]

La bourgeoisie d'Etat dominait totalement les processus de production dans les entreprises étatisées, accaparant ainsi la plus-value. La situation était plus complexe dans le secteur agricole, puisqu'en dépit de l'étatisation de la propriété du sol, l'agriculture était (et est restée) essentiellement aux mains d'entrepreneurs privés ou de producteurs individuels.

C'est une bourgeoisie agraire, dont certains éléments pouvaient également appartenir à la bourgeoisie d'Etat et/ou à la bourgeoisie commerciale (grands riziculteurs, éleveurs et planteurs), qui intervenait dans les types de production régis par des rapports de production capitalistes. Les tentatives faites lors du lancement du Plan triennal en 1960, pour créer dans le domaine agricole des entreprises d'Etat avaient rapidement tourné court. Les différentes composantes de la bourgeoisie (et par conséquent la bourgeoisie d'Etat elle-même) et à travers elles l'Impérialisme, entretenaient des rapports d'exploitation avec la paysannerie par divers moyens: termes d'échange internes entre produits agricoles et manufacturés, écarts entre prix d'achat aux producteurs et prix de vente à la consommation intérieure ou sur les marchés extérieurs, etc. La bourgeoisie d'Etat se définissait par sa capacité à prélever une plus-value dont elle déterminait sans contrôle l'affectation, par son intervention donc au niveau des rapports de production. Elle allait représenter en Guinée la fraction essentielle du capitalisme national, étant donné le caractère revêtu par l'exploitation coloniale et le contexte international dans lequel le capitalisme ne pouvait se développer que sur la base d'un degré de socialisation relativement élevé. Le monopole de la bourgeoisie d'Etat sur les moyens de production "publics" était absolu, ses membres ne détenant d'eux que des droits limités et temporaires. L'étatisation avait engendré un appareil économique pratiquement approprié par le noyau dirigeant du Parti et de l'Etat. Cette appropriation donnait lieu à un type de gestion caractérisé par les traits suivants (Bettelheim, 1968: 45 à 101):

- Subordination des instances économiques aux instances administratives et politiques, elles-mêmes libres de tout contrôle populaire.
- Prédominance d'une hiérarchie verticale, de type administratif, dans les activités économiques.
- Prise de décision monopolisée par les instances politiques les plus élevées, donc mal placées pour prendre des décisions pertinentes.
- Le système des relations verticales créait des "chasses gardées", favorisait la concurrence entre secteurs, voire entre entreprises, et attisait ainsi les conflits entre intérêts individuels, ou de groupes, et les intérêts collectifs de la bourgeoisie d'Etat.
- Dans la mesure où toute bourgeoisie reproduit sans cesse la tendance à s'approprier privativement les moyens de production, la bourgeoisie d'Etat exerçait collectivement les droits réels du capitaliste sur la force de travail et les moyens de production, elle exploitait donc les producteurs mais les modes de réalisation de la plus-value impliquaient des formes de domination individualisées et concrètes sur les moyens de

production et de financement, sur l'utilisation de la force de travail. Ces formes de domination individualisées avaient pour effet des modes de réalisation individualisés de la plus-value. Les détournements de fonds et de produits, la spéculation, l'enrichissement individuel à partir des ressources publiques, étaient des modes de réalisation individuels rendus possibles par le monopole absolu de la bourgeoisie d'Etat. Monopole qu'elle ne pouvait exercer directement, en tant que telle, mais seulement par le truchement de groupes, d'individus, de "responsables" de tel ou tel secteur, investis de pouvoirs relatifs mais réels.

Comme l'a très justement souligné Mahmoud Hussein (1971: 171-172 et 191), les aspirations de la bourgeoisie d'Etat impliquaient la libération des tendances de ses composantes à l'appropriation individuelle. Et ces dernières pouvaient aller jusqu'à remettre en cause le fonctionnement de l'appareil d'Etat, menacé de dissolution, jusqu'à la paralysie du pouvoir d'Etat.

Dans les formations capitalistes avancées, le pouvoir d'Etat est détenu par la grande bourgeoisie qui assure le contrôle de l'appareil d'Etat et du secteur étatisé. Dans les formations sociales où le pouvoir d'Etat est aux mains de la bourgeoisie d'Etat, et constitue simultanément l'armature de l'appareil d'Etat, ce contrôle devient impossible.

Les modes de réalisation "collectifs" du surplus, ceux qui sont institutionnalisés (et appelés par l'existence de budgets, de plans, etc.) sont constamment menacés par les modes de réalisation individuels. La bourgeoisie d'Etat tend spontanément à se transformer en bourgeoisie "privée", et à renforcer cette dernière qui, du reste, est toujours présente aux côtés de la première. Cette tendance est cependant contrecarrée plar les exigences de survie de l'Etat, et de maintien de la domination de la bourgeoisie d'Etat, qui fait prévaloir le pouvoir d'Etat. En outre, les capitaux constitués par les particuliers, et donc soustraits à l'accumulation nationale, sont mis en valeur dans des opérations surtout spéculatives ou commerciales, ou s'associent à des capitaux privés étrangers pour réaliser des projets industriels de taille limitée.

En Guinée, l'existence d'une monnaie nationale et d'un système bancaire constituaient des conditions nécessaires au fonctionnement d'un tel système. La politique de création monétaire avait été fonction des déficits budgétaires, de l'incapacité du secteur public à organiser son expansion à partir de ses propres ressources. La "bureaucratie" (qui composait l'appareil d'Etat) exerçait le pouvoir d'Etat. Cette "bureaucratie", qui se présentait empiriquement comme telle, n'agissait fondamentalement comme classe sociale que dans la mesure où elle tendait à se nier comme véritable bureaucratie. A cet égard il n'est pas sans intérêt de suivre l'évolution des classes exploitées par la bourgeoisie d'Etat.

Dans l'agriculture, le nombre de salariés avait diminué de plus de 50% après une décennie d'Indépendance, tandis que les rémunérations étaient restées constantes pendant cette période (après une phase de hausses importantes de 1952 à 1959). Les salariés agricoles étant le plus souvent des semi-prolétaires, ils furent d'autant plus touchés par le blocage des salaires que la crise des productions d'exportation ne leur permettait pas de se transformer en salariés à plein temps, alors que l'agriculture dans son ensemble voyait sa situation se dégrader et que l'inflation s'aggravait. Le manoeuvre agricole recevait un salaire de 28 F.G. en 1967, 31 F.G. au bout d'un an. Les salariés d'une importante plantation d'ananas recevaient en 1967 une rémunération mensuelle de 4 à 5 000 F.G., soit 50 à 60% du revenu du manoeuvre travaillant en milieu urbain (Rivière, 1978: 241).

Les agriculteurs étaient désavantagés par l'évolution des termes de l'échange entre produits manufacturés (importés ou fabriqués en Guinée) et les produits agricoles. L'extension progressive (puis accélérée à partir de 1967–1968) de la pénurie et du marché noir les excluait pratiquement de l'accès aux biens manufacturés, du fait de la faiblesse de leurs revenus et de leur éloignement de la capitale.

De 1959 à 1970 la production vivrière avait stagné, les exportations de café et de bananes (qui avaient suscité des entrepreneurs nationaux dès 1958) avaient régressé. Les palmistes et l'ananas, par contre. avaient progressé avec une pointe (25 000 tonnes) pour ce dernier produit au début des années soixante-dix. Le trafic frauduleux qui s'était instauré avait plus enrichi les intermédiaires que les paysans ou même les planteurs. Dans le secteur bananier un grand nombre d'Européens, après l'Indépendance, avait vendu leurs plantations à des Guinéens ou des Libanais. En 1960, les bananeraies guinéennes fournissaient le 1/4 de la production totale pour 1 800 planteurs environ.

En 1967 les 2/3 de la production étaient assurés par 4 coopératives européennes ou assimilées, employant 7 000 salariés. Les plantations dirigées par des nationaux travaillaient pour la plupart avec des salarriés familiaux dont le nombre n'excédait pas 5000 personnes. Il faut remarquer que tous les produits d'exportation, à l'exception de l'ananas (dont la culture était aux mains de producteurs étrangers), étaient achetés à des cours nominaux supérieurs aux cours internationaux.

Au taux de change officiel donc, la Guinée vendait sur les marchés extérieurs à des prix inférieurs aux prix d'achat aux producteurs. Mais nous avons vu l'importance des écarts entre le taux de change officiel et le taux réel. Même en tenant compte du caractère spéculatif du taux de marché noir, le prix d'achat au producteur (étant donné la dévalorisation du F.G.) était sensiblement inférieur au cours mondial, et permettait ainsi le prélèvement d'une fraction importante de la plus-value produite.

La pénurie profitait aux intermédiaires, au commerce privé. Parallèlement à la stagnation de la production, il faut rappeler l'échec de la coopération, lancée en même temps que le premier Plan (le Plan triennal), et l'accentuation de la différenciation sociale dans les campagnes. Fréquemment les responsables des coopératives utilisèrent pour leur compte personnel les tracteurs fournis aux coopératives, ou les prêtèrent à des paysans riches utilisant de la main-d'oeuvre salariée. Lorsque les Centres de modernisation rurale furent liquidés (les C.M.R. devaient tenir lieu d'écoles techniques pour les coopératives et exécuter avec leur matériel les travaux demandés), ce fut souvent au bénéfice de la modernisation de l'équipement d'exploitations privées.

En ce qui concerne les produits vivriers (le riz notamment qui constituait la base de toute l'alimentation), le système des prix d'achat aux producteurs, des prix de vente à la consommation par le secteur d'Etat, la pénurie de ces produits, leur rationnement et le marché noir qui en résultait représentaient une source également importante de surplus.

Dès la période du Plan triennal, la paysannerie fuyait la campagne pour les centres urbains (surtout jusqu'en 1964–1965), ou se repliait sur l'autoconsommation (phénomène très net à partir de 1966-1967). Le nombre de salariés dans l'agriculture diminuait de moitié (plus de 15 000 personnes). Or le nombre des emplois industriels créés par l'industrie de transformation n'excédait pas 6000. Le pouvoir d'Etat décida donc, à partir de 1963, d'utiliser des méthodes policières pour juguler l'exode rural, considéré officiellement comme "un facteur négatif qui prive la campagne de bras valides et occasionne la surpopulation des centres urbains" (Min. de l'agriculture, Rép. de Guinée, 1963: 21). Il fut recommandé de faire périodiquement procéder à des rafles pour arrêter les "faux chômeurs" (selon la terminologie officielle), et de les utiliser à des tâches productives: cultures vivrières, travaux routiers, etc … Ces travailleurs prisonniers devaient être nourris sur la base de 75 F.G. par jour (ce qui représentait, par rapport au S.M.I.G. agricole, moins de trois heures journalières de travail payé). On insistait particulièrement sur l'affectation de ces détenus à des travaux agricoles qui permettaient d'assurer un meilleur ravitaillement des centres urbains, notamment de Conakry la capitale. Ces détenus, après leur première arrestation, devaient travailler trois mois, avant d'être ensuite dirigés vers leurs villages d'origine (le temps de travail forcé était porté à douze mois en cas de récidive) (Ibid.). Dans les villes de garnison, l'encadrement, l'hébergement, et l'entretien des détenus, étaient assurés par l'armée.

Au cas où le nombre de chômeurs appréhendés viendrait à dépasser les besoins en main-d'oeuvre pour la production vivrière, on envisageait d'affecter une fraction de cette force de travail à la production de l'ananas. Mais deux problèmes se posaient alors: le premier était de ne pas mettre en concurrence ces travailleurs forcés (les rapports officiels évitaient soigneusement le terme) et les salariés ordinaires des plantations; en second lieu, la production d'ananas réclamait une main-d'oeuvre qualifiée, alors que ces détenus n'étaient "disponibles" que trois mois.

Cette politique de lutte contre l'exode rural fut appliquée pendant trois ans environ. A partir de 1966 la paysannerie s'enferme de plus en plus dans l'autoconsommation, ou émigre vers les pays voisins. Dès lors ces méthodes n'auront plus de raison d'être. Ces tentatives de la bourgeoisie d'Etat pour freiner l'exode rural nous paraissent très significatives des rapports qu'elle entretenait avec la paysannerie semi-prolétarisée. Les mesures que nous venons d'exposer visaient à assurer le ravitaillement des centres urbains à moindres frais pour la bourgeoisie, ou à augmenter la production de denrées susceptibles de rapporter des devises, toujours au prix d'une surexploitation de la force de travail.

En définitive, il fallait distinguer (Rivière, 1978: 257-258) les gros producteurs (riziculteurs, éleveurs, maraîchers, planteurs de bananes organisés en coopératives leur permettant d'obtenir crédits, engrais et insecticides, d'écouler leur production), les petits exploitants (planteurs de café, producteurs de biens vivriers), le prolétariat agricole. Seules, ces deux catégories étaient exploitées ou même surexploitées, la surexploitation étant entendue comme un processus conduisant à la non reproduction de certains travailleurs comme supports de la force de travail social, à leur rejet hors du procès de production (Cournanel, 1979: 71-72). Les premiers partageaient le surplus d'origine agraire, produit par le prolétariat agricole, avec la bourgeoisie d'Etat et selon les cas avec la bourgeoisie commerciale. Par contre les petits exploitants, endettés et incapables de s'équiper, ne recevaient que le salaire (ne dépassant pas un strict minimum vital) qu'ils s'attribuaient à eux-mêmes, déduction faite de leurs frais de production (Marx, 1960: 185). Une partie de leur surtravail "est donnée gratuitement à la société et n'entre pas dans la fixation des prix de production ou dans la création de valeur en général" (Marx, 1960: 185). L'autre fraction de leur surtravail se partageait entre la bourgeoisie d'Etat et la bourgeoisie commerciale. Cette catégorie des petits exploitants était à l'origine du prolétariat et du semi-prolétariat. La régression du secteur agricole dans la première décennie suivant l'Indépendance, conduisait à un véritable rejet hors du secteur agricole national d'une partie de la force de travail.

A partir de 1970 deux évolutions sont à souligner: (1) Les années 1970–1977 seront plus favorables à la croissance agricole (Hodgkinson, 1982: 473, 474 et 477). Progression de la production vivrière et assimilée, quasi-doublement de la production bananière par rapport aux années soixante, augmentation des exportations de palmistes. Le café a poursuivi son déclin, l'ananas est passé de 25 000 (en 1970) à 15 000 tonnes, mais globalement l'agriculture semblait avoir connu une indéniable progression. (2) Durant cette même phase, les Pouvoirs révolutionnaires locaux (P.R.L.) installés depuis 1968 allaient organiser la production et l'écoulement de la production agricole à travers la mise sur pied de brigades "qui groupent, sur la base d'un volontariat plus ou moins respecté, les personnes nécessaires à la réalisation de leurs tâches" (Leunda, 1973–1974: 172). Selon l'auteur de cette description (qui relayait les intentions de l'idéologie officielle), "l'institution ... est susceptible de guider ... vers un développement auto-soutenu débouchant à long terme sur une certaine forme de collectivisme".

Le commerce privé disparaissait pratiquement en Guinée de 1975 à 1977. Contribuant directement à l'activité agricole (à travers les P.R.L., les investissements financés par l'aide étrangère, les sociétés mixtes constituées avec le capital étranger, la constitution de fermes agro-pastorales d'arrondissements), la bourgeoisie d'Etat avait souhaité évincer le capital commercial privé et amorcer une restructuration de la société rurale. Celle-ci revenait à renforcer la main mise du pouvoir d'Etat sur la production et sa circulation, à conduire brutalement agriculteurs et éleveurs vers un statut de quasi-salariés. Une évolution

qui ne s'accompagnait pas pour autant d'un meilleur approvisionne-
ment des campagnes en biens manufacturés. Economiquement elle
signifiait pour les intéressés une détérioration supplémentaire de leur
niveau de vie, si l'on tient compte des possibilités que leur donnait la
libre disposition de leur production (vente clandestine à meilleur prix
au commerce privé, échanges en nature, exportation clandestine).

Paysannerie et éleveurs allaient réagir contre cette tentative, non
seulement par les méthodes habituelles (évasion de la production,
auto-consommation ou exportations clandestines), mais par une résistance plus ouverte relayée ensuite par celle du commerce privé (manifestation des femmes à Conakry, émeutes de 1977). Cette réaction
contraignit le régime à s'engager en 1978 dans une nouvelle phase de
libéralisme, à rétablir le commerce privé et la possibilité pour les agriculteurs de commercialiser leur production.

La situation du prolétariat urbain, et plus généralement des travailleurs ne disposant que de leurs salaires (ce qui n'était pas le cas de la
bourgeoisie d'Etat) s'était aussi spectaculairement dégradée depuis
1960. En 1959, quelques mois après l'Indépendance, le S.M.I.G. était
passé de 31 à 36 F C.F.A. pour la première zone, de 25 à 30 F pour la
deuxième zone de salaires. Après la création du franc guinéen, ces
salaires payés désormais en monnaie nationale, mais sans changement
de leur valeur nominale, allaient rester constants jusqu'en 1965. A
cette date, le S.M.I.G. passait de 36 à 42 F.G. en milieu urbain.

A compter de 1967, le paiement des heures supplémentaires était
supprimé. Nous avons vu par ailleurs l'importance du processus inflationniste; on peut estimer que durant la décennie 1960-1970, le coût
de la vie avait été multiplié par 4 au moins. Nous avons effectué des
calculs tendant à montrer que le pouvoir d'achat alimentaire du
S.M.I.G. en 1968, était inférieur à celui de son homologue en 1951
(Cournanel, 1971: 133).[5] Nous n'envisageons ici que le pouvoir d'achat
alimentaire, car la fraction socialisée du salaire était pratiquement
nulle. Vêtements, tissus et chaussures, étaient introuvables ou 4 fois
plus chers que dans les pays environnants. Les dépenses alimentaires
absorbaient donc l'essentiel du revenu mensuel (et ce dans des conditions de rationnement drastique). Précisons par ailleurs qu'entre 1957
et 1966 le nombre global des salariés avait baissé, particulièrement
celui des ouvriers et manoeuvres qui représentaient le prolétariat
urbain. L'industrie de transformations mise en place dans les années
soixante avait apporté environ 6 000 emplois. En 1979, ce secteur
manufacturier n'employait que 7 000 personnes, soit 0,3% de la pop-

ulation active (Europe - Outre-Mer, 1979: 34). Ces entreprises ont toujours connu les mêmes problèmes: déficits, détournements, fonctionnement à un faible pourcentage de leur capacité de production.

De 1968 à 1971 le niveau de vie se dégradait encore, et il est probable que cette tendance se soit maintenue. M. Sékou Touré a annoncé en 1980 une augmentation des salaires de 10 à 20% rendue possible par la politique d'austérité relative pratiquée après 1975. Mais que pèse cette hausse quand le P.I.B. en francs courants a été multiplié par 25 en 18 ans et seulement par 2,5 en francs constants?

Le prolétariat employé dans les entreprises minières contrôlées par le capital étranger, connaissait à l'origine des conditions de vie nettement plus favorables: doublement des salaires dans la période 1962–1966, économats des entreprises important de l'étranger des denrées alimentaires vendues en F.G., et à des prix inférieurs aux prix de revient (calculés au taux de change officiel bien sûr).

Ces avantages disparaîtront par la suite.

Nous n'avons pas abordé la législation sociale ou la législation du travail. Il nous semble en effet que la situation économique réduisait singulièrement leur portée. Dès 1966 d'ailleurs, le rapport de l'Office de la main-d'oeuvre signalait le non-respect systématique de la réglementation relative aux avis d'embauche, de mutation, aux rémunérations, etc. Les décrets plaçant la gestion du personnel de toutes les entreprises sous la tutelle du Ministère du travail n'étaient pas respectés. Ajoutons qu'un décret de 1967 prohibait désormais le paiement d'heures supplémentaires dans les entreprises d'Etat. Bref, si la législation adoptée après l'Indépendance paraissait séduisante, elle ne pouvait que rester lettre morte, ou se modifier dans un sens plus réactionnaire.

Sur le plan syndical, le IIIe Congrès du P.D.G., en 1967, s'était prononcé pour l'intégration de la Confédération nationale des travailleurs guinéens (C.N.T.G.). Comme l'écrit C. Rivière (1978: 211):

Après cette phagocytose, l'on comprend qu'en avril 1969 s'effectue une révision des statuts des syndicats, et on saisit le sens politique de la campagne menée à cette époque pour contraindre les travailleurs à s'affilier à l'organisation syndicale unique. En poussant les travailleurs à se syndiquer, le gouvernement resserre son contrôle politique sur chaque citoyen puisque le syndicat est un organe du Parti. Il rend plus efficaces ses décisions et donne l'illusion d'une meilleure unanimité populaire.

Lutte des classes et parti unique

Les crises politiques qui ont jalonné l'histoire de la Guinée depuis l'Indépendance, ont été autant de manifestations de la lutte des classes, lutte toujours étroitement liée aux fluctuations de la stratégie de développement et de la situation économique. La recherche d'une croissance auto-entretenue et l'adoption d'une "voie non capitaliste", recevaient le soutien actif des syndicats et de la gauche (dont les thèses étaient celles du Parti Africain de l'Indépendance (P.A.I.), lequel avait demandé à sa section guinéenne de se dissoudre dans le Parti Démocratique de Guinée après l'Indépendance) (Condé, 1972: 168). Mais toute une série de démarches contredisait au même moment la réalité de cette orientation: nature des nominations aux postes de responsabilité ou des candidats présentés à la première élection des organismes du Parti après le référendum, prise en main antidémocratique des syndicats et des mouvements de jeunesse, fluctuations significatives de la politique extérieure (Benot, 1972: 391-393).

C'est au niveau du plan que la bataille décisive allait s'engager. A la Conférence de Kankan, réunie pour adopter le Plan triennal, Sékou Touré intervenait pour réaffirmer: "Nous ne sommes pas un régime communiste", et encore, "Nous nous définissons par l'Afrique et c'est l'Afrique que nous choisissons. On nous affirme que nous devons nécessairement choisir entre le capitalisme et le socialisme, mais je m'excuse, et - soit dit entre nous - nous sommes pratiquement incapables de définir ce qu'est le capitalisme, ce qu'est le socialisme" (Benot, 1972: 267-268).

L'allocution du Président était au mieux décisive dans la mesure où elle marquait à quel point le Plan était un enjeu déterminant (de la lutte sourde qui durait depuis plus d'un an), et dans quel sens le pouvoir souhaitait trancher. Le renforcement de la bourgeoisie d'Etat et la croissance de la bourgeoisie commerciale entraînèrent rapidement une pression sur le niveau de vie des travailleurs. Fin 1961, se produisait un violent affrontement entre le pouvoir et les syndicats, avec pour conséquence le démantèlement de la tendance marxiste qui contrôlait la majeure partie des syndicats composant la C.N.T.G. (Confédération nationale des travailleurs guinéens).[6] Il est significatif que les syndicalistes arrêtés aient été traités de partisans "d'un égalitarisme poussé au-delà de toute mesure" ou encore, de "pseudo marxistes" (Benot, 1972: 274).

A partir de 1962, l'interpénétration des capitaux publics et privés, les mesures de libéralisation adoptées dans le secteur commercial, accéléraient l'ascension de la bourgeoisie "privée" (essentiellement commerciale). Elle avait un rôle important à jouer dans le cadre d'une politique de croissance fondée sur l'appropriation d'une plus-value en provenance des activités productives nationales, la bourgeoisie d'Etat faisant le lien entre le capital commercial (situé "au-dessus" de la production agricole) et le marché international. Après le tournant de 1962, la bourgeoisie d'Etat choisit de dépendre de la rente minière et de se lier plus explicitement au capital international. Elle croyait pouvoir dorénavant prendre ses distances vis-à-vis d'une bourgeoisie commerçante qui, après avoir connu (de 1960 à 1964) un essor spectaculaire, devenait politiquement dangereuse.

En 1964 et 1965, des mesures économiques et politiques (limitation du nombre des commerçants, ce qui aboutissait à favoriser la concentration, tentative de vérification de l'origine des biens acquis, exclusion des commerçants des postes de responsabilité politique, répression du "complot" de 1965 qui manifestait l'existence d'une bourgeoisie privée également soucieuse d'accéder au pouvoir politique) frappaient cette fraction de la bourgeoisie et ses alliés dans la bourgeoisie d'Etat.

De 1967 à 1969 s'ouvrait une nouvelle période de crise. La gravité de la situation économique et financière (stagnation, inflation, généralisation du rationnement) va exacerber les conflits de classe. Le pouvoir d'Etat décidait une série "d'économies" (réduction des salaires, suppression des primes d'ancienneté et des heures supplémentaires dans les entreprises) qui, touchant surtout ouvriers et employés, soulevait le mécontentement des syndicats sans donner lieu à un conflit ouvert. Le problème sera réglé par étapes: intégration de la C.N.T.G. au Parti Démocratique de Guinée (P.D.G.) en 1967, implantation du Parti dans l'entreprise en 1968, affiliation syndicale obligatoire des travailleurs. Le syndicat devenait plus qu'une courroie de transmission: un élément supplémentaire de contrôle politique et de centralisation des revendications. Remarquons que l'offensive continue menée contre la classe ouvrière a correspondu à une diminution des effectifs de celle-ci.

Parallèlement éclatait un conflit politiquement beaucoup plus violent au sein de la bourgeoisie d'Etat. Comme nous l'avons vu, la croissance de la bourgeoisie d'Etat impliquait la constitution de "chasses gardées", de capitaux privés, et donc l'extension du champ ouvert à l'investissement privé. Mais les difficultés économiques que connaissait la Guinée restreignaient de plus en plus les possibilités d'expansion de la bourgeoisie d'Etat, à un moment où le pouvoir contrôlait de près le secteur privé. La lutte entre factions (la bourgeoisie commerciale soutenant certaines d'entre elles) devenait plus sévère, et l'intégration dans la bourgeoisie d'Etat des nouvelles générations posait un problème difficile à résoudre dans une économie en complète stagnation. L'enjeu de cet affrontement était crucial: la conquête des principaux domaines politiques et économiques du secteur étatique, mais aussi la possibilité d'une libéralisation économique à l'intérieur, et par conséquent d'une ouverture tous azimuts au capital étranger (alors que le régime en place entendait limiter cette ouverture à certaines formes de coopération avec le capital étranger, dans des domaines définis). Cette lutte impliquait on ne peut plus clairement la possibilité d'un changement de l'équipe au pouvoir.

L'épanouissement de la bourgeoisie d'Etat impliquait un style de gouvernement moins dictatorial, mais aussi, à terme, la dissolution du pouvoir d'Etat tel qu'il existait dans le pays. Les procès de 1969 et les purges de 1971 frappaient des éléments de la bourgeoisie d'Etat et de la bourgeoisie "privée". Mais la bourgeoisie d'Etat n'était pas attaquée en tant que telle. Elle allait faire l'objet d'un renouvellement profond qui, en mettant provisoirement fin à la lutte entre fractions, réglait le problème de l'intégration des nouvelles générations (Rivière, 1975: 254). Nous sommes sur ce point parfaitement d'accord avec Claude Rivière lorsqu'il écrit: "l'épuration des sympathisants de la prétendue 'cinquième colonne', en 1971, a été l'occasion d'un renouvellement radical des élites et a apporté une réponse brutale à une question cruciale".

En 1968-1969, la menace venait de l'intérieur. En 1970, un débarquement tentait de renverser le régime, et ce dernier profitait de la conjoncture pour mener à bien l'épuration entreprise en 1969, lors des procès de Conakry. A compter de 1973, l'accent mis sur les Pouvoirs révolutionnaires locaux dans tous les domaines de la vie sociale, sur leur rôle dans la planification de la production rurale et sa commercialisation, allaient susciter une forte opposition: dissimulation et évasion de biens (produits agricoles vivriers et d'exportation, troupeaux), accélération de l'émigration des hommes. Les Peuls constituant la majorité de la population, étaient aussi les plus nombreux parmi les émigrés installés dans les pays limitrophes. En effet la dominance du microfundium au Fouta-Djalon avait toujours provoqué un exode rural particulièrement important chez les Peuls. La situation de la

Guinée expliquait que ce mouvement se fasse en direction de l'étranger. Ajoutons que le bétail constituait un moyen traditionnel d'accumulation dans la société peule. La résistance des éleveurs à la tentative de "collectivisation" poursuivie par l'intermédiaire des P.R.L., ne pouvait que produire des contradictions avec des segments de cette ethnie.

S. Touré souhaitait enfin éliminer Monsieur Diallo Telli, la dernière personnalité politique (peule de surcroît) du régime ayant une dimension internationale propre. En dépit des déclarations sans cesse réitérées contre le racisme et le tribalisme, la crise économique avait renforcé les rapports noués en fonction de la parenté, plus largement de l'ethnie. C'était évident en milieu rural où la paysannerie s'enfermait dans l'autoconsommation. En milieu urbain les rapports de parenté permettaient aux plus défavorisés de faire face aux pénuries les plus criantes, d'atténuer partiellement leur situation de classe.

Au sein même de la bourgeoisie d'Etat, les rapports les plus étroits se nouaient en fonction de la parenté et de l'ethnie. Des études (Charles, 1968) ont fait apparaître la prédominance des Malinkés dans l'administration régionale et dans les entreprises nationales.

La stagnation, en freinant l'accumulation du capital, réactivait les rapports pré-capitalistes.

Il était tentant pour le pouvoir d'atteindre ses divers objectifs (freiner l'exode des hommes et des biens, mater la résistance aux nouvelles méthodes d'extorsion du surplus, éliminer des personnalités politiques peules et faire pièce à l'opposition réfugiée à l'étranger) en arguant d'un hypothétique complot peul. Comme l'a déclaré S. Touré: "On n'a pas besoin de parler de la justesse d'une ligne politique, c'est le résultat qui atteste cette justesse" (Touré, 1969: 344). Ce pragmatisme sans principe s'est révélé en l'occurence peu payant. La thèse du complot peul n'a guère suscité les échos attendus auprès des autres ethnies.[7]

En 1977 la marche des commerçantes à Conakry (le commerce privé avait officiellement disparu depuis deux ans) et les émeutes qui secouèrent plusieurs villes guinéennes contraignirent le gouvernement à modifier sa politique: suppression de la police économique, rétablissement du commerce privé. Sékou Touré annonçait une large coopération avec les pays capitalistes, se rapprochait une nouvelle fois de la Côte d'Ivoire et du Sénégal, entreprenait d'établir des relations avec les Etats du Proche-Orient et du Golfe Persique notamment. En dépit d'attentats perpétrés en 1980 et 1981, d'une opposition qui pourrait être d'origine interne, le nouveau cours de la politique guinéenne ne paraît pas s'être modifié.

Le parti unique, le Parti Démocratique de Guinée, a joué un rôle de tout premier plan dans le refoulement des contradictions de classe. Son implantation dans la société guinéenne avait été intimement liée à la pénétration des rapports marchands et de rapports de production capitalistes, à la reprise d'initiative suscitée par près d'un demi-siècle de colonisation. Le P.D.G. fut, dans sa phase ascendante, représentatif de la communauté d'intérêts de différentes classes dans leur lutte contre le colonisateur. Néanmoins, des clivages importants se produisirent au sein du Parti sous l'influence d'évènements maintenant bien connus: collaboration avec les autorités coloniales, désapparentement du Rassemblement démocratique africain (dont le P.D.G. représentait la section guinéenne) et d'avec le Parti Communiste Français, rupture avec la C.G.T. française et création de la Confédération générale des travailleurs africains (C.G.T.A.). Ces clivages avaient pour fondement la nouvelle stratégie du R.D.A. dans les années cinquante.

Après l'Indépendance, les partis qui avaient combattu le P.D.G. sur une base réactionnaire se sabordent, et leurs membres rejoignent le P.D.G. qui confie immédiatement à nombre d'entre eux des responsabilités importantes. Le P.A.I., dont la création était récente, se réclamait du marxisme-léninisme et soutenait une thèse diamétralement opposée à celle du P.D.G. sur l'existence des classes sociales en Afrique. Mais l'analyse du P.A.I. concluait à la nécessité de la formation d'un Front National (conclusion plus tard renforcée par les thèses sur la démocratie nationale de la Conférence tenue à Moscou en novembre 1960, des 81 partis communistes et ouvriers). On comprend que dans ces conditions, et en dépit de divergences idéologiques importantes, la section guinéenne du P.A.I. ait rejoint à son tour le P.D.G.

La situation interne de la Guinée, la conjoncture internationale en 1958-1960, favorisaient un équilibre relatif des classes sociales, équilibre qui se caractérisait par le fait que le maintien et le développement de rapports de production capitalistes passaient par l'émergence puis l'hégémonie d'une bourgeoisie d'Etat. Ce qui impliquait une autonomie relative du pouvoir d'Etat, particulièrement marquée dans un premier temps, et donc le recours à des méthodes dictatoriales et à une mise en tutelle complète de la bourgeoisie d'Etat et des autres classes, au nom de la survie de l'Etat et de l'intérêt national.

Le P.D.G. va constituer un instrument essentiel pour le pouvoir d'Etat. S'ingérant absolument dans tous les domaines, fussent-ils les plus traditionnellement "privés", il permet au Bureau politique national (B.P.N.), qui coïncide avec les membres essentiels du gouvernement, de se saisir de toutes les questions (individuelles ou collectives) sus-

ceptibles d'avoir des incidences politiques. B. Charles (1967) a clairement établi la prédominance de l'exécutif dans le système politique
guinéen, c'est-à-dire, en définitive, celle du Président de la République
(également Secrétaire général du Parti) et du B.P.N.

En 1964, le Parti comptait 10 250 comités de base, et donc autant
de dirigeants à ce niveau, 10 250 comités spéciaux de femmes (avec
132 500 responsables), 10 250 comités de jeunes (et 132 500 responsables), 177 comités directeurs de sections et 2 125 dirigeants, etc.
(Horoya, 1964), soit un élu pour 11 habitants. L'adhésion au Parti
étant obligatoire, et l'intervention de ce dernier indispensable pour
des actes aussi vitaux que les mariages, les divorces ou le ravitaillement, cette proportion de 1 pour 11 habitants ne traduisait pas un
fonctionnement particulièrement démocratique du Parti, mais l'étendue
du quadrillage politique réalisé par son entremise.

Ce processus de contrôle politique s'est accompagné d'une diminution spectaculaire du noyau dirigeant. En 1964, alors que le B.P.N.
comprenait encore 15 membres, des "ministres délégués" furent créés,
sortes de "Sur-ministres" qui supervisaient chacun une des quatre
grandes régions naturelles. Le VIIIe Congrès du Parti, en 1967, réduisait le B.P.N. et regroupait divers ministères rebaptisés secrétariats
d'Etat.

En 1976 existaient huit domaines: domaines du Président, du Premier ministre (Armée, Affaires étrangères, Planification, Contrôle
financier), de l'Interieur et de la Sécurité (qui englobe également la
Justice et le Développement régional), de la Culture et de l'Education,
du Social (Santé, Affaires sociales, Travail et Fonction publique), du
Commerce et des Communications, de l'Economie et des Finances
(comprenant aussi l'Industrie, les Mines, les Banques), et enfin le
domaine rural. Chaque domaine était contrôlé par un membre du
B.P.N., six de ses huit membres ayant toujours appartenu à cet organisme depuis l'Indépendance.

La réduction du nombre des membres du B.P.N. coïncidait avec la
personnalisation spectaculaire du pouvoir au bénéfice de S. Touré
(Président de la République et Secrétaire général du Parti). Le monopole politique conféré au P.D.G. conduisait à une contestation radi-
cale de toute liberté d'association (Benot, 1972: 350)[8], d'expression (y
compris culturelle et scientifique), de réunion, dans un contexte de
lutte exacerbée.

La libéralisation introduite à partir de 1978 s'est accompagnée de
modifications institutionnelles significatives: les domaines étaient
supprimés pour permettre à chaque ministre d'assurer véritablement

la responsabilité de son département. Le nombre de membres du Bureau politique national passait de 7 à 10, le Comité central voyait ses effectifs tripler (de 25 à 70), une Assemblée Nationale élargie était élue en 1980, tandis que la décision était prise de pourvoir par élection les postes de Gouverneur de Région.

Un processus de déconcentration relative du pouvoir semblait devoir succéder au style de fonctionnement des annés soixante-dix.

CONCLUSION

Le socialisme était devenu l'objectif officiel du régime à partir de 1967, alors que le niveau de vie du prolétariat s'était considérablement réduit et que la paysannerie émigrait ou s'enfermait dans l'auto-subsistance. Classe ouvrière et paysannerie étaient placées, dans l'imaginaire, aux commandes de la vie économique et sociale. Au même moment se préparait le renouvellement de la bourgeoisie d'Etat et se poursuivait la liquidation de la bourgeoisie privée. En 1963 déjà, un an après avoir écrasé la gauche marxiste, S. Touré avait prétendu que la Guinée s'orientait vers un "développement socialiste à partir des réalités paysannes" (Benot, 1972: 275). Du reste, comment envisager une transition vers le socialisme quand l'idéologie officielle se refusait à une analyse de la lutte des classes en termes de rapports de production, et assimilait la bourgeoisie à une collection d'individus manifestant une attitude critique vis-à-vis du pouvoir d'Etat?

En dépit d'un secteur public omniprésent (en dehors de la production agricole), la Guinée ne s'est jamais engagée dans une voie de développement non capitaliste. Le bilan est éloquent après deux décennies d'indépendance, qu'il s'agisse de l'évolution de l'agriculture, de l'industrialisation, de la planification, du rôle dévolu à la classe ouvrière et à la paysannerie dans le fonctionnement des instances économiques et politiques.

Le véritable problème à l'ordre du jour est de mettre en place les mécanismes propres à permettre un développement plus rapide du capitalisme, et il nous paraît indispensable à cet égard de nuancer nos analyses antérieures (Cournanel, 1968 et 1976: 50). Le rythme moyen de croissance enregistré depuis 1959 est trop faible (tout au plus une multiplication par 2,5 du produit national en 20 ans) étant donné la modestie du point de départ.

Nous avions avancé l'hypothèse que toute tentative pour créer un capital (au sens marxiste du terme) national à partir du secteur public avait pour corollaires l'inflation et la stagnation, dans des formations sociales telles que la Guinée. L'argument développé était que les capitaux constitués par les particuliers n'étaient pas assez importants, considérés isolément, pour financer des actions susceptibles d'accélérer la croissance du produit national.

De ce fait, ils étaient essentiellement investis dans des opérations commerciales ou spéculatives. Néanmoins, dans la mesure où ces capitaux provenaient de ponctions sur les moyens destinés à l'accumulation collective (assurée par la bourgeoisie d'Etat), leur constitution ralentissait sensiblement le rythme de croissance. Ce raisonnement est loin d'être satisfaisant. La stagnation n'est pas une conséquence inéluctable de l'instauration du capitalisme d'Etat. La période (1960-1965) où la croissance du produit national guinéen a été la plus rapide a coïncidé avec un élargissement simultané de la bourgeoisie d'Etat et de la bourgeoisie privée (surtout commerciale, mais elle commençait à investir aussi dans le domaine manufacturier, même si ces tentatives n'ont pas eu le loisir de se multiplier).

C'est là que réside le problème posé à la Guinée. Dans le cadre des rapports de production hérités de la colonisation, en l'absence donc d'une stratégie de transition vers le socialisme, il n'est pas possible à la bourgeoisie d'Etat de supprimer les autres fractions de la bourgeoisie, tout en assurant un rythme satisfaisant de croissance.

La matérialisation des projets miniers est trop lente pour autoriser la bourgeoisie d'Etat à négliger le surplus d'origine agricole, comme elle avait cru pouvoir le faire jusqu'aux années soixante-dix. Mais la décennie écoulée montre également que la bourgeoisie d'Etat ne peut résoudre le problème en écartant le capital commercial et en intervenant directement au niveau de la production. En définitive il était faux d'écrire, comme nous l'avons fait (Cournanel, 1976: 50), que le développement de la bourgeoisie privée limitait les possibilités d'accumulation nationale et de croissance. C'est l'inverse qui est vrai.

Dans la mesure où la constitution de capitaux privés est indissociable du capitalisme d'Etat, toute tentative pour faire uniquement "disparaître" la bourgeoisie privée, conduit à renforcer les rapports de production pré-capitalistes (surtout dans les campagnes) et à développer l'économie souterraine au détriment de la création d'entreprises capitalistes dans le pays (commerces, petites usines de transformation, plantations, etc.), fussent-elles de taille modeste.

En retour, les mesures volontaristes prises contre le capital privé, les déclarations fracassantes sur un socialisme mythique, leurs effets sur la situation économique interne, toujours préoccupante, parfois catastrophique, ont certainement joué un rôle important dans les réticences du capital étranger.

Quinze ans après, le même problème se pose dans des termes identiques: l'élargissement simultané (même si des compromis sont indispensables pour assurer le maintien d'un secteur public important) de la bourgeoisie d'Etat et de la bourgeoisie privée est indispensable mais il implique des changements politiques au plus haut niveau.

Etant donné le discrédit dans lequel la logomachie du P.D.G. risque d'avoir jeté les notions mêmes de révolution et de socialisme, un développement accéléré tant du capitalisme d'Etat, que du capital privé national, avec toutes leurs implications, le rapprochement (monétaire et commercial notamment) avec les formations sociales voisines de l'ouest Africain, créeraient sans doute les éléments indispensables pour une transition ultérieure.

NOTES

1. Le franc C.F.A. (des Colonies françaises d'Afrique) fut créé en 1945. Sa valeur fut portée à 2 francs métropolitains en 1948. Cette parité s'est maintenue et donc par rapport au nouveau franc français, la valeur est 1 nouveau franc: 0.02 franc C.F.A.

2. La valeur du franc guinéen créé en 1961 était de 1 F C.F.A.: 1 F.G.

3. Le Syli valait en 1972 0,20 franc français, ou 10 F C.F.A. En 1979 il représentait 0,223 F F ou 11,13 F C.F.A. De 1973 à 1975 la valeur du Syli par rapport au dollar américain était de $1 U.S.: 20.46 Sylis. Il est rattaché depuis 1975 aux droits de tirage spéciaux, D.T.S.; 1 D.T.S.: 24.68 Sylis. En octobre 1980, 1 Syli valait officiellement 11 F C.F.A. La valeur du Syli en mars 1982 était la suivante: $1 U.S.: 22.02 Sylis, 1 Syli: 10 F C.F.A.: 0.20 franc français.

4. En dépit du grand intérêt des analyses sur la bourgeoisie d'Etat contenues dans cet ouvrage, nous tenons à souligner notre désaccord avec l'optique générale de cet ouvrage.

5. Or le pouvoir d'achat en 1951 correspondait à celui de 1938! Il ne s'agit pas d'un phénomène extraordinaire. En décembre 1963 au Ghana, le taux de salaire réel tombait au dessous du niveau atteint en 1939 (Fitch et Oppenheimer, 1966: 97).

6. Ce conflit prolongeait celui de 1957, pendant la phase d'autonomie interne, entre le gouvernement déjà dirigé par S. Touré, les syndicats et la gauche au sein du Parti Démocratique de Guinée (et dont les positions coïncidaient avec celles du P.A.I. créé seulement en 1957).

7. De violents affrontements ethnico-politiques s'étaient produits avant l'Indépendance. Il n'est pas exclu que les autorités aient spéculé sur les résurgences de vieux antagonismes.

8. Les remarques de Benot ont été rédigées avant l'intégration de la C.N.T.G. dans le P.D.G., en 1969.

OUVRAGES CITES

ALTHUSSER, L. (1970). "Les appareils idéologiques d'Etat." La Pensée, juin.

AMIN, S. (1973). Africa South of the Sahara. Europa Publications.

———(1971). L'Afrique de l'Ouest bloquée. Paris: Minuit.

BALIBAR, E. (1974). Cinq études du matérialisme historique. Paris: Maspero.

BELL, G. (1963). Le pôle électro-métallurgique de Fria. Paris: Cahiers de l'Institut de Science Economique Appliquée, Série F, no 18, septembre.

BENOT, Y. (1972). Idéologies des Indépendances africaines. 2e édition. Paris: Maspero.

BETTELHEIM, C. (1970). Calcul économique et formes de propriété. Paris: Maspero.

———(1968). La Transition vers l'économie socialiste. Paris: Maspero.

———(1950). Mémorandum no 1, objet: Orientation générale de la planification guinéenne, Conakry.

Bulletin d'Afrique (1981). no 10453, avril.

Cecchi et Co. (1963). The Climate for Private Investment in Guinea. The Basis for Industrial Growth, Conakry.

CHARLES, B. (1968). Cadres guinéens et appartenances ethniques, Paris: Thèse, Sorbonne.

———(1967). "La Guinée" dans Mabileau et Meyriat (eds.). Décolonisation et régimes politiques en Afrique Noire. Paris: Colin.

CONDÉ, A. (1972). Guinée: Albanie et l'Afrique ou néocolonie américaine? Paris: Git-Le-Coeur.

COURNANEL, A. (1979). "L'analyse du capitalisme périphérique," Tiers Monde, no 77, janvier-mars.

———(1976). "Le capitalisme d'Etat en Afrique: le cas guinéen," Revue française d'études politiques africaines, mars.

———(1971). "Situation de la classe ouvrière en République de Guinée," Partisans, Paris, septembre-octobre.

———(1968). Planification et investissement privé dans l'expérience guinéenne. Paris: Thèse non-publiée.

Economiste du Tiers Monde (1974), novembre-décembre.

Europe - Outre-Mer (1979), septembre.

FITCH, B. et M. OPPENHEIMER. (1966). Ghana: End of an Illusion. Monthly Review Press.

HODGKINSON, E. (1982). Africa South of the Sahara, 1981-1982. Europa Publications.

Horoya (1964). Organe quotidien du P.D.G. 19/11/1964.

Horoya (1976). Collections de Horoya, République de Guinée.

HUSSEIN, M. (1971). La lutte des classes en Egypte, Paris: Maspero (2e édition).

Industries et Travaux d'Outremer (1980), mai.

Industries et Travaux d'Outremer (1981), janvier.

Jeune Afrique (1981), 13 mai.

LATREMOLIÈRE, J. (1975). "La Guinée pays minier - réalités et perspectives", Afrique Contemporaine, no 81, septembre-octobre.

LEUNDA, X. (1974). "Nouvelles institutions rurales en Guinée", Bruxelles: Civilisations, nos 1-2, Année 1973-1974.

Marchés Tropicaux et Méditerranéens (1981 a), 24 avril.

————(1981 b), 17 juillet.

————(1980), 10 octobre.

————(1974), 19 avril.

MARX, K. (1960). Le Capital, Tome VIII. Paris: Editions Sociales.

Moniteur Africain (1973). 30 août.

MOUSSA, P. (1957). Les chances de la communauté franco-africaine. Paris: Colin.

Organisation des Nations Unies (1973). Yearbook of International Trade Statistics, 1972–1973.

Organisation des Nations Unies. (1975). Conseil Economique et Social. Comité des Ressources Nouvelles. EC 7/51 - 13 février.

PRÉ, R. (1951). L'avenir de la Guinée française. Editions Guinéennes.

Revue de Développement Economique (1964). Conakry, no. 1, janvier.

République de Guinée, Ministère de l'Agriculture (1963). Conférence économique de Mamou du 18 au 20 avril. Rapport sur la préparation de la campagne agricole 1963.

RIVIÈRE, C. (1975). Dynamique de la stratification sociale en Guinée. Paris: Librairie Champion.

————(1978). Classes et stratifications sociales en Afrique. Le cas guinéen. Paris: Presses Universitaires de France.

RYELANDT, B. (1970). L'inflation en pays sous-développés. Origines, mécanismes de propagation et effets des pressions inflatoires au Congo, 1960–1969. Mouton.

TOURÉ, S. (1969). Défendre la révolution. Conakry.

6

SOCIALISME, CAPITALISME, ET PRECAPITALISME AU MALI (1960-1982)

JEAN-LOUP AMSELLE

Grâce à un certain nombre de travaux effectués récemment (Jones, 1976; Ernst, 1976; Martin, 1976; Jacquemot ed., 1981; Bagayogo, 1982 et Maharaux, 1982), on connaît maintenant avec suffisamment de précision l'évolution politique et économique du Mali depuis la fin de la Deuxième Guerre mondiale et particulièrement la période dite "socialiste" qui s'étend de 1960 à 1968.

Aussi plutôt que de me livrer à un rappel historique classique concernant la période coloniale et le début de la colonisation pour brosser ensuite un tableau de ce pays depuis 1960, je préfère dégager quelques grands traits qui serviront à caractériser la "philosophie" du Mali indépendant et qui pourront également le cas échéant, s'appliquer à d'autres pays africains.

LE SOUDAN COLONIAL (1946–1960)

En 1946 avec la création des partis et syndicats, les différentes classes sociales et forces politiques qui travaillaient le Soudan colonial en profondeur, trouvent soudain à s'exprimer. Ces partis, le Parti soudanais du progrès (P.S.P.) et l'Union soudanaise du rassemblement démocratique africain (U.S.R.D.A.) avaient un recrutement assez marqué bien qu'ayant tous deux à leur tête des bureaucrates. Le premier dirigé par Fily Dabo Cissoko, un chef de canton lettré qui après l'indépendance défendra les intérêts des commerçants, bénéficiait du soutien des notables locaux et des aristocrates ruraux et recevait de l'administration coloniale tout l'appui nécessaire.

L'U.S.R.D.A. avait également à sa tête des bureaucrates et représentait fondamentalement ceux qui constitueront plus tard la bourgeoisie d'Etat. Elle noue une alliance tactique avec les commerçants qui financent le mouvement et utilise les paysans et les rares ouvriers comme masse de manoeuvre. Défendant des thèmes progressistes comme la suppression des travaux forcés, le relèvement des prix au producteur et enfin la libération totale du colonisateur, elle réussit à attirer à elle la majeure partie de la paysannerie. Les commerçants qui souhaitent se débarrasser des maisons de traite françaises, des Libano-syriens, et obtenir des prêts que les banques leur refusent, adhérent également à ses positions nationalistes (Amselle, 1977: 239-260). C'est ainsi que l'U.S.D.R.A. finit par l'emporter sur le P.S.P. aux élections de 1959 et décide alors de supprimer la chefferie de canton.

LE MALI SOCIALISTE (1960-1968)

Lorsqu'en 1960, le Mali obtient l'indépendance, la petite bourgeoisie d'enseignants, de commis et de syndicalistes issus de l'aristocratie ouvrière qui dirige l'U.S.R.D.A., s'installe au pouvoir. Là, comme du reste dans bon nombre de pays en voie de développement, en raison de la faiblesse de l'industrialisation, de la domination du capital étranger et de la prédominance du milieu rural, l'accumulation ne peut se faire que par le biais de l'Etat et du commerce, les deux secteurs fonctionnant d'ailleurs bien souvent en symbiose.

C'est dire que cette petite bourgeoisie, en accédant aux responsabilités suprêmes, prend d'emblée la forme d'une "nomenklatura" selon l'expression de Voslensky (1981), c'est-à-dire d'une nouvelle classe de privilégiés dont le pouvoir politique n'est pas la résultante de la détention de moyens de production et d'échange mais bien au contraire dont les instruments d'accumulation sont fonction de la place occupée dans l'appareil d'Etat.

Lorsqu'elle arrive au pouvoir, cette "nomenklatura" a réussi à éliminer totalement la classe rivale, l'aristocratie terrienne, grâce à la suppression du parti politique qui représentait les intérêts de cette dernière: le P.S.P. Toute sa tactique va donc consister à se débarrasser de la bourgeoisie marchande et à pressurer la paysannerie pour se constituer en tant que classe. Pour ce faire, cette "nomenklatura" va se parer des oripeaux du socialisme. On ne reviendra pas en détail sur les origines du "socialisme" au Mali; il est certain que les communistes français en poste au Soudan ont grandement contribué à l'essor de l'U.S.R.D.A., de la lutte anti-coloniale et également de la diffusion de la vulgate marxiste-léniniste dans sa version stalinienne. Cependant il ne faut pas surestimer l'influence du marxisme même stalinisé sur la pensée des dirigeants socialistes maliens. Ce qu'ont apporté à l'U.S.R.D.A. le parti communiste français et, derrière lui, le Komintern ou le Kominform, c'est d'abord un modèle d'organisation, le parti unique, et l'idée que le secteur d'Etat et la planification doivent jouer un rôle moteur dans l'économie. La vision léniniste d'une paysannerie arriérée a pu également jouer un rôle négatif dans les conceptions politiques des leaders maliens mais toute aussi importante a été, comme en témoigne l'oeuvre d'un des plus grands idéologues du régime, Seydou Badian Kouyaté (1964), la théorie du "socialisme africain" qu'on retrouve à des variantes près chez Senghor, N'Krumah et Nyerere.

Selon cette théorie, l'Afrique d'avant les Blancs aurait été essentiellement rurale, communautaire et égalitaire. Les paysans auraient vécu dans des collectivités villageoises harmonieuses que seule l'empreinte coloniale serait venue oblitérer.

Tels sont les deux pôles de l'idéologie qui animait les dirigeants socialistes maliens au moment de l'indépendance. En quoi cette idéologie était-elle adéquate au projet socio-économique conscient ou inconscient qui était le leur?

Tout d'abord, la priorité donnée au secteur d'Etat, à la planification et à l'essor étatique des forces productives permettait de faire pièce au secteur privé, c'est-à-dire aux maisons de traite françaises qui seront éliminées, mais surtout à la bourgeoisie marchande qui avait été déjà gravement lésée par l'éclatement de la Fédération du Mali en 1960.[1] En ce sens la création de l'Office des produits agricoles du Mali (O.P.A.M.) et de la Société malienne d'importation et d'exportation (S.O.M.I.E.X.) limita grandement la capacité économique et donc politique des commerçants maliens et en particulier de ceux qui fonctionnaient dans l'orbite de ces vieilles maisons de commerce. La constitution de ce secteur d'Etat qui était relayé par des coopératives au niveau villageois permettait également à cette "nomenklatura" naissante de prélever par le biais de la commercialisation forcée des céréales, donc de son achat à bas prix, des "investissements humains" et des "champs collectifs", ce qu'on peut appeler à la suite d'I. Bagayogo (1982: 133) une "rente bureaucratique".

Cette rente bureaucratique était d'autant plus facilement perçue qu'elle s'appuyait sur l'idéologie du "socialisme africain" qui a été évoquée plus haut. La méconnaissance intéressée des milieux ruraux maliens et la projection fantasmatique d'un modèle homogène et communautaire sur les paysans, permettaient de nier leur organisation sociale effective (lignages, clans, chefferies) et de leur imposer un réseau d'encadrement qui facilitait leur exploitation. La radicalisation économique du régime se traduisit par la création, en 1962, d'un franc inconvertible, ce qui ne tarda pas à provoquer un affrontement entre la "nomenklatura" et la bourgeoisie marchande. Celui-ci se produisit en juillet 1962 lorsque les commerçants défilèrent dans Bamako aux cris de "Vive le C.F.A.". La manifestation fut suivie de l'arrestation et de la condamnation à mort des leaders de l'aristocratie terrienne déchue: Fily Dabo Cissoko et Hamadoun Dicko qui étaient devenus les représentants de la classe marchande ainsi que celle d'un riche commerçant de Bamako, Kasoum Touré.[2]

Dès lors, la classe marchande malienne cessera d'exister en tant que force politique organisée même si elle continuera, comme par le passé, à contrôler les campagnes et même si par son action économique elle contribuera à saper les fondements du régime "socialiste".

Ayant abattu à la fois l'aristocratie terrienne et la bourgeoisie marchande, la bureaucratie naissante allait pouvoir accomplir son destin historique, c'est-à-dire se constituer en tant que classe.

Il s'agira dans un premier temps de peupler et de développer l'appareil d'Etat abandonné par le colonisateur français, ensuite d'assurer la "reproduction élargie" de ses propres effectifs en créant un tissu industriel et commercial d'Etat.

Ainsi entre 1960 et 1968, le plus souvent avec l'aide des pays de l'Est, l'U.R.S.S. et la Chine notamment, un grand nombre d'entreprises publiques verront le jour: Société Nationale d'Exploitation des Huileries du Mali (S.N.E.H.M.), Société des Conserves du Mali (S.O.C.O.M.A.), Societe Nationale pour l'Exploitation des Abattoirs (S.O.N.E.A.), Ateliers et Chantiers du Mali (A.C.M.), Société Nationale d'Entreprises et de Travaux Publics (S.O.N.E.T.R.A.), Régie des Transports du Mali (R.T.M.), Air Mali, Compagnie Malienne de Navigation, Pharmacie Populaire, Librarie Populaire et, bien sur, la S.O.M.I.E.X. et l'O.P.A.M. déjà citées (Constantin et Coulon 1978).

C'est ce tissu industriel et commercial d'Etat qui fournira la structure d'accueil du peuplement de la "nomenklatura". En 1968, il comptera 9000 personnes et occupera une place privilégiée dans l'économie malienne (Constantin et Coulon 1978).

L'industrialisation du Mali à cette époque n'est pas dictée par des raisons strictement "économiques", c'est-à-dire par la volonté de réaliser une accumulation de type capitaliste comportant la réalisation d'un profit, elle obéit davantage à des motifs politiques, à savoir trouver des emplois à des "clients".

En ce sens, il s'agit d'une "industrialisation clientéliste et extensive" qui consiste moins à accroître la productivité qu'à trouver des postes à des protégés. Et c'est pourquoi toutes les critiques que l'on peut faire au caractère inefficace et pléthorique de la bureaucratie malienne d'avant et d'après le coup d'état de 1968, sont d'une certaine façon sans objet puisque cela revient à la juger selon des critères de rationalité capitaliste alors qu'il est sans doute préférable de l'évaluer selon ses propres normes de fonctionnement: celles d'une bureaucratie analogue à celle des pays de l'Est (Voslensky, 1981) et soumise en plus à des principes de prédation et de redistribution remontant à l'époque précoloniale.

Parallèlement à la constitution de cette "nomenklatura" en bourgeoisie industrielle et commerciale d'Etat, la bureaucratie malienne, sous prétexte du "retour à la terre" et de fidélité aux traditions agraires des civilisations soudano-sahéliennes, se transforme en une bourgeoisie agraire et crée des grandes plantations autour des villes en utilisant de la main-d'oeuvre salariée.

Pendant les huit années où elle a été mise en oeuvre, cette politique a réussi à mécontenter à peu près tout le monde, hormis ceux qui occupaient les sommets de l'Etat. L'ensemble de la population a en effet subi les tracasseries de la milice populaire dont les membres recrutés hâtivement et lancés sans aucune formation dans des tâches de contrôle et de police surent rapidement se faire haïr. Lié à l'existence de cette milice, le climat de suspicion et de délation entretenu par le gouvernement provoqua l'hostilité de nombreux Maliens. Enfin les souscriptions présentées comme volontaires mais qui étaient en fait de véritables impôts firent perdre progressivement au régime le capital de confiance dont il disposait au moment de l'indépendance. Mais à côté de ces causes d'ordre général, il en existe d'autres qui rendent compte de la désaffection des différentes couches sociales.

Les fonctionnaires, tout d'abord, qui auraient dû être le pilier du socialisme malien, ont vu leur niveau de vie baisser après l'indépendance, surtout après la dévaluation du franc malien de 50% en avril 1967 et la suppression des logements de fonction en juin de la même année. En outre, ils furent soumis plus que d'autres aux souscriptions de tous ordres qui se traduisaient souvent par des retenues de salaires.

L'armée a vu également son niveau de vie baisser entre 1960 et 1968 mais elle avait des raisons supplémentaires d'en vouloir à ce régime qui avait créé une milice la menaçant dans son prestige et sa fonction et qui, dans le souci d'en faire une armée populaire, l'obligeait à se livrer à l'agriculture. Les contrôles portant sur les biens privés ("opérations taxis, villas"), entrepris à la veille du coup d'état ne pouvaient que la décider à passer à l'action.

Toutefois le résultat majeur de cette politique fut de créer un fossé entre la "nomenklatura" et la paysannerie, cette dernière exerçant en permanence une résistance passive se muant parfois en mouvements de révolte ouverts (Amselle, 1978; Bagayogo, 1982: 222–223). Elle provoqua également l'opposition larvée des commerçants qui certes disparaissent, comme nous l'avons vu, en tant que force organisée mais qui manifestent néanmoins leur mécontentement en fuyant le pays et en exportant illégalement leurs capitaux.[3] Dans le même temps, ces marchands rendent de réels services aux paysans en les ravitaillant avec des produits importés introuvables dans le circuit étatique et en leur achetant les céréales et l'arachide à des prix supérieurs à ceux pratiqués par les organismes officiels. Ils provoquent ainsi l'affaiblissement de l'économie malienne et se rapprochent des paysans à qui ils apparaissent comme des protecteurs face à un appareil d'Etat coercitif.

LE MALI MILITAIRE

Plus que tout autre facteur, l'alliance entre la paysannerie et les commerçants explique l'effondrement du Mali socialiste le 19 novembre 1968 alors que beaucoup d'observateurs estimaient que ce régime était un des plus solides d'Afrique. La politique mise en oeuvre par les militaires contentera, dans un premier temps, les paysans en supprimant les champs collectifs ainsi que la commercialisation forcée des céréales.[4] Elle sera également plus favorable aux investissements privés tant nationaux qu'étrangers. Le nouveau régime donne ainsi satisfaction aux commerçants, bien que ceux-ci n'aient pas participé directement au coup d'Etat, en assouplissant les conditions d'exercice du commerce et en incitant les négociants à rapatrier leurs avoirs déposés à l'étranger pour les investir dans les entreprises locales. Depuis 1968, une vingtaine d'entreprises industrielles ont été créées par des Maliens, ces derniers travaillant seuls ou en association avec des investisseurs étrangers et essentiellement dans les industries agricoles, alimentaires et de biens de consommation (Maharaux, 1982). Cette percée incontestable des opérateurs privés maliens sur le marché industriel doit néanmoins être nuancée. Dans certains cas, en effet, ceux-ci ne doivent leur entrée dans ce secteur qu'au retrait de capitaux étrangers. Le groupe Agache-Willot a ainsi revendu ses parts dans l'usine textile ITEMA aux commerçants Bathily en raison des pertes qu'il encourait. D'autres entrepreneurs maliens comme Mamadou Saada Diallo (industrie chimique et alimentaire) et ceux détenant des parts dans la SOMASAC (entreprise de sacherie) et dans la SOMAPIL (piles) connaissent également des difficultés (Maharaux, 1982: 146; Mazier, Jacquemot et Gamet, 1981).

En fait la libéralisation du commerce et des investissements privés dans l'industrie a surtout profité aux capitaux étrangers, qu'ils soient d'origine occidentale, asiatique ou libano-syrienne. Ces capitaux se sont investis dans plusieurs unités industrielles qui se sont ajoutées à celles, peu nombreuses, qui existaient déjà avant 1968. Ces entreprises ont pour caractéristique essentielle d'être des industries légères, induites et à profit élevé. Citons parmi elles la Société Scierie Atelier Garage (scierie et atelier de réparation pour camions et voitures), SIVINEX (embouteillage de vin), I.M.A.C.Y., filiale de la C.F.A.O. (construction de cycles), SOMABIPAL (biscuiterie et pâtes alimentaires), Mali Industrie (fabrication de fenêtres), SEGMA (émaillage et galvanisation), SOMAPA (parfumerie) etc. On peut également mesurer le degré de pénétration du capital étranger par l'existence de nombreuses sociétés combinant du capital expatrié et du capital étatique malien. C'est notamment le cas d'ITEMA jusqu'en 1979 (Agache-Willot 52%, Etat malien 48%), de la petite unité industrielle de l'Opération pêche (FED, PAM, Etat malien), de l'Union laitière de Bamako (UNICEF, PAM, Etat malien), de la SEPAMA (huilerie, Hobum Afrika Hambourg 51%, Etat malien 49%), de la SOCAM (conserverie CFDT, Coopérative agricole de Camaret 10%, Etat malien 90%), et de la SMECMA (matériel agricole, CODAMM 16, 6%, Etat malien 83, 34%). Si le grand changement par rapport à la période socialiste a été la croissance des investissements étrangers, il n'en reste pas moins que parallèlement le secteur industriel d'Etat a connu depuis 1968 un développement important. Souvent ces entreprises industrielles avaient d'ailleurs été conçues sous l'ancien régime mais elles ont été néanmoins reprises à leur compte par les militaires. C'est notamment le cas de la Société des Tanneries du Mali (TAMALI), de la Société des Ciments du Mali (SOCIMA), de la Rizerie de Sévaré, de la COMATEX (usine textile) dont la dernière unité a été installée en 1975 et de l'exploitation de l'or de Kalana (SONAREM). De nouvelles réalisations ont également vu le jour comme celle des phosphates de Bourem (SONAREM). La poursuite de l'édification du secteur industriel d'Etat après 1968 ainsi que le maintien des Sociétés et Entreprises d'Etat qui existaient auparavant ne manifestent pas simplement le désir de sauvegarder les "acquis du peuple", de défendre le socialisme et de conserver au pays son rôle de non-aligné, image que précisément le régime de Moussa Traoré voulait jusqu'à une époque récente accréditer dans l'opinion malienne et internationale. Elles obéissent également à une rationalité politique et économique évidente qui consiste à assurer, comme sous le régime de Modibo Keita, une base sociale à la "nomenklatura", en réservant des postes à des privilégiés et en permettant le prélèvement de la rente bureaucratique faite en grande partie de détournement, de concussion et de prévarication.

Comme on peut le constater, c'est toujours le modèle de "l'industrialisation clientéliste" qui prévaut et non la préservation des intérêts du peuple malien auquel auraient été fournis des biens et des services à des prix très bas. On retrouve ce modèle clientéliste ainsi que l'association de l'Etat et des capitaux étrangers dans l'agriculture. Jusqu'en 1968, en dehors de la Compagnie française des textiles (C.F.D.T.) et de l'Opération arachide du Bureau de développement de la production agricole (BDPA), organisme dépendant du Ministère français de la Coopération, créé en 1967, l'essentiel de l'exploitation de la paysannerie était l'oeuvre de l'OPAM, de la SOMIEX et du réseau des coopératives.

Depuis cette date, le pays s'est couvert d'opérations de développement toutes placées sous la juridiction de l'Etat malien mais également toutes financées en grande partie, sinon en totalité, avec des capitaux étrangers. Ces opérations de développement rural (ODR), au nombre d'une vingtaine, ne profitent, en fait, qu'à quelques privilégiés. Ainsi, l'O.A.C.V. (Opération arachide et culture vivrière) qui a vu le jour en 1974 et qui bénéficie d'un financement de la Banque Mondiale et du FAC (Fonds d'aide et de coopération, organisme financier du Ministère français de la Coopération) est-elle censée fournir des intrants aux paysans, assurer leur encadrement et commercialiser l'arachide.

Le bilan de cette opération effectué après huit ans de fonctionnement révèle que celle-ci n'a bénéficié qu'à l'Etat malien, au personnel de cet organisme ainsi qu'à quelques "paysans pilotes" qui sont, en fait, pour la plupart, des commerçants, des marabouts et des paysans riches, c'est-à-dire des producteurs ayant des liens avec l'appareil d'Etat.[5]

Une situation analogue prévaut à l'Opération riz de Segou, où l'essentiel des périmètres irrigués ont été attribués à des fonctionnaires et des commerçants. Il en ira probablement de même pour les terres situées en aval du barrage de Selingué.

L'UTILISATION DU SURPLUS

Les politiques d'aide mises en oeuvre par les grandes puissances depuis l'indépendance ont eu plusieurs effets sur la vie économique du Mali. Tout d'abord la venue d'un grand nombre de diplomates, de coopérants et d'experts a entraîné la création d'un marché nouveau pour les fonctionnaires et les commerçants maliens.

C'est ainsi que la demande de logements a été fortement stimulée et que les classes dirigeantes y ont répondu en faisant construire de somptueuses villas louées à des prix mirobolants. En outre la fourniture d'une aide financière et budgétaire a provoqué le gonflement de la masse monétaire mise en circulation, ce qui a permis son détournement à des fins d'accumulation et de consommation par ceux qui se trouvent à proximité des circuits fiduciaires, (trésor, douances, etc. . . .) et a nourri l'inflation.

De même le matériel destiné à l'agriculture—camions, tracteurs, land rovers—a été récupéré par les bourgeoisies qui l'ont utilisé sur leurs propres plantations ou l'ont reconverti en luxueuses voitures d'un usage plus commode en ville.

Le détournement et la concussion sont désormais des pratiques généralisées au Mali: tout ce qui peut se vendre est vendu, depuis les permis de conduire jusqu'aux actes judiciaires en passant par les médicaments. Le salaire correspondant au poste occupé est sans commune mesure avec les revenus réels perçus par l'agent en fonction de la position de pillage qu'il occupe dans l'appareil d'Etat.

On voit ainsi se dessiner les véritables ressorts des classes au pouvoir: voitures, vergers, villas, virements, les "4 V" selon une expression en vogue au Mali. Le prélèvement de la rente bureaucratique provenant des revenus extra-salariaux de la "nonmenklatura" donne, en général, lieu à des processus d'accumulation et de consommation qui se déroulent dans un ordre déterminé. Le démarrage se fait d'abord dans des entreprises de transport privé qui prospèrent particulièrement à Bamako depuis le démantèlement de la compagnie publique de transports urbains (TUB). Les gains de celles-ci financent par la suite en tout ou en partie de la construction immobilière ou de la plantation fruitière ou légumière. Le reste est consommé en biens et agréments de luxe représentés par les "V" des vacances à l'étranger et du vidéo-cassette fort prisé à Bamako bien qu'il n'existe pas de réseau de télévision, sans compter l'entretien d'une nombreuse clientèle sociale. Cependant, il faut noter qu'à la différence des pays occidentaux où l'accumulation se traduit par l'extension du mode de production capitaliste, dans des pays comme le Mali, et en dehors des quelques entrepreneurs privés maliens évoqués plus haut, le prélèvement de la rente bureaucratique ne débouche sur aucun processus productif. Le détournement et la corruption ne sont, en fait, que des moyens d'accéder à un statut déterminé, lequel se manifeste par un certain nombre de signes.

Dans une telle économie, ce ne sont ni la production ni le profit qui sont déterminants dans les processus d'accumulation qui ont pour origine le pillage de l'appareil d'Etat. Il serait, d'ailleurs, préférable de remplacer le terme accumulation par celui de prédation et de définir la circulation de biens et d'argent qui en découle comme de la redistribution, pour mettre en relief le lien qui existe entre la "nomenklatura" malienne actuelle et sa devancière, l'artistocratie terrienne et guerrière, à qui elle emprunte nombre de ses comportements.

LA SÉCHERESSE

Le processus de captation du surplus s'est considérablement accru à partir de 1973, quand a débuté la sécheresse qui se poursuit actuellement. Depuis cette date, des flots d'aide alimentaire sont déversés sur le Mali. Pour la période 1973-1978, celle-ci s'élève à 460 592 tonnes (Thenevin, 1980: 25). Comme il était prévu dans les accords, une bonne partie de cette aide (surtout des céréales) a été revendue à la clientèle solvable, ce qui a permis de renflouer la trésorerie déficiente de l'OPAM ou, ce qui revient au même, a été purement et simplement détournée par les classes au pouvoir. Comme le fait remarquer Thenevin (1980: 82), l'aide alimentaire présente en effet sur les autres types d'aide un avantage considérable dans la mesure où sa destination et son utilisation ne sont assorties d'aucun contrôle de la part des organismes donateurs. Alors que les opérations de développement en milieu rural, par exemple, sont soumises à l'évaluation d'experts envoyés par les pays développés, l'usage de l'aide alimentaire dès lors qu'elle est accordée, est laissée à la libre disposition du pays receveur.

Au Mali pendant toute cette période, on assiste à des phénomènes massifs de captation et d'utilisation ostentatoire de l'aide alimentaire

C'est ainsi qu'on peut noter la croissance du parc automobile et de la construction immobilière avec, à Bamako, les célèbres "million bugu" (litt. le quartier du million), "avenue" et "palais de la sécheresse" selon les noms que leur donne le peuple malien.

Cette catastrophe naturelle est également l'occasion pour le gouvernement malien de procéder à la liquidation de fait d'une fraction de la population, à savoir les nomades. Le détournement de l'aide alimentaire condamne, en effet, à mort une grande partie des éleveurs qui vivent dans la région septentrionale du pays et qui, pour de multiples raisons, sont beaucoup plus durement touchés par la sécheresse que les paysans (Amselle, 1981).

LES RÉACTIONS

Ce processus massif d'enrichissement de la classe dominante malienne aussi bien dans sa composante bureaucratique que marchande, incite le gouvernement à anticiper les réactions de la couche sociale qui est la plus active politiquement parce que sans doute la plus démunie, c'est-à-dire les masses urbaines et particulièrement bamakoises.[6] Celles-ci voient, en effet, leurs conditions de vie durement touchées par l'inflation, le blocage et le paiement différé des salaires.[7]

A l'occasion du coup de force de 1978, tombent ainsi les premières "victimes de la sécheresse" du côté des classes dirigeantes: Karim Dembélé, Kissima Doukara et Tiekoro Bagayogo. Comme le dit bien I. Bagayogo (1982: 132), ces arrestations font partie des campagnes de moralisation qui fonctionnent comme un moyen pour le chef de l'Etat de se refaire une virginité politique. Chaudement applaudies par les citadins, elles permettent pour un temps de masquer l'extorsion dont est victime la plus grande partie de la population. La première réaction des Maliens qui ne soit pas due à l'initiative du régime sera celle des étudiants qui en 1979-1980 se révoltent contre le pouvoir à cause de la nature dictatoriale de celui-ci mais également pour des raisons strictement corporatistes: celles relatives au droit d'obtenir automatiquement un emploi dans la fonction publique à l'issue des études supérieures.

Ces manifestations d'étudiants qui entraîneront la participation des masses urbaines se poursuivront jusqu'en 1980. Elles se solderont par une répression sanglante et la fermeture de la quasi-totalité des établissements. En octobre 1981, les écoles rouvriront leurs portes sans que les étudiants aient obtenu quoi que ce soit.

Ce mouvement, qui exprimait avant tout les intérêts des étudiants, manifestait également le consensus de la société malienne face à un droit précis, celui pour quiconque de devenir fonctionnaire à l'issue d'un cycle d'études. Or ce droit, considéré comme intangible depuis la période coloniale, se heurte maintenant aux dures réalités des contraintes budgétaires. Si le modèle de développement extensif et clientéliste de la "nomenklatura" malienne a pu fonctionner sans trop de peine pendant les années qui ont suivi l'indépendance, il atteint ses propres limites alors que les effectifs de la fonction publique en 1980 s'élèvent à 62 000 (FMI: 1981) soit 40% des salariés pour une population de 7 millions d'habitants environ. Ce pourcentage est certes peu important si on le compare à celui d'un pays comme la France par exemple mais il est considérable si on le rapporte aux capacités économiques du Mali et à l'inefficacité de cette bureaucratie.

Or, en 1982, les ressources de l'Etat malien, elles-mêmes alimentées par les pays arabes et le Trésor Français à travers le compte d'opération, sont épuisées. L'appareil d'Etat est, en effet, devenu une coquille moderne et vide, les sommes destinées au Trésor malien, par exemple, étant détournées au passage par les agents qui se trouvent aux différents niveaux de la hiérarchie administrative.[8]

Le régime se trouve donc à la croisée des chemins. Il lui est impossible de continuer à assurer sa reproduction élargie sur la base du clientélisme car les bailleurs de fonds, grandes puissances ou organismes internationaux, ne sont plus disposés à assurer la croissance indéfinie de la fonction publique malienne.

LIBÉRALISATION ET PRIVATISATION (1981-1982)

Le gouvernement doit donc trouver une autre base sociale que celle des nomenklaturistes s'il veut assurer sa pérennité. Ceci passe bien évidemment par un dégraissage de la fonction publique et c'est ainsi qu'il faut analyser les propos du chef de l'Etat demandant de démissionner aux fonctionnaires mécontents de voir baisser leur pouvoir d'achat et de toucher leur salaire avec retard.

Ce changement de base sociale du régime est sans nul doute à mettre en relation avec les pressions exercées par le FMI et la Banque Mondiale sur des pays comme le Mali (Mazier, Jacquemot et Gamet, 1981). Dès avant l'arrivée de Reagan au pouvoir, les experts de ces institutions, à la suite du rapport d'E. Berg (1981), insistaient pour que le gouvernement malien renforce l'efficacité du secteur public et s'en remette davantage au secteur privé. Ces recommandations furent rapidement suivies d'effet avec la décision de restreindre le rôle de l'OPAM et de libéraliser le commerce des céréales en janvier 1981 puis de libéraliser le commerce de l'arachide en janvier 1982. Il en va de même pour ce qui est des sociétés et entreprises d'Etat, hormis de rares exceptions (SONATAM—tabacs et allumettes, SMECMA—matériel agricole, Pharmacie Populaire, Librairie Populaire); les entreprises publiques ou mixtes du secteur secondaire ou tertiaire ont aujourd'hui une exploitation chroniquement déficitaire. Pour 1979, le déficit consolidé des 24 SEE est de 14,5 milliards de FM soit 12,8% du chiffre d'affaires global. Les cas les plus dramatiques sont ceux de la SOMIEX, de l'EDM (énergie), d'Air Mali, de la COMATEX, de la SEPOM et de la SEPAMA.

Ces entreprises sont actuellement soumises au diagnostic de la Banque Mondiale et à un plan de redressement draconien prévoyant la fermeture d'ateliers ou de magasins, la compression des effectifs jugés pléthoriques et la hausse des prix de vente et des tarifs. La SOMIEX va se voir amputée de son activité dans le commerce de détail, les tarifs intérieurs d'Air Mali vont être augmentés et la flotte hétéroclite, rationalisée; EDM va devoir accélérer le recouvrement de ses impayés et relever ses tarifs afin de réduire le montant considérable de ses arriérés. Aucune SEE ne pourra plus bénéficier de l'aide de la Banque Centrale pour financer les déficits structurels d'exploitation et les concours du Trésor (y compris les exonérations de taxes et les remises fiscales) seront également strictement contingentés.

Quant aux sociétés considérées comme ni stratégiques ni rentables, elles vont être soit fermées (SEMA équipement), soit ouvertes au capital privé autochtone ou étranger, ouverture pouvant aller jusqu'au désengagement total de l'Etat (SEPOM, CMTR—transports, TAMALI, SONETRA, Hôtellerie du Mali).

Bureaucrates contre commerçants: l'éternelle donne de la politique malienne

Cette politique de libéralisation économique dont le foyer se situe dans les pays capitalistes s'est déjà concrétisée avec l'entrée du capital étranger dans certaines entreprises du secteur d'Etat. Le Grand Hôtel, par exemple, qui a été transformé, est maintenant entre les mains d'une société privée étrangère. Des négociations sont également en cours avec TAMALI et la SEPOM. Cette ouverture constitue donc une victoire du capitalisme mondial, représenté par le FMI et la

Banque Mondiale, mais également de la classe marchande malienne qui depuis son élimination de la scène politique en 1962, grignote patiemment les positions de l'appareil d'Etat soit en fonctionnant en symbiose avec lui (commerçants servant de prête-noms à certains dirigeants) soit en contrant carrément sa politique économique et en proposant des services plus efficaces à certaines couches de la population et notamment aux paysans. La libéralisation du commerce des céréales et de l'arachide d'une part et l'exclusion de la SOMIEX du commerce de détail d'autre part marquent ainsi la reconnaissance de fait, par le régime, du rôle joué depuis très longtemps par les commerçants dans ces secteurs.

Cependant en dehors de la reprise en main du commerce des biens primaires et de celui de détail, il n'est pas certain que les commerçants maliens, pas plus d'ailleurs que les investisseurs étrangers, se lancent à corps perdu à la conquête des dépouilles du secteur d'Etat. Les commerçants ayant investi dans le secteur industriel sont peu nombreux et ont déjà connu des déboires. Le capital privé malien expatrié peut hésiter à s'engager dans une zone enclavée et à faible pouvoir d'achat. Il en va de même pour les investisseurs étrangers pour lesquels le Mali ne peut pas constituer un enjeu important. De surcroît, la question reste entière: qui acceptera de prendre en charge à la fois le passif des SEE (que l'Etat ne peut pas apurer) et les actifs constitués souvent d'équipements obsolètes?

LE COÛT SOCIAL DE LA LIBÉRALISATION

Le changement de base sociale du régime qui se traduit par l'abandon des fonctionnaires et la prise en charge des intérêts des commerçants comporte, comme on peut s'en douter, certains coûts sociaux pour de larges fractions de la société malienne.

Tout d'abord la libéralisation du commerce des céréales et de l'arachide va pratiquement supprimer la concurrence qui existait entre l'OPAM et l'OACV d'une part et les commerçants d'autre part. Cette concurrence profitait directement aux paysans puisque les commerçants achetaient à un prix supérieur à celui des organismes officiels. La preuve a contrario est fournie par le prix d'achat offert par les commerçants aux paysans pour le maïs à l'automne 1981 et qui était de 25 à 50 francs maliens le kg alors que le prix officiel était de 90 FM. Il en va de même pour l'arachide que les marchands ont achetée 45 à 50 FM le kg dans la région de Kita au moment du paiement de l'impôt en 1981 alors que le prix officiel était de 90 FM.[9]

La limitation ou la suppression complète de la commercialisation officielle provoque donc la baisse du pouvoir d'achat des producteurs et le transfert de la rente agricole aux commerçants sans que les consommateurs des villes ou des zones rurales déficitaires en profitent, si ce n'est pour l'année 1982, pour l'arachide où la surproduction a permis à de nombreuses familles maliennes de renouer avec la consommation de ce produit.

Du côté de l'industrie, de l'administration et de l'enseignement, la dénationalisation passe par la compression des effectifs dans les entreprises, la réduction du recrutement des fonctionnaires et la baisse du volume des bourses scolaires. L'assainissement du secteur d'Etat restant implique la hausse des prix de vente à court terme. Le risque est grand par conséquent que l'opération chirurgicale de redressement préconisée par le FMI et la Banque Mondiale exacerbe les tensions sociales actuelles, en milieu urbain tout particulièrement, et qui tiennent déjà à la baisse continue du pouvoir d'achat (entre 1973 et 1980, hausse des prix de 50% contre des augmentations de salaire de 30% en moyenne).

Cette politique de libéralisation, d'austérité et de vérité des prix aurait dû déboucher logiquement sur la réintégration du Mali dans l'Union Monétaire Ouest-Africaine, décision qui avait été déjà envisagée dans le cadre des accords monétaires en 1967. Cette réintégration aurait peut-être comporté quelques avantages pour l'économie malienne: rigueur dans l'octroi des crédits, consolidation des comptes d'opération des 7 pays membres, alignement progressif des prix régionaux, élimination des exportations clandestines, mais elle supposait également, avec le retour du CFA, une baisse des salaires de moitié alors qu'il était certain que les prix n'auraient pas été divisés par deux. Là encore les commerçants auraient été les principaux bénéficiaires de cette mesure.

Quoi qu'il en soit, en juillet 1982, cette décision n'a toujours pas été prise en raison de l'opposition de certains pays membres de l'UMOA et peut-être de la France. La réforme de 1981-1982 est donc bancale alors que le Mali est en cessation de paiement (Mazier, Jacquemot et Gamet, 1981).

BILAN

Vingt-deux ans après l'indépendance, la situation de ce pays est donc extrêmement grave. L'industrie créée depuis 1960 reste embryon-

naire et faible. L'agriculture de grande exportation, et particulièrement celle de l'arachide, s'effondre complètement en raison de la
faiblesse des cours mondiaux et de l'inefficacité, de la corruption et de
la brutalité des agents de l'OACV. Même la culture du coton qui était
la seule, sous l'impulsion de la CMDT, à s'être véritablement déve-
loppée depuis l'indépendance connaît un déclin depuis quelques années.
Il ne reste donc aux paysans qu'à se tourner vers l'agriculture marchande vivrière d'intérêt local ou interafricain, c'est-à-dire essentiellement le mil, et à partir en migration. Cependant les débouchés du
mil ne sont pas illimités[10] et les migrations ne sont pas elles-mêmes
indéfiniment extensibles en raison de l'interruption de l'immigration
en France et de la crise que connaît la Côte d'Ivoire, principal exu-
toire du Mali.

Du côté des classes dominantes, on peut noter le caractère pléthô-
rique, parasitaire et autoritaire de la "nomenklatura" qui de ce point
de vue fait moins bien que sa devancière coloniale, ce qui fait regret-
ter aux Maliens les plus âgés la période d'avant l'indépendance.

Dans l'état de délabrement que connaît l'économie malienne, seuls
les commerçants témoignent d'une certaine efficacité et reçoivent
pour cette raison les éloges des experts reaganiens du FMI et de la
Banque Mondiale. Mais c'est oublier que l'efficacité des commerçants
ne peut apparaître qu'au regard de l'incurie dont font preuve les
bureaucrates. Il suffit que l'Etat se retire d'un secteur pour que le
poids que les commerçants font peser sur la population se fasse
pleinement sentir.

La situation politique et économique du Mali est donc bloquée
depuis plusieurs années sans qu'on voie se dessiner quelque issue que
ce soit. Contrairement à ce que beaucoup affirment le problème n'est
pas d'ordre économique: ce n'est pas, par exemple, la découverte de
gisements pétroliers ou uranifères qui changerait quoi que ce soit aux
conditions de vie de la majorité de la population. Bien au contraire, la
rente pétrolière ou minérale aurait pour effet, comme on a pu le constater dans d'autres pays d'Afrique, au Nigeria, par exemple, de
provoquer l'abandon de l'agriculture et d'accroître la corruption.

Le blocage du système malien est avant tout d'ordre politique. La
digestion de l'appareil d'Etat moderne par des pratiques précoloniales
(prédation-redistribution) est l'effet du sous-développement industriel
qui empêche l'apparition d'une structure sociale fondée sur la détention des moyens de production et d'échange modernes. L'Etat préda-
teur-redistributeur devient ainsi la source d'un vaste réseau de clientèle
englobant de larges secteurs de la population. En effet, si seule une

minorité de bureaucrates profite réellement du pillage de l'appareil d'Etat, il n'empêche que le processus de redistribution touche de larges effectifs et que par ailleurs, fait plus important, il n'existe aucune alternative à ce modèle clientéliste, lequel est profondément ancré dans les structures de base de la paysannerie.

L'ensemble de la hiérarchie sociale étant structuré par des relations de clientèle, on comprend aisément qu'une conscience de classe ou de groupe puisse difficilement apparaître et déboucher sur un changement de régime. Ceci explique également que les seuls mouvements sociaux de quelque ampleur, comme celui des étudiants en 1979-1980, soient des mouvements corporatistes et que la masse de la population, c'est-à-dire la paysannerie, reste à l'écart de la vie politique malienne.

Les seuls changements qui peuvent se produire sont ceux qui interviennent au sommet de l'Etat, soit par l'élimination d'une des fractions comme en 1978, soit, comme cela a failli se produire à plusieurs reprises, par le renversement du chef de l'Etat lui-même. Mais jusqu'ici, celui-ci se tient solidement accroché à son poste et il n'est pas sûr, au demeurant, que beaucoup de Maliens ne préfèrent pas voir rester en place une équipe qui pendant 14 ans a réussi à capter une part importante de surplus plutôt que d'assister à l'arrivée au pouvoir d'un sous-officier démuni et avide de toucher le "prix de sa vie".[11]

NOTES

1. L'éclatement de la Fédération du Mali avait entraîné l'interruption des échanges avec le Sénégal.

2. Ils furent supprimés quelque temps plus tard au Sahara.

3. Ils contribuent ainsi au retour du franc malien dans la zone franc et à sa dévaluation en 1967, épisode qui marque en fait le glas du régime.

4. La commercialisation forcée des céréales sera rétablie peu de temps après.

5. Enquête personnelle, avril-mai 1982.

6. Voir à ce sujet l'excellent article d'A. Marie (1981).

7. Les fonctionnaires maliens sont couramment payés avec trois ou quatre mois de retard.

8. En janvier 1982 circulait à Bamako la photocopie d'un chèque d'un pays arabe destiné au Trésor malien et endossé par le chef de l'Etat.

9. Enquête personnelle, avril-mai 1982.

10. Sans compter, comme nous l'avons vu, que les prix seront moins rémunérateurs puisque n'existera plus la concurrence entre l'OPAM et les commerçants.

11. En bambara, *nisongo*, littéralement le prix de la vie. Cette expression désignait l'esclave qu'on avait capturé au combat et par extension, le tribut et l'impôt. Ainsi le pouvoir est-il "prix de sa vie" puisqu'on risque celle-ci pour s'en emparer.

OUVRAGES CITES

AMSELLE, J-L. (1981). "Famine, prolétarisation et création de nouveaux liens de dépendance au Sahel: les réfugiés de Mopti et de Léré." Politique Africaine I (1): 5–22.

———(1978). "La conscience paysanne. La révolte de Ouolossébougou juin 1968, Mali." Revue canadienne des Etudes Africaines. 12(3): 339–355.

———(1977). Les Négociants de la Savane. Paris, Anthropos.

BAGAYOGO, I. (1982). Emergence d'une bourgeoisie agraire au Mali: l'exemple des planteurs de la région de Bamako. Thèse pour le doctorat du 3e cycle. Paris: E.H.E.S.S.

BERG, E. (1981). Le développement accéléré en Afrique au Sud du Sahara. Washington: B.I.R.D.

CONSTANTIN, F. et C. COULON. (1978). "Entreprises publiques et changement politique au Mali," in Les Entreprises publiques en Afrique Noire. Paris: Pédone.

ERNST, K. (1976). Tradition and Progress in the African Village: The non-capitalist transformation of rural communauties in Mali. London: C. Hurst.

FMI (1981). Mali—Recent economic developments. 111 p. dactyl.

KOUYATE, S.B. (1964). Les dirigeants africains face à leurs peuples. Paris: Maspéro.

JACQUEMOT, P. [ed.] (1981). Mali, le paysan et l'état. Paris: l'Harmattan.

JONES, W.I. (1976). Planning and Economic Policy: Socialist Mali and her neighbors. Washinton: Three Continents press.

MAHARAUX, A. (1982). L'industrie au Mali. Etude géographique de l'industrie d'un grand pays sahélien enclavé. Thèse pour le doctorat du 3e cycle Paris: E.H.E.S.S.

MARIE, A. (1981). "Marginalité et conditions sociales du prolétariat urbain en Afrique. Les approches du concept de marginalité et son évaluation critique." Cahiers d'Etudes Africaines, 81–83, XXI-1-3: 347–374.

MARTIN, G. (1976). "Socialism, economic development and planning in Mali, 1960–1968." Revue canadienne des Etudes Africaines 10(1): 23–47.

MAZIER, J., P. JACQUEMOT, et B. GAMET (1981). Evolution et Perspectives de l'économie malienne. Rapport de mission 12–21 novembre 1981. Paris, Ministère des Relations Extérieures. Ministère de la Coopération et du Développement. Service d'Etudes du Développement, dactyl.

THENEVIN, P. (1980). L'aide alimentaire en céréales dans les pays sahéliens. Paris: Ministère de la Coopération Service des Etudes et questions internationales.

VOSLENSKY, M. (1981). La Nomenklatura. Les privilégiés en URSS. Paris: Le Livre de Poche.

7

THE FISCAL CRISIS OF THE STATE
The Case of the Ivory Coast

BONNIE K. CAMPBELL

The study of the fiscal crisis of the Ivorian state that occurred at the end of the 1970s may serve as a starting point for the analysis of the contradictions in the patterns of accumulation which have characterized the political economy of this country.

The Ivory Coast's political stability during the first two decades after independence for which it is cited as a model reflected the capacity of the dominant ruling class to reproduce and enlarge its own basis. Their ability to do so has been based above all on the access they have maintained to the revenue drawn from export agricultural production. The revenue from this sector ensured the reinforcement and enlargement of the politically dominant group which began as a planter class. With time, the mechanisms and sources of appropriation of this class became more varied and its social basis more diversified. Substantial amounts of revenue were transferred as well, from the export agricultural sector via state institutions to subsidize the activities of the nascent foreign dominated industrial sector, which emerged within the framework and as the extension of the colonial trading network.

If during the first decade and a half of independence there appeared to be complementarity between the activities of the export agriculture and industrial sectors, the increasing subordination of the export sector to the needs of the industrial sector by the late 1970s and the new lines of

Author's Note: I wish to thank Henry Bernstein for his helpful comments and careful editorial work on this chapter.

social differentiation which emerged as part of this process revealed the limits of this pattern of accumulation.

To summarize schematically what is in fact a far more complex process:

(1) The expansion of the industrial sector has been based on ever increasing transfers from the export agriculture sector.
(2) These transfers, obtained through price and subsidization policies have entailed the stagnation and even the decrease in real terms of producer prices, which in the long term impedes continuing expansion of agricultural output and productivity, and limits the development of the internal market.
(3) While the full consequences of this process may take time to become apparent, the underlying contradiction of the Ivorian experience manifested itself by the end of the 1970s at the locus where the transfer from the export to the industrial sector occurs and consequently where the struggle between conflicting interests and forces, both internal and external, takes place: the state.
(4) Moreover, the past process has involved among other things, a specific pattern of state investment, employment and local capital formation, each of which was dependent on the capacity of the group controlling the local state to increase public revenues. In this area as well, the contradictory nature of the process and its limitations had become apparent by the late 1970s. It is the manifestations at the level of the state, and the implications of these limits and contradictions which are the central object of this chapter.

The following analysis will concern the relations between the circuits of realization, distribution and investment in the export agriculture and industrial sectors, and the ways in which the state intervenes in these contradictory relations. It will consider the manifestations of the limits of past patterns of accumulation by examining unemployment and patterns of government spending. The latter reflect how the dominant group which controlled the state could, in the past, use state revenues from export crops to reproduce and enlarge its own class basis—a strategy that is no longer feasible.

This study considers one facet of much broader questions concerning the historical evolution of the various patterns of accumulation which have characterized the Ivory Coast and which would require an analysis of the conditions of production, exchange, and distribution in the agricultural and industrial sectors. The latter much more global study would give a central place to the process of realignment of class forces to which the following presentation can only allude, while nonetheless emphasizing that theoretical advance is contingent on further empirical work.

To facilitate the analysis, the presentation will be based on three periods, not for their importance in time, for they are moments in the same historical process, but because these general periods typify different phases in the patterns of accumulation that have characterized the Ivory Coast and that may be identified in very approximate terms as follows:

(1) *The colonial period (late nineteenth century to 1960): Colonialism and export agriculture.* The colonial period was characterized by the application of extensive techniques to cash crop production, i.e. forced labor in the context of land abundance and direct coercion on the part of the colonial administration. This period may be thought of in terms of a "surplus drain" model of accumulation. The obstacles to the prolongation of this form of primitive accumulation were to be temporarily overcome by the emergence of a local planter class.

(2) *Export agriculture and import-substitution industry: the 1960s and 1970s.* While the former period was prolonged as far as the use of extensive techniques in the export agricultural sector and very far-reaching foreign control over the commercial and nascent industrial sectors were concerned, through state intervention changes occurred at the beginning of the 1970s in the level of accumulation and finance, notably in import-substitution activities, without, however, being accompanied by changes in the organization of production. In the absence of a local *bourgeoisie d'affaires* or local entrepreneurial class, whose emergence has been clearly suppressed by the dominant planter group, this state involvement opened areas for a process of local capital formation under the umbrella of the state, and consequently the gradual broadening of avenues of appropriation and of the basis of the dominant planter class itself.

(3) *The limitations of the present phase and the fiscal crisis of the state: the current period from the late 1970s.* Overcoming the limitations of the past pattern of accumulation will require the adoption of a mode of organization of productive activity capable of increasing productivity in both the agricultural and industrial sectors. The current phase of restructuring (involving the extension and deepening of capitalist relations of production leading to a process of expanded reproduction) will

involve new alliances with international capital and new lines of social differentiation and class formation with inevitably crucial effects at the level of the state.

THE COLONIAL PERIOD
(LATE NINETEENTH CENTURY TO 1960)

Colonialism and Export Agriculture

The establishment of a permanent colonial presence and the beginning of export crop production for the metropolitan market were closely related. Although they came relatively late to the Ivory Coast, no other process has affected more profoundly all aspects of that country's history.

The introduction of cash crops into the forest zone of the south-east was to alter the original agrarian system based on subsistence agriculture in a context of land abundance. It was to create new labor requirements, encouraging an influx of immigrant workers that led to a process of growing differentiation among agricultural producers. The internal dynamics and contradictions of the development of cash crop production in the Ivory Coast have yet to be fully analyzed. The following is a brief summary of the features of this critical historical period.

While there were attempts by French colonial administrators (present in the area since 1893) to induce Africans to engage in commercial agriculture, the results at the very beginning of the twentieth century were of limited success. The drop in world market prices for palm oil at this time discouraged many Africans from processing this crop for export. In response the governor introduced coercive methods. However, apart from an experimental coffee plantation at Elima, other attempts to diversify crops for export at the turn of the century were unsuccessful. Altogether only twenty-nine tons of coffee were produced in 1905 and only six tons of cocoa in 1910.

The completion of French military "pacification" in 1917 removed obstacles to the extension of cash crops for export. Until about 1925, the Ivory Coast's main contribution to the French economy continued to be timber and palm oil, after which export crops were diversified. Simultaneously the colonial authorities attempted to introduce a European planter economy. After 1918, the colonial administration encouraged the settlement of European *colons* in the Ivory Coast (unlike Senegal). These mostly French *colons* together with African planters produced about 1000 tons of coffee by 1920. During the next decade cocoa production remained far more substantial than that of coffee. By 1930 the Ivory Coast and other colonies produced more cocoa than France could absorb, and since France imported most of its coffee from other monetary zones, coffee growing was encouraged by means of premiums and preferential prices. Through the intervention of the colonial administration production of coffee exceeded that of cocoa by 1945 and it continued to expand rapidly.

The introduction of coffee and cocoa production brought about far-reaching changes in the original agrarian system. While traditional subsistence agriculture in the forest zone of the south-east was of a slash-and-burn type, the cash crops introduced were perennials requiring higher labor inputs, particularly during the seasonal peak of October to February (Lee, 1980: 609). Although land was abundant enough for cash cropping and traditional agriculture to coexist, the supply of family labor was an effective constraint. Additional labor, made available either through colonial recruitment policies or subsequently through immigration, has been from the beginning a necessary condition for the expansion of cash cropping.

When the French colonial administration first assumed control in West Africa, it instituted a system of unpaid labor services for public works such as road building (Campbell, 1978: 69–74). European plantation owners were able to recruit sufficient agricultural labor by making arrangements with African chiefs whereby the latter provided teams of workers in return for a 'gift.' This system was effective until the mid-1920s, when increasing production by both European and African growers led to problems over the recruitment of labor. This drew the administration more closely into regulating conditions of export crop production, particularly in establishing privileges in favor of the French planters. By 1943 African planters were debarred from employing recruited labor, which was reserved exclusively for work on European plantations. In some cases Africans were even removed from their own plantations to be recruited for European enterprises. Other administrative and commercial policies worked, if not explicitly to discourage African planters, at least to privilege the Europeans. The latter, for example, succeeded in securing higher prices than the African planters, through the collaboration of the administration with the trading companies.

The long-term importance of these systematic privileges can hardly be over-estimated. Because the consequences of forced labor were experienced so pervasively by the entire population, it was around this issue that the anti-colonialist movement began to form. African planters, and particularly those with the largest plantations who stood to benefit greatly from the abolition of colonial recruitment policies, had strong reasons to struggle against certain aspects of French colonialism, especially when labor became even more scarce with the outbreak of World War II.

It was the African planters who were to supply the political leadership of the anti-colonialist movement. Their combination of national and sectional interests had far-reaching implications for the outcome of the movement and for the orientation of political and economic changes in the Ivory Coast after political independence. The dissatisfaction of African planters with the discriminatory practices of the colonial administration led them to withdraw from the only existing planter organization, the European-dominated *Syndicat Agricole de la Côte d'Ivoire,* and to form the *Syndicat Agricole Africain* in September 1944. The 20,000 African members of the S.A.A. were not subject to administrative labor recruitment. However, since only those planters owning two hectares of coffee or three hectares of cocoa could be members of the organization, many smaller African planters remained subject to forced labor. The S.A.A. challenged not only the European planters but also the European middlemen by signing contracts directly with the big trading firms, and its members began to compete more belligerently with the European planters in the recruitment of labor. At first, the S.A.A. simply favored the more equitable distribution of laborers between the two groups of planters. Soon, however, the S.A.A. took a stand against the very principle of forced labor.

This explains the popularity of the S.A.A. and the support which it was able to mobilize in the campaign for the abolition of forced labor. But the breadth of such support, although it provided the basis for a mass party, certainly does not imply that the objectives of the S.A.A. were in any sense "popular." The Syndicat had been created at the initiative of the largest planters, who stood to gain most handsomely from the abolition of forced labor. It was constituted from the top down. Its eight co-founders appointed agents at the level of every sub-division, the latter typically leading planters themselves who were also county-chiefs and literate in French. One of the co-founders was Felix Houphouët-Boigny, whose ethnic group, the Baoulé, formed the largest bloc of members. Consequently he was easily elected president of the S.A.A. at its founding congress in 1944. At this congress the most important resolutions adopted were: to secure premiums for African producers; to organize co-operative sales in order to eliminate middle-men; to obtain a quota of imported cloth and agricultural implements; to secure a more equitable allocation of labor for its members. The evident narrowness of the economic interests on which the S.A.A. was founded, was to play a crucial role in the outcome of the anti-colonialist struggle.

The suppression of forced labor by the law of 5 April 1946 and the removal of certain discriminatory aspects of colonialism reinforced the position of relatively privileged social groups, notably the larger African planters. The political concessions conceded particularly after 1946 may be seen as a result of the interaction of changes taking place in both the metropolitan and the colonial areas. After World War II economic and social changes in metropolitan France necessitated a redefinition of colonial relations that was to be brought about through colonial eco-nomic development plans, greater investments, and the decentralization of certain responsibilities and powers previously concentrated in metro-politan France. In turn this encouraged the formation of a local group whose interests lay in a continuing close relationship with the metropoli-tan power.

While the economic basis of the group which assumed power at independence depended on the continuation of relations established under colonialism, the nature of—and constraints on—the political power it exercised internally were to have very profound social, politi-cal, and economic implications for changes within the Ivory Coast. What were the origins and interests of this group?

Although in the 1930s the number of Africans who became planters needing hired workers was not very large (and the average yield per planter during this early period was quite small) their methods of cultivation enabled them quickly to outstrip the production of Euro-pean planters. In fact, by the end of World War II African planters produced 95 percent of cocoa and 82.78 percent of coffee in the Ivory Coast (Gbagbo, 1982: 66).

The origins of the group of larger planters lay in the pre-colonial ruling group, which used its powers during the colonial regime to appropriate land for private use. From the creation of the S.A.A. many of its local agents in the plantation belt were official chiefs. This made it easier for S.A.A. delegates to reach agreements with the northern chiefs who supplied workers, incorrectly described as "voluntary" labor. After the abolition of forced labor, the group of African planters grew in size and importance. Moreover, rising coffee and cocoa prices after 1946 encouraged an increase in the area of coffee and cocoa cultivated. By 1960, approximately 500,000 hectares were devoted to coffee and 200,000 hectares to cocoa production, of which 97 percent was undertaken by Africans (Gbagbo, 1982: 127). The expansion involved not only an increase in the number of planters but also increasing differentiation among African planters. With regards to cocoa production 80 percent of plantations in 1960 were family holdings of between 2 and 10 hectares (Gbagbo, 1982: 127). There emerged during this period a group of larger cocoa and coffee planters, estimated at about 20,000 by the mid-1960s, who controlled about one quarter of land under cocoa and coffee, and employed about two thirds of wage labor in agriculture (Amin, 1967: 277).

As direct figures on the size of holdings and the numbers employed in the cultivation of these crops for the period 1945–1960 are not available, one may understand how a controversy over the importance and interests of this group has arisen in the literature concerning the Ivory Coast. While the expansion of production involved different forms of labor recruitment (seasonal workers, permanent laborers and even sharecroppers), there is no doubt that the interests of the wealthier planter group "became those of employers, as they shared activities with European entrepreneurs and with the wealthier traders and transporters" (Morgenthau, 1964: 215). It is in this sense, that one may refer to an emerging Ivorian agrarian bourgeoisie during this period. In using this term, our concern is not so much to defend a static description of the characteristics of this group for which empirical evidence is badly lacking, as to understand the process which led to the emergence of new relations of production in the Ivorian context.

The growth of the Ivorian planter class from several hundred families in 1950 coincided with—and in fact is largely explained by—the end of forced labor. Moreover, in spite of the narrowness of the economic interests on which it was founded, the importance of the S.A.A. grew beyond the confines of its membership. After the war its membership lists were used to draw up electoral registers, and during the first election campaign it served as an admirable machine to promote the candidacy of its president, Houphouët-Boigny.

The role which the planter bourgeoisie was to play in Ivory Coast politics is especially clear in relation to the ruling party. The Ivorian branch of the territorial *Rassemblement Démocratique Africain* (R.D.A.), the *Parti Démocratique de la Côte d'Ivoire* (P.D.C.I.) founded by Houphouët-Boigny in 1946, had begun as a *Comité d'action poli-*

tique du Syndicat des planteurs S.A.A. Later the same year about one third of the party's 80,000 estimated members and supporters belonged to the S.A.A.

The emergence and consolidation during the post-war period of a wealthy planter class which assumed the leadership of the anti-colonialist movement was an essential condition for the perpetuation of the past pattern of growth. The fact that the planter group remained closely linked to metropolitan markets and supplies ensured the continuation of close relations with the metropolitan power and the continued presence of French economic interests. It is important to look more closely at how this was maintained.

The Financial and Administrative Organization of Export Agriculture

Marketing organizations. During the period of political decolonization (1946–1960), an elaborate set of highly centralized structures and regulations firmly controlled by France were created to link the French and Ivorian economies tightly together and to provide mechanisms to ensure further increases in output. These structures had become necessary by World War II, as the mode of accumulation conditional on a highly repressive colonial administration and military presence appeared to have reached its limit. The monopolistic organization of colonial trade in primary products by private trading companies had squeezed producers to the point of undermining their reproduction and hence further increases in output. In view of the levelling off and even the decrease of agricultural production by the end of the war as a result of forced deliveries (Meillassoux, 1964), France created bodies to overcome obstacles to expanding production and hence accumulation. As of 1946, *Caisses de soutien*—a form of marketing board—were established for various cash crops such as cotton, ostensibly to guarantee a minimum return to peasant producers; however, since they also guaranteed the profit margins of the private trading companies, the *Caisses de soutien* became an alternative means of taxing the peasant producer and ensuring the profits of the trading companies.

The two leading export crops of the Ivory Coast, coffee and cocoa, were taxed with an export duty of 15 percent, of which two-thirds went to the colonial regional budget of *l'Afrique occidentale française* (A.O.F.), and the remaining third to the special coffee and cocoa account of the Ivory Coast to be used in the agricultural development of the colony (Gbagbo, 1982: 128).

In 1955, the latter accounts were replaced by *Caisses de Stabilisation* responsible for the marketing of cash crops so as to adapt supply to demand, to set minimum sales prices and to ensure the repatriation of all foreign currency to metropolitan banking institutions (Gbagbo, 1982: 128–129). Also in 1955 a special metropolitan fund, the *Fonds National de Régularisation des Produits Outre-Mer,* was established in order to advance funds to the overseas Caisses, creating a pattern of subsidization not only of peasant producers but especially of the private trading interests and, indirectly, the local colonial administration (Lawson, 1975: 209). This pattern represents an interesting precedent for the post-independence period, when the role of the Caisses became increasingly important. The creation of semi-public metropolitan export promotion agencies together with the role played by the metropolitan stabilization funds reinforced the already integrated and often monopolistic colonial economic agencies. To control production and/or collection of the crop made it considerably easier to organize its export marketing:

> If the firm which produces or at least collects the coffee, or cocoa, or palm oil, is at the same time a European sales agent, the problem of finding outlets is eased. Such a firm becomes, as it were, its own Produce Marketing Board. Moreover, in seeking investors the Ivory Coast will always see a special point in dealing with firms which already specialise in trading in local natural resources [Barnes, 1969: 170].

However, metropolitan subsidies contributed only exceptionally and partially to the support operations of the Ivorian Caisses, in which reserves were held, while the latter benefited the colonial trading companies at least as much as the peasant producers. Moreover, the majority of the funds used for support operations in the Ivory Coast came from local resources: either from surpluses accumulated in favorable periods or, more frequently (and increasingly), from import taxes and duties and from subsidies from local budgets, which meant at the expense of African tax payers and consumers. In view of the continuity of the structures involved, and looking ahead, one may note that since independence the Caisse's responsibilities have broadened to include other agricultural products including cotton, palm products and sugar. It assumed the name of *Caisse de Stabilisation et de Soutien des Prix des Productions Agricoles* (CSSPPA), and in 1964, was legally incorporated as a wholly owned public enterprise *(société d'état)*, albeit with governmental rather than entrepreneurial functions. The CSSPPA plays an important role both in establishing producer prices and in marketing major export commodities. It sets producer prices based on its forecasts of export prices, the level of its own reserves, and estimated producer costs. The price set is the minimum that may be offered by exporters. The products are purchased by private accredited exporters who are assigned quotas and can obtain bank credit on the basis of these quotas. When the world market price is above the price paid to the exporter, the CSSPPA receives what is in effect a tax revenue. Export duties are based on a standard value *(valeur mercuriale)* which at the end of the 1970s and the beginning of the 1980s was far below the world market price. The setting of the standard value effectively determines which portion of the overall surplus accrues to the Treasury directly in the form of export duties and which portion stays with the CSSPPA.

The Ivorian Caisse differs fundamentally from equivalent marketing organizations in the anglophone African countries in its intimate relationship with the private sector: "The originality of the system which exists in the Ivory Coast stems from the fact that it permits the private sector to maintain its traditional role in the purchase, sale and distribution of products" (Delaporte, 1970: 10). Consequently, it has preserved virtually intact the marketing structures inherited from the colonial period. These structures have ensured the colonial orientation and also determined the terms of exchange for producers of agricultural export commodities in the post-independence period.

The Franc zone: Commercial and monetary policies. Equally important in ensuring the continuity with the colonial period were the commercial and monetary policies of the Franc zone established in 1953 with the aim of ensuring privileged access for metropolitan products in colonial markets. The closely integrated economic relations and high degree of protection assured private interests by this centralized and hierarchical monetary framework, were of critical and lasting importance to the country's economic orientation long after the granting of political independence. Commercial, monetary and industrial policies governing economic relations within the Franc zone remained closely interrelated.

Part of the arrangement linking dominant planter interests in the Ivory Coast closely to the metropolian power was the agreement on the part of France to give preferential treatment to two important Ivorian exports, coffee and bananas. The coffee treaty, signed for a period of five years, 1961-1966, and renewed subsequently with modifications, was particularly important in that it stipulated the annual purchase by France of 100,000 tons (70 percent of the country's production at the time) at above world prices then prevailing (Lawson, 1975:207).

The Ivorian Code of investment was enacted in 1959, the year before independence. The lavishness of its terms are considered to be the most liberal for the former French West African colonies (Baulin, 1982: 88). As with the creation of the marketing boards, the conditions of the Code reveal certain functions which state agencies and regulations were to perform, previously accomplished in the colonial period by private merchant capital. The new roles assumed by public bodies created a favorable framework within which private colonial interests, solidly entrenched at independence, could redefine their form of activity.

The elaboration of a hierarchical commercial and monetary framework in the period of decolonization, reinforced by measures like the Investment Code which encouraged short-term profit strategies rather than local industrial transformation, supplied the conditions permitting long established colonial trading interests to maintain their position in the Ivorian market. Because of the manner in which investment in local industry was initiated, industries were integrated into commodity circuits dominated by metropolitan commercial capital. In fact, at least at the beginning of the independence period such industrial involvement was often undertaken by these commercial capitals. Moreover, in keeping with the logic of the colonial period, a precondition for their establishment was the updating of monopolistic control and the exclusion of potential competitors, most notably African competitors.

The exclusion of a potential competitor in the form of a local entrepreneurial class was an essential condition for the political consolidation of the emerging Ivorian agrarian bourgoisie that assumed the leadership of the independence movement on the promise to end forced labor, and that gained political control at independence. Moreover as Baulin notes (1982: 158), "by preventing from the beginning the economic consolidation of a local entrepreneurial class, as a means of blocking its access to power, the planter class was acting in the interests of foreign investment."

As will be seen, this strategy remained a *leitmotif* of the manner in which the dominant class was to confront the question of the Ivorization of the economy, in a manner compatible with the reproduction of its own political basis, over the first two decades of independence.

THE 1960s AND 1970s

The Expansion of Agricultural Commodity Production and Class Formation in the Export Agriculture Sector

In 1960 coffee and cocoa exports accounted for 78 percent of the value of the country's total exports. By 1979, the two crops still represented 58 percent of the value of exports (Ivory Coast, Ministry of Agriculture, 1980: 171). At the end of the 1970s, coffee and cocoa were responsible for the monetary income of between 400,000 and 600,000 households, and consequently the livelihood of well over 4 million people in a population of 8,262,000 in 1980.

The other chief export crop during this period had been timber but the lack of reforestation depleted resources to such an extent, that the volume of timber transactions whether for export or local market, declined consistently from the late 1970s. The country's exports include certain other crops promoted in the interest of diversification, among which pineapples, bananas, cotton, rubber, and palm oil are regarded as successful.

The development of commercial export agriculture historically assumed land abundance, and access to a large labor reserve in the savannah belt of the Ivory Coast, as well as Bourkina Fasso and Mali, rather than increases in the productivity of labor or land:

> Given the indications of a generally stagnant level of agricultural technology and the large inflows of labour into the plantation section, we are inclined to agree with the assessment that "the over-all increases in incomes and in output per head in agriculture in recent years have been due not so much to improvements in technology as to the migration (from regions of low productivity) of people—partly coming from outside the Ivory Coast—to the relatively more productive forest areas [I.B.R.D., 1970: 19, quoted by Lee, 1980: 614].

Similar conclusions concerning the persistence of extensive techniques can be drawn from studies of at least one crop cited as a success in diversification schemes: cotton. The analysis of the conditions which have permitted the expansion of cotton production also throws some light on the process of differentiation which accompanied increases in output. During the campaigns to promote cotton in the 1970s, the area cultivated increased from 51,400 ha. to 122,983 ha. In the absence of widespread intensification of techniques (in 1980 75.5 percent of Ivorian cotton production was still based on hand labor), the ability to mobilize extra family labor and increasingly to hire wage labor, were the dominant means at the end of the 1970s for extending cotton production (Campbell in Barker, 1984).

In looking at the pattern of rural differentiation in the plantation sector, our concern is not so much to enter into the debate concerning the appropriateness of the term *bourgeoisie de planteurs,* as to raise questions concerning the manner in which increases in output have permitted certain producers to secure and combine the elements of production necessary for further concentration and expansion of production, and to increase productivity (if and when this has occurred). This entails investigating the interrelation between changes in productive techniques, size of landholdings, and the extension of wage and other forms of contractual labor, to the extent that data are available.

First, there is a strong correlation between the distribution of land and other aspects of differentiation, notably those concerning cropping patterns and output mix. The adoption of cash crops such as coffee and cocoa is itself correlated with size of landholding, since small farms under one hectare show only very limited adoption of cash crops (Lee, 1980: 630). The adoption of improved farm machinery is also directly related to the size of landholdings. Figures made available by the rural survey of the Ministry of Agriculture suggest a high degree of inequality in the size of holdings in 1973-1974:

> The top 11 percent of landholders [of holdings of more than 10 hectares] operated 34.3 percent of total cultivated land in 1973-1974 . . . .
> The average size of the 89 percent of total holdings which were less than 10 hectares in size was 3.8 hectares, whereas the average size of the top 11 percent of holdings was 15.5 hectares [Lee, 1980: 627 and 630].[1]

The pattern of land distribution in the export agricultural sector has implications for the extension of improved productive techniques, given the critical sociopolitical conditions of access to credit necessary for further extensions and improvements. While large landholdings no doubt serve as backing for credit, the distribution of credit is also a function of political affiliation and access to the centers of political power, which the large planters are in a far better position to possess. What is more, the distribution of credit has been used in the expansion of the dominant ruling class to regulate who would be able to join the group of larger planters (Baulin, 1982: 150).

The slowness and contradictory nature of the emergence of wage labor in the plantation sector has led some to conclude that because medium and small planters participate directly in production, their activity cannot be characterized in terms of capitalist relations of production (e.g., Gastellu and Affou Yappi, 1982: 149–179). Analyzed within its specific historical circumstances, the slowness of the expansion of wage labor appears to suggest that relations of production, while determined by capitalism, have not been completely transformed by it. Certain non-capitalist relations persist in various forms of labor contracts such as the *abusan,* a type of share-cropping arrangement whereby the worker is paid a one-third share of the harvest. Another arrangement involves wages being paid at the end of the year, while yet another form is for payment to be made for specific tasks, performed under the supervision of the owners. The variety of phenomenal forms, however, should not obscure the developement of wage labor.

Moreover, in the Ivorian plantation sector, an estimated 70 percent to 80 percent of hired workers are migrants from neighboring countries, particularly Bourkina Fasso and Mali.[2] The availability of low paid foreign migrant labor has been of critical importance in explaining the relations of production in export agriculture. While its availability has no doubt showed a process of differentiation (including "proletarianization") among Ivorians, it is an important factor in the persistence of the low level of rural wages, and in the perpetutation of extensive techniques of production (Lee, 1980: 635).

The impact of the massive influx of migrant workers on rural wages can be documented, as can the resultant differentials between wage levels in export agriculture and in the nascent industrial sector. While the hourly S.M.I.G. *(Salaire minimum interprofessionnel garanti)* in the secondary sector increased from 37 CFAF in 1958 to 158 CFAF in 1979, an increase of 427 percent, wages of agricultural workers in coffee, cocoa, cotton, and rice, increased from 19.50 CFAF an hour in 1958 to 400 CFAF a day in 1979, an increase of 156 percent, presuming the work day was limited to eight hours (Baulin, 1982: 87).[3] The effect of very low agricultural wages, and rates of increase, on the development of the domestic market must be examined in relation to the conditions of production and exchange of the industrial sector.

The Conditions of Production of Import-Substitution Industrialization: The Case of Textiles

As noted, nascent industrial activity in the late 1950s and early 1960s emerged most often as the extension of the operations of colonial trading interests. In textiles it was the leading trading companies, *Compagnie française de l'Afrique occidentale* (C.F.A.O), *Société commerciale ouest africaine* (S.C.O.A.), *Compagnie du Niger Français* (United Africa Co.), and *Compagnie Optorg*, which supplied the capital for the early phases of dyeing and printing operations based on imported raw cotton cloth. Figure 1 shows the commercial structure and capital holders which controlled the textile industry of the Ivory Coast in the early 1970s (Campbell, 1974: 414). As will be seen, this first phase of import-substitution emerged in the highly protected environment of colonial markets. Moreover, the newly created industrial activities benefited from the extensive concessions set out in the Code of investment and destined to minimize the operating costs of foreign investors.

Local industrial activities in the 1960s and 1970s are best understood as essentially mercantile ventures, established to avoid tariff levies, and to facilitate the sale of inputs, spare parts, imported equipment, and so on. Their profitability was largely dependent on the fact that they exchanged intermediary products with other subsidiaries of the group to which they belonged.

The economic survival of such firms has been possible, as a study of the Ivorian textile industry pointed out, because of subsidies (very favorable purchase price of locally produced cotton, duty free imported products, low taxation on local value added, and the like), and protection (very high customs duties on competing imports, and subsidization of exports sold at a lower price than on the internal market) (Ivory Coast, Ministry of the Plan, 1980, Vol. I: 171).

By way of illustration, in 1973–1974 the local textile industry benefited from a 75 CFAF rebate per kilogram on local lint cotton through the state marketing operations. For 1978–1979, this rebate represented an annual subsidy to local industry of 1.3 billion CFAF (Ivory Coast, C.I.D.T. 1981).[4] Second, since local textile firms benefited from the concessions of enterprises granted priority status, they were permitted to import all intermediary products duty free. In 1979

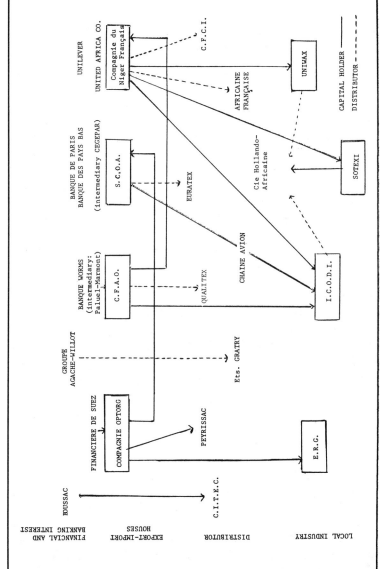

Figure 1: The Commercial Structure and Capital Holders of the Textile Industry in the Ivory Coast in the Early 1970s

nine firms in the cotton and synthetic textile and clothing branches still benefiting from priority status were exempted duties worth over two billion CFAF.[5]

Such measures illustrate the importance of the state in ensuring a highly protected market, and in this sense directly assuming functions previously performed by merchant capital. The Ivorian state also supplied important support to local industrial activity in numerous other ways, notably in putting up capital, in facilitating access to credit at a low rate, and in applying a low rate of taxation.

The expansion of state economic intervention from the early 1970s included the Ivorization of the capital of certain formerly private or semi-public French extension agencies such as the *Compagnie française pour le Développement des Fibres Textiles* (C.F.D.T.), which had complete control of Ivorian cotton production. This body was converted in 1973 into the *Compagnie Ivoirienne pour le Développement des Textiles* (C.I.D.T.), when the Ivorian government bought 55 percent of the shares. However, in view of the fact that the C.F.D.T. has retained official control over all aspects of technical expertise, the sale of Ivorian cotton on the world market, and consequently a critical aspect of the financing of the CIDT (as well as retaining 45 percent of the shares), state participation has not fundamentally altered the orientation of productive activities of the new C.I.D.T.

Industrial activities in the Ivory Coast in the 1970s continued to follow market strategies of short-term profitability, involving massive transfers of funds abroad whether in the form of repatriated profits, or payment for costly imports (inputs, licences, foreign expertise, and so forth). The dominant place retained by commercial capital in the activities established in the 1960s, and its relative autonomy vis-à-vis industrial capital, together with the highly protected framework created by state industrial and commercial policies, explain the perpetuation of similar conditions of production throughout the 1970s, and the adoption of the logic of accumulation that they entailed, even by the most recently established firms. Moreover, the multiplication of import substitution processing plants belonging to the same parent company in the neighboring countries of the region, explains the creation of excess capacity on a regional basis. Under these conditions, it becomes apparent why the high priced goods resulting from such productive activities have provoked problems of realization and consequently difficulties in ensuring operation at full capacity.

The example of the textile industry illustrates the conditions that have resulted in the perpetuation of a highly protected industrial structure, which is uncompetitive internationally. Research undertaken in 1972 revealed that average operating costs in the Ivorian textile sector were 80 percent higher than those of similar activities established in internationally competitive conditions (Campbell, 1975). This corresponds to the figure established by a World Bank Mission at the same time, to be the average rate of effective protection for the Ivorian industrial sector in general.

The same degree of protection and types of extremely advantageous concessions continued to be accorded to foreign investors throughout the 1970s.[6] New studies carried out at the end of this period on the synthetic fabric sector revealed a striking continuity and suggest that Ivorian production in this sector is twice as costly as the equivalent competing imports which are debarred entry in order to protect the local industry. Systematic adoption by the state under the pressure of foreign industrialists, of higher and higher tariff duties, of a hypothetic *valeur mercuriale* or tax base on which duties would be calculated, and finally of a decree prohibiting imports without the granting of a licence (which in the case of textiles was passed in 1976 and which in practice meant an embargo on imports), are only some of the measures used to exclude competing products.

The consequences of such a structure are extremely far-reaching. The cost of local goods places restrictions on their realization on the local market, as it does on the possibility of exporting them, and leads to severe capacity underutilization. Prices are set by a uniform system *(prix homologués),* to ensure that the least favored enterprises would not be at a disadvantage vis-à-vis those firms benefiting from concessions under the Code. The result is to sanction the operating costs of the least competitive firms, and to guarantee super-profits to those which had the most privileges (Campbell, 1975).

In view of the embargo on competing imports, the local market for textiles, particularly with regard to synthetics, polyester and knitted wear, is increasingly supplied by goods imported fraudulently. The quantity of synthetic fabrics imported illegally by the end of the 1970s was estimated to be the equivalent of local output, that is, approximately 4 million meters.

This pattern, which may be generalized to other sectors of industrial activities (notably shoes, car and motorbike assembly plants, plastics, processed coffee, and so on) means that the local population pay very high prices for essential manufactured goods, restricting the development of the local market, and that the state loses revenue which would accrue from duties on competing imports.

An indication of the importance of foreign interests and notably French interests in the economy is suggested by the fact that in 1978, 53 percent of capital in commercial enterprises was controlled by French capital and 30 percent of the industrial sector was in the hands of French nationals. French nationals controlled 45 percent of business turn-over of the modern sector of the economy, and French interests were responsible for 81 percent of profits (Africa Confidential, 1979).

On the one hand, massive transfers of funds externally were to be the counterpart, as has been noted, to attracting foreign capital to the secondary and tertiary sectors. Until the end of the 1970s, the growing importance of such transfers was masked by the receipts from coffee, cocoa, and wood exports. The conjunctural drop in world prices after 1978 was to reveal the structural contradictions of the short term growth strategies of the past.

Annual private transfers from the Ivory Coast between 1950 and 1965, in constant 1965 value, had increased three and a half times, from 7 billion to 25.2 billion CFAF. During the same period, the relative size of private transfers remained fairly constant at about 11 percent of the country's GNP reflecting the fact that half of national urban income as a whole continued to accrue to private firms, individual entrepreneurs and non-African salaries. By 1969 foreign transfers had increased to almost 29 billion CFAF. The consequence of the size of the transfers was to become manifest in the country's negative balance of payments position as of 1971. The overall deficit since that year was largely due to unilateral private transfers—a net drain which was to reach 131.5 billion in current CFAF by 1980.

Concerning the place occupied by foreign capital in industrial activities, the deliberate policy whereby nascent industrial operations were to remain the *chasse gardée* (preserve) of foreign interests was, as has been noted, essential to the attempt on the part of the dominant planter class, to stall the ascension of a local *bourgeoisie d'affaires*. Changes in the scale of finance at the beginning of the 1970s were made possible by a clear policy of state intervention, described officially as "state capitalism." Through its Ministry of the Plan, the state bought in 20 to 30 percent of share capital in numerous private enterprises at the beginning of the 1970s. This state participation did not involve any significant change in the organization of production or the degree of foreign control, as we have seen. Insofar as it established any basis for promoting Ivorian industrial capital, this was under the umbrella of the state, and in such a way as to be compatible with, and permit the enlargement of, the dominant alliance that remained under planter leadership.

Moreover, the extensiveness of foreign control over industry helps explain why investment by Africans tends to be in activities like transport, real estate, and the like. Moreover, the control exercised by foreign interests over the industrial structure provides further elements for the analysis of the conditions for the formation of local capital. This process was to take place through the intermediary of the local state and as a means to ensure the enlargement of the dominant ruling alliance, giving rise to what has been called *couches affairistes non-entreprenantes* (a non-enterprising business class).[7]

If the logic of production of the early industrial activities finds its origins in the extension of the commercial sector, it is in the growing transfers from the agricultural export sector necessary to pay for the continuation of this pattern of industrial activity that the tensions become most manifest.

The Conditions of Exchange in the Export Agricultural Sector

During the 1960s and 1970s there occurred a deterioration of the terms of exchange for producers of the chief export crops. As we shall see, this has restricted the possibility of extending agricultural production and increasing productivity. Various studies, which will be examined in more detail, confirm the deterioration of the terms of exchange for Ivorian producers of coffee and cocoa, as well as the drive by the state through the Caisse, to increase continually its revenues from this critical sector.

The relative stability of producer prices of coffee from 1960–1961 to 1973 (with only a slight increase for cocoa prices) together with rapid price inflation of commodities on which agricultural producers depend suggests a net loss of real income. Producer prices of coffee rose between 1973 and 1977. However, with the decision to impose industrial shelling of coffee in 1978 and to prevent its processing by cultivators, the price received by the latter was 150 CFAF per kilogram. The differential between this price and the declared producer price of 250–280 CFAF per kilogram is appropriated by industrial processors of cherry coffee. Producers suffered a further disadvantage as the price of cherry coffee they received was based on a ratio of 2 to 1 for cherry to green coffee, whereas the actual ratio is about 1.9 to 1.

The fact that producer prices were kept stable for the years immediately following 1979–1980 while price inflation of manufactured goods continued, has meant that coffee producers suffered a drop in real income of approximately 30 percent. Producer prices of cocoa levelled off from 1977, resulting in a similar deterioration of the terms of exchange, although cocoa producers have not been affected quite as badly as those producing coffee.

Part of the explanation for the deterioration is the continuing contribution of export crops to state revenues through the operations of the Caisse, even after the fall in world prices after 1978. In 1961–1962 the total revenue drawn from coffee and cocoa producers by the Caisse was 400 million CFAF. In 1974–1975 this had increased to 59.4 billion CFAF (Gastellu and Yappi, 1982: 175, quoted from J.-C. Berthélémy: 14).

If one examines the returns to producers as a proportion of world prices for the chief export products, coffee and cocoa, one is presented with a clear picture of the increasing weight of state levies. During the period 1960–1965, it has been calculated that this ratio was 0.61 for coffee and 0.67 for cocoa. By the period 1971–1975, the ratio had fallen to an average of 0.52 for both products (Lee, 1980: 639). Even after a slight recovery from the very low ratios in 1978 and 1979 of 0.33 and 0.39 respectively, the ratio in 1980 of 0.42 was substantially lower than between 1971 and 1975.

Bearing in mind that effective producer prices were 150 CFAF per kilogram of cherry coffee, the difference between producer prices and world export prices for coffee and cocoa in 1979, can be broken down as follows:

	In CFAF per kg coffee (green)	cocoa
Producer price	249.3	275.2
Droits uniques de sortie (D.U.S.)		
Export duties	55.8	50.6
Other non-defined "margins"	42.7	39.5
Contribution to the CSSPPA	295.0	323.3
Export price (F.O.B.)	642.8	688.6
Fixed costs	19.4	18.6

Variable costs	17.9	25.4
Adjustments	17.1	–7.9
Average export price (C.I.F.)	697.2	724.7

The low yields of the Ivorian export agriculture sector are explained officially by technical factors, rather than by the organization of marketing and the deterioration of terms of exchange for producers. By 1980, officials estimated that only 5 percent of the existing stock of coffee trees had been planted in the last five years. As much as 60 percent of the stock was over 15 years old and 28 percent was more than 25 years old (The Financial Times, 1980: vi).

Similar problems exist with cocoa production. Given the increasing costs of inputs (the cost of fertilizers for the older trees has increased five-fold in recent years), and the five or six years delay between planting and the first harvest, only planters in a very favorable position—notably in terms of access to credit—are able to replant. As existing studies (e.g., Gastellu and Yappi, 1982) reveal, the returns to the vast majority of growers are insufficient for them to assure the maintenance and general upkeep of their farms, not to speak of their renewal and investments in improved techniques. Decreasing returns to export crop producers have critical importance not only for state revenues and for the extension of the internal market but for the expansion of the industrial sector as well.

The Conditions of Distribution in the Rural and Urban Sectors

The obstacles to the extension of the Ivorian pattern of industrialization may be identified at various levels. The terms of exchange of export agricultural crops, and their effects for real incomes in the countryside, establish an immediate level of contradiction in the process of commodity circulation. To take up again the example of textiles, although the productive capacity of cotton prints and wax prints of the Ivorian textile industry by 1980 was between 80 and 100 million meters, the local market absorbed only around 50 million meters. The balance of local consumption, with the exception of wax prints which could be imported legally, was supplied by illegally imported fabrics.

Moreover, as the highly protected activities of the industrial sector depend on ever increasing subsidies, this requires ever increasing state revenue. In the 1960s and early 1970s, state operations were financed to a substantial degree from the levies of the *Caisse de Stabilisation*. In 1970, for example, the Caisse was estimated to supply 34 percent of public revenue. According to the World Bank, over the period 1965–1966 to 1974–1975, about one-third of total coffee and cocoa export earnings went to the public sector (as quoted in Lee, 1980: 637–638). With the drop in world prices from 1978 the relative importance of levies on export crops declined, and the other major source of revenue, indirect taxes, took on a proportionally more important role.

Although the question of state revenues will be examined in greater detail in the final section of this chapter, it is important to note here the central place of these two sources of state revenue, export and import duties on one hand and indirect taxes on local production on the other. Throughout the 1970s, they together contributed over two-thirds of state funds. By contrast, and reflecting the privileged accumulation of certain well protected sectors, the contribution of direct taxes was much less significant. The latter remained remarkably stable at approximately 10 percent of total state revenue. The relative importance of the various sources of Ivorian state revenues reveal the particular constellation of social and political forces within the state apparatus.

What must be analyzed in turn is the pattern of distribution of resources resulting from the forms of accumulation described above. This will be done in three stages, beginning with a brief presentation of income distribution in the rural and urban sectors. Second, I shall examine how the distribution of resources affects the capacity of producers to reproduce themselves. Finally, I shall consider the impact of the pattern of distribution on the capacity of the state to reproduce its range of activities and consequently it own class basis.

According to the 1981 study entitled *Prix, aides, subventions et taxes* commissioned by the World Bank, the official minimum guaranteed agricultural wage in coffee, cocoa, and cotton production increased from a range of 160–214 CFAF in 1970–1971 to 275–343 CFAF in 1980–1981. This represents less than a two-fold increase, while the official African cost of living index increased almost fourfold, from 144 to 503. In view of the massive influx of migrant workers, there is good reason to doubt whether the official minimum wage is indeed applied. On the optimistic assumption that it is, these figures nevertheless reveal an important drop in real wages in the plantation sector, which may be part of the explanation as to why workers prefer to be paid in kind according to the *abusan* system.

Studies undertaken on the impact of the extension of cash cropping in the northern savannah region of the Ivory Coast (notably cotton), suggest that the conditions of reproduction of peasant producers have changed significantly, not least through the intensification of labor. Increased centralized control over all aspects of production and marketing of cotton, in the 1960s and the 1970s has resulted in the neglect and decline of food crops in cotton growing areas, the loss of food autonomy,[8] new forms of subordination of women, changes in practices of collective help, and above all the emergence of new lines of social differentiation. (For a fuller treatment, see Campbell, 1984).

The failure of urban incomes to keep pace with the cost of living index is officially recognized in planning documents (Ivory Coast, Ministry of Finance, 1982: 26). In addition to declining real incomes and its implications for the development of the internal market, several other aspects of urban incomes should be emphasized. First is the relatively small proportion of urban workers employed by the private sector, compared with the state, and the low rate of growth of urban employment. Both these reflect the capital intensive nature of foreign-controlled industry (noted earlier), and the consequently enhanced role of the state as employer. A second major aspect is the erosion of real incomes of urban workers, the increasing differential between categories of workers, and, most important, the gap between salaries paid to nationals and to expatriates (Gouffern, 1982: 25, note 5).

The figures concerning annual private transfers given above, bring us to the heart of the contradictions of past patterns of accumulation in the Ivory Coast, and the limitations of short-term growth strategies, as they manifest themselves in fiscal terms. While state expenditure necessary to reproduce the costly pattern of growth increased, the sectors which had traditionally supplied state revenues were less and less able to meet its increasing exactions.

In the 1970s as the situation worsened, rather than mobilize local savings and attempt to stall the massive transfers of funds abroad (such as salaries, profits, and services), and to put an end to prestigious investment projects, the Ivory Coast multiplied its foreign borrowing. According to World Bank sources, the country's foreign debt increased from U.S. $388 million in 1969, $1.5 billion in 1975 and $4.2 billion in 1979 (Baulin, 1982: 167). By 1984 Ivorian foreign debt was officially estimated at $6 billion.

According to the World Bank, debt service as a ratio to the value of exports was 4.9 percent in 1969; 7.9 percent in 1972; 8.8 percent in 1975; 10.4 percent in 1977; 14 percent in 1978 and 25 percent in 1980 (Baulin,

1982: 167). As will be seen in the final section of this chapter, debt servicing charges were to increase even more rapidly at the beginning of the 1980s. As these figures reveal, by the end of the 1970s the contradictions of the past pattern of growth had become very evident. During the period studied, the country's stability reflected the capacity of its ruling class not only to reproduce, but also to enlarge the social basis of state power. The process had included specific patterns of state investment, employment and local capital formation, each of which was dependent on the capacity of the state to increase its revenues. In this area as well, the contradictory nature of the process and its limitations had become apparent by the late 1970s.

THE LIMITATIONS OF THE PRESENT PHASE AND THE FISCAL CRISIS OF THE STATE: THE CURRENT PERIOD FROM THE LATE 1970s

Principal Characteristics of the Present Phase

Evolving planter interests in the context of foreign industrial control. The particular pattern of surplus drain from the Ivorian economy perpetuated, if in a modified form, through the creation of foreign dominated and highly protected industrial activities, has depended on a specific pattern of surplus distribution within the economy itself.

The non-competitiveness of Ivorian industry may be illustrated with reference to any number of sectors, as for example the findings of a study comparing the cost elements of producing printed cotton cloth (Ivory Coast, Ministry of the Economy, of Finance and the Plan, 1978). The costs which explain this situation included very high expatriate salaries, royalties and fees for foreign technical services, equipment and inputs, and so on. To give but a very brief illustration of one of these cost elements—that of the cost of foreign salaries at the supervisory level (cadres) in the private sector—according to the Ivorian statistical centre, the Centrale des Bilans, in 1979 30 percent of the wage bill in the modern sector (excluding the civil service and banks) went to non-Africans. (For further details see Gouffern, 1982: 25, note 5).

The consequences of the pervasive and monopolistic place occupied historically by colonial and foreign interests are numerous, and particularly important with regard to the pattern of local capital formation. Concerning, for example, access to public funds to permit the extension or intensification of agricultural production, the conditions for obtaining credit depend not only on the way in which funds are used, but as well on who the larger planters or potential local investors are. The political continuity of the Ivorian leadership has depended on its ability to reproduce and enlarge its own political base. While its original planter base has become more varied and complex, as compared to the situation at political independence, the critical importance of the ruling party's ability to maintain political support from farmers (and not only from the larger planters) is evident in view of export agriculture's contribution to state revenues. Political links and access on the part of the larger planters have been maintained and are important to their success: "The 'entrepreneurial planters' *(planteurs entrepreneurs)* belong to a political and administrative elite; they live in the city and for them, it is capital which is the scarce factor" (Gastellu and Yappi, 1982: 150; our translation).

However, the political support of the planter class as a whole has been maintained in spite of the deterioration of the terms of exchange for agricultural exports, through concessions such as selective access to credit and the possibility of paying very low wages to mostly foreign agricultural workers. According to the 1981 study, *Prix, aides, subventions et taxes,* the daily minimum agricultural wage for workers in coffee, cocoa, cotton, and rice production was kept below that of other crops and for these four crops it ranged officially between 275 and 343 CFA francs or between U.S. $1.00 and $1.50 during the period 1978–1981.

Deterioration of the Terms of Exchange for Agricultural Exports and Lack of Reinvestment in Agriculture

The deterioration of the terms of exchange for agricultural exports has been discussed. This has had adverse effects on the capacity of small and medium producers to invest in techniques which would increase productivity. Moreover, available studies suggest that surpluses accruing to the largest planters have not been used for productive reinvestment in agriculture (Gastellu and Yappi, 1982). These studies undertaken in the Moronou and Ketté areas of eastern Ivory Coast, reveal that even on large farms where some agricultural equipment had been acquired, it remained insufficient according to the norms recommended by the agricultural extension agency responsible for coffee, the *Société d'assistance technique pour la modernisation agricole de la Côte d'Ivoire* (SATMACI). Surpluses appear above all to continue to be channelled outside the plantation sector, into transport, real estate, services, speculative activities, much as described by Samir Amin in the early 1960s (Amin, 1967: 91–107).

Noting the similarity with the situation in the 1950s, the former more recent study concludes:

> Productive investments [in agriculture] appear to be just as absent as they were. On the contrary, the larger planters make placements in various other sectors: in construction, which allows them to rent houses; in small commercial ventures, by setting up shops which they then entrust to young relatives; in artisanal production, through the purchase of sewing machines for the young women of the household; through usurious loans, which are lent to impoverished villagers . . . [Gastellu and Yappi, 1982: 172-173; our translation].

The Pattern of Government Financing

As illustrated by the 1979 example of the break-down of export prices for coffee and cocoa, the agricultural export sector has played a critical part in supplying state revenues, not least through the reserves of the CSSPPA. According to law, 60 percent of the Caisse's surpluses are to be paid into reserves, 30 percent are earmarked for transfers to the Ivorian Treasury and 10 percent to the *Banque Nationale de Développement Agricole*, B.N.D.A. By the mid-1970s however, relatively little was allocated to reserves and the major portion of the surpluses was used to finance government investment expenditure. In fact, as of 1974, the Caisse directly financed large-scale investment projects. By 1977, 50 billion CFAF was transferred to the Treasury and in 1978, a transfer of almost 59 billion CFAF was forecast. In spite of attempts to regularize this mode of financing in order to improve control over the Caisse's reserves, large amounts continued to remain outside the control of either the Caisse or the Treasury. The projects so financed were normally executed by the relevant technical ministries of the central government, but could in fact be executed by any person or organization designated by the President. The practice of carrying out large-scale investment programs outside the budget and hence without effective financial control represented, according to the I.M.F. in 1981, one of the most serious problems of financial management in the Ivory Coast. This was exacerbated by the fact that the Caisse was the most important source of domestic savings in the 1976–1978 period.

Major increases in government expenditure took place in years when export earnings were high but small increases were maintained even in poorer years of export performance through recourse to foreign borrowing. For example, the sharp increase in investment expenditure in 1976, 79 percent above the level in 1975, occurred when export earnings were beginning to rise rapidly due to favorable world market prices and increased production of coffee, cocoa and timber.

The year 1977 saw a departure from previous policy in that foreign borrowing increased sharply at the same time as export earnings were at the highest level ever reached. Caisse resources used to finance government expenditure more than tripled from 47 billion CFAF in 1976, to 145 billion in 1977, while at the same time net direct government borrowing rose from 35 billion CFAF to 77 billion. In a further departure, more than half the proceeds of the *Caisse Autonome d'Amortissement* direct foreign borrowing in 1977 were onlent by the C.A.A. to public enterprises with the remainder used to finance projects in the investment budget. Investment in public enterprises, much of which involved recurrent expenditure, accounted by this period for close to half of all public investment, reflecting a pattern of local capital formation to be discussed below. A consequence was a rise in the ratio of public external debt service to exports of goods and services to over 20 percent, a ratio which was to increase substantially with the attempt to perpetuate such a pattern of government financing as required by public investment policies.

The contradictory nature of this pattern that became manifest by the end of the 1970s was to have far-reaching implications not only for the continuing expansion of production in the agricultural export sector, but as well, for the economy as a whole.

With the severe indebtedness of the country, the revenues of the Caisse having decreased substantially as well, the portion of the investment budget attributable to loans increased proportionately. In the 1980 investment budget, the Caisse's contribution represented 121 billion CFAF or approximately 26 percent of the total budget of 467 billion. In view of the further worsening of the country's position in 1981, it was projected that of a proposed budget of 423 billion, the Caisse's contribution would be reduced to 23.6 billion, and that 304.9 billion would be funded through borrowing.

Having shown the limitations of the former pattern of financing state revenues for government operations in general, it is important in conclusion to consider the consequences of the previous pattern of government expenditure in the agricultural sector.

While it may be shown that approximately 30 percent of the investment budget, *(Budget spécial d'investissement et d'équipement),* has been devoted to agriculture over the decade 1970 to 1980, this was largely accounted for by the massive investment in the sugar program. The same project was subsequently described as a "fundamental error" in planning by President Houphouët-Boigny in his declaration to the Seventh Party Congress, 1 October 1980 (The Financial Times, 1980: vi).[9] In the Economic Plan 1981–1985, the allocation of the investment budget to agriculture was substantially reduced to 18.7 percent of the total.

The major contribution over the past two decades of the southern plantation region to the state budget has been noted above. However, in view of the increasing pressures on the state budget and the decrease in the proportion of the agricultural investment budget allocated to this region over the decade 1970–1980, the productive system has not been intensified and improved and there is an urgent need for a more rapid implementation of the renewal of crops. The implications for the whole economy if this situation is not remedied by an increase in public allocations, are recognized explicitly in official planning documents:

> The South, just like the Centre-West, is a region of surplus finance capacity which has been of great benefit to the State. However, we have seen to what extent the South has suffered rapid cuts in its share of agricultural development programmes since the beginning of the decade (1971–1980), and the real danger which exists today is that of the accelerated ageing of its productive system. A reversal of this situation is imperative and it will require a renewed allocation of a minimum of 12 percent of the public investment budget [Ivory Coast, Ministry of the Plan and Industry, 1981b: 51; our translation].

The persistence of a pattern of extensive production in the export sector during the first two decades of political independence, and the limits reached by this pattern at the beginning of the 1980s, should not be allowed to detract from the enormous wealth that has in fact been produced by the plantation economy. However, much of this has been transferred to the benefit of other areas of economic activity, above all to the industrial sector.

The Conditions of Production in the Industrial Sector and the Extension of Non-Agricultural Petty Commodity Production

Concerning the internal market, the high prices of basic necessities[10] bring about changes in the patterns of consumption which are themselves reflections of a more deeply rooted process of social differentiation. For reasons related to the high rate of unemployment (discussed below), only a very small minority of urban wage earners are in a position to attempt to obtain wage increases to compensate for increasing prices. Moreover in view of the extremely small official increases in the S.M.I.G. between 1980 and 1983 it may be shown that, just as in the case of civil servants, industrial workers have suffered a decline in real wages. Similarly, in the rural areas, as has been shown and according to the 1981 study commissioned by the World Bank, rural wages rose over the period 1970 to 1980 at only half the rate of the cost of living index.

In this context, the critically central role of the so-called informal sector becomes apparent. Far from occupying a residual place, petty commodity production outside agriculture provides a livelihood for an increasing proportion of the population, both rural and urban. A study of the regional impact of the creation of one of the three integrated textile complexes, that of Cotivo established at Agboville in 1976, reveals the very important extension of non-agricultural petty commodity production activities in the region and concludes that the extension of the artisanal sector appears as a necessary condition for the reproduction of the workforce at a lesser cost, and therefore the profitability of the modern firm (Dubresson, 1981–1982: 163).[11]

Excluding "traditional" activities in agriculture and stock farming, the artisanal sector represented an estimated 430,000 jobs in 1980 (Ivory Coast, Ministry of the Plan and Industry, 1981a: 12).[12] Of these jobs, 330,000 were in towns of over 10,000 inhabitants. Three-quarters of the jobs in the informal sector were urban; 100,000 jobs were rural, but of the latter, approximately 50,000 were activities of an industrial type. Without providing evidence for a directly causal effect, these figures do underline a very likely correlation between the spread of artisanal activities and the creation of salaried employment.

However, the contradictory role of petty commodity production, at times reinforced by the capitalist sector, at others absorbed when it becomes apparent that the market supplied by the former sector can be captured by the capitalist sector (often by the non-economic intervention of the state; de Miras, 1977), and the new patterns of accumulation and differentiation emerging within these sectors, merit far more empirical research than has so far been carried out.

The Manifestations of the Limits of the Current Phase of Accumulation

If in the past the dominant group which controlled the state could use an extensive mode of accumulation from agriculture to reproduce and enlarge its own class basis, by the end of the 1970s the evidence suggests that the prolongation of this strategy was no longer an alternative. In view of the central economic role of the post-colonial state as employer and investor, the limits of the former pattern of accumulation have implications for the dominant group's capacity to restructure the alliances on which its power has depended. The importance of these limits is conveyed by the fact that in 1980 the state employed over 100,000 people of the total 470,000 in the modern sector, as well as creating conditions for investment by supplying credit, putting up capital, guaranteeing markets, and so on. Since independence, the expansion of state employment and its wage fund, as well as the pattern of distribution and local capital formation dependent on state funds, have been essential components in the shaping of the alliances on which political stability has been based.

To cite but one example, after the "plots" against the government in 1963-1964, civil servant salary scales were increased systematically so that by 1970 they represented 500 percent of the S.M.I.G. in the secondary and tertiary sectors (Baulin, 1982: 154). The rate of expansion of employment and the wage fund depends on state revenue, whose expansion is held within fairly well defined limits by the rate of expansion of real output within the economy. By the end of the 1970s, it had become evident that the economy was increasingly unable to expand sufficiently rapidly to provide increasing urban employment, and sufficiently skilled employment for trained job seekers.

In 1981, a study produced by the Ivorian Ministry of the Plan and Industry (1981a: 10) projected that the percentage of persons able to find employment as compared to the active population of work age would decrease as follows: 51.6 percent (1975), 46.3 percent (1980), 41.5 percent (1985), 39.1 percent (1990). The same study projects available urban employment as a proportion of active population as 20.1 percent (1980), 16.7 percent (1985), 15.3 percent (1990). The number of people unable to find employment in 1980 was estimated at 223,000, and officially projected to increase to 432,000 in 1985 and 671,000 in 1990.

In addition, there is a growing gap between the number of job seekers who have more than primary education and the availability of appropriate jobs. To prevent an increasing rate of unemployment among those who have more years of education, the preparatory study for the Five-Year Plan (1981-1985) recommended that the rate of entry to post-secondary specialized training be reduced from 42 percent (the average between 1974 and 1977) to 32 percent in 1985, and to 15 percent in 1990 (Ivory Coast, Ministry of the Economy, of Finance and the Plan, 1979: 22).

A final and politically critical dimension of the question of employment, is the projected decreasing capacity of the modern urban sector to offer employment to more highly skilled Ivorians. This was already true for a growing number of students graduating with a social science as opposed to a pure science degree in the latter half of the 1970s. It was projected, however, that even under the optimistic hypothesis that all expatriate cadres in the social sciences be replaced by 1986 (in 1980 there were 4000 French *coopérants*, of whom 3200 were teachers), 24 percent of Ivorians, or approximately 5000 people with university training of at least two years literary or legal training, would still be unable to find suitable employment (Ivory Coast, Ministry of the Economy, of Finance of the Plan, 1979: 31).

By 1981, unemployed cadres (skilled professional, technical, or managerial personnel at a supervisory level) had already formed an association in order to put forward their grievances. The President of the country responded by convening the *Association interprofessionnelle de la Côte d'Ivoire*, the employer's association, and requesting that directors of firms hire approximately 700 unemployed Ivorian cadres (Gouffern, 1982: 23, note 2).

During the 1970s, while the number of civil servants increased, the budget for their salaries increased less than proportionally. Loss in *per capita* salary (exacerbated by inflation) reveals not only the squeeze on state expenditure by the end of the 1970s, but also changes in policies. During the 1970s, the strategy appears to have been one of favoring certain strategic groups of salaried workers at specific moments, such as the teachers who received important salary increases in the mid-1970s, rather than, as formerly, dealing with state employees *en bloc*.

Moreover, lack of expansion of the state wage fund becomes a contributing factor in limiting the expansion of state revenues, as indirect taxes represented an increasingly important portion of these revenues.

Together, indirect taxes on local production, with duties on imports and exports, have contributed, as noted, over two-thirds of state revenue: 65 percent in 1975; 81 percent in 1977 and 69 percent in 1981. The relative importance of indirect taxes levied on local production and imported goods in the total of state revenues, fluctuates with the contributions of export taxes and marketing operations of the *Caisse de Stabilisation*, and the *Caisse de Péréquation* that is responsible for assuring uniform internal prices for certain products such as rice and gasoline. With the drop in world prices for Ivorian major export crops after 1978, in 1979 indirect taxes from local production contributed a far larger amount than marketing board operations. The contribution from the latter rose from 19 percent of total state revenue in 1975, to reach 47.1 percent with high world prices of coffee and cocoa in 1977, and dropped to 12.5 percent in 1981.

By contrast, direct taxes which are drawn from corporate profits, personal income, and state lands, represent a very much less significant contribution. They have remained remarkably stable at approximately 10 percent of total revenue. The small size of the latter source contrasts rather strikingly with Kenya for example, where direct taxes in 1970 contributed 34 percent and in 1975, 35 percent of state revenues (Kitching, 1980: 417).

As noted, the expansion of state expenditure in the 1960s and 1970s became more and more dependent on foreign borrowing, while simultaneously intensifying fiscal pressures on traditional sources of revenue. The decrease in world export prices of coffee and cocoa after 1978 revealed rather dramatically the structural contradictions of the previous pattern of expansion whose remedies lay beyond conjunctural factors such as world prices. The costs involved were partially concealed for a time through a positive balance of trade (as in 1977, 1978, and 1979), but the latter was negative in 1980 and registered a deficit of 50 billion CFAF in 1981. This situation was exacerbated by the maintenance of a high level of private transfers at 131.5 billion CFAF (1980), 132.7 billion (1981) and 131.9 billion (1982).

In 1981 the country's public debt had reached 1420 billion CFAF, an increase of 40 percent over the previous year. Official calculations of the foreign debt service ratio were 31 percent (240 billion CFAF) in 1981, and 33.8 percent (317.5 billion CFAF) in 1982, while alternative calculations suggest 35 percent for 1981 and 39 percent for 1982.

Under the pressure of loan suppliers, public spending was reduced. The rate of increase of public investment which had depended increasingly on foreign borrowing since 1977, declined substantially as of 1979. In 1980 important changes were also made in the country's policies concerning public and semi-public corporations. In June 1980 of the 36 major state corporations, 15 corporations were dissolved and 11 were changed into public service corporations, that is, public utilities governed by the regulations of the civil service.

The operational budget which concerns recurrent expenditure (Budget général de fonctionnement) was reduced in real terms (in constant CFAF value) as of 1979. Between 1979 and 1983, the public investment budget was cut by approximately half (in constant CFAF value), with the far-reaching if indirect effects that these contractions entail for the expansion of public employment and the wage fund.

To bridge the gap between revenue and expenditure, including the need to meet interest payments on previous borrowing, the government turned more and more to external borrowing. In view of existing levels of taxation of export agriculture, there remained little scope for raising taxes, as the IMF study noted in 1981, without leading to even further decreases in output and demand. To give but one example of each, prices to palm oil producers have dropped so much in real terms that peasant producers are abandoning this industrial crop in favor of food crops such as cassava for self-consumption and for sale. An attempt to increase the value-added tax on bottled non-alcoholic beverages in 1981–1982 that increased prices proportionally, provoked an immediate decrease in consumption. The complaints of the firms producing these products led to the abandonment of the attempt to increase indirect taxes by this means.

What effects does the squeeze on the state budget have for the capacity of the ruling group to reproduce and enlarge its own basis? The previously consistent policy of impeding the emergence of a local industrial capitalist class which might rival foreign interests was modified to a limited extent through highly circumscribed policies of Ivorization and a pattern of local capital formation dependent on the local state. The critical links which exist between the Ivorian state and the process of local capital formation may be illustrated in three ways.

First, by the links which exist between local investors and state structures. Several studies reveal that at least two-thirds of Ivorian investors or promoters of small industries were members of the civil service or held political positions (Chevassu and Valette, 1971; quoted in Campbell, 1983: 831). After the 1971 state decree on Ivorization, 80 percent of the Ivorization of bakeries took place and by the mid 1970s, 66 percent of Ivorians owning bakeries were members of the civil service (De Miras, 1977: 83). The same author notes that where artisanal production was efficient, its disappearance and replacement by industrial firms, as in the bread industry, cannot be explained by strictly economic mechanisms.

Second, by the links which exist between private investment and state participation; in at least one-third of the firms in which there are private Ivorian interests, there is also state participation. This reflects the state's deliberate policy of buying shares and transferring them to Ivorian investors. It was in order to facilitate this process that the Abidjan Stock Exchange was created in April 1976. After two decades of independence, policies for the promotion of Ivorian initiatives and interests remained in perfect conformity with the orientations adopted by the dominant ruling group at independence. The promotion of local investors was indissociable from state intervention.

Third, by the use of public funds, services, equipment, by guaranteeing protected markets, access to credit, influence, and so on, as the necessary means (in view of monopolistic control by foreign interests) of setting up a process of local "parallel" accumulation. The use of public funds in local private capital formation partly explains the lack of centralized control over financial decision-making, noted earlier, which had assumed critical proportions by the late 1970s. The official estimate for 1980 of the debt for the operational budget was 20 billion CFA francs; for the public investment budget, 50 billion CFA francs; for the C.A.A., 20 billion; for the Caisse, 30 billion; and for public corporations approximately 100 billion (of which the SODESUCRE represented 64 billion): a total of 220 billion CFA francs.

The Conditions Necessary for Surpassing the Limits of the Past Pattern of Accumulation

What has been labelled "parallel accumulation" *(coulage)* or corruption, appears not so much as the sign of dysfunctions or errors of past policies, but rather reflects the specificity of the condtions of accumulation in a post-colonial context, and notably the narrowness of the internal base of local accumulation, and the conditions for the retention and reproduction of political power in the Ivorian context.

Overcoming the contradictions of this model entails nothing less than abandoning the economic mechanisms and forms of accumulation which in the past permitted the economic ascension and access to power of the dominant ruling group, which have permitted this group to reproduce the ruling alliances on which its power has depended.

Overcoming the limitations of this model entails the adoption of a mode of organization of productive activity, capable of increasing productivity through the intensification of techniques in the agricultural sector and the adoption of productive, as opposed to marketing strategies in the industrial sector. Without such an overhaul, the structural contradictions that have given rise to indebtedness, non-competitive local production, and inability to supply the local market or to export, and so forth, will inevitably worsen. The pattern of revenue transfer on which the Ivorian experience was based was recognized by the country's new creditors before the drop in world prices made its limitations blatantly obvious: "The industrial sector, on the whole, is subsidised, and it is the forest and agricultural sectors which supply the means to do so" (World Bank, as quoted by Baulin, 1982: 166).

Short-term attempts to overcome the present obstacles to continued accumulation have entailed massive foreign borrowing which has been forthcoming from essentially North American sources, suggesting the displacement of traditional suppliers of funds by the mid-1970s. This new phase of penetration of international capital would seem to require a significant development of productive forces, involving increases in productivity which in turn entail changes in the organization of production.

Within this context one may understand the centrally important role of the World Bank in financing development in the Ivory Coast, particularly from 1975. In 1981, the $150 million loan for a program of structural readjustment, brought the total of World Bank funding to the country to $906 million. According to the country's President, this sum was to reach $1 billion in 1983 (Fraternité Matin, 29 April 1983).

The place occupied by foreign borrowing in Ivorian finances has given the country's creditors very important leverage, above all concentrated in the World Bank, which leads and coordinates the interests of other creditors. The Bank is thus in a key position to influence the orientation of development policies beyond the usual supervisory role it plays in the projects if funds. As with all I.B.R.D. loans, the terms of the agreements are associated with conditions which must be "satisfactory to the Bank" concerning the selection of consultants, their qualifications and experience; the selection of contractors, the timing of the implementation of programs, and even the adoption of new statistical instruments and methods of calculation. By the end of the decade, as the country's economic difficulties became all the more apparent, the Bank stepped more fully into the arena of decision-making. A central area of its recommendations linked to structural readjustment funding, concerned the exercise of tighter control over certain very protected activities, notably concerning pricing and subsidy policies, as outlined by the 1981 study, *Prix, aides, subventions et taxes.* In this example, one can see a direct challenge to certain functions formerly assumed by the state in favor of private interests, dependent for their perpetuation on the privileges and forms of accumulation inherited from the colonial period.

Moreover, the Bank's intervention not only in financing development, but also in contributing to defining its objectives, creates new areas of economic activity for private, as opposed to public capital, and openings for suppliers of foreign capital linked more closely to the Bank-IMF group, where previously European and essentially French interests had been dominant.

This new phase of capital penetration would seem to require both changes in the mode of accumulation and finance and increasingly, changes in the organization of production as well. To this end there is an important need for associating nationals with the new objectives and projects that previously have been held almost exclusively by foreigners. It is within this context that one can see the fuller significance of policies recommending the acceleration of Ivorization, whether it be for instance, the promotion of local capital formation or the training of nationals according to the norms of the new suppliers of loans and foreign capital, etc. Moreover, a proposed strategy for changes in the mode of accumulation is made explicit in the 1981 IMF report which recommends a process of "financial deepening and the spread of the capital market," notably through the creation of a domestic market in government securities. Just as at the time of political decolonization, when a particular phase of capital penetration had as its counterpart an internal process of differentiation with the emergence of a dominant planter group closely linked to metropolitan markets and resources, current attempts to restructure the process of accumulation call for the consolidation of new local forces as economic partners and political allies. In terms of control of state power, it will be important to analyze the impact of new foreign interventions, whether they be those of international financial organizations, public or private capital, on the constellation of forces within the ruling alliances. More fundamentally and underlying the political process is the question of the emergence of new social relations and new contradictions within the dominant local groups and between them and new categories of producers.

If one takes the example of the cotton programs whose objective is to stabilize output and to offset the initial costs by gradual intensification of techniques, the extension of production entails the emergence of a new category of cultivators identified in planning documents *agents cibles,* target groups of producers, "young modern cultivators." Their consolidation is a central objective of the cotton extension programs which aim:

> To train young peasants and especially selected cultivators in order that they may become individual agents—dynamic elements at the village level and in the training centers created in each zone [Ivory Coast, Ministry of Agriculture 1981: 5].

The new cultivators will no doubt benefit from the intensification of cotton production but their own "success" depends on the emergence of new patterns of wage labor. Research on the cotton extension programs suggests that if in the short term the emergence of a group of wealthier producers will serve to stabilize the new forms of production and to keep down the cost of cotton to the local textile industry, the conditions and techniques introduced to this end will entail the accentuation of social differences and contradictions within the cotton growing areas.

More generally, the extension of capitalist relations of production and new lines of differentiation manifested in a new phase and type of expansion of the domestic market and the accelerated formation of an at least partially proletarianized urban and rural wage force are the conditions for the current phase of penetration of international capital and the related process of local capital formation.

CONCLUSION

While this analysis has not considered explicitly the political dimension, the following are clearly critical determinants of trends about which one may only hypothesize at present.

The specific forms which the extension of wage-labor relations will take and the new patterns of social differentiation which will emerge in the Ivorian context are the result of a historical process, specific to that country and on which empirical research has yet to be done. Similarly, the moving constellation of forces within the dominant groups controlling the state apparatus may be seen, in addition to multiple and complex other forms of cleavages of a regional and ethnic nature, and so on, as an extension and a reflection of this same process of the restructuring of the current phase of accumulation. More specifically, one might well expect cleavages between those who seek to use state institutions to prolong the forms of accumulation left by the colonial period as opposed to those strengthened by new sources of foreign credit and capital, for whom such practices merely seek to impede the process of expanded reproduction on which their interests depend.[13] These cleavages and alliances are far from static. They are continually being redefined, depending on issues, giving rise to policies which at times appear inconsistent and even contradictory.

In the case of the Ivory Coast, what certain commentators have seen essentially as a period of transition of political leadership, is in fact a far deeper process involving the attempt to restructure the past phases of accumulation as a condition for overcoming the obstacles to the continuation of this process. The current phase of attempted restructuring involving the extension of capitalist relations of production and new lines of social differentiation has inevitable and crucial repercussions at the level of the state, which is the site of struggle among the complex competing forces involved. During this process, one cannot speak of the hegemony of national as opposed to international capital, or a fraction of one of these whether it be the dominant planter group or an emerging fraction of the urban based *bourgeoisie d'affaires,* linked to a particular set of foreign partners, for, as Gavin Kitching points out in his chapter in this volume, it is precisely the question of hegemony which is one of the central issues at stake. The outcome of this unresolved historical process will depend at least as much on the struggles between internal dominant groups, and in particular their struggles with other emerging classes in Ivorian society, as on the strategies of dominant foreign interests which, far from being monolithic, are themselves in competition with each other.

NOTES

1. E. Lee suggests that in 1973–1974 there were over 60,000 planters operating on more than 10 hectares. "There were 20,000 holdings of between 15 to 40 hectares in size, almost 400 of between 40 to 100 hectares in size and, . . . 550 holdings of over 100 hectares which were not included in the statistics for the traditional sector" (Lee, 1980: 630). In spite of the predominance of holdings under 10 hectares, the forest belt producing cash crops in the Ivory Coast is generally referred to as the plantation sector, and the term will be used in this context throughout this chapter.

2. In 1980, the foreign population in the Ivory Coast was well over 2 million and in view of the rate of increase, it was estimated that it would reach almost 3 million by 1985.

3. The currency unit of the Ivory Coast is the CFA franc *(Colonies françaises d'Afrique).* A fixed parity exists between the CFA franc and the French franc: one French franc = 50 CFA francs. The CFA franc floats against the US dollar. In the early 1960s, the rate fluctuated with variations at approximately one US dollar = 250 CFA francs. Subsequently the rate was as follows (den Tuinder, 1978: xix):

1969	=	US $1	=	CFAF 256
1970	=	US $1	=	CFAF 278
1971	=	US $1	=	CFAF 278
1972	=	US $1	=	CFAF 252
1973	=	US $1	=	CFAF 223
1974	=	US $1	=	CFAF 241

| 1975 | = | US $1 | = | CFAF 214 |
| 1976 | = | US $1 | = | CFAF 230 |

Since that date and particularly since 1981, fluctuations have been important.

1977	=	US $1	=	CFAF 245
1978	=	US $1	=	CFAF 224
1979	=	US $1	=	CFAF 212
1980	=	US $1	=	CFAF 210
1981	=	US $1	=	CFAF 260
1982	=	US $1	=	CFAF 327
1983	=	US $1	=	CFAF 376

Calculation based on *Revue de la Banque du Canada*, 1983, Table 65.

4. The size of annual subsidies for the period 1973–1974 to 1977–1978 are given in Ivory Coast, Ministry of the Economy, of Finance and the Plan, and Ministry of Commerce (1978: 13).

5. The figure (2,054,920,134, FCFA) for the year in question is based on calculations from 12 months of customs records, which give figures for the nine firms with priority status (Blue Bell Inc., Cotivo, Gonfreville, Mice, Socitas, Sotexi, Uniwax and Utexi), concerning the value of the *droits de douane* (custom duties) and *droits fiscal d'entrée* (import duties) on a monthly basis.

6. To illustrate these concessions one may cite the example of the new firm Blue Bell Côte d'Ivoire. BBCI began operations in the mid-1970s with the object of producing blue jeans for export on the basis of denim to be produced by COTIVO. The latter belongs to the same economic grouping initiated by the engineering interests Schaeffer and Co., which associates ICODI-COTIVO-BBCI. The share capital of BBCI is divided among ICODI (30 percent), Riegel Textile Corp. U.S.A. (19 percent), and Blue Bell Inc. U.S.A., the principal client of Riegel and a manufacturer of jeans (51 percent). In order to encourage the establishment of foreign capital, the new firm was granted exemptions on (1) all duties on imports of industrial equipment; (2) duties on imports of raw materials and means of production, each of the above for 10 years; (3) income tax for 5 years. Furthermore, by Article 13 of the firm's founding agreement dated 25 January 1974, the state has guaranteed that no other Company will be allowed to produce the same commodities which BBCI produces, blue jeans, for a five-year period.

7. A detailed analysis of this process is provided by de Miras (1982: 181–229). See also Baulin (1982: 157–161).

8. Rice imports to the Ivory Coast increased from 1636 tons in 1975 to 242,441 tons in 1980, and to over 350,000 tons in 1981. This massive increase reflects a variety of factors including the dissolution in 1977 of the parastatal body responsible for rice production, Sodériz.

9. The cost of six sugar complexes is estimated at 300 billion CFA francs.

10. Ivorian prices for synthetic fabrics before tax, were by 1982 twice as high as C.I.F. prices to Abidjan of South East Asian equivalent imports, and 60 percent higher than American products with the result that over half of the local market was supplied by fabrics imported fraudulently (Gouffern, 1982: 26, note 7).

11. The wage relationships resulting with the creation of 1500 new non-expatriate jobs by this firm, have further ramifications to which little attention appears to have been paid so far. There has resulted through the establishment of Cotivo, new relations of indebtedness and consequently, new forms of subordination of workers to the firm. This has taken place through the advance of very important portions of the total wage bill (30 percent to 40 percent in 1981) for *crédit scolaire* (loans to pay school fees), before the work year begins, to permit workers to send at least certain of their children to school. The importance of this new type of subordination of wage labor to capital, which rests on the educational aspirations of the population as a means of upward social mobility, reflects the role of the dominant ideology in shaping new social relations of production and merits further analysis. This example underlines the active role of ideology as a determinant factor in establishing the terms of new wage-labor capital relations, and consequently the conditions of reproduction of the emerging salaried labor force.

According to studies in preparation for the 1981-1985 Economic Plan, employment in the artisanal and traditional sectors over the period 1976 to 1980 had grown at an annual average of 6 percent, as compared to 5.7 percent for the industrial sector and 4.5 percent for the agricultural sector. It was expected that this rate would increase to 6.5 percent during the period 1981-1985.

12. According to a study (de Miras, 1977) of the period 1965–1970, the number of jobs in the traditional and modern sectors for all areas of economic activity (Branches 03 to 27) had evolved as follows:

	Artisanal	*Modern*
1965	134,300	190,400
1970	191,270	153,530

13. A particularly vivid example of the displacing of former, traditional capitalist interests which were the legacy of the commercial strategies of the colonial trading houses, by new international groups following productive strategies, was the buying in of the majority of shares of the French interests, Blohorn, by Unilever. Concerning the question of local control however, the announcement of the take-over specified: "This transaction will take place through the buying back by Unilever of Blohorn S.A. shares held by non-nationals" (Fraternité Matin, 1981: 2).

REFERENCES

Africa Confidential (1979). August 1st, 20(16).

AMIN, S. (1967). Le développement du capitalisme en Côte d'Ivoire. Paris: Editions de Minuit.

BARNES, L. (1969). "Expansion without growth: Ivory Coast," Ch. 13 in African Renaissance. London: Victor Gollancz.

BAULIN, J. (1982). La politique intérieure d'Houphouët-Boigny. Paris: Editions Eurafor-Press.

CAMPBELL, B. (1974). "The social, political and economic consequences of French private investment in the Ivory Coast, 1960-1970." D. Phil. dissertation, University of Sussex.

CAMPBELL, B. (1984). "Inside the miracle: cotton production in the Ivory Coast," pp. 143-171 in J. Barker (ed.), The Politics of Agriculture in Tropical Africa: Transnational, National and Local Perspectives. Beverly Hills, CA: Sage Publications.

———(1983). "Etat et développement du capitalisme en Côte d'Ivoire" pp. 301-314 in Entreprises et Entrepreneurs en Afrique, XIXe et XXe siècles, Vol. 2. Paris: L'Harmattan.

———(1978). "Ivory Coast," pp. 66-116 in J. Dunn (ed.), West African States: Failure and Promise. A Study in Comparative Politics. Cambridge: Cambridge University Press.

———(1975). "Neocolonialism, economic dependence and political change: A case study of cotton and textile production in the Ivory Coast 1960 to 1970." Review of African Political Economy 2: 36-53.

CHEVASSU, J. and A. VALETTE. (1975). "Les industriels de la Côte d'Ivoire. Qui et pourquoi?." Office de la Recherche Scientifique et Technique Outre-Mer, Côte d'Ivoire, Série d'Études Industrielles, 13.

DELAPORTE, G. (1970), Quinze années bien remplies au Service du Pays, Information Service, Caisse de Stabilisation de Côte d'Ivoire. Abidjan: May.

DUBRESSON, A. (1981-1982). "Régionalisation de l'industrie et croissance urbaine: le 'Mammouth' Cotivo à Abgoville (Côte d'Ivoire)," Cahiers de l'Office de la Recherche Scientifique et Technique Outre-Mer, série Sciences Humaines 18(1): 149-164.

FAURE, Y.-A. and J.-F. MEDARD. (1982). Etat et Bourgeoisie en Côte d'Ivoire. Paris: Editions Karthala.

Financial Times (1980). Ivory Coast, A Financial Times Survey. London, December 15.

Fraternité Matin (1983). Abidjan, April 29.

———(1981). Abidjan, December 2.

GASTELLU, J.-M., and S. AFFOU YAPPI. (1982). "Un mythe à décomposer: la bourgeoisie de planteurs," pp. 149-179 in Y.-A. Fauré and J.-F. Médard, Etat et Bourgeoisie en Côte d'Ivoire. Paris: Karthala.

GBAGBO, L. (1982). Côte d'Ivoire. Economie et société à la veille de l'indépendance, (1940-1960). Paris: L'Harmattan

GOUFFERN, Louis (1982). "Les limites d'un modèle? A propos 'd'Etat et bourgeoisie en Cote d'Ivoire.' " Politique Africaine, 11(6): 19-34.

Ivory Coast (1981). Compagnie ivoirienne pour le Développement des Textiles (C.I.D.T.), Rapport annuel d'activités, Campagne 1979-1980, Abidjan.

Ivory Coast, Ministry of Agriculture (1981). Organisation et Gestion du Développement, Commission 2, Mission d'Identification. Projet Nord et Nord Ouest, Bouaké: 12 March.

Ivory Coast, Ministry of Agriculture (1980). Statistiques agricoles, Direction des Statistiques Rurales et des Enquêtes Agricoles, Abidjan.

Ivory Coast, Ministry of the Economy, of Finance and the Plan (1979). Préparation du Plan de Développement Economique, Social et Culturel, 1981-1985, Fasciule IV, Education et Emploi, Direction Générale de la Planification, Direction du Plan, Abidjan.

————and Ministry of Commerce (1978). Mémorandum Textile pour la Communauté Economique Européenne. Abidjan, December.

Ivory Coast, Ministry of Finance (1982). Budgets Economiques de l'Année 1982, Direction de la Prévision, Abidjan.

Ivory Coast, Ministry of the Plan (1980). L'industrialisation des régions en Côte d'Ivoire, Direction générale du Développement Régional, Ferrault, P., Heymann, Y., Thenevin, P., Zaslavsky, J., 2 vol., May 1980, Abidjan.

Ivory Coast, Ministry of the Plan and Industry (1981a). Contribution à l'atelier sur l'utilisation des indicateurs socio-économiques dans la planification nationale et régionale, September.

Ivory Coast, Ministry of the Plan and Industry (1981b). Analyse régionale des actions de l'Etat réalisées au cours des dix années de lois programmes 1971–1980, Direction du Développement Régional, Abidjan: September.

KITCHING, G. (1980). Class and Economic Change in Kenya: The Making of an African Petite Bourgeoisie. New Haven and London: Yale University Press.

LAWSON, G.H., (1975). "La Côte d'Ivoire: 1960–1970. Croissance et diversification sans africanisation," pp. 199–238 in J.D. Esseks (ed.), L'Afrique de l'indépendance politique à l'indépendance économique, Edition F. Maspero and Presses Universitaires de Grenoble.

LEE, E., (1980). "Export-led rural development: the Ivory Coast." Development and Change, Vol. II: 607–642.

MIRAS, C. de (1982). "L'entrepreneur ivorien ou une bourgeoisie privée de son état", pp. 181–229 in Y.-A. Fauré and J.-F. Médard, Etat et bourgeoisie en Côte d'Ivoire. Paris: Karthala.

————(1977). De l'artisanat au secteur de subsistance. Conditions de Production et de Reproduction du secteur de subsistance. Office de la Recherche Scientifique et Technique Outre-Mer, Sciences Humaines, Petit Bassam, Ivory Coast.

MEILLASSOUX, C. (1964). Anthropologie Economique des Gouro de Côte d'Ivoire, Paris: Mouton and Cie.

MORGENTHAU, R.S. (1964) Political Parties in French-Speaking West Africa. Oxford: Clarendon.

Revue de la Banque du Canada (1983). Ottawa, Bank of Canada, December, Table 65, p. S 127.

TUINDER, B. den (1978). Ivory Coast. The Challenge of Success. A World Bank Country Economic Report. Washinton: Johns Hopkins University Press.

About the Contributors

JEAN-LOUP AMSELLE has a Doctorate in Sociology from the Sorbonne University. He is currently Maître-assistant at the Ecole des Hautes Etudes en Sciences Sociales, where he is Secretary of the Centre d'Etudes Africaines. Mr. Amselle is the author of *Les Négociants de la Savane* (Anthropos, Paris, 1977), *Le sauvage à la mode* (Le Sycomore, Paris, 1979), and the editor of *Les migrations africaines* (Maspero, Paris, 1976).

BJÖRN BECKMAN is Associate Professor of Political Science at the University of Stockholm. He has carried out research in West Africa since 1967 and has also taught at universities in Ghana and Nigeria. He is the author of *Organising the Farmers: Cocoa Politics and National Development in Ghana* (Scandinavian Institute of African Studies, Uppsala, 1976), and many articles on agrarian political economy, and theories of imperialism, underdevelopment, and the state. He is currently researching agricultural projects in northern Nigeria.

HENRY BERNSTEIN is Lecturer in Third World Studies at the Open University in England. He has taught at universities in Tanzania and Turkey as well as in Britain, and is author of many articles on peasant economy under capitalism, state and peasantry in Tanzania, African historiography, and theories of development and underdevelopment. He has edited *Underdevelopment and Development: The Third World Today* (Penguin Books, fourth printing 1981), and, with Hazel Johnson, *Third World Lives of Struggle* (Heinemann, London, 1982), and is an associate editor of *Third World Book Review*.

BONNIE K. CAMPBELL teaches at the Department of Political Science at the University of Quebec at Montreal, and has done extensive research on the political economy of the Ivory Coast. Her work on this subject is published in a wide variety of journals and in the form of an essay in *West African States* (edited by John Dunn, Cambridge U.P., 1978). She is the author of *Libération nationale et construction du socialisme en Afrique. Angola/Guinée-Bissau/Mozambique*, (Eds. Nouvelle optique, Montreal, 1977), and *Les enjeux de la bauxite. La Guinée face aux multinationales de l'aluminium*, (Presses de l'Université de Montréal and Institut Universitaire des Hautes Etudes Internationales de Genève, 1983).

ALAIN COURNANEL has a *Doctorat d'Etat* in Economics and is *Diplomé d'Etudes Supérieures* in Sociology. He has taught at several universities in Africa and Europe, most recently at the University of Paris I from 1975 to 1980. He is currently employed as an economist in a French public corporation. He has contributed to numerous journals, including *Revue Tiers-Monde, Revue française d'études politiques africaines, Partisans,* on subjects related to development theory, Guinea, capitalism, and class struggle in Africa.

PETER GIBBON has a Ph.D. in sociology from Manchester University (1972) and has taught in Ireland and Tanzania. He is currently teaching sociology at Sheffield City Polytechnic, England, and is the author of *Origins of Ulster Unionism* (1975) and co-author of *The State in Northern Ireland 1921–1972* (1979).

JUDY KIMBLE worked and studied in Lesotho from 1974 to 1979. She teaches in London, where she is also an active member of the Anti-Apartheid movement, and WISH (Women in South African History). She recently completed her Ph.D. dissertation on "Migrant Labour and Colonial Rule in Lesotho," and has contributed to such journals as the *Review of African Political Economy, Feminist Review, Journal of Peasant Studies,* and *Journal of African Marxists.*

GAVIN KITCHING is Lecturer in Sociology at the Polytechnic of North London. He has carried out extensive research in Tanzania and Kenya, and is currently interested in Brazil. He has written three books, *Class and Economic Change in Kenya.* (Yale University Press, New Haven, 1980); *Development and Underdevelopment in Historical Perspective: Populism, Nationalism and Industrialization* (Methuen, London, 1982); and *Rethinking Socialism* (Methuen, London, 1983).

MICHAEL NEOCOSMOS holds a Ph.D. from the University of Bradford (1983) and has taught at Bradford and the University of Dar es Salaam, Tanzania. He currently teaches sociology at Sheffield City Polytechnic and Huddersfield Polytechnic, England.